Emasculating Warriors

A Nation At War
With Its Warriors

Dwight Horn
CAPT, CHC, USN

Book Reviews

Steve Fisher, Colonel, USMC Infantry (ret), 28 years

In this book, what Navy Captain Dwight Horn provides is amazing and the most thought provoking, and analytical examination of warriors that I have ever seen. With historical examples, thorough research, and, most significantly, personal experience, Chaplain Horn details the vastly complex experience of killing in combat. He explores the motivation and the human toll on the young men and women we send to fight our nation's wars. He deals with the horrors, sacrifices and morality of war from a warrior's perspective. All Americans should read this book. We owe it to our warriors.

James Herrera, Colonel, USMC (retired), 35 years

This body of work is provocative, bold and greatly needed; it adds an essential element to the understanding of warfare and the profession of arms. It provides a stark reminder that a nation's ignorance, indifference, and misplaced attention are the greatest threats to its warriors. I have had the privilege of serving alongside warriors for over three decades. I have witnessed the complexities of combat and marveled at the dichotomies involved: audacity, humility, violence of action, and compassion. There is no compromise when it comes to right purpose and right action.

Acknowledgements

This work comes out of my reflections with the Marines of 3rd Battalion 5th Marine Regiment. I was humbled to serve with them in the Battle of Fallujah. They opened my eyes to many things, and showed me the clearest example of what it is to be professional and sacrificial to country, cause and truth.

It is important as well to thank my Parents, John and Betty Horn, for their belief in me and their endless support of my academic pursuits. I would not have accomplished this without their investment in my life. I also thank my wife, Cyndee, for her endless support and work on this project, my faithful writing companion Mochi, Parker for help with the cover and my l&lsil Cathy for her help. A mention goes as well to my other children, Turner, Connor and McKenzie for all that they have taught me and for how they have endured my own post war challenges.

Preface

Emasculating Warriors, a Nation at War with its Warriors, is a book that directs attention to an issue our nation is having with those it sends to war. The idea behind the title is not to be taken literally, nor is it meant to say that there are only male warriors. It is also not intended to mean that our nation is in some actual and deliberate battle with those we send to war. The title is a provocative way of calling attention to the fact that research has clearly identified that veterans of war suffer from Post Traumatic Stress Disorder and depression, that they have had a 41% higher suicide risk than the general U.S. population (U.S. Dept. V.A.), and that many struggle with marriage, drug and alcohol abuse, homelessness, incarceration and other such things. Given these things and others to be seen in the book, it is time to recognize that something is not right in terms of how veterans are responding to involvement in war.[i] This work addresses the matter by exposing underlying issues that corrupt combatants and by providing insight into how we can avoid repeating all of this in subsequent conflicts.

The study begins by examining the challenges service members have as a result of combat. It looks closely at the psychological and physiological trauma of war and shows the many ways that these things can influence behavior both in combat as well as in the transition back to civilian life. The analysis itself becomes fascinating as it offers a rare glimpse into what war is like and how alien the experience really is for those who have never been through it.

From there, a novel presentation is offered regarding the nature of warriors. Those who fit this profile are highly unique. Not everyone in combat is a warrior. Many proofs are provided to substantiate this. The evidence comes from a broad spectrum of books and journals about war, and they are most importantly founded in my personal anecdotes from almost 24 years as a chaplain and from my time in the Battle of Fallujah.

Once warriors are identified, attention is given to separating warriors from those termed as other "war-types." This clarification becomes important. It begins to show why there is so much mental trauma in those sent to war. To treat all preparing for war in the same way and even to expect all to participate in war in the same way, overturns natural predispositions. How can that not lead to major problems? It does, and making the point is central.

One topic of paramount importance in this discussion is killing. Leading writers on war believe that killing is the principal issue which becomes troubling to "all." I contend that this is not true and establishing this alternate position and exposing the popular myth is vital. In the end, what is provided shows clearly that there are a select few, warriors, who are not only comfortable with killing, but even seek out that experience. Yet, when a nation does not see this, when leading authorities (authors, academics, politicians) say otherwise, and when the military overlooks this and forces all members to train and participate in killing, a wealth of calamitous issues arise. This is a part of what it means to emasculate warriors, to be a nation at war with its warriors. We have failed to prepare properly warriors for the experience of war, and we corrupt their very psyche, abilities and nature because of it. We do the same for non-warrior types who also end up going through some of the same things but for very different reasons.

Yet, as the next section of the book goes on to show, what we have seen so far about those who fight in wars is not even the entirety of the discussion. There is another critical part of understanding the process of war and the preparation for it that is overlooked and it is the most critical part. It has to do with ensuring that all those who fight must be able to align their mission with a moral cause for war. That is the most critical issue to consider when it comes to war, and presently, it is not adequately addressed.

Showing this, and sorting out the issues involved, takes three chapters; a chapter on finding a moral basis for war, a chapter on developing a construct by which to apply that moral basis for war, and a chapter on showing what happens to people when morality is altogether disregarded.

Finally, the book concludes with the challenge for every person to realize that going to war is not a matter solely for those who fight. All have responsibility to stand for truth and defend what is believed to be right. One is not exempt from what happens in war when its nation fights. All must own their part. Essential, though, in this is to prepare those on the front lines of battle. They will suffer the most from the experience.

As a nation and military, therefore, we must do all we can to equip combatants to stand in consonance with their natures and purposes as defenders of justice. We need just fighters in a just battle for a just cause! Anything less than this is unjust.

Of note, this material does not offer an anti-war message but rather a call to action on the nation's part to either prepare those who fight for war or to have the decency not to send them. Never has this message been more critical to address than now with so many world wars on the horizon.

Endnote

[i] National Coalition for Homeless Veterans, "Background and Statistics,"
http://nchv.org/index.php/news/media/background_and_statistics, (29 December, 2017), and Public Health, "Suicide Risk and Risk of Death Among Recent Veterans,"
https://www.publichealth.va.gov/epidemiology/studies/suicide-risk-death-risk-recent-veterans.asp, (3 June, 2015).

Table of Contents

Section IV   War is a National Effort

Section I

Cost of War on Veterans

Chapter One
Emasculating Warriors: The Overall Problem

Chapter Two
Awakening to the Veteran's Struggle: Fracturing Identity

Chapter Three
War and Biological Change

CHAPTER ONE

EMASCULATING WARRIORS:
THE OVERALL PROBLEM

Medical experts on veterans have noted that "the potential effect on service members of their war experiences may manifest indefinitely into the future in the form of emerging psychiatric illnesses."[1] This, as they have further stated, will be a long-term problem: "Many of the experts, including those in the Department of Defense (DOD), say that 25 to 40 percent of the soldiers who come back from war will experience post-traumatic stress disorder (PTSD) so severely that they may require treatment, primarily counseling and medications, for many years, if not for the rest of their lives."[2] It is time to regard what the professionals are saying and figure out why we are having these issues. What are we missing about the impact of war and how can we turn this around?

Emasculating Warriors refers to a process whereby a failure to comprehend this select group brings confusion for who they are, condemnation for what they do, and overall failure in providing for their needs. While there are some who desire to overturn this in order to be of better support, the challenge is greater than imagined. To show why is as easy as thinking about who would really want to be a warrior in the first place. Who desires to separate from loved ones for long periods of time and chooses to live in austere conditions? Who wants to give up personal freedom and allow others to dictate most aspects of life? Who is willing to have

1

an "always on duty" work schedule, missing births, birthdays, anniversaries, holidays and the like? Even more, and of greater inability to grasp, who is interested in dying for countrymen who might not honor their service, or who wants to be killed for those of other nations who might well be indifferent toward the sacrifice? Who is willing to do these kinds of things?

Most of us have a simple response to this: "not me." Now you see how far away you are from understanding the warrior. Yet, that rift grows wider still. For you have not come to the greatest mystery of all when it comes specifically to the warrior. It relates to something about this person which defies explanation for others. It has to do with the act of killing another human. For the warrior, killing is exhilarating. It is seeing a human being and with excitement and blood pulsing through the body, it is shooting that person with every intention to kill. This is what the warrior wants. This is where he excels. And with this, you begin to see just how wide the chasm of understanding is between you and the warrior.

I know in saying these things what many are thinking: this is preposterous. No one really thinks like this. But, not only is that wrong, there is more. Consider this too. Once that warrior has killed another, a guttural cry of elation is sounded for the kill. It is a feeling of ecstasy like no other, a true sense of accomplishment and pride. This is what represents the heart of a warrior. It is a mindset that only a warrior has and since very few people naturally fit this profile, even of those who go to war, this community lives outside of what most are able to understand. It all becomes a part of being a nation at war with its warriors.

Our ignorance inspires countless ill-founded books, misguided policies and empty rehabilitative programs that try to help warriors by providing counsel and training that does not speak to this community. That has been a big mistake. It is one that needs immediate correction not only for the warrior community but for all of the others who go into combat with them. For when you fail to realize how training for war needs to regard people in their uniqueness, or when you expect that all in the military should even go to front-line combat, or most significantly when you overlook teaching on what should be foundational in equipping the mind and spirit for combat, it will create all manner of internal strife. That these things are happening for all who go to war, warriors and non-warriors alike, is something that should be evident. Numerous controlled studies reveal the impact of war on veterans. A New England Journal of Medicine study offers this: "The recent military operations in Iraq and Afghanistan, which have involved the first sustained ground combat undertaken by the United States since the war in Vietnam, raise important questions about the effect of the experience on the mental health of members of the military services who have been deployed there. Research conducted after other military conflicts has shown that deployment stressors and exposure to combat result in considerable risks of mental health problems, including post-traumatic stress disorder (PTSD), major depression, substance abuse, impairment in social functioning and in the ability to work, and the increased use of health care services."[3]

As is seen, warriors and those who fight with them are struggling. Solidifying this more is another study which stated this: "Combat exposure results in substantial morbidity lasting decades and accounts for significant and multifarious forms of dysfunction at the national level."[4] What kinds of maladies are cited in this study which are attributable to combat exposure: post-traumatic stress disorder, major depressive disorder, substance abuse disorder, job loss, current unemployment, divorce or separation, and current spouse or partner abuse.[5]

As you see, a perilous situation is before us. Many who are going to war are not reacting well to the experience. It is leading to a burgeoning health crisis: "PTSD and depression among returning service members will cost the nation as much as $6.2 billion in the two years following deployment — an amount that includes both direct medical care and costs for lost productivity and suicide. …Unless they receive appropriate and effective care for these mental health conditions, there will be long-term consequences for them and for the nation."[6] This situation is bleak with long-term effects. "Things will only get worse because the bulk of our fighting force is still in uniform and still reporting to military doctors. We sent 1.6 million soldiers into Iraq and Afghanistan and 900,000 are still on active duty. When they hang up their uniforms, the VA [Veterans Administration] estimates that its clinics may see an additional 750,000 new vets and half a million of them may begin visiting the nation's 200 walk-in neighborhood Vet centers."[7] The tidal wave is yet to come ashore.

What might be interesting to note too in this discussion is that this intense struggle does not reside simply with Iraq and Afghanistan War Veterans. It goes back beyond these wars. Consider one story about a veteran named Jake.[8] For him, there is one day after the next that passes without a way to overcome the pain of war. Not even sleep takes the suffering away. Jake recounts what this is like. He says that he will fall asleep, exhausted from a long day and a continuous state of sleep deprivation, but then, he will quickly rise in terror, dripping in sweat and shaking. The pattern is overwhelming. On one particular day, he recounts that he had enough of this. So after waking up from such a nightmare, he grabbed his loaded pistol, released the safety and put the gun to his face. "Tears began again to trickle from his eyes. He pushed the barrel up under his chin as his index finger danced around the trigger, grazing it slightly. …His breathing became rapid; his entrenched hand began to quiver. Time passed. …He exhaled and yelled out, 'If there is a God I need you now…not tomorrow, not next year…right now, God!'"[9]

This moment passes for Jake like so many others while the rest of us remain oblivious to what happens behind the closed off walls of these veterans' lives. When will we awaken to these struggles? What does it take for us to know that many veterans can live after war on the edge of despair in solitude, an existence partly of their own making and partly of all others who fail to see the suffering? These veterans do not want to die. Suicide is just the only imaginable way to deafen, once and for all, the anguish that tears at every fiber of being. In the case of Jake, an important question to ask is how long has he endured this torture? The answer is shocking: decades! As he says,

I'm just tired of living. I have trouble sleeping; I have nightmares and flashbacks about things that happened decades ago in Nam. The only way I can get to sleep is by filling up with pills and booze...I have a VA psych doc, but he only has time to see me every other month and then for just a few minutes. He gives me more pills or ups the dosages and sends me home. ...What the hell do they know about the stink of body decay and death and emotional pain of watching a buddy die in my arms? But for all the years I have been coming to the VA for so-called treatment, nobody seems to really care, I mean really care about what happens to me.[10]

How is it possible that one can serve this country in war but end up feeling abandoned? There is no good answer. Yet, it is what Jake says next, however, that ought to shame even more all who sent him to war:

I feel friendless! I feel alone in this battle. ...If I killed myself no one would miss me. It would end my pain. I will never forget the devastating agony and helplessness I felt the day my Marine buddy was killed by a sniper's bullet, blood gurgling out of his neck and down his face from his nose; my first smell of blood; the touch of hot fluid running through my fingers as I tried to stick my finger in the wound to stop the flow. ...It is all one can do to live with the memories of war from combat and now a battle must be fought back home against those I served and protected. 'Ooh-rah... that's bullshit.'[11]

Search the internet and find other stories like Jake's. Army Special Forces soldier Bill Howell is a striking example. As soon as he returned home, it was evident to his wife, Laura, that all was not well. In her words, her husband went from being a good officer and dad to being someone that did not even resemble the man that she knew. On the final day of his life, he came to the door, and when she approached him she realized: "The guy standing in that door that night was not my husband. He in no way resembled him…, The look in his eyes was, 'Who are you?' It was death."[12] In this broken state of being, fueled principally by war trauma and in part by alcohol and medication, he not only beat his wife but then, went and got a gun and forced his wife to watch as he shot his brains out. Too dramatic? Perhaps it is, but it is a sad reality for some veterans and their families.

Granted, there are naysayers about all of this, even in the military ranks, who will say that behavior is complicated and the verdict is out in terms of what absolutely can be attributed to combat exposure. Hence, do not blame the war in all of these situations. In truth, they are right. There are always many attributable factors that bring people to crisis, and some as we will consider do not suffer from their experience of war but thrive in that milieu. Regardless, do not dismiss the impact of war for many. There are controlled studies as cited that show a link. As a Chaplain, I have seen a definite link between combat and abnormal or immoral behavior. Even more, investigative journalists have searched out the impact of war on veterans and have reported a definitive link. The New York Times did its own study and published a series on veterans who came home from war troubled and in the cases they reviewed, misbehavior and criminal activity were deemed directly attributed to war; there were one-hundred and twenty one cases in all.[13] Beyond all of this though, try telling family members who have seen loved ones struggle after war that combat experience played a minimal or non-attributive role. It would be impossible to do. A heartbreaking story comes out of Camp Pendleton:

At first, Jonathan Schulze tried to live with the nightmares and the grief he brought home from Iraq. He was a tough kid from central Minnesota, and more than that, a U.S. Marine to the core. Yet his moods when he returned home told another story. He sobbed on his parents' couch as he told them how fellow Marines had died, and how he, a machine gunner, had killed the enemy. In his sleep, he screamed the names of dead comrades. He had visited a psychiatrist at the VA hospital in Minneapolis. ...He told a staff member he was thinking of killing himself and asked to be admitted to the mental health unit, said his father and stepmother, who accompanied him. They said he was told he couldn't be admitted that day. The next day, as he spoke to a counselor in St. Cloud by phone, he was told he was No. 26 on the waiting list, his parents said. Four days later, Schulze, 25, committed suicide. [14]

This story alone ought to compel us as a nation to expend every effort to know why we are failing veterans when they need us the most. Without the resources required, this Marine, Jonathan Schulze, turned to drugs and alcohol. [15] He became violent and could not keep a job. His attempts at seeking help went unanswered. Suicide became his answer because he perceived that his country remained silent to his suffering.

Sadly, not much has seemed to change since Jonathan Schulze took his life. Our outreach to veterans seems to have grown worse:

In a scathing appraisal, ...the troubled Veterans Affairs health care system concludes that medical care for veterans is beset by "significant and chronic system failures," substantially verifying problems raised by whistleblowers and internal and congressional investigators. ...Since reports surfaced of treatment delays and of patients dying while on waiting lists, the VA has been the subject of internal, independent and congressional investigations. …More than 56,000 veterans have had to wait at least three months for initial appointments, the report said, and an additional 46,000 veterans who asked for appointments over the past decade never got them.[16]

Amazingly too, in spite of all that we have just seen about veterans, the challenges they face are greater still. There are those whose struggles cause them to end up on the streets. Although it is always difficult to get exact counts, it is estimated that there are between 529,000 and 840,000 veterans who are homeless at some point in the year.[17] This is horrendous. Worse still are those who end up in the prisons:

There are about 140,000 veterans in American jails today, according to the Justice Department, and 60% have substance abuse problems. About 25% were inebriated at the time of the violation that landed them in prison. Experts say many are "self-medicating," countering the strains of their service – PTSD, emotional stress, mental fatigue, family disruption – with drugs or alcohol.[18]

This book is offered to help prevent the problems this nation is having with its warriors and those who serve with them. *Emasculating Warriors* is written as a clarion call. It provides insight into the lives of those who fight in wars which can be used to help citizens mobilize nationally and sacrifice personally to reach into the lives of veterans and institute new ways to identify those who should be in war and train them for the experience. That is what we must do. If we are going to call men and women to war, we at least owe them the courtesy of understanding what we are asking, knowing what it means to prepare them properly, and then, supporting them in every way when they come home.

The picture offered herein portrays a true portrait of the lives, struggles, heroism and suffering of these men and woman as I have lived with them, observed them, supported them and read about them. It challenges many of our convictions, but hopefully it forces us to see life through a lens that makes the warrior and non-warrior alike understandable. Then, realizing all of this, if we are not prepared to care for these people that we send to war, it just seems right that we must stop sending them. The consequences are too great otherwise. Reading this book is the first step toward moving a nation to support its veterans. Get ready for the challenge.

Endnotes

[1] Mayo Clinic. "War's impact can haunt veterans long after combat." Science Daily, http://www.sciencedaily.com/releases/2012/11/121108181138.htm, (November 8, 2012).

[2] Eric Newhouse, Faces of Combat: PTSD and TBI, (Washington: Issues Press, 2008), p. xi.

[3] Charles W. Hoge, M.D., Carl A. Castro, Ph.D., Stephen C. Messer, Ph.D., Dennis McGurk, Ph.D., Dave I. Cotting, Ph.D., and Robert L. Koffman, M.D., M.P.H., "Combat Duty in Iraq and Afghanistan, Mental Health Problems, and Barriers to Care", http://content.nejm.org/cgi/content/full/351/1/13#T1, (July 1, 2004).

[4] Holly G. Prigerson, PhD, Paul K. Maciejewski, PhD, and Robert A. Rosenheck, MD, "Population Attributable Fractions of Psychiatric Disorders and Behavioral Outcomes Associated With Combat Exposure Among US Men", http://www.pubmedcentral.nih.gov/articlerender.fcgi?artid=1447389, (January 2002).

[5] Ibid.

[6] Rand Corporation, For Release, "One In Five Iraq and Afghanistan Veterans Suffer from PTSD or Major Depression", http://www.rand.org/news/press/2008/04/17/, (April 17, 2008).

[7] [clarification added] Eric Newhouse, Faces of Combat: PTSD and TBI, (Washington: Issues Press, 2008), p. 32.

[8] As reported by Victor Montgomery in Healing Suicidal Veterans, (New Jersey: New Horizon Press, 2009), pp. 166-170.

[9] Ibid., pp. 169-170.

[10] Ibid., p. 184.

[11] Ibid., pp. 164-165.

[12] Mark Benjamin and Dan Olmsted, "Exclusive: Green Beret's strange suicide", http://www.upi.com/Business_News/Security-Industry/2004/05/11/Exclusive-Green-Berets-strange-suicide/71431084296160/, (May 11, 2004).

[13] Special Series, War Torn Part I, "A series of articles and multimedia about veterans of the wars in Iraq and Afghanistan who have committed killings, or been charged with them, after coming home",

http://www.nytimes.com/interactive/2008/01/12/us/20080113_VETS
_DATABASE.html, (January 12, 2008).

[14] Kevin Giles, "Jan. 27: This Marine's death came after he served in Iraq", http://www.startribune.com/local/11605966.html, (January 29, 2007).

[15] Caitlin A. Johnson, "Vet Kills Himself After VA Turns Him Away", http://www.cbsnews.com/stories/2007/03/13/earlyshow/main256253 7.shtml, (March 13, 2007).

[16] Jim Kuhnhenn, "VA review finds 'significant and chronic' failures", http://bigstory.ap.org/article/obama-hear-update-veterans-affairs-problems, (June 27, 2014).

[17] Veteransinc.org, "Statistics", http://www.veteransinc.org/about-us/statistics/, (June 24, 2015).

[18] Ari Melber, "For vets, rehab rather than prison", http://www.msnbc.com/the-cycle/vets-rehab-rather-prison, (July 19, 2014).

CHAPTER TWO

AWAKENING TO THE VETERAN'S STRUGGLE: FRACTURING OF IDENTITY

War has the potential of impacting a person so that they are no longer recognizable once they return home. Family members are often the first to notice: "Something was wrong. They put on civilian clothes again and looked to their mothers and wives very much like the young men who had gone to [war]. But they had not come back the same men. Something had altered in them. They were subject to sudden moods and queer tempers, fits of profound depression alternating with a restless desire for pleasure. Many were easily moved to passion where they lost control of themselves, many were bitter in their speech, violent in opinion, frightening."[1] What is this about? What kind of transformation of the soul can war induce?

In the children's story, Alice in Wonderland, the central character, Alice, tumbles down a rabbit hole and quickly her sense of meaning in life is jumbled as a new world opens up. She is faced with unknown surroundings and fixtures, talking animals and animated objects. She also confronts her own physical changes. It leaves her uncertain about her identity and this is made evident in a conversation she has with a caterpillar. This insect is a fitting selection given that it unquestionably experiences its own metamorphosis.

In the opening of this dialogue, the caterpillar says to Alice: "Who are you?"[2] Alice replies, "I – I hardly know, sir, just at present – at least I know who I was when I got up this morning, but I think I must have been changed several times since then."[3] The caterpillar asks her to explain what she means by her words and Alice struggles to do it. All she can think to say is "'I can't explain myself, I'm afraid, sir ...because I'm not myself, you see!"[4]

This dialogue reveals that Alice is failing to grasp her sense of self. All references and meaning that she once knew about the world and herself changed in a moment, once she fell down the rabbit hole. From here, she really does not know who she is. Her experience has left her uncertain about truth.

As we touched on in the last chapter, many who have gone to war are facing crisis. In many cases, it is one dealing with identity, struggling to figure out who they are and how to exist in this new post war reality. A significant reason is that like Alice their old references for life have changed. Their bodies, brains and spirits have fallen into their own metaphorical rabbit hole and resultantly, many fail to know who they are. Their disorientation is as profound as Alice's. But sadly, for these people, their reality is not fictional. They are facing a true existential crisis. It ends up leading to poor decisions in conduct and behavior. Often, the actions are insignificant or unnoticed. However, veterans find themselves doing things that are entirely unnatural to their state of being prior to war. Yet, how would we expect otherwise?

War is a world unto itself. It can severely impact a person in every aspect of being so that the person struggles with self-identity. The degree to which this happens can depend on many things. Here are just a few: one's nature as coupled with mental and spiritual disposition toward war, intensity of combat, duration of combat, proximity to danger, preexisting trauma, family support, repeated combat tours, failure to process prior trauma, faith, sense of mission, leadership, unity and cohesion with others, physical injury, seeing others injured and suffer, degree to which one felt death was imminent, responsibility for loss of combatants, killing of civilians, moral failings, view of killing, support from country, access to support, willingness to use drugs and alcohol, fear of losing sanity, fear of losing family, fear of losing career, and sense of honor about mission.

This short list shows how many things can play a part of the total transformation from combat. When one is impacted in one or more of these ways, it soon can become impossible for the person to make a decision in his or her so called 'right mind'. The consequences are seldom good. What is amazing is how little any of this is known and appreciated. A nation sends its people to war and when they come back the expectation is that they are fine or at least functional. Hence, the standard procedure at the end of a combat tour is to get the troops back home, ask them if they have any problems with some hope that they will admit them, give them some time off, and then, the push is to prepare them for their next combat tour or else to release them to the civilian world. Overlooked is how dramatically different these veterans can be and how quickly their inability to cope with fractured identities can lead to crisis.

Benjamin Sebena was a Marine who served two tours of duty in Iraq. He saw hellish combat, purportedly having killed 68 people in battle, watching friends die and on occasion being responsible to clean their blood and body parts from vehicles. Also, he suffered traumatic brain injury and lost body parts from a mortar explosion. After having been diagnosed with post-traumatic stress disorder, he was honorably discharged in 2005.[5] Tragically, after this point, although he stated that his wife was "the one love of my life,"[6] he shot her 5 times in the head.[7] He was sentenced to life in prison for his crime. No consideration was given to the fact that Sebena was definitively not Sebena in the sense that he was prior to war. Consider on this, the words of the judge in this case, who though weighing the war issues, stated "thousands of other war veterans don't come home and kill their spouses."[8] This judge's words, while technically true, reveal how great the failing is to consider how war can fracture the sense of self and literally change one's orientation and stability in life. Does anyone really think that Sebena would have done this if he never went to war?

Ann Jones, the author of *"They Were Soldiers: How the Wounded Return from America's Wars: The Untold Story*, offers insight into what many as a result of fractured identities face in their return from combat. The picture she gives is not positive. It is one, nonetheless, that comes from her time of having been embedded as a journalist in Afghanistan, having spent time interviewing the wounded from war, and from having done extensive research on the subject.

One issue that Jones examines is the connection between war and marital strife, the issue related to Sebena. What she makes clear is that more service members than you might think do come home and end up destroying their marriages and/or killing their spouses.[9] She offers an impressive catalogue of what one can find in an internet search on this, and it is devastating. Ultimately, it includes not just accounts of spouses being murdered but all manner of mayhem where family members, acquaintances, and strangers fall prey to the wrath of a veteran. The picture she paints is even bleaker as she looks at failed attempts at diagnosing veterans and the drugs and alcohol used by veterans to kill the pain. A huge problem exists from her perspective with returning veterans, and it is not being addressed.

Jones does paint a dark picture. It is not a complete picture of those who go to war, however. There are many noble veterans who return home and contribute successfully to the service and society. But in saying this, let us not discount Jones' findings either. She is speaking, I think, of a large group who do return with minor to severe mental and spiritual issues from war, and for some reason this picture of what happens is just not known to the extent that it should be. What makes this all the more surprising, even as Jones relates, is that "We have been down this road before...."[10] This same reality was also uncovered in the Vietnam War:

After they returned home, in the process of establishing a personal identity and constructing new values, most veterans had to deal with rejections and criticisms by a non-accepting society. Many individuals struggled in trying to achieve self-unity which led to PTSD. The returning veteran needed social support, affection, and a positive welcoming from his community in order to work through the war experiences while establishing his sense of identity. Because he was unable to share his war experience with his family and friends, this led to loneliness and alienation and sometimes complete hatred of oneself.[11]

These words, particularly noting the words regarding identity crisis, show that as a nation we need to be better prepared in terms of understanding what it means to send people off to war. If veterans lose their sense of being because they struggle internally with experiences that plague and control them, and if they attempt to anesthetize themselves from these toxic experiences with alcohol, drugs, blame-shifting, suicide or criminal behavior, and if we then fail to provide treatment and simply punish and judge them for the resulting misguided behavior, have we really achieved justice? Perhaps the words of Ron Kovic, both the character from the movie "Born on the Fourth of July" and the real-life Vietnam veteran upon whom the story is based are more accurate than we would want to believe: "People here, they don't give a shit about the War. To them it was just a million miles away. We got the shit kicked out of us and for what? For bullshit lies?"[12]

History should teach us something, or we are doomed to repeat it. It seems like we prefer our bruises:

"The *New York Times* 'found 121 cases in which veterans of Iraq and Afghanistan committed a killing in this country, or were charged with one, after their return from war.' ...After tracing this 'cross-country trail of death and heartbreak,' the *Times* concluded with an admission: that its research had probably

16

uncovered only "a minimum" of such cases.' Only a month later, it found 'more than 150 cases of fatal domestic violence or [fatal] child abuse in the United States involving service members and new veterans' since the war began in October 2001."[13]

This ought to anger us. It is unacceptable. How can we take valiant young men and women who step forward to serve honorably their nation, a group that is merely one percent of the national population and a group that is willing to sacrifice every comfort of life and die, and then fail them when they need us the most? How can we do this to their families, loved ones that entrusted them to our care?

On 24 May, 2006, I was called into my Colonel's office and briefed on an event that was going to transpire that evening. It concerned what ended up being seven Marines and a Sailor who were being investigated for the murder of an Iraqi national. They were being flown back from Iraq to Camp Pendleton. They were attached to 3rd Battalion, 5th Marine Regiment, and 1st Marine Division. When I heard this news I was shocked. This was the battalion out of which I just rotated. I was in the Battle of Fallujah with these Marines in 2004. I could not believe it. More surprising still was that three of these coming back were lay-leaders for me in 2004. Lay-leaders are those appointed in a command as volunteers to work with Chaplains to assist with religious services. The only way to become a lay-leader is to be a person of strong faith and upstanding character.

Considering who I knew some of these men to be, I questioned how could they or any of these men for that matter, men whom I had seen serve so valiantly in battle, be investigated for murder? It did not seem possible. Then I found out the charge which made it all the more untenable in my eyes. As was widely reported through all news outlets and which is still available today on line,

17

these men were accused of kidnapping, binding and killing Hashim Ibrahim Awad, a 52-year-old man.[14]

Charging documents released by the Marine Corps on June 21 allege that "the men also stole an AK-47 assault rifle and staged the scene to make it appear that Awad was in the midst of planting a roadside bomb when he was killed in Hamdania, Iraq."[15] That ostensibly, if it happened, is criminal behavior. Who would deny this? Yet as much as I knew this, I also felt like if this indeed happened as reported then something else had to be missing in my grasp of this situation. Could war be so life-changing for some in certain situations and could war create the conditions where a person of noble character could become ignoble?

The answer I have found through the years, not speaking about this situation at all, is yes, and the reasons for it I have discovered are that in many cases we have failed to understand and train for the moral complexities that arise in war, and we have not realized how war mentally and spiritually impacts those we send. None of this excuses the veteran for misconduct, but it certainly puts some of that blame on us as well. We need to be far better at understanding what it is to be in war and to equip people for that experience. Think about this with the example from US Marine Corporal William Wold. He was in the Battle of Fallujah. From one firefight as his squad was pushing south into the city, he offers the following recounting:

'It was a fucking small room, dude. It was fucking small!' He shakes his head. 'Thirty-five fucking rounds. I was fucking scared dude. I fucking grabbed my nuts.' Then, with one hand, he does so again, and lets out a big 'Ohhh!' 'I was told to go the room,' he says, 'and my first Marine went in... he saw a guy with an AK, I told him to shoot the guy, then I shot the six guys on the left... and my other Marine shot two other guys.'[16]

That is an evocative account of the kind of mayhem a veteran confronts and the electric emotional state that results just when one recounts the experience. It is powerful to read and this was not Wold's only time to have had that kind of erupting adrenaline rush from danger.

On another occasion, a vehicle penetrated the perimeter of a military position where he was and following the orders of his senior officer, he fired upon the vehicle. It was something that had to be done in accordance with Rules of Engagement (ROEs) to protect the position and keep the other service members safe. However, after having fired on the vehicle, Wold found that in the vehicle there were several dead occupants, some of whom were children. Wold did what had to be done to protect his Marines, but that was of little consolation as he pulled the children out of the vehicle.

Put yourself now in Wold's shoes. What would you do with these memories? It is likely the same thing that Wold tried; i.e., bury them in the deep recesses of the mind so as never to think of them again. What Wold found, however, was what many find in these kinds of situations; it is impossible to silence the tormenting grief and guilt. Consequently, he lost his sense of self, an identity shattered. He could not let go of his war experiences. Thus, "...back in the safety of his childhood home surrounded by his adoring family, the dark secrets and all the guilt emerged from his mind.[17] The tragic end was Wold's death. The internal strife, without the proper measures in place to protect against it, led to the typical pattern of pills, booze, and destructive behavior which finally culminated in a lethal dose of prescription medicines.[18]

It was a death as his mother saw it that was a result of a failure on the part of the Marines. Her son loved the Marine Corps and this she could not deny, but "[s]he also knew that the uniform was just the surface of a much more complex story, a story of belief, duty and honor yes, but also about how guilt over killing in the pursuit of those ideals could lead to ruin."[19]

19

These sentiments as expressed by Corporal Wold's mother are very much like those of Karl Marlantes, a Vietnam Marine. He stated, "'When I did eventually face death – the death of those I killed and those killed around me...,' 'I had no framework or guidance to help me put combat's terror, exhilaration, horror, guilt and pain into some larger framework that would've helped me find meaning in them later.'[20] Wold and Marlantes faced their own identity crisis and found no way of resolving it at the time.

This is disastrous. If we refuse to take the time to educate ourselves and all in the military on the deeper questions on war and killing, if we do not bring all resources to the table to help address these issues that strike at the core of our souls, we simply should never send anyone to war. It is like sending someone down the rabbit hole and hoping for the best. That should never be the case.

Sebena, mentioned at the beginning of this chapter for shooting his wife in the head, stated to a church group in recounting his war experience: "I've been to dark places."[21] There is no doubt about the truth of this. This Marine lost himself. He went down the rabbit hole and could not recover from his tortured identity. He is not the only one as we are beginning to see:

A stunning number of parents feel that the soldier who came back to them is not their real son or daughter - as in those old sci-fi films about aliens who assume human bodies and betray their presence only by a peculiar gleam in the eyes. Many family members and friends are vaguely afraid. They don't want to confront the veteran they love when things are bad - when the vet is drinking or drugging or beating up his girlfriend - for fear of making things worse. And when the vet seems somewhat better, parents and wives don't want to rock the boat. So every day is a surprise. Life becomes chaotic. Lived on tiptoes. It's exhausting. Parents may come to blame each other, and wives to blame themselves. Small children are diagnosed with anxiety disorders. Someone has to take care of these vets.[22]

Someone should care for these veterans and that someone is us. Jonathan Shay, a noted psychiatrist who worked extensively with veterans, writes in his book, *Achilles in Vietnam*: 'When you put a gun in some kid's hands and send him off to war, you incur an infinite debt to him for what he has done to his soul.'[23] In total agreement, we are indebted to veterans and need to address the deeper questions of truth. The identity crisis of veterans is our crisis as well.

What is it that lies behind this identity crisis as far as the experience of being in war is concerned? What causes a person to go off to war with an optimistic sense of self and purpose only to come home in turmoil with a shattered sense of self? What is it actually like to go through the rabbit hole of war? This is what we address next.

Endnotes

[1] Ann Jones, They Were Soldiers: How the Wounded Return from America's Wars: The Untold Story, (Chicago: Haymarket Books, 2013), 127.

[2] Robert Stockton, The Millennium Fulcrum Edition, 3.0, Lewis Carroll, Alice's Adventures in Wonderland, "Advice from a Caterpillar," Chapter V, http://www.cs.cmu.edu/~rgs/alice-table.html, (14 December, 2009).

[3] Ibid.

[4] Ibid.

[5] Dinesh Ramde, "Benjamin G. Sebena Gets Life For Killing Police Officer Wife", http://www.huffingtonpost.com/2013/08/09/benjamin-g-sebena_n_3734411.html, (October 9, 2013).

[6] Isaac Stanley-Becker, "Benjamin Sebena gets a chance at release from life sentence", http://www.jsonline.com/news/crime/benjamin-sebena-to-receive-life-sentence-friday-b9972146z1-218976331.html, (August 10, 2013).

[7] Ramde,http://www.huffingtonpost.com/2013/08/09/benjamin-g-sebena_n_3734411.html, (October 9, 2013).

[8] Ibid.

[9] Ann Jones, They Were Soldiers: How the Wounded Return from America's Wars: The Untold Story, (Chicago: Haymarket Books, 2013), 124.

[10] Ibid., p. 127.

[11] Josh Hochgesang, Tracye Lawyer, Toby Stevenson, "The Psychological Effects of the Vietnam War", https://web.stanford.edu/class/e297c/war_peace/media/hpsych.html, (July 26, 1999).

[12] Ibid.

[13] Ibid., 125.

[14] Figueroa, Teri, and Walker, Mark. "The 'Pendleton 8': A look at the 7 Marines and Navy corpsman charged in Hamdania incident", The North County Times, July 23, 2006, http://www.nctimes.com/articles/2006/07/23//news/top_stories/21_08_547_22_06.txt (March 3, 2009).

[15] Ibid.

[16] Kevin Sites, "The Unforgiven", http://aeon.co/magazine/psychology/how-do-soldiers-live-with-their-guilt/, (November 2004).

[17] Ibid.

[18] Kevin Sites, "Killing Up Close", http://www.vice.com/read/killing-up-close-0000001-v20n1/page/1, (January 28, 2013).

[19] Kevin Sites, "The Unforgiven".

[20] Ibid.

[21] Gordon S. Johnson, "Iraq Vet Accused Of Killing Wife Suffers From PTSD", http://tbilaw.com/blog/iraq-vet-accused-of-killing-wife-suffers-from-post-traumatic-stress-disorder/, (29 December, 2012).

[22] Mark Karlin, "'They Were Soldiers' Author Discusses High Cost of War for America's Veterans", http://www.truth-out.org/news/item/19992-how-easily-americans-forget-the-physically-and-psychologically-wounded-veterans-of-the-post-9-11-wars-a-national-shame#, (13 November 2013).

[23] Kevin Sites, "The Unforgiven", https://aeon.co/essays/how-do-soldiers-live-with-their-feelings-of-guilt, (09 April, 2014).

CHAPTER THREE

WAR AND BIOLOGICAL CHANGE

"Some 300,000 U.S. troops are suffering from major depression or post-traumatic stress from serving in the wars in Iraq and Afghanistan.... 'There is a major health crisis facing those men and women who have served our nation in Iraq and Afghanistan,' said Terri Tanielian, the project's co-leader and a researcher at the nonprofit RAND. 'Unless they receive appropriate and effective care for these mental health conditions, there will be long-term consequences for them and for the nation.'"[1]

In Chapter 1, we considered briefly the difficulty that exists in understanding those who go to war and the overall impact of combat on veterans. The return home, as we saw, proves overwhelming to many. In the last chapter, we viewed these issues again, but this time we looked more closely at it in terms of how combat can impact the soul of a person, resulting in an identity crisis. This inner fracturing of self and the turmoil that one experiences in this state is something that leads to chaos and we have to learn how to help people avoid this. At this point, we add to what we have examined by looking specifically at the effect of combat on the body; the biological impact of trauma from war. This is something little considered in weighing the postwar behavior of veterans, even though it brings great changes.

As a Chaplain, I was very naïve in terms of my own sense of what war would be like. When arriving in Iraq in September 2004 as a member of 3rd Battalion, 5th Marines (3/5), we were flown to a base called Taqqadum (TQ). The next day, those in my group or "stick" as it is called were loaded in the back of what are called seven tons, Medium Tactical Vehicle Replacement, essentially large transport vehicles used to haul any and everything. Our destination was Camp Fallujah. This base was about twelve miles from TQ and just on the outskirts of the city of Fallujah. As we were gearing up for the transport, it did not take long to realize how dangerous this trip would be. Our briefing by the convoy commander was serious. Weapons were to be Condition 1 (magazine inserted, round in the chamber, bolt is forward, ejection port cover is closed, and the weapon on safe), readied for fire if and when a threat appeared.

We were told to be on the lookout for VBIED's (Vehicle Born Improvised Explosive Devices) as well as IED's (Improvised Explosive Devices, the typical road side bombs). Little did I know that this battalion providing the escort recently lost seven Marines to a VBIED: "The bomb detonated as the convoy traveled down a barren stretch of road nine miles from Fallujah, U.S. officials said. Two Humvees were reduced to smoldering wreckage."[2]

The threat was real. We were traveling through hostile territory and should be prepared for anything. Prior to leaving TQ, we rehearsed possible situations: mounting and dismounting vehicles, defensive positions and preparing for casualties. Then, we were ready to go.

The drive to Camp Fallujah proved mostly uneventful and eerily quiet. There were few cars on the road, only occasional people to be seen and the buildings and houses passed along the way bore the marks of having been bombed heavily and strafed with gunfire. I imagined what must have happened in this area during the Invasion of Iraq in early 2003. I would not have wanted to be on the receiving end. We did have one incident along the way when a car did get close to the convoy and almost got fired upon. Fortunately for all, it backed away.

Once we arrived at Camp Fallujah, the fact of war became real. Not more than a few minutes after having gotten off of the

25

seven tons, mortar rounds landed about one hundred feet from the large tent area where we stayed. It was very strange as I looked over to see and hear the two explosions and then, the puffs of smoke. I stared at the scene in disbelief, and even as the dust was settling, my first reaction was no reaction at all; I failed to be alarmed. I asked one of the Marines who had been escorting us about it and he said it was a typical greeting from the insurgents. The enemy was well aware of our arrival and wanted to let it be known. The next group from our battalion that came in from TQ got the same welcome message. It became routine.

We were in this area for about two weeks. On one occasion, I remember sitting in one of the very large, open bay tents. I was there with some of our Marines, talking and playing cards. Without notice or warning, mortar rounds came in. This time the rounds were extremely close. The sound and vibrations shook all of us. We hit the deck and looked at one another in amazement. We were new to this and in tents, made of canvas, not hardened defenses. Also of note, these tents were next to the refueling depot. The imagination allows for numerous possibilities. The enemy had my attention.

While none in our battalion was ever hurt by the insurgent's fire during this period, other mortar rounds came onto the base while we were staged in this area, killing and wounding Marines. We were in war and as we were discovering, it was situation where the impact was beyond physical. One Marine came to medical in need of support. This Marine was a true hero in my eyes. During the 2003 Iraqi War, he was seriously injured by an RPG (Rocket Propelled Grenade). The Marine next to him in this attack was killed. In spite of that incident, however, and the severe injury he suffered, he wanted to return to Iraq with us on this tour to serve his country and be there for his Marines. I had the deepest admiration for him. Yet, after a few days of exploding mortar shells near our position, not surprisingly he was losing his ability to focus and function, living with extreme and constant agitation. This condition is well documented in studies that show how Post Traumatic Stress

Disorder (PTSD) as resulting from severe life-threatening events brings about a state where internal changes occur that cause people to react more quickly and explosively to subsequent fearful episodes.[3] Their biological systems have been compromised. That is what this Marine was facing and he needed to get out of Iraq. Fortunately, he did. He returned to the States to serve our battalion in the Remain Behind Element (RBE). I have no doubt, though, that he felt guilty about returning. As a leader in his platoon, he was there to keep his Marines alive. Now he was letting them down as far as he saw it. Here is a casualty of war about which few ever think. A warrior considers that he is invincible, wants to confront the enemy and has a loyalty to his men. He wants nothing more than to take on this challenge by going back to the fight. Yet, in this case, with this Marine, once he does, he realizes that he cannot do it. That decision makes him question the core of his being: What is wrong with me? Why can't I overcome this? Am I afraid? These questions are ridiculous to those on the outside, and what more could this Marine have done to prove himself, having already suffered severe injury in battle? Yet, the decision to go home in this way will nonetheless likely end up being an incessant mental plague. The saddest part is that no one will ever know. This Marine and others like him will suffer in silence. The memories will plague them. In the end, without proper help, these people will slowly lose themselves. How many veterans like this end up on the streets of our nation being judged harshly, while no one knows that right there before them is a hero who just needs help to quiet his demons?

Finally, our Battalion left Camp Fallujah and headed over to what was to be our base for the next seven months, Camp Baharia. We were taking over for Second Battalion, First Marines, First Marine Division (2/1). They had suffered heavy casualties in their time. The promise for us was to be nothing less. The gravity of it all became more real when I toured the chapel area. In it was a memorial wall for the Marines of 2/1 that had died in combat. There was no doubt that war was going to change all of us. Those days

27

were to come. For the moment, we were gaining familiarity with our base and getting our feet wet.

Routinely at this new camp, even as it was on Camp Fallujah, the insurgents in the city would make us keenly aware of their presence by sending in haphazardly aimed mortar shells. The damage was usually minimal, but they got lucky at times. On one occasion, a mortar hit right next to the building where our dog-handlers stayed, about eighty feet from the chapel. These Marines and their dogs were inside at the time, one Marine just having gone indoors. I, however, was outside and heard the scream of the incoming round. I immediately squatted down. It all happened so fast: boom! I turned in the direction of the sound, toward the dog handler's house, and saw a ball of fire. The mortar hit right next to the dog-handlers' HUMVEE (High Mobility Multi-purpose Wheeled Vehicle). It was quite damaged. It took a little while for my nerves to calm.

In spite of the proximity of this base to the danger, however, I considered it a good place to be. The structures in which we stayed were hardened buildings for the most part and there was food, electricity and showers. Life was good as far as it could be.

For the first few weeks at Camp Baharia, we essentially remained inside the wire; that is, we stayed for the most part on the protected base. That position held certain dangers, obviously, but they were incomparable to living outside the wire. Yet, it did not take long for the Marines to grow tired of this base. They wanted more action. Their daily runs outside the wire on patrol only gave them a taste of what they really came for; i.e., to be up close and personal with the enemy. Also, as strange as it might seem to most, the "comforts" on base—chow hall, air-conditioned sleeping areas, internet and the relative safety—held little allure for these Marines in comparison to the chance to live in fox-holes right next to the insurgents. That thought was much more exciting as it gave them the promise of getting into regular fire-fights with the enemy and killing them when they could. Thus, with the adventurous spirit moving them, one company of Marines after the next went out and established a forward position. They truly loved that transition.

Their decision to move out had implications for me. It meant that if I was going to see them, I had to go outside the wire too. Honestly, I had trepidation about it. As soon as 3/5 moved out to the enemy, they were 'get-n-some,' as they loved to say: firefights, attacks, counter-attacks, IED explosions and the like. Our Marines were reaching out and touching the enemy and some of our Marines were getting wounded in the process. But now, if I was going to support these Marines, it meant that I would be thrown into the midst of that action. It was unsettling to say the least. Yet, I vowed that I would be with these warriors wherever they wanted me to go and whenever. Hence, outside the wire I went.

The first time I went off base, it was very odd. As it happened, it was not to visit our forward Marines, but it was disconcerting nonetheless. The only way to describe it is to say it was like being in the Wild West. I was traveling with Marines from the Civil Affairs Group (CAG). Their mission was to go to a local college and see what might be provided by way of assistance. As a chaplain, my role was to be a kind of dignitary, showing our spiritual face in a culture where religious leaders are highly regarded. This was one of several missions like this I attended.

Once I went outside the wire, it was game on. Everyone was tense and their weapons were set to fire and respond in accordance with Rules of Engagement (ROE's) to any provocation. All were on constant alert from any threat: IED's, VBIED's, ambushes, sniper fire and the like. Every moment, every situation, every road, every Iraqi, every building, every bridge, every dirt mound, every piece of discarded trash or animal carcass or dead human under which a bomb could be placed, and every car represented the potential for death.

What does this mean in terms of the human body? Consider the graphic provided and note the many physical changes that occur in an instant.[4] Then, as you look at how all of these systems are

29

impacted by one threat, keep in mind that this emotional ramping up of the body is continuous in combat. The combatant is always on alert status. It is as if he is a policeman driving around the city with his siren constantly blaring, gun drawn, hyper-vigilant throughout the day. Imagine the impact of that on the body long term.

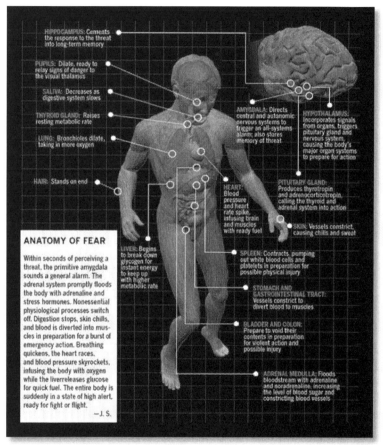

As I travelled on this day with CAG to the College, in this hyper emotional state, we travelled down the Main Supply Route (MSR). This road bordered the city of Fallujah to the East and Camp Baharia to the West, running North/South. We moved at a steady clip but eventually got stuck in traffic. Yes, as odd as it sounds, while the insurgents held the city of Fallujah, with the famed leader Abu Musab al-Zarqawi likely there, citizens were all about too.

Fallujah was home to about 300,000 people. With limited ability or options to leave this chaos, they lived their lives as best they could in a war zone. It was a sad existence given that the insurgents made their lives a living hell: kidnapping, torturing and executing whoever they wanted. But there was not much else the citizens could do. The entire country was on a war footing.

The reason for the traffic we were experiencing at this time was because an American Military unit had set up a surprise roadblock ahead in the hopes of nabbing terrorists who might have been out and about. It was one tactic the Americans used on occasion and it did work. For us, however, being caught in this extended line of cars and trucks was dangerous since we had become sitting ducks for the insurgents. We had to get out of this situation. The CAG Commander took over and ordered us out of line, and much to my complete surprise, off the MSR. Without hesitation, we went flying down the embankment of this road. The descent was about a forty degree drop at a fairly high rate of speed. These areas were favorite spots for buried IED's; it was not a maneuver taken lightly by anyone. Once down the embankment, we screamed alongside the MSR in what seemed like a wild roller coaster ride with the undulating desert terrain creating a mild up-and-down gut-check. Then, after having adjusted to this, we went shooting right back up the MSR just beyond the check-point. It was exciting as you can imagine.

We eventually arrived at the school and the meeting occurred without incident. I enjoyed my role as a dignitary, but sadly felt that our overall visit was not received well. It was strange. We were there to offer money to finance projects for the school but it seemed as if we really were not welcomed or at least were viewed suspiciously. Nonetheless, after about an hour, we returned to the base.

As time passed from weeks to months, I experienced these kinds of rides out of the base many times. Each trip was filled with its own adrenalin rush, fear, excitement, and anxiety. Yet how could it be otherwise when you are flying around in a HUMVEE, with a gunner in the turret, having everyone suited for combat and awaiting the insurgents' next strike?

An important point to make here is that moments like this begin to change the way you view life, the way you experience it, and the emotions that become a part of your daily existence. "In the war zone, soldiers are taxed physically and emotionally in ways that are unprecedented for them…., especially the behavior and emotional effects of circulating norepinephrine, epinephrine and cortisol (stress hormones), which sustain the body's alarm reaction (jitteriness, hypervigilance, sleep disruption, appetite suppression, etc.)."[5] Given enough time, these biological states that consume you can end up making you into a new person because the "[s]tress symptoms that develop during an operational deployment sometimes continue long after return from the war."[6] A neurobiological model developed to explain these long term changes is allostasis. It proposes "…the shifting of set points in biological systems under severe or prolonged stress, resulting in the inability of those systems to return to their previous baseline levels once the source of stress has been removed. This model has been used to explain how stress can lead to lasting depression or anxiety symptoms, including some of those characteristic of PTSD."[7] Fortunately, with proper counsel and rest mental changes will go away "by a year and a half after returning from combat, suggesting that the brain can largely heal itself."[8] However, that is not the experience today of military service where one tour during war often follows another. Hence, the warfighter pushes on and the body changes to a new state that is seldom good for the warfighter.

One neuroscientist, Daniel Amen, provides an example that shows the long term impact of biological war trauma. It concerns a Vietnam Veteran he treated. The allostatic change in this person was in his basal ganglia, an area of the brain surrounding the emotional center, the Limbic Brain, which is responsible for the smooth interaction of emotions, thoughts and movement. This is a portion of Amen's account:

> Mark, a fifty-year-old business executive, was admitted to the hospital shortly after he tried to kill himself. ...He was angry, hostile, frustrated, distrusting, and chronically anxious. His coworkers felt that he was "mad all the time." He also complained of a constant headache. Mark was a decorated Vietnam veteran, an infantry soldier with over one hundred kills. He told me that he lost his humanity in Vietnam and that experience had made him "numb." In the hospital, he said that he was tormented by the memories of the past. Mark had post-traumatic stress disorder (PTSD). ...In working with Mark, I often felt that his experiences in Vietnam had reset his basal ganglia to be constantly on alert. Nearly every day for thirteen months of the war, he had had to be "on alert" in order to avoid being shot. Through the years, he had never had the chance to learn how to reset his brain back to normal.[9]

This story makes one wonder how many veterans exist with hidden injuries to their brains, causing them all manner of physical and social dysfunction. Sadly, the number is likely larger than is realized.

One day I went out with a group of Combat Engineers that supported our Battalion. They were headed up to the Thar Thar Bridge. The exact mission, besides distributing supplies and visiting outposts, was to check the banks of the Thar Thar River for weapons caches. Once we got to the river, we got out of the vehicles and started a slow and methodical walk along the banks of this canal. The Marines were very careful to eye and scour the river banks, farmlands, fields and groves for any danger signs. We stopped at many points along the way to check out possible hidden weapons caches. In the end, we found nothing and had no contact with the enemy. On our way back to the base, we hit the Northeast point of

Fallujah, about a mile from our turn off point to the base, and all hell broke loose. The insurgents, holed up in houses on the outskirts of Fallujah, started firing. Bullets went whizzing by. The HUMVEE in front of us got hit by a round and the turret gunner in a vehicle behind us received shrapnel wounds.

I was not prepared for this. Bear in mind that the HUMVEE I was in was not an up-armored type and not even fitted with make-shift up-armor. Those upgrades and the better combat equipped HUMVEE's would come later. Additionally, I was on the side of the vehicle receiving the fire, with a thin sheet-metal type door that came up to my rib cage and without a window of any kind. Behind me in the open-air cargo bay were five Marines. They were sitting on benches that lined both sides of the rear of the vehicle and they were exposed from the waist up.

Hearing the sounds of the shots and the bullets zinging past was stupefying. Without having had any training for this, I was somewhat detached from the reality of it, my thoughts frozen in a state of uncertainty. I had no idea what this was that I was hearing. It took me what seemed like minutes to figure it out, but it was truly only seconds. When the sound finally did register and I realized that the insurgents were firing upon the convoy, randomly trying to hit anything, I got scared. I looked over at the driver who was equally exposed and alarmed. I could see the tension in his face and arms. He was gunning the vehicle and leaning back as far as he could, trying to gain the best cover possible while valiantly ensuring that we got out of there safely.

My plan, when I finally formulated it, was far less gallant. All I could think to do was slide down in my seat for cover, hoping however foolishly, for this thin sheet metal door to provide cover. I remember being slightly embarrassed as I surreptitiously melted down in my seat. I did it slowly because I did not want anyone to see that I was afraid. Is that not really strange on many levels?

Anyway, as I did this, a deafening sound broke out just behind my head. I went from one unnerving and explicable experience to the next. What was that sound? It happened so fast and the sound was so unfamiliar that even as my mind tried to place it, I was entirely baffled. It was not until we got beyond this area that I understood what happened. While I was sliding down, the Marines behind me in the open cargo bay rose up from their limited cover and started to fire every round they had at the insurgents. One had a M249 SAW (Squad Automatic Weapon) firing 750 rounds a minute. The others joined in with their M-16's.

When the firing finally stopped and we cleared the area, the Marine with the SAW was elated. He yelled out – "I got him, Did you see that? I got the guy in the window, yeah! I got him; I saw him fall down." The others joined in the revelry, congratulating one another on "get-n-some." I was not so jubilant. I was rather in suspended shock and suffering from severe hearing-impairment. This was truly the Wild West!

I had other opportunities to get out and see war first hand in these opening months of being in Fallujah. I always went when asked. Sometimes, however, I was forbidden to go. For example, once before the Battle of Fallujah started, I had a mission commander ask if I wanted to go with his unit that evening on a mission. My rule was that if someone asked me to come on a mission, I would go. Hence, I said, "Sure." I got the time from him as to when they were stepping off and then, I told him I would meet him later.

Later that day, and well before the mission, the Executive Officer (XO, second in Command), a good man, a true warrior with two purple hearts soon to come, called me to his office. He asked me in very colorful language what the #*&$@ I was doing going on this mission. I told him that I was asked to go and always wanted to support the Marines whenever requested. In a bewildered tone, he explained the mission. It was nothing short of harried combat: rifles blazing, machine guns roaring, TOW missiles (Tube-launched, optically tracked, wire-guided anti-tank rounds) firing and Marines doing what they do best, "locate, engage and destroy the enemy." He asked me with a somewhat wry smile what I thought I was going to do on this mission with the implication being that I did not have a weapon.[10] I really did not have an answer other than to say support the Marines as I could. He concluded the meeting with "You're not going!" I did not argue the matter. I assumed that God was using the XO to place me where I needed to be.

That night when the mission went down, I went to watch the Marines head out. Then, I went to the top of the chapel as I often did to see our Marines in action. Fallujah was right next to our base and from the top of the chapel building I could hear everything and see the tracer rounds and explosions. What I saw had an impact on me, even from a distance. The rapid and forceful sounds of the deadly assault, the sights of tracers flying through the air, bombs exploding with their yellowish and red flames, and the fire and smoke raging, even in the short distance was sobering. We were aiming deadly weapons at real targets, wanting to kill the enemy. Our Marines were out there, putting their lives on the front lines of battle to destroy those very people who by this time had ruthlessly tortured and killed Iraqis, the Blackwater contractors, innocent civilians from America and other aid-workers. I stared in awe at what I was witnessing.

There is something important to gather at this point which will move us forward in the remainder of this chapter. It is this. In relaying these stories to you about combat, you might start to think that you have a picture of what it was like to be in war. Yet, you do not. You can read these stories and others, and see them portrayed in movies. It will impact you, but not as profoundly as if you were there. Think of this current raid in Fallujah. What is missing for you is what happens inside a person who actually lives that experience. In this regard, a reader cannot feel and be impacted even as I was in watching the event. Yet, that too is further removed from how those Marines right there in the action processed this event. Granted, each of us has an impact, but the more real that experience, the greater the effect. This is critical to understand as we think about the true impact of war on a person. Let me make this even clearer by giving you an extreme picture of what combat can do.

One day while still in Fallujah, I heard the story about a Marine who was plagued by an explosion that he was in, one that killed many in his platoon. It was a dreadful experience. What did he go through that none of us can truly appreciate? One is the actual sensual impact that this Marine had: smells, sounds, sights, tastes from ingested matter in the air, and the physical sensation of the explosion and ricocheting objects. Next, was the lapse of time where life was detached; a mind suspended in confusion by the event. On top of this was the pulsating heart that felt like it would explode, pounding feverishly, signaling the utter intensity of the situation. Still more was the body's reaction of fear, stimulated by chemicals flowing through the veins, helping the body gain control of the situation, shutting needless organs down and coursing blood to vital life-saving systems. Another was the adrenalin that heightened senses and empowered the blood engorged muscles for keen action. Soaking sweat and sheer panic engulfed the body too as a byproduct of the internal hormones released, increasing in intensity as fearful thoughts fired in the mind, wondering what might be next. Beyond this was the primal surveying of surroundings, ensuring adequate protection, ascertaining personal injury and dealing with it, wondering if someone else was injured, wounded and in need of help. Then, there was the settling of dust, smoke, and explosive powder. Finally, with additional surges of bodily chemicals as the brain stimulated the ability to be better alert and prepared, there was the growing desire to get up and find the wounded, injured and dead. This is what that experience was like for that Marine. Yet, that was only stage one. The next stage for him was worse.

Once the area was considered safe from a secondary explosion or enemy fire, the Marine got up and looked around to gain a close look at what happened. It was at this time when he spotted pieces of bodies, heard moans and cries of the wounded. As the Marine tried to prioritize what to do, he saw something that impacted him as deeply and horrifically as the explosion itself. It was a body part that belonged to his best friend. That was all he saw of his friend, nothing else to be found. Instantaneously, from this and all else encountered, the Marine metamorphosed. His outlook on life, understanding of himself, belief about the mission, even his engrained sense of being a Marine, all began to fray and disassemble. Rising prominently amidst the inchoate sense of being was anger. It was fueled ceaselessly by this macabre scene and anything that reminded him of it. From that day on, there were continual nightmares, grief and growing questioning about what he was doing in Iraq. Sleeplessness, rage, loss, frailty were internal issues that only made life seem more senseless. This Marine had become someone he did not recognize.

Daniel Goleman, in his book about the mind, talks about the biological impact of significant experiences by saying that the greater a moment affects us, the greater it becomes etched in a part of our brain that deals with emotions, the amygdala. Because of this, he says, "...that's why we are more likely, for example, to remember where we went on a first date, or what we were doing when we heard the news that the space shuttle Challenger had exploded. The more intense the amygdala arousal, the stronger the imprint; the experiences that scare or thrill us the most in life are among the most indelible memories."[11]

Taking what Goleman says and looking at this Marine, we see why his trauma had such great effect. His brain had changed. He was living with a growing agitation that was brought on by these physiological changes.[12] This helps to explain why veterans can act so inappropriately or oddly on occasion. Their normal orientation to life has been altered. To get an even better sense of this, let us look further into this.

The amygdala is key in emotional response.[13] It responds to sensory stimuli via the thalamus even before there is time for the thinking part of the brain, cortex, to formulate what the best logical response to a situation might be. While this might seem like a poor design of the body, why not think before you act, it is actually quite important because the amygdala is our rapid response creator. When it gains information that it deems as dangerous to the body, it will throw the body into a fight or flight response immediately so as to save the body. For instance, when you are walking through the woods on a trail and suddenly go into panic mode, jumping into the air because your peripheral vision catches sight of an object that appears to be a snake, that reaction can save your life. You never thought about what to do. You just did it. This is good because if it was a rattlesnake that you saw, then your reaction enabled you to avoid being bitten. A problem can arise at this point, however. When that same sensory information is seconds later analyzed by the rational brain, and it is determined at this point not to be a snake but a stick, then you feel a little foolish for reacting as you did.

That is what the amygdala does. It reacts to protect, but not in a fully reasoned manner. Knowing this explains why we jump when someone comes up from behind and yells, Boo!" The inexplicable sound and potential danger scared us into reacting. For those in war, imagine what happens when an IED explodes next to them, bullets go flying by, they get shot or their combat buddy dies. Those are extreme situations of terror for the body.[14] At that point, the amygdala responds instantaneously, causing a chain of internal chemical reactions that enable bodily systems to shut down or turn on so as to put in place life-saving measures. Yet, here is a problem. In these kinds of situations, because the trauma is so great, the amygdala not only causes the flight/fight reaction automatically, but it also imprints those experiences and much of the sensory information related so deeply into its own memory cells and with messages that call for high levels of stress hormones to be sent out that in subsequent experiences that have one or more similar sensory cues, a person will jump right back to that exaggerated level of response. They will do this whether these new situations warrant that kind of reaction.

Michael Scott and Stephen Stradling, in their book on counseling PTSD, state it this way: "If a memory is burned into the amygdala with enough force, it may be almost uncontainable and trigger such dramatic bodily reactions that a person may subsequently re-experience the precipitating trauma complete with full sensory replay that characterize PTSD. Le Doux ([J. Le Doux],1998) has suggested that the amygdala-based system can produce a sort of physical reminiscence reconstituting the body state, palpitations, sweating and so on that arose with the original trauma."[15] Consider on this, the experience of a Vietnam veteran, 24 years after the trauma initially occurred:

I can't get the memories out of my mind! The images come flooding back in vivid detail, triggered by the most inconsequential things, like a door slamming or the smell of stir-fried pork. Last night I went to bed, was having a good sleep for a change. Then in the early morning a storm-front passed through and there was a bolt of crackling thunder. I awoke instantly, frozen in fear. I am right back in Vietnam, in the middle of the monsoon season at my guard post. I am sure I'll get hit in the next volley and convinced I will die. My hands are freezing, yet sweat pours from my entire body. I feel each hair on the back of my neck standing on end. I can't catch my breath and my heart is pounding. I smell a damp sulfur smell. Suddenly I see what's left of my buddy Troy, his head on a bamboo platter, sent back to our camp by the Viet Cong. Propaganda messages are stuffed between his clenched teeth. The next bolt of lightning and clap of thunder makes me jump so much that I fall to the floor.[16]

For this veteran, the experience is one that transports him entirely back to a moment of trauma. What is fascinating is how completely immersed in that moment of the original trauma the veteran becomes. That is the power of the brain: "During the retrieval of emotional memories, many of the brain structures involved in the encoding processes are reactivated (Dolcos et al., 2005), and the remembrance process involves literally returning to the brain state that was present during that episode (Danker and Anderson, 2010, p. 87)."[17]

"Complete immersion" back to a moment of trauma as a result of a PTSD flashback is not the only experience veterans have, however. One Afghanistan veteran describes his flashback episodes as being in the present but having old behaviors and sights return: checking for snipers in his workplace, superimposing images of dead people and parts onto those around.[18] He further states, "Whenever I look at people, I know what they're going to look like dead. I know what they look like with their brains blown out or jaws blown off or eyes pulled out. When I look at somebody I see that to this day."[19]

Researchers at Cornell and N.Y.U. compared brain scans of people who were near the WTC [World Trade Center – 9/11 period] during the attacks and people who were farther away. *Both studies found that those who were closer continue to show heightened activity in the amygdala, the part of the brain that regulates emotional intensity and creates emotional memories.* In the Cornell study, … people within two miles of the site that day have a hyperactive amygdala as compared with people who lived 200 miles away… The N.Y.U. team similarly found that when asked to recall the events of 9/11, twice as many people who were near Ground Zero had elevated amygdala activity as compared with people who were five miles away in midtown Manhattan. Slow recovery of a highly active amygdala, the Cornell researchers say, could increase susceptibility to mental health problems later in life. [italics added]
Karen Frenkel, "Continuing Effects of 9/11," http://www.sciammind.com/print_version.cfm?articleID=1878E9 0B-E7F2-99DF-3F4B426F6533D13A, (August, 2007).

Gaining this insight, helps understand why veterans feel like they are going insane. They come home, drive down the road, see a dead dog on the side of the road and freak out. That one sight reminds them of that moment when they were driving down a road in Iraq saw a dead dog on the side of the road and then, boom, an IED. Now their body, just like it was in Iraq, is presently coursing with stress hormones that make them edgy, hyper-vigilant, restless and ready to attack. How is one supposed to live like this, especially considering that it is not just one kind of sensory data like that of smell that that can trigger PTSD but all the sensory information from a traumatic moment can be captured and later become a trigger for PTSD.[20] Overall, veterans can endure flashback behavior through a multitude of sensory stimuli as the amygdala is activated.[21]

There is more on all of this, though, that should be realized. What also brings about this condition where flashbacks occur is the fact that the trauma associated with PTSD impacts not just the amygdala, but the relationship that it has with the medial prefrontal cortex (mPFC).[22] The mPFC is responsible for rational control and when it is not activated properly because of prior trauma and the impact that it can have on the brain a person can go through a flashback without the mPFC engaging to bring context or self-restraint to a situation.[23] Interestingly then, that can lead to a situation where one is not only brought back to a moment of trauma but feels in that time like that experience is actually happening all over again, in all of its lurid detail.[24] The amygdala, at these times, simply acts disinhibited and apart from knowing the appropriateness of its response.[25] It is acting without thinking.

Yet, as if all of this is not bad enough to make you think you are going crazy, it is further reported that a person can re-experience a traumatic stress condition but never be able to identify later why: "...the amygdala can store non-conscious memories so that the person may have no explanation for the sensations."[26] For this person, there was no discernible connection in his mind between the sudden onset of stress and the event in which it occurred: "... fear related memories can be stored by the brain/body system with no reasoning attached to them. They have never been elevated to a conscious level."[27] Can you imagine how disconcerting all of this can be? To hear a sound, flip back to a war mindset, grab a rifle and go without being aware of what is really happening would be a terrible reality to be in.

Charles Heads back in 1977 became famous with regards to living out a flashback.[28] In trying to find his wife who left him four days earlier, he arrives to his sister-in-law's house. He is not let in so he goes Rambo; weapon in hand, kicking in the door, and moving in to find his wife. His brother-in-law is down a hallway flashing a gun and this begins a firefight. Heads unloads his weapon firing repeatedly, goes back out to his car, gets a rifle, comes back in firing, and ultimately kills the brother-in-law. Though he is found guilty in his first trial, in an appeal trial, for the first time ever for a U.S. trial case, he pleads not guilty by reason of insanity based upon 'Vietnam Stress Syndrome' and won. In his case, "Medical experts contended that Mr. Heads believed he was 'cleaning out a hooch,' or hut, in Vietnam when he kicked in a door and shot his victim."[29] In the eyes of his lawyers, "Heads was reverting to survival tactics and could not have known right from wrong when he killed....".[30] This position has been echoed by others in review of this defense: "If [a person's] crime [was] one of violence, such as murder or assault, and he indeed believed that he was in combat in Vietnam, then it could reasonably be concluded that he did not know his actions were wrong as he believed he was attacking or killing the enemy."[31] It is amazing to realize the sensitivity of the brain and what trauma from war can do to it. With just this focus on the amygdala, and the brief consideration of the mPFC, you begin to see what can happen inside veterans as a result of war.

To complicate this issue even more, however, realize that these impaired physical processes do not work in isolation from other factors going on in the life of combatants. Here we are talking about personal or psychological issues. For instance, combatants live with endless thoughts about the loss of friends. They are exhausted from a lack of rest that disrupts reasoning ability. They can grow in desire for revenge to lessen the guilt of not having protected those who died. Thus, because of these kinds of things, as combatants move out on patrols and come across anyone resembling the enemy, they can regard the locals with keen vigilance, trigger ready, wondering at times if these people are either insurgents or sympathizers of this enemy. Any faint spark of danger, any trigger that might activate the amygdala, might well cause them to act. Their lives count on it. Their newly found determination not to lose anyone else focuses them all the more. They scrutinize with laser focused determination all that they contact. Then, it is not until they have moved away from these threats that they can calm down some, only a little because other threats remain. But through that entire process, what no one really considers is how infinitesimally close to death the situation was. It would have only taken minimal provocation or some sensory cue to activate the amygdala and then, that same situation would have ended differently, something in the moment would have caused the combatant to react or overreact:

In this sequence every successive anger-provoking thought or perception becomes a minitrigger of amygdale-driven surges of catecholamines, each building on the hormonal momentum of those that went before. A second comes before the first has subsided, and a third on top of those, and so on; each wave rides the tails of those before, quickly escalating the body's level of physiological arousal. A thought that comes later in this buildup triggers a far greater intensity of anger than one that comes at the beginning. Anger builds on anger; the emotional brain heats up. By then rage, unhampered by reason, easily erupts in violence. At this point people are unforgiving and beyond being reasoned with; their thoughts revolve around revenge and reprisal, oblivious to what the consequences may be.[32]

That is the threat that comes from being a human being in war. Consider closely what this looks like as it was lived out by a Vietnam Veteran. His frustration with losing friends, the constant fear of death and other combat challenges created an intoxicated psychotic rage. This is a description of that state:

I really loved fucking killing, couldn't get enough. For every one that I killed I felt better. Made some of the hurt went away. EVERY TIME YOU LOST A FRIEND IT SEEMED LIKE A PART OF YOU WAS GONE. Get one of them to compensate what they had done to me. I got very hard, cold, merciless. I lost all my mercy.[33]

Obviously, this approach to war is not right. It likely causes many to be angry in hearing that this kind of thing goes on. However, I would say that before any gets overly pious in attitude, let us go back to where we started this examination on the brain and recognize as indicated that this story of war for most is just that, a story. The reality of combat is removed in the telling. What would it take to bridge this gulf that exists between that traumatized combat veteran and all those on the outside? True understanding comes in knowing what it is to see your best friend next to you in one moment and in the next, to see him lifeless, headless, limbless, eviscerated or entirely vaporized in red mist. It comes in dealing with the utter grief, loneliness and loss of this friend. It comes in feeling endless blame for not having been the one to die, for not protecting your friend, for not seeing the enemy in the situation. It comes in the sleepless nights, nightmares, cold-sweats and exhaustion. It comes in the refusal to rest and sleep because of the terrifying chance that you might relive that moment, seeing pieces of your dead friend, having his leg or arm torment you, hearing his voice crying out, feeling with ghoulish clarity his blood, flesh or hair covering your face and body. It comes in trying to overcome the pain, but in having to face it day after day after day where nothing seems to help. It comes in having

45

this endless loop of the same thoughts that you cannot get rid of. You feel like your head will explode. You think you are going crazy and nothing enables you to stop it, nothing. It comes in knowing what it is to crawl deeper and deeper into a hatred for all who caused you to be in this living hell: the insurgents, the local populace, the military, the President, your country, God. It comes in knowing isolation as your only friend and medicated induced comas as your only rest. It comes in being afraid to speak to anyone because you know that your thoughts are criminal; you know that to share them you would be considered psychotic, one in need of being locked up or dishonorably and disgracefully discharged. It comes in being fed up with the arduous living conditions, sleeping in filth and mire, having the same old food, being sent on endless missions that make no sense and which always seem to awaken you from the perfect sleep only to go out into the rain or heat or cold for another miserable day of your life to chase ghosts. It comes in the constant sounds and threats of war as bullets, bombs and explosions ever destroy your nerves and mind. It comes in never being able to let down, be alone, or get away. It comes in living with a broken body where physical injuries and sicknesses are constantly nagging. It comes in knowing what it is to grow increasingly disinterested in relationships, appearance and concern for others. It comes in losing touch with life altogether, existing in apathy, not caring whether you live or die, hating everything, where killing at least brings some measure of relief, even if it is short-lived. It comes in being tormented incessantly with this living hell where suicide or racing toward enemy fire seems to be the only escape. One question to ask yourself now is that if you had walked in these combat boots, would your grasp of reality with a physiologically compromised state be much different? Might you find yourself on the slippery slope of immorality? Would you find yourself asking for a little understanding if you acted out criminally? Would you hope that people would want to understand why you are the way you are rather than just sending you off to jail? If you answer anything but yes to these questions, it just shows that you have not walked in those combat boots!

Shay says something interesting here that presses the point even more: "Repeatedly, veterans have described their officers, comrades, and even CHAPLAINS urging them to exact a price in blood from the enemy for their fallen friends—to get "payback."[34] This is astonishing to read, is it not? From the outside looking in, you ask how is it possible for military leaders or more inexplicably chaplains, the voice of moral reason, to urge killing for the sake of revenge? How could anyone even raise the issue of killing for vengeance and not justice? That is not honorable, we say. It is, I admit, shocking to hear, even as a Chaplain who has been in war and who has grieved over the loss of brave young Marines from my unit. Yet even still, I would say that not all experience combat in the same way, and I am not beyond imagining that given the right circumstances, I too might get to a place of being physically, emotionally, mentally, and spiritually compromised such that I would act immorally. At the end of it all, the real point is that if we are going to judge combatants for their actions, we damn sure ought to understand them first. Then, and only then, are we of value to those who fight. It is not about locking up combatants when they fail to reach our lofty non-combatant views of truth. It is about helping veterans before, in, and post-war to gain the right mindset to navigate the mine-fields that come with war. What I am really calling for is for us to do our best to understand the combatants' experiences for what they really are. This is what enables us then to help them, to oversee their inner soul before, during and post war. This is what provides the insight to remove them from combat when needed and to allow them to heal mentally, emotionally, physically and spiritually. This is what is needed to stop them before they reach a state of irrationality. If we held to this kind of approach and sought this kind of understanding, then we would truly support our combatants in the fight. We would walk with them through the battle to the extent that we are called to do so and are able. We would be as much a part of this fight as the combatants we send out. We would also, and most critically so, be forced to receive our own rightful share of blame when these fighters fail.

Think again back to the Marines from 3/5. One Marine from this group was Robert Pennington. An article from the time on him follows:

At the age of 21, Robert Pennington was already on his third tour in Iraq. He had seen his best friend killed in house-to-house fighting in Falluja in 2004. He had fired on a car that failed to stop at a checkpoint and killed an Iraqi child -- an act that his superiors called unfortunate but in accord with the rules of engagement. But on April 26, 2006, in the town of Hamdaniya, the young Marine lance corporal and the seven other members of his squad stepped over the line. Frustrated by the Iraqi police's revolving-door releases of a suspected insurgent that U.S. forces had arrested three times, the squad decided to execute the man. A barking guard dog at the home of their intended target, a suspected cell leader known as Gowad, thwarted the marines, who instead broke into the house of Gowad's lieutenant, Hashim Ibrahim Awad, and shot him. ...At their trials this year Pennington testified, "We were sick of their rules and decided to write our own." Pennington's attorney, David Brahms, described his client's act as a "pre-emptive strike." Brahms, a retired brigadier general and a former senior legal adviser for the Marine Corps, told National Journal that among the marines in Hamdaniya, "there was a level of frustration and fear that it was only a matter of time until the [insurgents] did something that would kill or maim one of their own. So they said, 'We've got to do something. We're trained to take the fight to the enemy.'"[35]

Given what you now know about combatants and the insight from this article about what Pennington went through in combat, put yourself in his place as a combatant, as best you can, understanding

48

trauma as outlined, and convince yourself that you would have acted differently in the case of Hashim Ibrahim Awad. To the untainted eye and disaffected brain, the action is judged to be immoral. The sterile "facts" point to a willful miscarriage of justice. Yet from all that we now see, it is possible to uncover how blurry the lines of justice can become when rationality and internal states are compromised from combat. This is not to excuse injustice or say that moral truth is relative. It is rather to open your mind so that you can comprehend the incomprehensible. This is what we are after. But if that understanding is still not clear in Pennington's case, let us take one more attempt to make it so. Start with the impact of just one combat tour. As one widely read author on veterans, Dave Grossman, says; "War is an environment that will psychologically debilitate 98 percent of all who participate in it for any length of time. And the 2 percent who are not driven insane by war appear to have already been insane—aggressive psychopaths—before coming to the battlefield."[36] Combat changes you. This fact is becoming ever clearer:

> The number of troops with new cases of post-traumatic stress disorder jumped by roughly 50 percent in 2007 amid the military buildup in Iraq and increased violence there and in Afghanistan. Records show roughly 40,000 troops have been diagnosed with the illness, also known as PTSD, since 2003. Officials believe that many more are likely keeping their illness a secret. ...More troops also were serving their second, third or fourth tours of duty, a factor mental health experts say dramatically increases stress.[37]

Given the change that combat brings, it seems obvious that Pennington needed time off, time to readjust from just one combat tour. This was not afforded to him, though, as he kept pressing from one tour to the next. He was now on his third tour and this dramatically increases stress as stated above. Yet, still there is more.

Adding to all of this profoundly for Pennington was the fact that he lost his best friend in combat. That too would have been difficult to overcome. But what about the most profound thing mentioned in the article regarding the fact that Pennington shot an Iraqi child who was in a vehicle? This kind of incident is devastating to the mind of a combatant. I sat with a Marine who had this same experience when I was in Fallujah. It was not Pennington, though we were together in 3/5 on that combat tour. There are no words to describe what this moment was like. As I sat next to this Marine, trying to console him, I knew my words fell away vainly like water poured on an inverted cup. The Marine stared vacuously off into silent grief and horror as others around us just looked down upon this Marine with sympathy. It is likely that to this day, with every mention of Iraq, every time someone calls him a war hero, every time he sees a kid, particularly one who looks like the dead Iraqi child, this Marine anguishes. There are likely 30 or more triggers from that moment that pop up to haunt him, pulling him right back in an instant to when he shot at the car. No doubt he has fastidiously and with ardent desperation worked to bury the details of that moment, never wanting to recall it again. Some use alcohol, some drugs, some rage against others and some just commit suicide; the pain is too overwhelming.

Staff Sergeant Jimmy Massey, an Iraqi war veteran, who also killed civilians in cars as they refused to stop when approaching his position, reports in a radio interview about the never ending trials of letting go: "I'll be honest with you, there isn't a waking moment of the day that I don't think about it and think about what we have done over there."[38] Shay, in working with veterans who have experienced the killing of women and children, says this: "It would be no exaggeration to say that the guilt and remorse of such acts of war can drive veterans insane after they get home."[39]

For Pennington, all of his combat issues thrown together must have made his life a living hell. Considering this, listen to the words of a forensic psychologist, Glenn Scott Lipson, who testified on behalf of Pennington at his trial. He stated the following in regards to what he considered to be Pennington's impaired decision-making ability: "The way the brain functions actually changes after trauma, …He was [chronically] in a state of fight-or-flight, and with that level of arousal, it undermines the ability to deliberate rationally."[40]

Given this discussion, do we see now that if veterans are internally fueled with intense emotional trauma, the chances of them being rational is severely limited at best and completely lost at worst? That is not to excuse criminal behavior; it is to show that we need to put measures in place before one reaches that point. That means we need to understand the biological impact of war in such a way that we are able to provide veterans the help that they need before it is too late. For as we are seeing, "If the trauma is prolonged, extreme or repetitive, it can actually physically injure the brain. The best analogy is that the amygdala stays in the alert state so long that it gets 'stuck there'. …The neuron pathways in the amygdala lose their 'elasticity' or ability to recover."[41] In this state, the person becomes overly sensitive because the amygdala is altered and set to create rage. It does not take much to set this person off. "The longer the vigilant state lasts the higher the chances of permanent damage."[42] How about 6 months or more in a combat zone where every minute might be your last, with about a month off once returning home, to combat training right after this to prepare for the next deployment, and then of course, going back to the war zone. Do this once and see how your response to life changes. Do this two or more times with extreme trauma involved, and where does this leave a person? The evidence is not favorable:

> More than 600,000 Americans have served multiple tours in Iraq and Afghanistan. "Psychological trauma is cumulative," explained Dr. Paul Ragan, a former Navy psychiatrist who is an associate professor of psychiatry at Vanderbilt University. More deployments can mean more mental stress, and for some, more mental illnesses, he said. Army surveys show that for those

soldiers deployed once, the rate of anxiety, depression and post-traumatic stress disorder is 12 percent. For those deployed three or more times, the rate is 27 percent. "People who have psychiatric symptoms, actively symptomatic with PTSD or depression, are being sent back to the very situation that caused their PTSD and depression," Ragan said.[43]

Let me push these issues one more level by discussing another incident from war, one having to do with a different battalion. In this situation, the combatants of this battalion were accused of having murdered not one but many non-combatants. How could something like this have happened? A very possible contributing factor is what we have been discussing regarding what happens to the mind in combat, being driven by feverish emotional states. Let us consider this situation, therefore, and see why from yet another situation people in war do things that do not make sense to those removed from the experience.

The essence of this situation concerns what happened in Haditha, Iraq. According to the reports, the following transpired:

Here's what all participants agree on: at around 7:15 a.m. on Nov. 19, a U.S. humvee was struck by a powerful improvised explosive device (ied) attached to a large propane canister, triggered by remote control. The bomb killed Terrazas, who was driving, and injured two other Marines. For U.S. troops, Haditha, set among date-palm groves along the Euphrates River, was inhospitable territory; every day the Marines found scores of bombs buried in the dirt roads near their base. ...According to military officials familiar with the investigation, the Marines say they came under fire from the direction of the Waleed house immediately after being hit by the ied.[44]

Other details surrounding this event are different depending upon whether one listens to the Marines' or Iraqis' account. What is clear from the information given in the *Time* magazine article, though, is that as this unit was returning to its base in the city, the IED exploded, and in the subsequent firefight that went from the street and into a house twenty-three people were killed: women, children and military aged men.[45]

Of additional note, I spoke to some of the Marines who were on the base where this convoy was headed or rather returning; the base was very close by, just around the corner. As I remember from what was said, at least one Marine mentioned how empty the streets were and how quiet it was that morning. At the time, this Marine said he did not think much about it. It was just something odd his mind registered about the morning. Afterwards, however, he considered that the reason for the calm was the storm to come; something big was about to happen. The locals, he surmised, knew it, and they stayed clear.

Given this information that you have heard about this incident now, let us consider what might have happened in Haditha. Let us go step by step to try and get in the minds of these Marines who experienced this IED. What are the different possibilities that explain this situation? First, it is possible apart from what we have considered that the Marines in question in this shooting decided to act criminally and take "justice" into their hands because they were mad or immoral. Some might want to say this, but I find it highly unlikely from what I know of Marines, having seen their character in battle. Thus, I do not find this explanation the least bit plausible. What happened then? I believe this is a case where numerous factors came together on that morning, and they likely caused these Marines to act out of a compromised state of mind. It is a condition in keeping with what we have been discussing. Goleman refers to something like this as emotional hijacking: a mental state where the thinking or reasoning mind is prevented from engaging as the emotional brain overwhelms and forces a fight or flight reaction, in this case fight. Goleman talks about it in this way:

At those moments, evidence suggests, a center in the limbic brain proclaims an emergency, recruiting the rest of the brain to its urgent agenda. The hijacking occurs in an instant, triggering this reaction crucial moments before the neocortex, the thinking brain, has had a chance to glimpse fully what is happening, let alone decide if it is a good idea. The hallmark of such a hijack is that once the moment passes, those so possessed have the sense of not knowing what came over them.[46]

We have all had times similar to this when we do something out of an intense emotional state and regret our response, claiming that we failed to think about what we were doing. In fact, we did fail to think as Goleman describes it; the intense emotion caused the rational mind to fail.[47] For combatants, it can happen because they live in a heightened emotional state that is further fueled by negative combat experiences and thoughts and thus, it only takes minimal provocation to reach a boiling point.

Considering this now with these Marines in the Haditha incident, think about all that was going on, and how this incident might have gone down. For starters, what if just a few or several of the following factors were true about these Marines prior to the incident: 1) on a second or third combat tour; 2) had personal problems going on stemming from separation from family and loved ones; 3) lost friends and fellow Marines in combat; 4) experienced IED's and firefights before, especially during this tour; 4) had a growing sense that the Iraqi civilians were not being forthcoming with information about the insurgents; 5) were physically and emotionally spent from their time in combat thus far; and 6) had already experienced their own allostatic changes from previous trauma.

Now, take one or a few of these factors and place on top of that any one of these additional factors from the morning of the explosion: 1) tired from a zero dark thirty wake-up call for the mission that morning; 2) on edge because they knew the possibility that an IED might blow up on their trip or that they might come under attack; 3) possibly hungry; 4) maybe unsettled because they too noticed the unusual lack of activity on the streets that morning; and/or 5) perhaps since the mission of that morning was just about over, they had started to let down emotionally and this would have had a secondary effect when the explosion occurred of causing their body now to overreact once it primed back up for action.[48]

Now, take one or a few of the first set of factors, add one or a few of the other set of factors and most monstrously, think about a third set of factors that could have alone entirely overloaded their emotional system: 1) the sudden, extremely loud and violent explosion of the IED, shaking the body so violently that it blackens every sense; 2) the internal impact of such an explosion on the physical and emotional systems; 3) the brain trauma from pressure waves and from striking the head against things inside the HUMVEE; 4) the disorientation, shock and confusion; 5) the chemicals rushing through the system as the emotional brain (limbic system) was preparing the body for this life-threatening situation; 6) the gruesome site and disbelief in seeing the dead Marine, their friend and combat buddy, bloody, mangled and lifeless; 7) the site of other Marines wounded in action; 8) the sudden realization, after coming out of mental numbness that they were under enemy fire; 9) even more intense fear rising as the screaming limbic system is heightening the alert status, making the brain hyper alert and attuned to any information that will help to zero in on the location from where these deadly bullets are coming; and 10) the intense anger that starts to take over as the brain is now processing the reality of the situation, your Marine-friend-warrior has just been blown up, you have just been blown up and now those "fucking son of a bitches" are still trying to kill me. AAAaaaaaaaahhhhhhh, just imagine the intensity and insanity of this kind of situation.

At this point, we have three sets of factors impacting the combatant to varying degrees. When is it possible to say that these Marines may well have been extremely challenged in being able to see this situation for what it actually was? Goleman in another book, *Working with Emotional Intelligence*, offers this:

> The reason a small hassle can drive us over the brink if we are already overwrought is biochemical. When the amygdale hits the brain's panic button, it induces a cascade that begins with the release of a hormone known as CRF [Corticotropin-releasing factor] and ends with a flood of stress hormones, mainly cortisol. The hormones we secrete under stress are enough for a single bout of fight or flight—but once secreted, they stay in the body for hours, and each successive upsetting incident adds more stress hormones to the levels already there. The resulting buildup can make the amygdale a hair trigger, ready to hijack us into anger or panic at the least provocation.[49]

What Goleman is talking about here is how the body builds its emotional levels so that something seemingly innocuous under most circumstances can push one over the edge; acting, but oblivious to the consequences. For the Marines on this morning, if their emotional state was already primed from any of the first two sets of factors listed above, the final set of factors, none of which was slight in the least, might well have broken them: the IED, death of the Marine and in-coming fire from the insurgents…. Granted it is still hard for any of us to imagine that these Marines as the reports indicated fired upon women and children. Yet, do not be too quick to judge for believe it or not we are still not done in understanding the fullness of what these Marines faced. For instance, after the explosion, recovery from that experience, and then the movement toward the place (a house) where they perceived the enemy to be firing upon them, they then faced the daunting situation of having to work their way into that house where they believed the enemy was just waiting to kill them. How overwhelming would that thought have been to them, thinking that every step could be their last! What awaits me beyond this door? Will I die as I charge through? Are there explosives rigged up? Is this an ambush? Are there snipers on the surrounding rooftops? In this state of questioning as they moved to engage the enemy, they did not have the luxury of announcing their entry to the house. Why would they do this anyway as that would get them killed? Hence, they must have gone into that house on the offensive, believing as I am sure they did, that the enemy was just behind any or possibly every door. The emotions must have been pulsating at seismic levels.

With all of this in mind, I can easily see these Marines blasting through doors and firing into rooms almost in a haze, not quite believing that anyone other than the insurgents would be there. That is how I believe it happened that women and children in this situation got shot, being behind one of those doors. It was not right for this to happen. These Marines unquestionably never wanted this to occur. Yet, it did and I understand it for all that is stated. This is war, and it is war when you are fighting insurgents who have callous disregard for whatever might happen. They purposely planted and detonated this IED in front of a civilian home. If they wanted to engage the Marines with any concern for the locals, they could have planted this IED elsewhere or attacked in some place to protect women and children. As it was, drawing the civilians into the fire was a part of their sadistic plan and what they dementedly must have considered to be their success.

In sum, with the example of Haditha, I truly believe from what we realize about the body and how it works, that these Marines went on the offensive to engage those who were attacking them and who had just killed and injured others. Their motivations were right, as far as they could even weigh them given their traumatized condition and the exigencies of their situation.

Understanding these biological factors and how they can lead to terrible consequences is vital. We must do more to protect the bodies and minds of those who fight. Having combatants fight in a compromised physiological state cannot be optimal as we see. It cannot be good. In fact, as the studies on how the body works show, it seems clear that the longer we allow combatants to go on fighting when they are compromised physically and mentally, the more poor judgment and a growing irrational state of mind will move these people from a righteous mission to inglorious behavior.

Chris Hedges, in an article entitled, "The Death Mask of War," offers some interesting testimonies of war where it seems that criminal action is tied closely to heightened emotions that stem from trauma. He says, "The rage soldiers feel after a roadside bomb explodes, killing or maiming their comrades, is one that is easily directed over time to innocent civilians who are seen to support the insurgents."[50] Hedges goes on to offer icy and anger driven accounts from soldiers about the reality of this. One soldier, Camilo Mejia, describes how Iraqi families were fired upon "routinely" for getting too close to check points and he adds, "this sort of killing of civilians had long ceased to arouse much interest or even comment."[51] In other words, the practice of unjust killing was becoming routine because the soldiers had lost any sense of justice about what they were doing. Meija goes on to say that units "nonchalantly opened fire in crowded neighborhoods with heavy M-240 Bravo machine guns, AT-4 launchers and Mark 19s, a machine gun that spits out grenades. The frustration that resulted from our inability to get back at those who were attacking us... led to tactics that seemed designed simply to punish the local population that was supporting them."[52]

Should this kind of behavior shock us? Absolutely. Is it criminal? Yes. Yet, as I am pressing, what if this behavior does result in part from anatomical changes stemming from PTSD? We know that there is this inviolable link between PTSD and emotional rage. "Increased physiological arousal including irritability, hyperarousal, anger and hypervigilance are also associated with PTSD (APA, 2000). Heightened levels of anger in PTSD have also been found in previous studies (Andrews, Brewin, Rose, & Kirk, 2000; Olatunji, Ciesielski, & Tolin, 2010). In particular, anger control, the tendency to express anger inwards and the tendency to express anger through verbal or physical behaviour have been found to distinguish individuals with PTSD from those suffering from more general anxiety disorders."[53] If, then, PTSD is a contributing factor in these situations, it at least makes the sordid behavior like this somewhat comprehensible to those on the outside. It shows the potential for emotions to drive action.[54] The rational part of the brain, the mPFC, becomes hyporesponsive, and so it fails to inhibit the amygdala, and the amygdala simultaneously becomes hyperresponsive, leading to this difficulty in emotional regulation and contextual processing.[55] "[T]rauma exposure sets off a cascade of neural changes that culminates in a state of amygdala hyperresponsivity to trauma-reminiscent and other threat-related stimuli."[56] These are "[k]ey features of PTSD, including emotional numbing and heightened and prolonged experience of fear, anxiety, and other negative affective states,"[57] and they, "suggest that poor emotion regulation plays a key role in this disorder and contributes significantly to behavioral dysfunction."[58]

Is this possibly what we see happening with Meija's soldiers; i.e., being enraged by what was occurring and having problems thinking clearly through the full consequences of what they were doing?[59] Perhaps it is, and hopefully, without excusing the behavior, we are given insight into the soul of those who fight. That is highly beneficial in that as we gain knowledge about these dynamics in war, we are better equipped to stop this kind of thing from going on. If punishing and locking up combatants is our only response, we become nothing other than a nation at war with its warriors.

Before we leave this discussion, it certainly sounds from what is being offered that criminal activity is rife on the front lines of combat. I do not think that this is the case. In fact, a great example of this comes in the story of one unit under the leadership of Lt. Col. Steven Russell that got into a firefight in Iraq. This story shows the full complexity of fighting this kind of enemy, the emotional entanglements involved for combatants, and how one can adroitly navigate to justice in dealing with the enemy. This is the report:

59

"…we saw a white Nissan truck come fishtailing around the corner," said Russell, now retired. "In really just a flash of a second, I saw the silhouette of a rocket-propelled grenade in the back, and I yelled at my driver, 'Cut him off!' So he headed the vehicle straight at him and rammed him; and as he rammed him, I leapt out and began firing." In seconds, Russell and his driver had shot all four armed men in the truck. "Once I realized I was out of danger," Russell recalled, "I instinctively let out a very guttural yell. I can't describe it." Then Russell switched modes completely. "One of them was a very big guy, and he didn't die immediately," he said. "I called a medic. It was clear he was not going to make it, but it was our duty as decent human beings. Once we had them down, we bore them no malice, even though they had tried to kill us." Some of Russell's men, stoked with fear and adrenaline, struggled to make the same switch. "One of my soldiers fired a round at one of the insurgents who was down and incapacitated," Russell said. "I remember shouting, 'Cease fire, cease fire! We will show quarter!'" In the final moments of that big insurgent's life -- after Russell shot him but before he died of his wounds -- the Iraqi had changed from a legitimate target to a protected person under international law. In fact, the duty of warring parties to care for, not kill, wounded soldiers no longer able to fight was the subject of the first modern treaty on the law of war, the original Geneva Convention of 1864.[60]

It is truly amazing to see the struggle that exists for combatants as they engage in a firefight where emotions are sky-high, death is staring at them in the face, and the enemy is trying to kill them. Most do their best to remain faithful to their mission. Yet, this is not easy when the intensity of combat reaches fever pitches. Put yourself in this combatant's shoes and think if you would always act perfectly:

I mean, fuck, each patrol is a driving version of Russian Roulette. ...And you sure do not want to shoot someone who does not mean you harm. But you also do not want to take a chance; you do not want to hesitate, for more than just your own life is at stake. So you have to decide, in a split second, whether or not to shoot. Is it just an innocent car that just happens to have no passengers? Is it a terrorist? Maybe. But you must decide quickly. Decide! Is it a car just going fast, heading in your direction, or is it a terrorist careering forward, belted into a bomb with wheels? Decide! No time to contemplate! And how about that car with the shocks loaded down as if carrying lots of weight? Terrorist? Maybe. Decide, now! Lives hang in the balance! How about that car coming into the intersection from our right, the car that does not stop when you wave your non-firing hand? Who does not stop when you point your weapon? Who does not stop even when you finally take a warning shot into the street? Terrorist? Maybe. Decide—now!—because you have a micro-second remaining before you must shoot him in the chest. Decide! ...The clock is ticking! No time is left! ...I mean really, there are thousands of these scenarios each and every day, and each one comes down to this: the choice of life, or death. Do I save myself and risk killing an innocent? What about the Americans I'm with? It's all about how we weigh choices: how much risk am I willing to accept before I kill a possibly innocent person? And consciously or not, every American fighting an insurgency feels some version of this—the ever present press of a barrel to the temple, and then the "Click,' over and over again, hundreds, thousands, tens of thousands of times, over and over again, and knowing that sooner or later the universe will demand remittance. It's pure statistics. But if you focus on each and every choice, the countless chances of death, it will drive a person insane.[61]

Those we send to war do their best to remain just combatants in battle. Some do lose their focus. Some become traumatized and are not able to be perfect in the execution of their mission. Yet, thinking about all of this, I ask, do you really think that you would have an easy time being a virtuous and gallant knight? I can tell you from my own experience of being with warriors on the front lines of battle that in spite of these obstacles, our warriors tried. They felt it was their duty to abide by the ROE's, even though the enemy did not. They tried in every instance to be righteous warriors. Sergeant Scott Palmer shows how careful they were in the execution of this duty: "As a sergeant in the U.S. Army serving in Iraq, [he] recalls having his weapon aimed at a silhouette of what appeared to be an armed person standing in the tower of a building. Keeping himself from pulling the trigger prevented [him] from making what he said would have been the biggest mistake of his life, as the silhouette turned out to be a young boy holding a broomstick."[62] That is how far our warriors went to protect lives and ensure that they were indeed killing insurgents.

Truly, from all we see, what ought to astound, considering the complexities of war, the many variables involved in executing missions, as well as the impact of trauma on the body and mind, is that combatants most often do their jobs with absolute fidelity to their mission. That itself is a powerful testimony to the upstanding combatants that represent this nation. Do not overlook this. I was with a warrior in battle just after he walked into a room and saw insurgents hiding under a bed. He screamed out in shock as soon as he saw the men and I do not remember what he said, but the emotion in his voice was feverish. Yet, he did not shoot. He detained these men, turned them over, and pushed on in the city. That same warrior later died on these very streets a few days later. I am still amazed to think about that situation and his restraint in the utter shock and danger of the situation. Men like that are the ones we most often do not read about, or ever know their names, but they remain semper fidelis to their duty to serve those in need, even to their death.

Hopefully, what you are seeing through this is the extent to which sending people to war has the potential to cripple them. It is an important part of the picture that needs to be seen. We have looked at this closely through some stories that highlighted the impact that trauma has on the brain, most specifically on how trauma creates changes to the amygdala and to its interaction with the mPFC. We could spend some time on other parts of the brain too. For example, the hippocampus has been shown to be impaired by combat. According to Robert Sapolsky, a neuroscience researcher: "It's becoming clear that in the hippocampus, the part of the brain most susceptible to stress hormones, you see atrophy in people with post-traumatic stress disorder."[63] What this means ultimately is that this part of the brain, which is used to process and retrieve information, can degenerate in terms of size and memory functionality. The problems will appear in terms of being able to process information and thus, knowing how to act and react appropriately to situations, causing dangerous and deadly overreactions or under reactions.[64] This dysfunction has the chance of getting worse by increased traumatic exposure.[65] It only adds to the complexity of combat and shows how difficult it can be to engage the enemy, particularly when their goal is to obfuscate the battle.

But now given all of this, considering many aspects of how a person's brain can change from combat, do we not begin to see that we must institute a continual screening process, observing combatants to see if they are 1) acting significantly under the power of emotional behavior like hostility, rage, anger, guilt; 2) expressing thoughts focused on revenge; 3) making statements that fail to discriminate enemy from the civilian population; 4) overlooking, apathetic toward, incapable of articulating what the mission is, the reason for engaging the enemy; 5) having repeated physical ailments because of unseen but high cortisol levels; 6) physically exhausted from lack of sleep as adrenaline is always high; 7) accident prone; 8) abnormally behaving; 9) constantly edgy, trigger-happy, nervous to the point of sweating profusely, disconnected from the moment, not all there, withdrawn; and 10) having suicidal thoughts or gestures? These are just some of the indications of mental breakdown but each show a need for screening and perhaps removal from combat. The consequences of not doing this kind of thing can be great. Hear loudly what the experts are saying about the impact of trauma on the brain:

> The episodic memory of the experience may be stored in the right limbic system **indefinitely**. …Such unprocessed traumatic memories can cause cognitive and emotional **looping**, anxiety, maladaptive coping strategies, depression, and many other symptoms of complex PTSD. Because the episodic memory is not processed, a relevant semantic memory is not stored. Consequently, **the trauma survivor has difficulty using knowledge from the past experience to guide future action.** An individual who cannot learn from his experience is at **greater risk of behaving inappropriately, even violently.**[66]

CONCLUSION

To be a veteran in war or post war has great challenges. In one Marine's case, Gamal Awad, the struggles are unimaginable:

> …he needs to think of a reason each morning not to kill himself. He can't even look at the framed photograph that shows him accepting a Marine heroism medal for his recovery work at the Pentagon after the terrorist attack. It might remind him of the burned woman whose skin peeled off in his hands when he tried to comfort her. He tries not to hear the shrieking rockets of Iraq either, smell the burning fuel, or relive the blast that blew him right out of bed. The memories come steamrolling back anyway. 'Nothing can turn off those things,' he says, voice choked and

eyes glistening. ...His flashbacks, thoughts of suicide, and anxiety over imagined threats -- all documented for six years in his military record -- keep him from working. The disability payments don't even cover the $5,700-a-month cost of his adjustable home mortgage and equity loans. He owes more on his house than its market value, so he can't sell it and may soon lose it to the bank.[67]

Here is a Marine who served his country in many ways and is suffering. The trauma is real. It is not mysterious, strange or the result of insanity. "It is a normal reaction to undue and deadly stress."[68] That stress can as we have seen impact the brain, "...directing physiological and metabolic processes away from long-term management to immediate survival."[69] If this chemical state is maintained through constant trauma exposure or some horrific moment of impact to a person, the brain and body begin to break down.[70] We looked at how this process happens. Yet, what we looked at was in truth only a part of the picture. Other things can happen to the brain as well from trauma and the high stress levels created.[71] These impacts are equally as devastating to the person: obsessive-compulsive disorder, panic disorder, depression, body pain and/or fatigue.[72] But that too is not all. Stress also creates the conditions for an increase in heart rate, decrease in digestion, alteration in immune function, cellular break down, susceptibility to infection, and neoplasm with possible autoimmune diseases.[73] A person's whole life can change from war.

In realizing these things, let every citizen, elected official and military member work to provide what veterans need when they come home from serving their country. One aspect of this as we have considered in this chapter is giving great attention to what happens to the body as a result of combat. We must do better in trying to provide for the physical needs of those who return from war. Additionally, in considering the last chapter, we also need to be better about understanding how the mind of those who go to war can break, creating an existential crisis of being. Attending to this through psychological resources is important as well. Yet that is still not everything. What complicates this matter more has to do with the issue which we will address next. It is related to the concept of a warrior and the fact that not everyone falls into that group. This has massive implications when it comes to war. Exploring this idea, therefore, will become monumental and provide many insights into why some do well in combat, succeeding and remaining pure to the mission, and why many others fail from the same experience. Let us turn to this now.

Endnotes

[1] The Associated Press, "Mental health injuries scar 300,000 troops," http://www.msnbc.msn.com/id/24183188/from/ET/, (April 17, 2008).

[2] Jackie Spinner, "7 Marines Killed in Blast Near Fallujah, Apparent Suicide Attack Is Deadliest for Troops Since April; 3 Iraqis Slain", http://www.washingtonpost.com/wp-dyn/articles/A64921-2004Sep6.html, (September 7, 2004).

[3] Most of the early clinical investigations of the pathophysiology of PTSD identified a relationship between severe stress exposure, increased peripheral sympathetic nervous system activity, and conditioned physiologic and emotional responses. Since the early 1980s, a series of well-designed psychophysiologic studies have been conducted that have further documented heightened autonomic or sympathetic nervous system arousal in combat veterans with chronic PTSD. Combat veterans with PTSD have been shown to have higher resting mean heart rate and systolic blood pressure, as well as greater increases in heart rate, when exposed to visual and auditory combat-related stimuli compared with combat veterans without PTSD, patients with generalized anxiety disorder, or healthy subjects. Dennis S. Charney, Ariel Y. Deutch, John H. Krystal, Steven M. Southwick, Michael Davis, "Psychobiologic Mechanisms of Posttraumatic Stress Disorder", Arch Gen Psychiatry. 1993;50 (4):294-305. (April, 1993).

[4] Graphic is found at http://hardanxiety.blogspot.com/fight_or_flight.html. The Fight-or-Flight.

[5] Brett LItz and Susan Orsillo, "The Returning Veteran of the Iraq War: Background Issues and Assessment Guidelines," Excerpt from the Department of Veterans Affairs National Center for PTSD, http://www.ncptsd.va.gov/ncmain/ncdocs/manuals/iraq_clinician_guide_ch_3.pdf, (2 June, 2009).

[6] Charles Figley and William Nash, Combat Stress Injury: Theory, Research, and Management, (New York: Routledge, 2007), p. 49.

[7] Ibid., p. 84.

[8] Additionally note, "post-deployment brain scans showed lower activity in the midbrain, a region known to be involved in working memory, compared with the brains before deployment. What's more,

midbrain tissue showed signs of damage and weaker connections with another brain region, the prefrontal cortex. The midbrain and prefrontal cortex are involved in working memory and attention, among other things." Laura Sanders, "Military combat marks the brain", Science News, Vol. 182, Issue 7, (10/6/2012).

[9] Daniel Amen, Change Your Brain, Change Your Life, (New York: Three Rivers Press, 1988), pp. 90-91.

[10] Just for information, Chaplains are non-combatants and by U.S. Military policy do not bear arms or give orders to bear arms.

[11] Daniel Goleman, Emotional Intelligence, (Bantam Books, New York, 1995), p. 21.

[12] 'Neurocircuitry models of PTSD implicate the amygdala, medial Prefrontal Cortex (PFC), and hippocampus (Rauch et al, 1998b, 2006). According to some models, the amygdala is hyperresponsive in PTSD, which may account for exaggerated fear responses and the persistence of traumatic memories. Abnormal hippocampal function may contribute to deficits in contextual processing, as well as impairments in memory and neuroendocrine dysregulation.' Lisa M Shin and Israel Liberzon, "The Neurocircuitry of Fear, Stress, and Anxiety Disorders", Neuropsychopharmacology (2010) 35, 169–191; (22 July 2009).

[13] It is simplistic to identify the amygdala alone as the stress/emotion controller. More is involved: "First, the amygdala has a pivotal role in mediating the effects of stress on the consolidation and recall of memories. Second, these effects are not confined to the amygdala: stress also modulates memory mechanisms involving other brain regions that are sensitive to stress hormones. Such findings suggest that stress exposure can induce amygdala activation, in concert with excitatory and inhibitory effects on other brain regions, to create a brain state that on the one hand promotes the long-term storage of memories of these emotionally arousing events and thus preserves significant information, but on the other hand impairs memory retrieval and working memory." Benno Roozendaal, Bruce S. McEwen & Sumantra Chattarji, "Stress, memory and the amygdala", Nature Reviews Neuroscience 10, 423-433 (June 2009).

[14] One veteran describes his first moment of terror as such: "The first time Chris Monroe's unit was shot at…He pissed himself. He froze for a few seconds. And then he began shooting wildly. 'I went

through magazine after magazine after magazine, emptying my gun. I wasn't aiming at anything—I don't even remember what it was. Just blurs in the distance. Much too far away to hit anything.' When the firefight was over, he covered up the stain on his pants by low-crawling through some nearby mud and tried to look past the querying looks of his friends. He was utterly humiliated." This reaction shows the power of the amygdala to shut down the rational brain in response to life-threatening danger. Erin Finley, "Fields of Combat: Understanding PTSD Among Veterans of Iraq and Afghanistan", (Ithaca: ILR Press, 2011), Chapter 3.

[15] Michael J. Scott and Stephen G. Stradling, Counseling for Post-Traumatic Stress Disorder, (Thousand Oaks: CA, SAGE Publications, 2006), p. 29; also confer, Israel Liberzon, Stephan F. Taylor, Richard Amdur, Tara D. Jung, Kenneth R. Chamberlain, Satoshi Minoshima, Robert A. Koeppe, and Lorraine M. Fig, "Brain Activation in PTSD in Response to Trauma-Related Stimuli", Biological Psychiatry, Volume 45, Issue 76, (1 April, 1999).

[16] Dennis S. Charney, Ariel Y. Deutch, John H. Krystal, Steven M. Southwick, Michael Davis, "Psychobiologic Mechanisms of Posttraumatic Stress Disorder", Arch Gen Psychiatry. 1993;50 (4):294-305. (April, 1993).

[17] Tania Storm, Marianne Engberg and Christian Balkenius, "Amygdala Activity and Flashbacks in PTSD: A Review", https://www.lucs.lu.se/LUCS/156/LUCS156.pdf, (2013).

[18] Erin Finley, "Fields of Combat: Understanding PTSD Among Veterans of Iraq and Afghanistan", (Ithaca: ILR Press, 2011), Chapter 3.

[19] Ibid.

[20] "Several studies have reported increased amygdala activation in PTSD relative to comparison groups in response to trauma-related imagery (Shin et al, 1997; Shin et al, 2004a), combat-related sounds or smells (Liberzon et al, 1999;Pissiota et al, 2002; Vermetten et al, 2007), trauma-related photographs or words (Driessen et al, 2004; Hendler et al, 2003; Morey et al, 2009; Protopopescu et al, 2005), fear conditioning (Bremner et al, 2005), and fearful facial expressions (Bryant et al, 2008b; Rauch et al, 2000; Shin et al, 2005; Williams et al, 2006). Exaggerated amygdala activation in PTSD has also been found at rest (Chung et al, 2006; Semple et al, 2000) and

during the completion of neutral attention and memory tasks (Bryant et al, 2005; Shin et al, 2004b)." Lisa M Shin and Israel Liberzon, "The Neurocircuitry of Fear, Stress, and Anxiety Disorders", Neuropsychopharmacology (2010) 35, 169–191; (22 July 2009).
[21] "Intrusive recollections of the trauma come in many different forms. Many people fail to realize that "flashbacks" are not just visual and often lack a narrative component. Flashbacks are fragmented sensory experiences involving affect, vision, tactile, taste, smell, auditory, and motor systems (van der Kolk & Fisler, 1995). Without a visual image to anchor an experience as belonging to the past tactile, affective, kinesthetic or olfactory sensory fragments, traumatized individuals are prone to experience the flashback as belonging to present. Stabilization consists of learning how to correctly interpret the intrusive sensory fragments of traumatic experience." Cf., Bessel van der Kolk, "The Assessment and Treatment of Complex PTSD", http://www.traumacenter.org/products/pdf_files/complex_ptsd.pdf, (2001).
[22] Lisa Shin, Scott Rauch and Roger Pitman, "Amygdala, Medial Prefrontal Cortex, and Hippocampal Function in PTSD", Annals of the New York Academy of Sciences. 2006, Vol. 1071 Issue 1, pp. 67-79, (2006, July 15).
[23] "Individuals who re-experienced their traumatic memory and showed concomitant psychophysiological hyper arousal, exhibited reduced activation in the medial prefrontal - and the rostral anterior cingulate cortex and increased amygdala reactivity. Reliving responses are, therefore, thought to be mediated by failure of prefrontal inhibition or top-down control of limbic regions." Ruth Lanius, Mark Miller, Erika Wolf, Bethany Brand, Paul Frewen, Eric Vermetten, and David Spiegel, "National Center for PTSD, Dissociative Subtype of PTSD", http://www.ptsd.va.gov/professional/PTSD-overview/Dissociative_Subtype_of_PTSD.asp, (3 January, 2014). Also, cf. Israel Liberzon and Chandra Sekhar Sripada, "The functional neuroanatomy of PTSD: a critical review", Progress in Brain Research, Vol. 167, (2008). Also confer, David R. Euston, Aaron J. Gruber, Bruce L. McNaughton, "The Role of Medial Prefrontal Cortex in Memory and Decision Making", Neuron,

Volume 76, Issue 6, p1057–1070,
http://www.cell.com/neuron/abstract/S0896-6273(12)01108-
7?_returnURL=http%3A%2F%2Flinkinghub.elsevier.com%2Fretrie
ve%2Fpii%2FS0896627312011087%3Fshowall%3Dtrue&cc=y=,
(2012, December 20).

[24] If the mPFC fails to discriminate contextual cues, it brings about
an "...inappropriate expression of trauma-related memories and
emotions, thus contributing to re-experiencing phenomena. Cues
resembling trauma are not perceived in the current context but rather
independent of it — as if trauma is the actual context." Israel
Liberzon and Chandra Sekhar Sripada, "The functional
neuroanatomy of PTSD: a critical review", Progress in Brain
Research, Vol. 167, (2008).

[25] Lisa Shin, Scott Rauch and Roger Pitman, "Amygdala, Medial
Prefrontal Cortex, and Hippocampal Function in PTSD", Annals of
the New York Academy of Sciences. 2006, Vol. 1071 Issue 1, pp.
67-79, (2006, July 15).

[26] Michael J. Scott and Stephen G. Stradling, Counseling for Post-
Traumatic Stress Disorder, (Thousand Oaks: CA, SAGE
Publications, 2006), p. 29.

[27] Tian Dayton, "Scared Stiff: The Biology of Fear",
http://www.tiandayton.com/scared-stiff-the-biology-of-fear, (3 July,
2015).

[28] Wellborn Jack, "The Vietnam Connection: Charles Heads'
Verdict",
http://heinonline.org/HOL/LandingPage?handle=hein.journals/ciiafe
n9&div=6&id=&page=, (1982).

[29] Deborah Sontag and Lizette Alvarez, "War Torn, Part III",
http://www.nytimes.com/2008/01/27/us/27vets.html?pagewanted=all
, (27 January, 2008).

[30] Associated Press, "Vietnam veteran wins insanity-defense case",
https://news.google.com/newspapers?nid=1310&dat=19811011&id=
d7RQAAAAIBAJ&sjid=VOIDAAAAIBAJ&pg=5727,2820890&hl
=en, (October 11, 1981).

[31] Thomas Hafemeister and Nicole Stockey, "Last Stand? The
Criminal Responsibility of War Veterans from Iraq and Afghanistan
with Posttraumatic Stress Disorder," Indiana Law Journal, Volume
85: Issue 1, (2010).

[32] Goleman, pp. 61-62.

[33] Ibid., pp. 78-79.

[34] [all caps added for emphasis] Jonathan Shay, Achilles in Vietnam, (New York, NY: Scribner, 1994), p. 264.

[35] Sydney J. Freedberg Jr., "Thin line separates aggressive fighting from war crimes", http://www.govexec.com/dailyfed/1007/101207nj1.htm, (October 12, 2007).

[36] Dave Grossman, On Killing: The Psychological Cost of Learning to Kill in War and Society, (New York: Back Bay Books, 1996), p. 50.

[37] Pauline Jelinek, "Number of troops diagnosed with post-traumatic stress disorder jumped roughly 50 percent in 2007," http://www.defenselink.mil, (May 27, 2008).

[38] Amy Goodman, "Ex-U.S. Marine: I Killed Civilians in Iraq", Rush Transcript," http://i1.democracynow.org/2004/5/24/ex_u_s_marine_i_killed, (May 24, 2004).

[39] Shay, p. 110.

[40] Sydney J. Freedberg Jr., "Thin line separates aggressive fighting from war crimes", http://www.govexec.com/dailyfed/1007/101207nj1.htm, (October 12, 2007).

[41] Sethanne Howard and Mark Crandall, "Post Traumatic Stress Disorder, What Happens in the Brain?", Washington Academy of Sciences, (Fall 2007).

[42] Ibid.

[43] Bob Woodruff, James Hill, and Jaime Hennessey, "Unstable Soldiers Redeployed to Iraq", http://www.veteranstoday.com/2008/10/24/unstable-soldiers-redeployed-to-iraq/, (October 24, 2008).

[44] Tim McGirk, Collateral Damage or Civilian Massacre in Haditha?, http://www.time.com/time/world/article/0,8599,1174649,00.html, (March 19, 2006).

[45] Ibid.

[46] Goleman, p. 14.

[47] Ibid., p. 9.

[48] "In the immediate days after a combat situation, a warrior can be at his most vulnerable. He may be so sleep deprived, confused, uncertain, and physiologically out of balance that he might respond to a subsequent combat situation with an inappropriate level of aggression." For a warrior on the front lines where there is so little rest, imagine the roller coaster of emotions that swing back and forth instantly. Daniel Goleman, On Combat: The Psychology and Physiology of Deadly Conflict in War and in Peace, (War Science Publication: 2008), p. 18.

[49] [clarification added] Daniel Goleman, Working with Emotional Intelligence, (New York: Bantam Books, 2006), p. 76.

[50] Chris Hedges, "The Death Mask of War", https://www.adbusters.org/magazine/72/The_Death_Mask_of_War.html, (23 July 2007).

[51] Ibid.

[52] Ibid.

[53] Anne Finucane, Alexandra Dima, Nuno Ferreira, and Marianne Nuno, Basic emotion profiles in healthy, chronic pain, depressed and PTSD individuals. Clinical Psychology & Psychotherapy [serial online]. January 2012;19(1):14-24. Available from: Academic Search Complete, Ipswich, MA. Accessed July 21, 2015.

[54] "Dysregulation of emotional responses due to amygdala hyperactivity resulting from PFC hypoactivity, has been suggested as one of the components of the PTSD pathology (Koenigs and Grafman, 2009; Shin, 2009; 6 Francati et al., 2007; Shin et al., 2006)", Tania Storm, Marianne Engberg and Christian Balkenius, "Amygdala Activity and Flashbacks in PTSD: A Review", https://www.lucs.lu.se/LUCS/156/LUCS156.pdf, (2013). Tania Storm, Marianne Engberg and Christian Balkenius, "Amygdala Activity and Flashbacks in PTSD: A Review", https://www.lucs.lu.se/LUCS/156/LUCS156.pdf, (2013).

[55] In addition, portions of the ventromedial prefrontal cortex (vmPFC), including the Rostral Anterior Cingulate Cortex (rACC), are hyporesponsive and fail to inhibit the amygdala. It is not clear which of the two regions 'drives' the overall outcome, but a hyperresponsive amygdala and hyporesponsive medial PFC may potentially lead to deficits in extinction, emotion regulation, attention, and contextual processing (Liberzon and Sripada, 2008).

Lisa M Shin and Israel Liberzon, "The Neurocircuitry of Fear, Stress, and Anxiety Disorders", Neuropsychopharmacology (2010) 35, 169–191; (22 July 2009).

[56] Israel Liberzon and Chandra Sekhar Sripada, "The functional neuroanatomy of PTSD: a critical review", Progress in Brain Research, Vol. 167, (2008).

[57] Ibid.

[58] Ibid.

[59] Ibid., "several studies have demonstrated reduced activation of the mPFC (BA 10 and 11) and ACC (BA 32) in PTSD subjects compared to traumatized controls (Bremner et al., 1999b; Shin et al., 1999, 2001; Lanius et al., 2001, 2003). Other studies have reported increased responsivity of the amygdaloid region (Rauch et al., 1996, 2000;

Liberzon et al., 1999b)."

[60] Sydney J Freedberg Jr., "Thin line separates aggressive fighting from war crimes", http://www.govexec.com/defense/2007/10/thin-line-separates-aggressive-fighting-from-war-crimes/25504/, (October 12, 2007).

[61] Lieutenant Colonel Bill Russell, god is not here: A soldier's struggle with Torture, Trauma and the Moral Injuries of War, (New York: Pegasus, 2015), pp. 119-120.

[62] Matt Rocheleau, "Veterans, grannies protest war", http://www.dailycollegian.com/2.10120/1.1345440-1.1345440, (February 3, 2009).

[63] Mark Shwartz, "We've evolved to be smart enough to make ourselves sick", http://news.stanford.edu/news/2007/march7/sapolskysr-030707.html, (7 March, 2007). Also confer, Charles Figley and William Nash, Eds., Combat Stress Injury: Theory, Research, and Management, (New York: Routledge, 2007), p. 85.

[64] "The de-contextualized nature of trauma memories in PTSD has been suggested to result from dys- or hypofunction of the hippocampus, as a consequence of the effects of stress and arousal mediated by the amygdala. Contrary to the amygdala, the hippocampus is exceedingly sensitive to stress (Kim and Diamond, 2002). A U-shaped relation between stress (and the release of stress hormones like corticosterone) and hippocampal function has been

suggested (Nadel and Jacobs, 1998; Kim and Diamond, 2002).Tania Storm, Marianne Engberg and Christian Balkenius, "Amygdala Activity and Flashbacks in PTSD: A Review", https://www.lucs.lu.se/LUCS/156/LUCS156.pdf, (2013).
[65] Robert Sapolsky, "Why Stress is Bad for Your Brain", Science, Volume 273, (August 1996).
[66] [boldness added for emphasis] J. Douglas Bremner, Bernet Elzinga, Christian Schmahl, and Eric Vermetten, Structural and functional plasticity of the human brain in posttraumatic stress disorder, http://www.ncbi.nlm.nih.gov/pmc/articles/PMC3226705/, (29 November 2011).
[67] [Reference added] Jeff Donn and Kimberly Hefling, "Wounded vets from Iraq, and families, now suffer economically," http://www.nctimes.com/articles/2007/10/01/military/5_20_889_29_07.txt, (29 September, 2007).
[68] Sethanne Howard and Mark Crandall, "Post Traumatic Stress Disorder, What Happens in the Brain?".
[69] "It is well documented that individuals with PTSD have altered cortisol levels, yet the direction of impairment (i.e., too high or too low) is mixed. Yehuda and colleagues showed that chronic PTSD was associated with loweredcortisol activity compared to those without a PTSD diagnosis and suggested that chronically high stress levels may exhaust the HPA axis. Other studies have found higher cortisol activity in those with PTSD. One research team found that compared to controls, Vietnam combat veterans with PTSD had higher overall cortisol levels. Another study documented that Croatian combat veterans had fewer glucocorticoid receptors (receptors that cortisol binds to) compared to healthy controls, which could also contribute to higher levels of circulating cortisol." Eileen Delaney, "The Relationship between Traumatic Stress, PTSD and Cortisol", http://www.med.navy.mil/sites/nmcsd/nccosc/healthProfessionalsV2/reports/Documents/ptsd-and-cortisol-051413.pdf, (July, 2015).
[70] Ibid., "Prolonged activation of the stress response can compromise the body's internal stability, resulting in HPA [hypothalamic-pituitary-adrenal] axis dysregulation and alterations in cortisol levels. Chronic illness and disease can then ensue due to cotisol's impact on the immune system." [acronym definition added].

[71] "Chronic failure to effectively modulate the stress response can impair the immune system, damage neurons in the hippocampus and prefrontal cortex, and contribute to a host of psychological and medical conditions, including depression, anxiety, asthma, and heart disease. The biology of resilience likely involves a complex network of brain circuits associated with emotion regulation, response to fear, social behavior, learning, memory, extinction, and reward.", Watson Southwick, "The emerging scientific and clinical literature on resilience and psychological first aid. A practical guide to PTSD treatment: Pharmacological and psychotherapeutic approaches", http://eds.a.ebscohost.com.library.gcu.edu:2048/eds/pdfviewer/pdfviewer?sid=63f7f891-aaf3-4e8e-a589-4aaa9460af38%40sessionmgr4001&vid=12&hid=4208, (July 18, 2015).

[72] Eileen Delaney, "The Relationship between Traumatic Stress, PTSD and Cortisol", http://www.med.navy.mil/sites/nmcsd/nccosc/healthProfessionalsV2/reports/Documents/ptsd-and-cortisol-051413.pdf, (July, 2015).

[73] Ibid.

Section II

Warrior's Identity

Chapter Four
Warrior's Nature

Chapter Five
Warriors in History

Chapter Six
Warrior's Traits as Witnessed in the Battle of Fallujah

Chapter Seven
Warrior's View of Killing

Chapter Eight
Separating Warriors from Non-Warriors

CHAPTER FOUR

WARRIOR'S NATURE

Some people are made for combat. James Gavin, an officer in the Army, was this kind of person. As he said of himself, "I went forth to seek the challenge, to move towards the sounds of the guns, to go where danger was the greatest, for there is where the issues would be resolved and the decisions made."[1] This description was one that others believed to be true about Gavin as well. He was considered to be driven, bold, inspirational, and oblivious to personal danger.[2] He "was an eager, ambitious professional for whom the war represented the greatest opportunity of his career. He behaved on the battlefield with the insouciance of a soldier emboldened by the experience of being fired upon without effect."[3] Even as a senior officer, he would be on the front lines engaging the enemy. As he said, "There is only one way to fight a battle or war, I am more than ever convinced. Fight intensely, smartly and tough. Take chances personally... [and] [h]it them quick and hit them hard."[4] What is it about Gavin and others like him that causes them to excel in war far beyond what others can do and well beyond what others would want to do? The answer lies in understanding the nature of the warrior.

By November of 2004, our Battalion had been at Camp Baharia for about two months. Our three companies had moved slightly forward and established positions against Fallujah, giving them ample opportunity to engage the enemy. Now, however, we were told that the time to take back Fallujah from the insurgents was to begin. All companies were brought back to the base for final planning, preparations, and the eventual movement to war.

On the eve of the assault, 7 November, 2004, when I reported to the staging area where our Battalion and a host of other units had formed, I saw the most impressive and intimidating display of military assault vehicles, gear and personnel that I had seen. There were hundreds upon hundreds of warriors in full combat gear, along with a raft of massive M1A1 tanks, LAV's, AAV's, and HUMVEES; all with varying assortments of mounted machine guns, rockets and cannons. These assets, along with the many assault vehicles that were to carry our troops into position, made for an overwhelming force. Additionally, we had air assets readied and they would be equally as crushing to the enemy: Apache helicopters, AC130 gunships, F18's with their assortment of laser-guided bombs.

As we awaited the final order to move out, I walked around and talked to the Marines, handed out various care items, offered religious ministry to those interested and checked on the state of mind of these warriors. I detected no hesitancy. They could not wait. They were ready to kill this enemy. They wanted to fight.

We left Camp Baharia just after midnight. In the early morning hours of 8 November, we got into our final places. Our Battalion was located on the northwest corner of Fallujah; we would push down through the city alongside the Euphrates River with other combat units lined up to our east, pushing down in their respective sectors. Around the city, encircling it in a ring of fire, were still other units. They were there to ensure that the insurgents could not get away once all the northern combat units began to push south. The entire operation required intensive coordination so as to avoid friendly fire as units fought close together.

As the three combat companies from 3/5 took positions along our forward line, situated just north of a train trestle that ran the entire length of the northern part of this city, the rest of us from 3/5 remained at our new location. It was, in military terms, a place known as a Forward Operation Base (FOB). It was placed on the grounds of an apartment complex that sat near the trestle and just behind where the combat companies had assembled. It would be from here that those not directly in the fight would monitor the war, offer logistical support and most critically provide the initial triage care. Intelligence reports indicated that the city was booby-trapped and that there were approximately three thousand hard core insurgents waiting to die. Given this, we knew that the number of wounded might well be significant. This was going to be a hard fought bloody battle. We were prepared and as ready as we could be, but it was definitely a sobering time as we waited for it to begin.

When every unit commander was ready and the final order was given to start the battle, the fighting began. Breaches were blown in the trestle and into the city went the warriors. It occurred at the break of dawn on 8 November. There were several names given to this battle: the Battle of Fallujah, Phantom Fury and Operation al-Fajr.

As the Marines and Soldiers from all units pushed forward, on the FOB we were anxiously awaiting the first reports on what was occurring, and had apprehensions regarding the welfare of our troops.

We were on edge. What about those warriors in the fight? Were they possessed by this anxious state of mind? Actually, no. These Marines could not wait. This was a historic time, one about which these Marines always dreamed. Their predecessors, the legends of lore, had their own battles and their chances to be warriors. Now it was their moment, an instance that would define existence. They were finally doing what they had joined the Corps to do. Instead of feeling uneasy or out of place, they were alive, loving life, doing what they do best: locating, closing with, and destroying the enemy. For warriors, there is no other pinnacle moment in life. To help you understand why, let me take you back to when I reported to 3/5. My experiences then will provide an important platform for uncovering the warrior nature. We will return to the details of this battle.

I reported as the chaplain to 3/5 on the Fourth of July, 2004. It was four months prior to the Battle of Fallujah. When I showed up to be with this unit, which was out of Camp Pendleton, the warriors were hard at work. They were training at a place about one hour north of Pendleton, March Air Reserve Base. This base had long since been mostly closed down due to the Base Realignment and Closure III. These Marines made the most of this situation, however, by using a now defunct residential site as a location to work on Close Quarters Battle (CQB). CQB is a specific type of fighting where the enemy is engaged at very close range, building to building, room to room and even to the point of hand-to-hand combat.

When I arrived I reported to the Command Post. I met with the Battalion Commanding Officer (CO). After that, I went to meet the Marines.

A concern I had in talking with these Marines, something which I believed would be a natural point of discussion, was about the upcoming deployment to Iraq. The word was out that this was going to be a difficult deployment. Although it went unstated, there was a sense that not all would be coming back. We were going to war. We were going to the front lines, the pointy edge of the spear as Marines often say. We were going, or I should say they were going and I was going to support them in this effort, to kill the enemy. It was one thing to train for this with the idea in mind that this would never really happen. It was quite another to realize that in a few months we would be right in the thick of combat, possibly being killed.

I walked around and tried to gauge what these men thought about this dangerous mission. This is where I first encountered the mindset of a warrior. It was nothing less than astonishing. When I asked the first Marine I ran into what he thought about going to Iraq, he said that he could not wait to get there.

83

When I asked why, there was no hesitancy in his answer or even thoughtful considerations of the possible dangers. His candid answer was this: "I want to go and kill those bastards."

Okay, what was I supposed to say to that? I had no idea. I, in no way, anticipated this response. Awkwardly, I finished up my conversation with this Marine after a few pleasantries and went off surprised. I guess I expected not a focus on killing or intensity about it but a concern for personal safety or issues related to dying. Yet, those thoughts did not seem to be present. Who knows, I wondered, maybe this was just a gung-ho Marine.

I continued on and found another Marine. I introduced myself and followed the same line of questioning. I asked him about going to Iraq. He likewise could not wait to get to there. I then asked as I did with the other Marine why he wanted to go to Iraq. He said, "I want to blow one of those assholes' brains out and watch them spill out all over the ground."

That was not what I was expecting to hear. Outwardly, I laughed. It was a reaction to the strangeness of what I was hearing and my feeble attempt to know how to reply. When I did gather myself, all I could think to say was "oh," and I shook my head agreeably as if to indicate this was a normal response or what I was expecting him to say. Then, without anything else to offer, I looked at the Marine next to him and asked him if he felt the same way about killing the enemy. He said, "Yes, I want to go and blow those motherfuckers away."

Much to my surprise, as I continued to make my way around this Battalion in an effort to talk to the Marines about war, I continued to discover the same thing. These men looked forward to going into harm's way for the chance to destroy the enemy. They were not controlled by personal fear related to war. They wanted to kill. Some had very graphic and colorful descriptions of how they wanted the enemy to die. Others were more matter of fact about their desire and need to kill. But all shared in this electric buzz that centered on being in war and engaging the enemy. This is the nature of a warrior. It is one that most do not understand and that leads to rampant confusion. To help in overcoming this, let us address what is unique to the nature of warriors. There are six attributes that I have outlined. I have particularly chosen them because individually and collectively, they seem to be what most defines what I saw about this group that makes them so unique and equipped for war.

The six are elitism, invincibility, hardness, self-sacrificing, gusto seekers and rigid moralists. Let us look at each in turn. In doing so, I will share mainly from my time of being with the Marines and what I have noted about this community. But do not overlook the fact that warriors fill all of our elite fighting forces. Yet, since Marines are certainly one of those, and since I served with them and observed these things through them, I will center a lot of the discussion on them. As we move forward, though, in subsequent chapters, this discussion on warriors and their communities will broaden and in fact, we will trace the broader community of warriors down through history. It will be a fascinating look into what is often overlooked.

Elitism

Joining the Marine Corps automatically puts one in a special group. Of all the military services, they are the smallest. As they often say about themselves—the few, the proud, the Marines. Yet, it is not numerical size that gives rise to their personal sense of importance. It rather relates to the special mission that is placed upon Marines; i.e., when it comes to war, they are counted on to be at the very forefront of battle. They are the first to charge in. Certainly, this is not something that most who join the military want, but it is the sole reason why many join the Marine Corps.

There is a commercial that is designed to seek out Marine recruits who have this desire to fight. The commercial is of a Marine on a chessboard and he is engaging in battle with a dark knight, ultimately slaying this knight and winning the game. For potential recruits, the appeal is to sign up to be a part of this select group. But after they do, recruits discover that just because they want to be in this group, it does not mean that they will be. Recruits have to show themselves to be worthy and earn their place as James Bradley recalls in his book, *Flags of our Fathers*:

> ...becoming a member of this elite force was not automatic. In boot camp the boys were cautioned: 'You are not Marines. You are recruits. We'll see if you will be worthy of the title of United States Marine!' Earning the title of Marines was an honor recruits strove for. As Robert Lane put it, 'You thought the Marines were the best and you had to be the best.'[5]

Certainly, part of the indoctrination to the Marine Corps is to test the mettle of a recruit. The process is grueling and what better way to show this than surviving the crucible: that final period of boot camp hell. But if you make it, if you pass all tests, your sense of identity as an elite fighter becomes crystalized. The magical moment to recognize this is graduation. It is then that you wear the uniform of a United States Marine. You are now like no other; you are a Marine. One recruit said this about the experience: "...We felt we were superior to any service member,... They made you into the best fighting man in the world."[6] Another recruit, Jim Lehrer, a famous newscaster, speaks of this too. He says about this experience that from "the special Marine warrior pride ingrained into him in boot camp: 'I learned that Marines never leave their dead and wounded behind, officers always eat last, the U.S. Army is chicken shit in combat, the Navy is worse, and the Air Force is barely even on our side."[7] That is the elite inner disposition and thinking that a warrior carries and which defines Marines. As yet another Marine stated, "You went into the Marines because you wanted to be the best,... We had the hardest training, hit the hardest spots. We were the best."[8]

You join the Marines because you want to be in the elite crowd. When you become a Marine, you are convinced that you truly are of the elite. It does not stop there, however. In the Marine Corps, there is a further narrowing of who really qualifies as the elite of the elite, at least in so far as the Infantry Marines are concerned; they are the front-line war fighters. For this group of Marines, to be of the true elite, one must not just be a Marine, but must become a 0311 (Infantry Rifleman) or have some other 03 Military Occupational Specialty (MOS). The reason is because this places the warrior not in a supporting role in combat, but right up front for the battle, at the "tip of the spear." That is the critical place to be. It is the place where a nation wants its best, engaging the enemy, seeking the kill and winning the war. It is not the place for the weak or the fainthearted. It is reserved solely for the Infantry Rifleman Marine, the elite of the elite.

But even here, as you might guess, as with any of the elite combat groups, the Infantry Marines simply being one, just being a front-line warrior is still not enough. There is more to the development of this elitist mindset. The determination of who is the "best of the best" is a process that gets quite intricate. This is how it breaks down in the mind of this Marine warrior. First, he wants to be in what he considers to be the best Infantry Division of the Marine Corps. Then, he has to be in the best Regiment of that Division. Then, he must be in the best Battalion of that Regiment. It keeps going from here: this Marine must be in the best Company of that Battalion; the best Platoon of that Company; the best Squad of that platoon; the best Fire-team of the squad; and then finally, yes, he has to be the best Rifleman of that Fire-team. This is not hyperbole. It is truthfully what that warrior is thinking. This warrior takes his status of being the best all the way down to this final end point. Every Marine warrior reading this is smiling now because he knows this is true, and he is thinking about how "he" was that person, and in fact, still is.

Notice importantly in this for the Marines, that this sense of exclusivity or superiority is not ultimately based in the history of a unit, in flattering words or in something like this. What makes these warriors believe this intractably is that all possess an innate sense that they truly are the best. This impulse is then honed and cemented in their military experiences to the point that nothing could convince them otherwise.

Being around that infectious self-assurance and audacious pride is intoxicating. It does not take long until you too believe that these warriors are truly the best in the world. I still have no doubt about it when it comes to Marines in general today, and I am also, and not unsurprisingly, convinced that my old unit, 3/5, was the elite unit in the Marine Corps. How could I not be when the history, lore, legends, awards, pictures, all of which were on display throughout the command post, built this belief in me? Seeing it every day too made me slowly believe how special this unit was.

This burgeoning belief was only further reinforced by the leaders in this command who had a way of talking and sharing information that made all of us think that we were the best and most important unit in the Marine Corps. Yet, if all of this was not enough to convince me of the elite status of this unit, I definitely came to believe it from what important officials outside of 3/5 said. Often we had Generals, Colonels, or dignitaries visit, examine our unit and give their motivational speeches. In their words to us, they always made it a point to say that 3/5 was the best battalion, the most disciplined, the most prized, and the most excelled in training and exercises. Once you hear this enough, you begin to define everything by it. I was convinced.

Let me give you an example of just how inset this sense was for me. It happened when I went to a presentation by Bing West. He wrote a book on the Battle of Fallujah, *No True Glory: A Front Line Account of the Battle for Fallujah*. During his talk on this battle, he focused on two battalions in the fight. To my astonishment, he never mentioned 3/5. I was highly agitated. How could he not talk about

3/5 when we, from my perspective, were the most important unit in that battle? Incontrovertibly, from all I that I heard, 3/5 was the main effort. Every senior military officer that came to speak to us prior and post that battle told us how critical and essential our unit was to this fight, and their words only confirmed what I already believed anyway. Given this, when Bing West excluded mention of 3/5 in his recounting of the Battle of Fallujah, I was dismayed. How could he do such a thing, I wondered?

After his speech, when the questioning portion of the presentation began, I stood up and laid out my frustration at West for not focusing on 3/5 and thus, as far as I was concerned, omitting key elements in this war, elements exclusive to the role 3/5 played. Most notably in mind was how after the battle had ended, 3/5 was given responsibility for the entire Northern section of Fallujah, the heart of the city, the residential and light commercial districts. It was a huge responsibility, spreading us thin, and at a crucial time.

We had four major tasks. One was to seal off the city to ensure that only its citizens returned and that insurgents could not filter in with them. Second, we had to clean up after the war, get the city ready and livable for its citizens. Third, we had to go back through the sectors controlled by the other battalions and ensure that they were clear. What we quickly found was that they were not. There were insurgents still in those parts of the city, ready and wanting to fight. In fact, we lost more men in what I call the second phase of the battle, when the battle was supposedly over, than in the initial fight. That was a huge effort. But even still, that was still only part of our mission. We also had a fourth task: overseeing the major Iraqi wide election process in Fallujah. The insurgents wanted nothing more than to squash this and the election support was quite involved. It too became a major undertaking. In sum, all of these objectives were crucial and daunting missions. To accomplish them required the best possible unit. It was no wonder to me why 3/5 was alone chosen to do this vital work. It was because 3/5 was the best unit in the Marine Corps. No one, but 3/5, I considered, could be trusted to do the job. Hence, we received it and it was all a part of validating the importance of this battalion. How then could Bing West omit mention of 3/5? It made no sense to me.

To his credit, when I spoke about my views to West, he allowed me to state my case. He, in fact, recovered himself somewhat by offering a few token things about 3/5 and about what this battalion did in the Battle. I was still annoyed. I felt my warriors and the requisite role they played in Fallujah had been overlooked. Now comes the interesting part. When the presentation was over, I started to leave. Before I got out of the theater, I had three Marine Colonels and two Marine Generals come up to me. Each offered support for my points. They praised me for speaking out and believed I was right. One of the Generals even told me that I ought to be promoted for speaking so boldly.

What did this do to my thinking? It convinced me all the more how deluded everyone was to think that 3/5 was not the best battalion. In fact, to this day, you cannot convince me otherwise: I saw those warriors in action and they were gallant and continued the storied history of their predecessors, incidentally, winning more Navy Crosses since 9/11 than any other battalion, six out of the sixteen awarded overall.[9] But what else would one guess?

Being elite is something that starts from within a warrior. He has an innate impulse that he is the best. This sense continues as he tests his skills and finds his place amongst others who feel the same way. Then, as they all join forces to fight the enemy, they do become an elite force. They all still perceive individually that they are the best at what they do, but then together, they envision themselves as superheroes. This is true no matter whether the warrior is a Marine infantryman as we have been talking about or a part of some other elite warrior group outside of the Marine Corps: SEAL, Ranger, Delta Force, Green Beret or something similar. All have this same sense about being the absolute best, the elite of the elite. They are convinced of it; nothing seems to shake that confidence. It is a central part of what leads them to war and allows them to overcome their enemy.

Invincible

Warriors view themselves as unassailable. It a belief that is never shaken and which is only assured all the more with each accomplishment and job done to perfection. It gets to the point where every victory is guaranteed because there is such a firm belief in oneself over and against the enemy. This belief centers around thinking that they are better at understanding the enemy and his tactics, better at overcoming physical challenges, better at breaching that enemy position, better at shooting, better at avoiding bullets, better at leadership, better at knowing what to expect, better prepared, better at maintaining composure, and better convinced that nothing will befall them. Even in the face of overwhelming odds, these warriors believe that they are incapable of failure. Where others will quit or cower, they see victory.

One place to show you this comes from the annals of 3/5. In the Battle of Belleau Wood, this battalion along with other Marine units played a part in one of the most important and storied victories of World War I. The location was about thirty miles outside of Paris. The Germans were dug in, heavily armed, well-fortified and seemingly impossible to defeat. As the Marines drew near to the site of Belleau Wood, the French soldiers retreating called for the Marines to do the same.[10] To this, a Marine Colonel replied: "Retreat hell, we just got here!"[11] For about one month, through horrendous fighting, massive losses, and casualties, the Marines kept assaulting the entrenched German Army in Belleau Wood. Finally, the invincible Marines won. As one Marine Commander declared: "Woods now U.S. Marine Corps entirely."[12]

What happened in this battle is best described through the eyes of the enemy. One message comes from an un-mailed letter found on the body of a dead German soldier. It read in part: "The

Americans are savages…they kill everything that moves."[13] Another message, this one from an intercepted German intelligence report regarding this battle, said this:

> The American 2nd Division may be rated as a very good division. [In particular] the various attacks by both of the Marine regiments were carried out with vigor and regardless of losses. The effect of our firearms did not…check the advance of their infantry. The nerves of the Americans are still unshaken…. The personnel may be considered excellent. They are healthy, strong and physically well-developed men. The spirit of the American troops is fresh and one of careless confidence.[14]

That careless confidence, that vigor regardless of losses is this invincible spirit. The Germans in this very battle gave a name to this spirit. It is a name that defines Marines to this day: *Teufel Hunden*—Devil Dogs. The name fits them well. I have seen that dogged spirit in action in my time with 3/5. It is an intrepid refusal to believe that you will lose the fight. One who possessed this inner fortitude from my time at 3/5 was Captain Brian Chontosh. He was a Navy Cross awardee from Operation Iraqi Freedom, the initial invasion of Iraq. In that war, on 23 March, 2003, Chontosh's platoon ended up in an ambush and as the write up for his award states:

> While leading his platoon north on Highway I toward Ad Diwaniyah, First Lieutenant Chontosh's platoon moved into a coordinated ambush of mortars, rocket propelled grenades, and automatic weapons fire. With coalition tanks blocking the road ahead, he realized his platoon was caught in a kill zone. He had his driver move the vehicle through a breach along his flank, where he was immediately taken under fire from an entrenched machine gun. Without hesitation, First Lieutenant Chontosh ordered the driver to advance directly at the enemy position enabling his .50 caliber machine gunner to silence the enemy. He

then directed his driver into the enemy trench, where he exited his vehicle and began to clear the trench with an M16A2 service rifle and 9 millimeter pistol. His ammunition depleted, First Lieutenant Chontosh, with complete disregard for his safety, twice picked up discarded enemy rifles and continued his ferocious attack. When a Marine following him found an enemy rocket propelled grenade launcher, First Lieutenant Chontosh used it to destroy yet another group of enemy soldiers. When his audacious attack ended, he had cleared over 200 meters of the enemy trench, killing more than 20 enemy soldiers and wounding several others.[15]

That is certainly an invincible spirit on display. I can say as well that I too saw the essence of this spirit when I spent time with Chontosh's company during the Battle for Fallujah, a little over a year later. As the India Company Commander, his job was to direct the movement of his men as they cleared one area after the next. While he could have lessened his involvement in direct firefights and likely avoided them altogether, he did not. When I was there to see it, as his Marines encountered the enemy, he went directly to the engagements. I was even told that in one of those encounters, he went in a house with some Marines, saw the enemy assembled unexpectedly not far from where he was and just pulled out his pistol and started firing at them. He appeared to be composed the whole time as it was reported to me. I am not surprised by this as I saw him act similarly when under fire and while walking the streets of Fallujah during battle. He displayed what was almost a cavalier looking spirit, although I truly think it was born in this ideology of invincibility.

Having this kind of unassailable spirit in the face of the enemy is a quality or belief system particular to warriors. Whatever the mission, they do not doubt that they will complete it. It does not matter how entrenched or determined the enemy is. Nothing is going to break their will. For instance, one Marine I know who was in a firefight jumped out from cover during it, exposing himself to a deadly hail of gunfire that just killed one of his own. Without protection, he took on the enemy, firing his machine gun (SAW) like a true-life Rambo, while another Marine crawled under his fire to retrieve a Marine that had just died in this conflict.

A few other Marines I had the honor of being with in Fallujah did similar things like charging into rooms filled with armed insurgents by themselves to kill the enemy once and for all. Still others picked up grenades lobbed at them by the enemy and threw them right back. Even more, other Marines have rolled or jumped onto live grenades, dying in the explosion to save their fellow Marines.

Who does these kinds of things? What compels a person to face certain death when all else would run or hide? It is the spirit of a warrior, an indomitable will that cannot and will not accept defeat. This is the very thing I saw in Marines during my time with them in Fallujah. As they charged forward in the fight, they were not hyped up on drugs like the enemy; they were not fighting for some post-death promise of glory and riches; and they were not even fighting for earthly rewards. They were just fighting because that is who they are! Invincible as testified most incontrovertibly by the fact that just as it was at the Battle of Belleau Wood so it also was when the Battle of Fallujah ended: "Fallujah now U. S. Marine Corps entirely."

The strength of warriors with their impervious attitude enables them to overcome amazing odds. They will attempt to do things that others consider to be foolhardy or insurmountable. If you spend any time around them, you will see this. One Navy nurse, Norma Harrison, who cared for those severely wounded in the Battle for Iwo Jima had her own testimony. It was recorded in James Bradley's book, *Flags of our Fathers*. That author mentions this about what she witnessed:

She saw many varieties of wounded and injured men. She administered to men of the Navy and the Army. But these Iwo Jima Marines would always be distinct in her memory. 'The difference was their spirit,' she said. 'Not one of them was ever beaten. The Marines had esprit de corps. They were burned and injured and full of shrapnel. They were hurting. But they were never beaten.'[16]

An inviolable will to achieve the task in front of them is what drives warriors forward. It is an attribute that has enabled them to overcome seemingly impossible assignments. At the Battle of Guadalcanal, a protracted fight that lasted for 3 months, a Marine made this assessment of what won the war for them:

For the amount of time we were there, we didn't do all that much fighting. But there were other things. The sickness and the heat especially. The living conditions were the worst on Guadalcanal. …The Japanese thought their indomitable will would provide them with the margin for victory. It did not occur to them—or they could not acknowledge—that the Marines and soldiers they were battling were equally indomitable and, in the end, victorious.[17]

This unwillingness to give up, in spite of the sufferings, is an undeniable part of the warrior constitution. It is a part of what drives them to war and victory. It is a trait feared by the enemy who realizes that facing these kinds of true warriors brings about a different kind of battle experience. This is confirmed well by a Japanese fighter during World War II. He stated this: "The Americans on this Island are not ordinary troops, but Marines, a special force recruited from jails and insane asylums for bloodlust."[18] That captures well this invincible spirit that looks in battle like one possessed of a demonic fighting spirit, a true devil dog. It is a dogged driving force within that will stop at nothing and do anything to win; defeat is not an option. That is the warrior.

Hardness

Having a resolute spirit or being hard as Marines will say of themselves is a way for them to talk about mental and physical toughness. Nurturing this quality begins at boot camp. Drill Sergeants, in their intimidating and unrelenting style, and through the rigors of training, break recruits down to weed out the weak. Constant verbal and physical challenges, along with a loss of freedom, extreme demands for order and discipline, punishing schedules and notably the crucible, a fifty-four hour non-stop test of will and physical shape, are all designed to see who is hard and who is not a Marine.

One Marine, 1st Lieutenant Robert Sullivan, who fought in the Pacific during WWII was described precisely as one who fit this ideal of hardness. Those who knew him best stated it this way:

> Sullivan was a big man, a former college football player, and a gung-ho Marine, a warrior who thrived on war. …He carried a Tommy gun, one of the few officers to arm himself with that weapon, because he liked combat. He wasn't satisfied with merely directing his men in battle; he wanted to take part in fighting, getting in among the enemy at close quarters, blasting them with automatic fire. He was fearless and **hard** and aggressive, and he had absolute confidence in himself and his abilities.[19]

As you can see, this description, which includes many attributes unique to warriors, has this one trait we are considering, being hard. It is a special quality that prevents Sullivan from quitting in spite of the circumstances. In truth, only death will overcome this warrior and that is, in the end, what happened. He died in Saigon, fighting the Japanese. This is what was said about him at the time: "We spoke of his bravery and toughness and his fierce delight in battle, and we all reached the same conclusion; sooner or later he would become a hero—even if he were killed in the attempt. Well, he did become a hero, and he was killed."[20]

I remember first seeing the characteristics of this kind of mental toughness in Marines during the arduous, long distance field marches or humps as the Marines called them. In my time at 3/5, these humps extended up and down the endless hills of Camp Pendleton. They could range from twelve miles to twenty plus miles. What made you hard with respect to these events was not just the hump, but also the carrying of your fully loaded sixty pound packs and your weapon systems. For some Marines too, those who had particularly heavy weapon systems, the added load meant carrying an extra twenty plus pounds. These Marines were really hard. Even harder, though, were a few Marines like our Sergeant Major who carried not only packs and weapon systems, but toted as well twenty pound mortar base plates or the equally heavy mortar canons just because. That is the epitome of hard. But if all that was not enough to steel the spirit and prove your mettle, once we completed these humps, when our feet were raw and blistered, after every muscle in the body was fatigued and agitated, then it was time to line up and go through the obstacle course. The pain of scaling up and down obstacles, climbing a twenty foot rope at the end, with every inch of the body regretting life in the moment was certainly enough to make you hard.

Why push yourself like this, especially considering that Marines did get hurt on these humps? Why beat down bodies like this and make these Marines trek for miles on twisted ankles, sore knees or bad backs? The reason is obvious—because you are hard. What destroys others brings great satisfaction to true warriors. Being hard is a part of the culture, proving it defines the culture, and not having this attribute rightfully removes you from the culture.

Undoubtedly, this kind of mental and physical hardness is vital to the warrior. To defeat a determined enemy means that you will need to endure what they cannot. In the Marine Corps, many of their greatest victories happened because the enemy never expected the Marines to be so hard. They wrongly calculated that the Marines would quit when the fighting got tough. What the enemy failed to realize was that they were not dealing with ordinary people, but with warriors. That makes all the difference. In Fallujah, I saw this. There were Marines who were shot and/or injured who should have been removed from battle, but they continued on never telling anyone about their wounds. They did not want treatment because they were in war. It was not until after the war that some of these injuries came to light.

One Marine in particular that I remember had a bullet wound that by the time it was revealed was on its way to healing. That is hard. Just as hard or perhaps harder were other Marines who were shot or severely injured, and they had to be removed from the Battle to receive emergent care. Yet after they got treatment, they refused to be evacuated from Iraq. Instead, they asked to be allowed to recover locally so that they could rejoin the fight when healed. I remember walking through the streets of Fallujah during the war with one such Marine. He had been shot, treated, convalesced and now was out leading a squad of Marines in war. It was amazing to see. What a warrior. He could have gone home rather than go back out on these deadly missions and if he had returned home, he would have returned as an America hero. It is not what he wanted. He stayed to fight. He carried on as the Marine that he was. That is hard core.

There is one more story that I want to mention as well on this topic because I do not know of another that exemplifies this quality more. This story begins on a Sunday morning in the city of Fallujah. My mission was conducting divine services for those scattered about the city. In the middle of one service gunfire erupted. A major battle had started just a few blocks away. This is what was going on. The following recounting comes from Corporal Jeremiah Workman. He was directly involved in the fight and later wrote down his experience. Here is the testimony of it:

We were in a full firefight. ...Insurgents are shooting out of windows, bullets are flying, hitting the ground all around us, and I post my guys as security but we don't know where the snipers are. So I run back into the house where the action is, I see my buddy on the stairs and the wall behind him is being shot up, missing him by inches – it was chaos. Then I see Sgt Kraft halfway up the stairs and he shouts, Marines upstairs! There's no way the two of us can do this alone. [So I go outside with Sgt Kraft] ...and I grab about 8 or 10 extra Marines. No one wants to go back in the house, so our Lieutenant says he'll take charge, and I'm right behind him. We get to the door, and he slides out of the way so that now I'm first, then the Lieutenant behind me, then Sgt Kraft.

[We are] Standing at the bottom of the stairs. Then he calls one, two, three – and you get a kick in the ass up the stairs. Bullets are flying. I get to the first landing and see there's no one behind me. I can see a couple of Marines up ahead, so I fire a couple of rounds. There's two bedrooms, one right and one left – with bullets coming from the right, and I think, I'm gonna die up here by myself. The thing is, once you're on the landing you have a wall protecting you – so I go to the landing and shout down to the guys to get up here. But the Lieutenant ordered me back down, so I dove head first downstairs and they picked me up. I know there are three Marines still up there who need to be pulled out. ...So we keep fighting and looking for our Marines. I'm being passed grenades and I'm throwing them but we're running out of ammo. We fight our way downstairs and out of the house to get more, then run back, with the Humvees close by.

[Once we enter again] Upstairs I see a good friend of mine, 33 years old, [Cpl Phil Levine], get whacked, shot in the arm, he's screaming – his whole arm smoking, blood everywhere, but he's so motivated he's shooting with his good arm. I bring Cpl Phil Levine out. He's still able to walk. When I come out of the house with Cpl Levine, another of our Marines comes out of house next, covered in blood. He falls over, I run up and grab him, drag him down the street by his gear, and they're still shooting out the window at him. He'd been trapped on the second story. Meanwhile Cpl Levine's smoking and asking for a pistol. …I get five more guys and run back into the house. Rifle fire and grenades everywhere – it's 11 o'clock in the morning but pitch dark with smoke. When we get upstairs we see insurgents coming out [of the] bedroom. Scared the living hell out of us – because we're shooting at them and we're lighting them up but they keep coming. It's like they're dead but they just keep moving, not dying, they keep shooting and not dropping.

Then we hit them with the AK47s and they start falling over. Later we found a bunch of cocaine and atropine on them. That made more sense. I want to see what's in the bedroom so I go in. I just figure whatever happens, happens. I take one step and they damn near shoot my leg off, and Sgt Kraft yanks me back. I have a grenade. I'm tired of these guys not dying, and just coming at us. So I pull the pin on the grenade and hold it. My plan is to detonate myself in that room and get 'em all. Run in and dive into the middle of them. But I take one step and throw the grenade into the room. We fire more rounds, then another grenade comes out and knocks us on our ass. I was almost unconscious, figured I was dying but was in no pain at all. I remember sitting against the wall, falling asleep, thinking, this is it. I was puking from dehydration. My battalion XO grabs me by the helmet and pulls me out. I'd taken out 24 insurgents. We'd killed eight high-value targets in that house. They were all wearing street clothes, pants, expensive watches, dressed as "normal" Iraqis. All foreign fighters. We found about 40 dead insurgents in the little area that we'd been fighting in: three houses, and we'd been in the middle house. Apparently the insurgents had been meeting in that house and had posted a guard who saw us pull in that morning. Instead of opening fire they figured, let's wait until they get into the house and then open up on them. Basically, we got ambushed.[21]

This is an amazing story. I remember talking to some of these Marines involved in that fight not long after the incident occurred, including Corporal Jeremiah Workman at one point. I was so humbled just to hear each recount what he did, what those around them did, and the many heroics that surrounded this story, some of which are not even recorded here as amazing as that seems.

Also of interest and worth offering on an aside is that on one of my many trips to the bookstore to find material from warriors on their experiences, to my complete surprise and joy, there on the shelf was a picture of the Marine whose thoughts are captured above: Corporal Jeremiah Workman. He wrote a book about this very incident: *Shadow of the Sword*. It is well worth the read.

To zero in on this firefight a bit more though, before moving on, let us consider a central figure in this fight, Corporal Phil Levine. I spoke with him several times about his involvement in this firefight. What fascinated me most and what was certainly in keeping with this scrappy New Yorker was how he would not let the fight go. As the story recounts, his arm had almost been shot off. It was limp by his side. Yet he kept on fighting. At this point, for most of us, if not all, the intense pain and loss of the use of an arm would have made for a good excuse to go and seek medical attention, thereby disengaging from the fight. Remember, as Workman said, his arm was smoking and there was blood everywhere. Yet, what might have appeared obvious to most of us, was not what Levine had in mind. After his arm was bloodied and hanging limp by his side, he went up to one of his superiors at the firefight, a Senior Staff Non Commissioned Officer, and demanded a pistol so he could run back into the house and kill the insurgents. This was not a one-time request or something done for show. It was an unrelenting and genuine demand to be given a weapon. He could not hold a rifle so he now wanted a pistol: "'Give me a pistol,'" he pleaded with anyone who would listen, even though he could still not lift his arm to use it. 'I will go out **hard**, fighting to the end.'"[22]

Why was Levine so insistent? A few years after this incident, he came by to see me and I asked him this very question. He mentioned something to the effect that he was not about to leave without getting his fellow downed Marines out of that house. He was going back in. His goal was to kill the insurgents and retrieve his Marines. Yet, though Levine wanted this, he was ordered to go and get medical attention. This he reluctantly did. But then once he arrived at the trauma center and the extent of his injury was made apparent, the surgical team wanted him to return to the states immediately. He was told that it was the only way that he was going to save his arm. Levine initially did not want to go, regardless of the cost. He wanted to stay with his Marines. Fortunately, reason finally won out, and Levine did return stateside to get treated.

Through this warrior's story, one unquestionably sees what it is to be a warrior, hardened to the point that no amount of pain or cost bends resolve. That is hard. It is hard-core. It is a unique aspect of the warrior and one that propels him to victory in battle when others would have quit long beforehand.

Self-Sacrificing

It is often said of warriors that the bonds they form in war make them indivisible. There is a loyalty to one another that is stronger in many cases than that found with extended family members and even spouses. They would do anything for one another. What all of this is getting at is an underlying motivation that inspires a warrior in battle. It is an inviolable attribute of self-sacrifice for others.

What makes this attribute even more unique is that this inner drive is such that warriors will even offer themselves for any in need.[23] Army Sergeant Dennis Weichel provides a prime example of this. While in Afghanistan his convoy comes across children in the road who are collecting brass bullet casings from spent rounds. The children are moved out of the road so the unit can pass by. As the convoy moves past, however, one child remains in danger with an armored vehicle bearing down quickly. Sergeant Weichel sees this, jumps in quickly to retrieve the child, but is then hit himself by this vehicle and killed. That is the spirit of a warrior. Not a moment of hesitation to die for someone he does not even know. The decision was made long before the event as that is just the nature of warriors.

Let us take an even closer look at this inner drive by considering an unbelievable display of it in battle. It concerns a Marine named Sergeant Rafael Peralta. His story is captivating and has an interesting twist in the end which makes it important to consider.

During the Battle of Fallujah, Marine Sergeant Rafael Peralta fought with 1st Battalion, 3rd Marine Regiment (1/3), a unit that was by our side, 3/5 Marines, as we pushed through the city. This Marine died in a close-quarters engagement and was posthumously awarded the Navy Cross. For the Marines who were with him in this firefight, men who saw Peralta sacrifice his own life for theirs, they felt like his heroic actions were deserving of more than a Navy Cross. They felt like he should have received the Medal of Honor, our nation's highest award. These Marines actually fought to have his award reconsidered.[24] They won this fight, but after the committee reviewed the award information, it was again determined that the Navy Cross was the appropriate award. The conclusion was still unsatisfactory as far as Peralta's supporters were concerned. In fact, his own mother was so upset by this situation that she refused to accept the Navy Cross on her son's behalf: "I don't want that medal," said Peralta's mother, Rosa. "I won't accept it. It doesn't seem fair to me."[25]

Setting aside for the moment the controversy surrounding this award, what exactly did Peralta do that shows how great the sacrificial nature of a warrior is? This is his story as provided by a Marine Corps Combat Correspondent who was present for the engagement:

…the Marines entered a house and kicked in the doors of two rooms that proved empty. But there was another closed door to an adjoining room. It was unlocked, and Peralta, in the lead, opened it. He was immediately hit with AK-47 fire in his face and upper torso by three insurgents. He fell out of the way into one of the cleared rooms to give his fellow Marines a clear shot at the enemy. During the firefight, a yellow fragmentation grenade flew out of the room, landing near Peralta and several fellow Marines. The uninjured Marines tried to scatter out of the way, two of them trying to escape the room, but were blocked by a locked door. At that point, barely alive, Peralta grabbed the grenade and cradled it to his body. His body took most of the blast. One Marine was seriously injured, but the rest sustained only minor shrapnel wounds. Cpl. Brannon Dyer told a reporter from the *Army Times*, "He saved half my fire team.[26]

Peralta certainly shows here what it is to be self-sacrificing. He is taking the point, leading his men into a house where the enemy might be. Being in that up front position is something that shows he is noble, courageous and willing to put the safety and well-being of others ahead of self. Then, moving to cover a grenade with one's body in order to save fellow warriors and dying as a result of it clearly shows one offering the ultimate sacrifice of self. This is indeed the heart of a warrior, one who will give all for those in need and those with whom he fights.

Considering all of this with Peralta, then, we can now ask how his sacrifice would not be considered worthy of this nation's highest award. The precedence for it in terms of jumping on a grenade to save others has been set.[27] Why is there a controversy? The question for the reviewing committee was centered on Peralta's final act to roll on this grenade. They wondered if, after Peralta was shot in the back of the head, he could have been capable of such an act.[28] From the autopsy reports examined, the committee felt that the shot to the head would have been fatal, rendering him incapable of any subsequent action like grabbing a grenade and rolling on it.[29] Additionally, the committee determined from the examination of Peralta's wounds that the grenade did not detonate under the body as reported by the eye-witnesses but must have exploded away from the body. Thus, while the committee did feel that his actions on that day were unquestionably valiant, as he led his men into this house and charged into a room filled with insurgents, they still felt that these acts fell short of the requirement for a Medal of Honor.

But what I want to ask is if there is something more to this situation that should be considered? I believe that there is. There is an interesting angle on this matter which has to do with habitual action. Let us consider this.

People often do things by what we call force of habit. This is also known as implicit memory. It is activity that is so to speak etched in the brain, acting out of rote memory. Some argue that this kind of habitual action requires some level of conscious processing in order to occur.[30] It is sort of a unified-mind process for all action. In this view, if we take the case of Peralta, we would conclude that because of his wounds, he might not have had the capacity for higher level thinking and thus, he might not have acted entirely as stated, specifically rolling on top of the grenade. Yet, there is another side to this. Some argue that there is a dual-mind process occurring where habitual action does not have to include higher levels of thinking.[31] Under this construct, if an act becomes fixed in the mind, specifically in the dorsolateral striatum,[32] as a result of repeated training,[33] then that action will occur automatically when the right stimuli is in place.[34] The full use of the conscious brain is not needed to make that decision, therefore.[35] The decision has already been formed in the mind.[36] Given all of this, could this explain what happened in Peralta's case? It is possible.

First, we start with this idea of the sacrificial nature of warriors. Those most possessed by this trait show it by placing themselves in front of their Marines; i.e., in the front of a stack of Marines as they charge into a house. As we know, this was where Peralta not surprisingly was.

Next, consider that Marines think a lot about grenade use and they think as well about what they would do if one is thrown in their midst, sacrificing themselves for those around is often at the top of the list. For example, consider this story from one Marine to whom I spoke. It was regarding his time at boot camp. He said that there was a segment of the training when he and his fellow recruits focused on how to react to incoming grenades. Heroics were not called for in these situations as he told me; i.e., picking up a grenade and throwing it back at the enemy or jumping on top of a grenade to save others. But, he did go on to say that in the minds of many, the thought is there of being a hero for the sake of others around. He then added to this, how can such a thought not cross your mind when five feet away is a placard that honors a Marine who jumped on a grenade, and just down from that is another Marine's placard describing the same kind of thing?

These are the heroes that surround us, one after the next, the Marine told me, and their impulses to save others is a message that is instilled in us. This Marine went on from there to tell me as well about what his Drill Sergeant relayed to all at that training. He said it had to do with something that happened when he, the Drill Sergeant, was a recruit at boot camp. As the story went, he and his fellow recruits were sitting around one day and they were receiving their own instruction on this very same topic of grenades.

A discussion broke out in this group about what each recruit would do if a grenade was thrown into their midst. One recruit in that group said without hesitation that he would unquestionably jump on the grenade to save others around. With that, the Drill

Sergeant, no longer back in his story but in the present moment, told this new class of recruits that the Marine about whom he was speaking was right over there, pointing to a nearby placard. I had chills in hearing the story. I can imagine how moved these recruits were as well in this moment, particularly the real warriors who already have that sacrificial spirit within.

Given all of this, and thinking about Peralta once again, an obvious warrior who embodied the warrior spirit of self-sacrifice, do we not think that he had already rehearsed in his mind many times over what he would do in that kind of situation if a grenade was thrown into a group of his Marines. Of course he did. It was as ingrained in his thinking as every other procedure to protect his men was.

In truth, Peralta must have thought about this kind of thing for years in the Marine Corps, having even gone through the motions, however subtle, etching his reaction into his mind. On account of this, therefore, I think it is very possible, regarding Peralta's supposed actions in the Battle of Fallujah that he did in fact act spontaneously to cover the grenade, even if he had lost conscious processing from a head injury. It was all a part of his habitually trained mind, something about which he did not need to "think." I know of no other explanation, and this is why. The Marines on scene for the firefight, those saved by Peralta, stated that this is indeed what happened; he grabbed the grenade and used his body to shield it.

Are they liars? Why would they be? I can think of no reason. So if they are being honest, is there then some way to reconcile what they stated with the evidence? I think that there is. Consider this account based upon habitual action. Peralta saw, perhaps involuntarily sensed, a grenade and by unconscious reflex, rote memory, he reached out for it. But, as this happened, let us say too, that he never got to that grenade before it exploded. He reached out, his men saw that act, and the grenade exploded before he reached it. In keeping with this, we could say as well that the Marines who

107

Peralta saved saw him reach out for the grenade, but then let us say that just after that initial reach they did not stand there and watch the rest of the action, but they instinctively dove for cover. They saw something in a flash, Peralta stretching out his arm to the grenade and then assumed confidently, what that action meant as they scrambled away. If this kind of scenario could be accepted, it reveals that Peralta was still displaying action commensurate with what is required for the Medal of Honor.

He started the process to save others by reaching out for the grenade, but being limited by injury, being limited by time, or both, he was not able to fully cover the grenade with his body. His body nonetheless shielded others and it did so because Peralta had trained his body to do so.

The report from the committee as stated discounts any version regarding Peralta having acted in that final moment to save his men. Yet, are they certain about what they claim? Do they have absolute evidence so as to overturn eye-witness accounts?

Interestingly, though they should, the report equivocates on this very thing. Notice how some of the conclusions are phrased:

1) "There is **some doubt** that Sgt Peralta, after sustaining the gunshot wound to the head, had the cognitive capacity to make the conscious decision to sacrifice himself..."; 2) "... death **likely** occurred before the grenade exploded";

3) "the gunshot wound to Sgt Peralta's head and autopsy evidence indicates that his effective blood circulation had **likely** stopped (meaning that he **may have** already been dead) before the grenade detonated"; and

4) "**None of these findings** in isolation **precludes** the possibility that Sgt Peralta performed a heroic action. However, the totality of the Medical evidence clearly places a "**margin of doubt**" on his neurological ability to perform this voluntary act."[37]

These statements express uncertainty on the committee's part as to the conclusion. So with the uncertainty, why reject what the eye-witnesses claimed:

> Leading an assault team during house-to-house fighting, Peralta is the first through the door. The sergeant instantly takes fire, is hit in the chest and head at close range, and falls to the floor as insurgents toss a grenade and flee. But before he takes his last breath and without hesitation, the dying Marine — as he was taught at boot camp and knew many before him had done — reaches out, grabs the grenade that would surely kill every man in the room, brings it tight into his body, and absorbs the impact.[38]

How are we not to believe that something of this order occurred? Consider too that even in the face of on-going controversy surrounding this issue, the Marine closest to Peralta still holds to what he stated and offers this: "I was within arms' reach of Peralta when Peralta put the grenade under his body.... If he hadn't done that, I would have been dead. Facts don't lie."[39]

The controversy surrounding this case will continue. In fact, after yet another review of this situation, Peralta was still not awarded the Medal of Honor. His award for the Navy Cross was instead reconfirmed.

However, notice something fascinating about the citation for this award. It will strike you as odd: "...After the initial exchange of gunfire, the insurgents broke contact, throwing a fragmentation grenade as they fled the building. The grenade came to rest near Sergeant Peralta's head. Without hesitation and with complete disregard for his own personal safety, Sergeant Peralta reached out and pulled the grenade to his body, absorbing the brunt of the blast and shielding fellow marines only feet away."[40] I am not sure how to understand these words since the words sound like something written only for a Medal of Honor citation, but as we know, they are for a Navy Cross.

Overlooking the striking questions here, what the controversy does not overturn is the way in which Peralta clearly displays the warrior spirit of self-sacrifice. He, like all warriors, chooses to be in the front, wanting to protect his men. This is integral to the warrior nature. It is what drives them in war. They fight for others, not themselves.

Always that means fighting for those by their side.[41] Always too that means fighting for those in need as one Soldier stated about his involvement in the Iraqi war: "'Liberating those people. Liberating Iraq. Seeing them free. They were repressed for, I don't know how many years, 30 something years. Just knowing that they are free now. Knowing that is awesome to me.'" [42]

In my time in Iraq, there was a phrase used by the 1st Marine Division that was promoted by its commander, Major General James Mattis, at the time. That phrase was "No better Friend, No worse Enemy." Those words epitomized the protector status of these Marines. They would fight to the death for anyone of any nationality, race, or religion. However, at the same time, do not dare to raise yourself up against them or those whom they are there to protect. It will be your death. What lies behind these words? It is this sacrificial spirit to do anything needed to help those in need, regardless of the outcome. Nothing will stand in their way. It is all a powerful part of what makes the warrior unique.

Gusto Seekers

Another characteristic that I find within warriors is how they are driven by a need to live life to the fullest. They love adventure or anything that enables them to feel the rush of excitement, the intense stimulation of their senses, and the sheer pleasure of an adrenaline surge: e.g., trying new activities, engaging in dangerous hobbies, exploring new horizons, living on the edge, tasting the thrill of a

110

harrowing moment or combat. One Marine recruit, in answering why he joined this service, offers this answer which shows the embodiment of this gusto seeker trait: "What drew me to the Marines? I'm not sure, but do clearly remember a poster of a Marine, charging up the beach, holding an '03 rifle over his head, wearing a World War I helmet, and the bold-lettered message: 'Join the Marines—First to Fight.' 'That's for me! I thought."[43] While some are comfortable in calm, safe or even self-indulging environments, this is clearly not the warriors' life.

A particularly striking moment for me in seeing this kind of zeal to live life to the fullest happened not long after we first arrived at Camp Baharia. One day, I was making my way around this base to visit the Marines and I noticed that there were about twenty of them assembled in an open area playing a game of football. While that itself is nothing remarkable, there were a few things in this game that stood out and definitely captured the warrior spirit. One was that this was not a game of tag or flag football. It was full-on tackle. Yet, note even more, the point in this game did not just seem to tackle the guy with the ball, but to punish an opponent for having the ball.

I watched for some time as these Marines ran at each other full-speed, delighting in hard hits and violent take-downs. On top of this, though, and definitely in keeping with the warrior mentality, was the fact that most of these Marines were playing this game with no shirts. And if all of this was not crazy enough, these Marines were playing the game on a hard-scrabble turf made of well-worn desert rock sand. Hence, as they played, if the initial pummeling received just for carrying the ball did not destroy your body, your body was still going to be punished when you hit the ground. I can still see this game being played in my mind, and I fondly remember it as a distinct part of the warrior culture.

Another important example of this mindset to live in the glory of the moment with a cavalier disregard for consequences came at an event our battalion had at the beach at Camp Pendleton. This was before we punched out to Iraq. This occasion was truly a warrior's celebration. It was an all-day and night festivity designed exclusively for the warriors of 3/5: food, fun, beer, motivational speeches, games and the like.

In terms of the games, aside from some of the more expected ones like the strong-man competition and tug-o-war, there was one signature event that stood out remarkably: a grappling tournament. The idea here was for two men to be locked arms-to-shoulders on their knees and readied for an all-out scrum, where the goal was to get the opponent to submit by tapping out. There were a few rules involved: no gouging or clawing at an opponent and no head-butting or striking with fists. Other than that, you could do what you needed to get an opponent to submit. I watched for hours as these contests went on. It was one match after the next as these warriors fought their way through a tournament bracket. It was a brutal challenge of skill, wit, determination, stamina and will to win. Winners and losers were covered with sweat and beach sand, some having intense body and facial abrasions from having endured forceful pile-drivers into the sand. There were points when I wondered if some of these guys would end up with broken bones or dislocated joints because in spite of the pressure applied against body parts to get opponents to submit, very few gave up, struggling instead to get free. Some actually did perform amazing escapes from what seemed well-executed holds, only then to gain equal footing or advantage.

You might think that the biggest and strongest man won this contest, but it did not prove to be. One of the smallest guys became our champion. His will to win and refusal to quit, in spite of the unbelievably exhausting series of matches, was humbling to see. He was also quite skilled at martial arts, and in the end, his combination proved to be the best. After the award ceremony, I remember this Marine walking gingerly off, numerous skin abrasions and no doubt with pain all through his body from a day of brutal contests. Yet to him, it did not matter. He was a warrior and had the adulation of all, the best of the best, a warrior's dream.

Sadly, another of the winners, a second-place finisher, was severely injured and permanently disabled later on by an IED while out on patrol in Fallujah, just before the actual battle for Fallujah began. Those sadder days were to come, but for the moment these warriors reveled in living life to its utmost extreme. It is something that I came to realize had to be a part of the warrior experience. They had to do it, and not doing it would have been to deny them an important opportunity to experience the joy of life. Yes, someone could have been severely hurt and prevented from deploying at this bash, but for the warrior, who thinks of this?

As I found in my time with these warriors, they craved doing things that pushed the outer edges of their comfort zones. Whether it was competitive games, outdoor adventure, learning new and physically challenging activities, or pushing the body to the limits of its conditioning, it was all a part of what defined them. This is the warrior's life. You can just imagine how important this would be for war. Every mission is that moment of getting the most out of life. There is no dread for the warrior in this. There is excitement. There is the chance to be enriched by an experience in life.

A Marine in battle who embodied this was General Smedley Butler. He engaged in combat with a seemingly compulsive spirit to live in that moment. It unquestionably made him a Marine's Marine—a title he certainly deserved given that he was only one of two Marines to have received the Medal of Honor, twice.[44] On both occasions, though being in the role of an officer who was charged to direct the efforts of others, he went far beyond that by taking positions in battle that exposed him to certain death. Rather than being killed, however, his fighting spirit enabled his men to gain the upper hand and defeat the enemy. His actions were truly heroic and unquestionably in keeping with this quality of pressing every situation to the edge. For warriors like this, it is not enough to be in a battle. It is not enough to direct that battle. It is not enough even to be on the front lines of that battle. Warriors, like Butler, have to be out in front, exposing themselves to deadly fire by leading the charge.

Listen to Butler express this very idea in his own words. The sentiments are captured in a letter that he writes to the then Commandant of the Marine Corps, General John A. Lejeune. He says about the Marine Corps: "We have a class of men in our ranks far superior to those in any other service in the world and they are high-spirited and splendid in every way. They joined because of our reputation for giving them excitement, and excitement from a marine's standpoint, can only be gained by the use of bullets and the proximity to danger."[45] Those words capture well not just Butler's own approach to war, but that of all like him who share this unusual warrior motivation. A phrase that certainly epitomizes this is carpe diem; that is definitely how the warrior lives.

Rigid Moral Code

In the book, *Les Miserables*, there is a character named Javert who is a Sheriff.[46] He believes in a rigid sense of justice, and as an enforcer of the law, he makes certain that all live by this standard. There is, for him, no place to compromise this moral order. However, the author of the book, Victor Hugo, develops a challenge for Javert and his Manichean worldview through a character named Valjean.

Valjean is both good and evil. But in his case, his goodness, which represents his current life, shines far superior to the petty evil of his youthful days. As Javert confronts this however, knowing fully of Valjean's sinister past, the struggle for him comes in knowing what to do. To maintain faithfulness to himself and what he knows is right, he must prosecute Valjean. Evil is evil and must be addressed regardless of circumstances. But as much as Javert thinks this, another side of him feels compelled to dismiss the infractions of Valjean since this man has redeemed himself by living an upstanding life. Hugo offers the dilemma within Javert to be this:

He saw before him two roads, both equally straight; but he saw two; and that terrified him—him, who had never in his life known but one straight line. And, bitter anguish, these two roads were contradictory. One of these two straight lines excluded the other. Which of the two was the true one?[47]

Unfortunately, in the story, Javert is not able to reconcile his bipolar moral impulses and so he takes his own life. Death is better for him than living in a world where evil is allowed to go unpunished regardless of the reason why.

The point of referring to this story is because it illustrates well what goes on within warriors when it comes to this same impulse of upholding moral rightness. Warriors, like Javert, have a very strong inner sense of moral truth, and they are compelled to stand for this. Hence, they will fight to uphold it. In war, they will die to ensure it. Compromise is not an option. They will rise to destroy that which destroys goodness.

For most, this kind of unrelenting inner moral drive is difficult to understand. For unlike warriors, people in general are willing to excuse injustice if it somehow means risking personal welfare. "Let someone else deal with it," they determine. Warriors, contrarily, cannot live like that. If no one deals with injustice, they will. They, like Javert, refuse to live in a world where injustice reigns. Let us look at this as it plays out in the life of warriors.

As to the inner moral code itself that drives this passion for morality, what is it for warriors? In the Marine Corps, there are core values that define this inner state of being. They are honor, courage and commitment. Honor is the idea of maintaining personal integrity by staying faithful to self, to one's commitments, and to one's inner virtue. Courage springs from honor in the sense that as one chooses to act on this virtue, he is enabled to maintain personal integrity in each and every circumstance of life. Commitment, then, is about the unrelenting passion and drive a person has to remain honorable and courageous, never giving up. Together, these core values are truly

115

what define Marines. They will remain faithful, *semper fidelis*, to their identity as warriors.

What is true about Marines is also true about warriors from other communities. Rick Fields in his book, *The Code of the Warrior*, traces this down throughout all warrior groups:

> The figure of the warrior is truly cross-cultural. ...In each of these traditions, the warrior is considered an essential part of society, a protector and a source of good. And in each of these traditions, the warrior is bound by a code, a rule, a way of life. This code of the warrior embodies ways to regulate and in some cases to transform or transcend aggression.[48]

Warriors as we see have an innate sense of what is right and they will stand for this regardless of the cost. Patrick Henry, a statesman for our country in its inception, forcefully shows this during the Revolutionary War. Overcome with the belief that the rights to personal sovereignty are being stripped away from the American colonies by Great Britain, and that all attempts to right these wrongs are being rejected, Henry stands before his peers and states his own willingness to address this moral dilemma. He says:

> If we wish to be free--if we mean to preserve inviolate those inestimable privileges for which we have been so long contending--if we mean not basely to abandon the noble struggle in which we have been so long engaged, and which we have pledged ourselves never to abandon until the glorious object of our contest shall be obtained--we must fight! I repeat it, sir, we must fight! An appeal to arms and to the God of hosts is all that is left us! ...The millions of people, armed in the holy cause of liberty, and in such a country as that which we possess, are invincible by any force which our enemy can send against us. Besides, sir, we shall not fight our battles alone. There is a just God who presides over the destinies of nations, and who will

raise up friends to fight our battles for us. ...There is no retreat but in submission and slavery! Our chains are forged! Their clanking may be heard on the plains of Boston! The war is inevitable--and let it come! I repeat it, sir, let it come. ...I know not what course others may take; **but as for me, give me liberty or give me death!**[49]

To this impassioned call from Henry, a nation rises to arms and one of those in attendance, George Washington, becomes a leader of the American revolutionary forces and guides his nation to liberty. As a true and noble warrior, he cannot do otherwise. In fact, to know his history is to see one who often is out in front of his men, drawing the enemy fire to himself as he leads the cause for moral truth.

John Paul Jones, yet another figure from the Revolutionary War of 1776, likewise shows this need as a warrior to fight for truth and freedom from unrighteous tyranny. During a battle at sea, when his forces are overwhelmed by a superior British Navy, he is asked if he wants to surrender. To this offer, he bellows: "I have not yet begun to fight."[50] Indeed he had not. He and his sailors, with these convictions to stand for truth or die, rallied from their position, and soon, the spirited group defeated the better equipped enemy.

Defeat for warriors in the face of unrighteousness is simply not an option. They cannot silence this inner fire to bring justice. They must stand for their convictions all the way to their dying breath.

Nathan Hale, yet another warrior from the Revolutionary War, shows the true power of this. When he is captured by the British and sentenced to death, he offers some final words that express perfectly what we are talking about here. He says, "I only regret that I have but one life to lose for my country."[51] What more can show this entrenched belief system that guides a warrior in battle? There is this inner will that refuses to be quieted, and that

117

must be defended for the sake of one's moral code. True warriors can live in no other way. Their moral call to duty will not let them.

Conclusion

Warriors are a different class of people. They are easily misunderstood because they approach the world uniquely. What is provided is a broad sketch of this group. The impetus for their zeal is their sense that they are the best (elitist), indomitable (invincible), capable of overcoming the physical and mental will of their enemy (hard), must care for others even if it means death (self-sacrificing), live on the edge of life and experience it for all that it has (gusto seekers), and refuse to let anyone or anything stand against what they believe to be ethically true (rigid moralists). This is the essence of what makes and moves warriors. They fight because they cannot do otherwise. It is who they are. Those who are not warriors clearly do not get it because they are not so possessed of these qualities. Yet, that does not mean that the warrior group does not exist. It does, and what is needed is true understanding of who they are in order for all to appreciate their individuality.

Many other descriptions could accompany this group: simple, raw, tough, uncompromising, rugged, individualists, resourceful, stubborn, hard-headed, jar-heads, devil-dogs, passionate, arrogant, confident, extreme, outdoorsy, faithful, loyal, etc.... Some of these words are subtle nuances of the attributes developed above. A few of the words listed show what the more positive attributes provided can look like from a negative point of view; e.g., elite versus arrogant. Still too there are other words that could be given which would bring out other subtle distinctions of the warrior or perhaps combine a few of the other concepts provided. Regardless, the six words developed in this discussion are selected because they seem to comprise the essence of warriors. As such, they show that which compels warriors to fight. Understanding this is vital, therefore, if we are to gain a sense of why warriors go off to war, what sustains them in war, and what will trouble or ennoble them post war, depending upon whether their actions were in keeping with their nature.

Endnotes

---

[1] Max Hastings, <u>Warriors, Portraits from the Battlefield</u>, (New York: Vintage Books, 2005), p. 238.

[2] Ibid., pp. 236-255.

[3] Ibid., p. 254.

[4] Ibid., p. 242.

[5] James Bradley, <u>Flags of our Fathers</u>, (New York: Bantam Books, 2006), p. 71.

[6] Ibid.

[7] Ibid.

[8] Ibid., p. 68.

[9] Gidget Fuentes, "6 Navy Crosses for Darkhorse," https://www.leatherneck.com/forums/showthread.php?t=47652, (June 11, 2007).

[10] Zachary Kent, World War I: The War to End Wars, (Berkeley Heights, NJ: Enslow Publishers, 1994), p. 74.

[11] Ibid.

[12] Michael Neiberg, Fighting The Great War, (Cambridge, Massachusetts: Harvard University Press, 2005), 328.

[13] Peter Bosco as revised by Antoinette Bosco, World War I, (New York: Facts on File, 2003), p. 93.

[14] Ibid, p. 97.

[15] Brian R. Chontosh Navy Cross citation, http://www.victoryinstitute.net/blogs/utb/2003/03/25/brian-r-chontosh-navy-cross-citation/, (16 December, 2017).

[16] Bradley, Flags of our Fathers, pp. 238-239.

[17] Lt. Col. Dean Ladd and Steven Weingartner, Faithful Warriors, A Combat Marine Remembers the Pacific War, (Annapolis, Maryland: Naval Institute Press, 2007), pp. 212-213.

[18] Jim Proser and Jerry Cutter, <u>I'm Staying with my Boys: The Heroic Life of Sgt. John Basilone, USMC</u>, (New York: St. Martin's Press, 2004), p. 190.

[19] [boldness added] Ibid, p. 438.

[20] Ibid, p. 439.

[21] [Information in parenthesis offered for clarity], Sergeant Jeremiah Workman, "24 Insurgents Killed, 3 Marines Rescued, 1 Navy Cross: A Reluctant Hero Is Made",

http://www.getthegouge.com/insider/waronterror/
stories.asp?print=Y&ID=264, (2009 U.S. NAVAL INSTITUTE).
[22] Norman Fulkerson, "Through the Valley of Death,"
http://www.tfp.org/through-the-valley-of-death/, (8 May, 2012).
[boldness added]
[23] MilitaryTimes, Honor the Fallen, "Army Sgt. Dennis P. Weichel
Jr.", http://thefallen.militarytimes.com/army-sgt-dennis-p-
weichel/6568133, (29 April, 2016).
[24] Gregg Zoroya, "Some upset Marine sergeant won't receive Medal
of Honor", http://www.usatoday.com/news/military/2008-09-17-
Medal-of-Honor_N.htm, (November 18, 2008).
[25] Dan Lamothe, "Honor or insult for a fallen Marine?",
http://www.marinecorpstimes.com/news/2008/09/marine_peralta_09
2808/, (September 30, 2008).
[26] Rich Lowry, "Sgt. Rafael Peralta, American Hero",
http://www.nationalreview.com/lowry/lowry200501110730.asp,
(January 11, 2005).
[27]
http://www.google.com/archivesearch?hl=en&q=medal+of+honor+g
renade&um=1&ie=UTF-
8&scoring=t&ei=YvbnSdmZLIOitwfi84iNBg&sa=X&oi=timeline_r
esult&resnum=12&ct=title.
[28] OFFICE OF THE SECRETARY OF DEFENSE, "Review of
Medal of Honor Nomination
(Sergeant Rafael Peralta (deceased), USMC), INFORMATION
PAPER",
http://media.utsandiego.com/news/documents/2012/03/01/DOD_rep
ort_on_Peralta_2008.pdf,
(2 June, 2008).
[29] Dan Lamothe, "Honor or Insult for a Fallen Marine?",
http://www.marinecorpstimes.com/news/2008/09/marine_peralta_09
2808/, (September 30, 2008).
[30] "Habits are behaviors wired so deeply in our brains that we
perform them automatically. …However, the brain's executive
command center does not completely relinquish control of habitual
behavior. A new study from MIT neuroscientists has found that a
small region of the brain's prefrontal cortex, where most thought and
planning occurs, is responsible for moment-by-moment control of

which habits are switched on at a given time." Cf., Anne Trafton, "How the brain controls our habits", http://newsoffice.mit.edu/2012/understanding-how-brains-control-our-habits-1029, (29 October, 2012). Cf. also, Carol A. Seger, and Brian J. Spiering, "A Critical Review of Habit Learning and the Basal Ganglia", http://www.ncbi.nlm.nih.gov/pmc/articles/PMC3163829/#, (2011). "…fully acquired habits are performed almost automatically, virtually non-consciously, allowing attention to be focused elsewhere."

[31] "The study of human consciousness has demonstrated that there are both conscious and unconscious systems. Other work, particularly in animals, has shown that there are habit and nonhabit systems and that these involve different brain regions and memory processes. Here we argue that habits can be equated with unconscious behavior and nonhabits with conscious behavior. This equation makes the extensive physiological literature on habit/nonhabit relevant to the less tractable issue of consciousness. On the basis of this line of reasoning, it appears that different parts of the BG [Basal Ganglia] and different memory structures mediate conscious and unconscious processes. It is further argued here that the unconscious system is highly capable; it can both process sensory information and produce behavior. The benefit of such a dual system is multitasking: The unconscious system can execute background tasks, leaving the conscious system to perform more difficult tasks." [Basal Ganglia offered for clarification], cf., John Lisman, Elizer Sternberg, "Habit and Nonhabit Systems for Unconscious and Conscious Behavior: Implications for Multitasking Journal of Cognitive Neuroscience", Volume 25, Issue 2, (February 2013).

[32] "An accumulating body of evidence suggests that rapid, goal-directed learning primarily involves the dorsomedial striatum, whereas the slower acquisition of habits, which are insensitive to changes in the reward value of the outcome, involves the dorsolateral striatum (Balleine et al., 2007; Yin and Knowlton, 2006). Importantly, goal-directed learning of new motor routines appears to be initiated in the dorsomedial striatum, whereas the long-term motor memory required to execute previously learned

sequences may be stored in the dorsolateral striatum.", cf., Anatol C. Kreitzer, and Robert C. Malenka, "Striatal plasticity and basal ganglia circuit function", Neuron, Volume 26, Issue 4, (26 November, 2008).

[33] Lisman and Sternberg., "Schneider and Schiffrin (Schneider & Shiffrin, 1977) showed that, when a task becomes highly practiced by human participants, it can be performed automatically and without attention. According to one major theory, nonhabit behavior involves the dorsomedial striatum, whereas the habit behavior involves the dorsolateral striatum (Yin & Knowlton, 2006)."

[34] "Although, in the initial stages of acquiring a skill and performing a behavior, intentions may be consciously and deliberately formed in response to environmental events, with repetition in constant contexts, they may (like behaviors) operate autonomously with minimal conscious guidance. As Heckhausen and Beckmann (1990) argued, 'intents resemble plans about how to act when predetermined cues or conditions occur. Once formed, however, the intents no longer require much conscious control. Instead, they are triggered as automatic or quasi-automatic operations.'" Judith A. Ouellette, "Habit and Intention in Everyday Life: The Multiple Processes by Which Past Behavior Predicts Future Behavior", Psychological Bulletin, Volume 124, Issue 1, 1998.

[35] Ibid., note the unconscious processing involved in driving, "It was shown that participants using cell phones often fail to report important targets, thus demonstrating inattentional blindness (Strayer, Drews, & Johnston, 2003). But if targets are not seen, why don't accidents occur more frequently? Certainly, continuous visual processes are required to keep a safe distance from other cars. Experiments done with an eye tracker show that, when drivers become deeply involved in a cell phone conversation, there is no reduction in the shifts of gaze to targets, although there is a reduction in the number of targets reported (Strayer et al., 2003). It follows that there is an unconscious system with considerable ability to produce the eye movements necessary for driving. We argue that it is this unconscious system that is driving."

[36] "...stimulus-driven "habitual" actions occur as an automatic response to sensory inputs with which the action has become associated, for example through reinforcement learning (Balleine &

Dickinson, 1998). Although apparently simple, the latter mechanism can produce very complex behavioral patterns combining basic learned responses (Donahoe, Burgos, & Palmer, 1993). …once a habitual action is learned it is elicited in response to a stimulus irrespective of what the value of the outcome may be." Fabian Chersi, Marco Mirolli, Giovanni Pezzulo, Gianluca Baldassarre, "A spiking neuron model of the cortico-basal ganglia circuits for goal-directed and habitual action learning", Neural Networks, Volume 41, (2013).

[37] Ibid., cf., OFFICE OF THE SECRETARY OF DEFENSE, "Review of Medal of Honor Nomination (Sergeant Rafael Peralta (deceased), USMC), INFORMATION PAPER". [bold print added for emphasis]

[38] Paul Szoldra, "Marine Sgt. Rafael Peralta Deserves the Medal Of Honor for What He Did in Fallujah or He Deserves Nothing", http://www.businessinsider.com.au/rafael-peralta-2014-1, 11 January, 2014.

[39] Hope Hodge Seck, "Eyewitnesses respond to claims challenging Peralta's MoH account", http://archive.marinecorpstimes.com/article/20140222/NEWS/302220009/Eyewitnesses-respond-claims-challenging-Peralta-s-MoH-account, (22 February, 2014).

[40] Military Times Hall of Valor, "Rafael Peralta, Awards and Citations, Navy Cross", http://valor.militarytimes.com/recipient.php?recipientid=3655, (July, 2015).

[41] Leonard Wong, Thomas A. Kolditz, Raymond A. Millen, and Terrence M. Potter, "Why They Fight: Combat Motivation in the Iraq War," http://25thaviation.org/history/id871.htm, (July, 2003).

[42] Ibid.

[43] Brady, Why Marines Fight, p. 34.

[44] United States Marine Corps, History Division, "Major General Smedley D. Butler, USMC", http://www.mcu.usmc.mil/historydivision/Pages/Who's%20Who/A-C/Butler_SD.aspx, (29 April, 2016).

[45] James A. Warren, American Spartans: The U.S. Marines: A Combat History from Iwo Jima to Iraq, (New York: Pocket Books, 2005), pp. 18-19.

[46] Victor Hugo, <u>Les Miserables</u>, New York: Dodd, Mead and Company Publishers, 1971.

[47] Ibid., p. 528.

[48] Rick Fields, The Code of the Warrior: In History, Myth and Everyday Life, (New York: Harper Perennial, 1991), p.3.

[49] [Emphasis added] Patrick Henry, "Give Me Liberty or Give Me Death", A Chronology of US Historical Documents, http://www.law.ou.edu/ushistory/henry.shtml, (March 23, 1775).

[50] Szandor Blestman, Ron Paul Revolution: We Have Not Yet Begun to Fight, http://www.americanchronicle.com/articles/view/42524, (November 09, 2007).

[51] Greg Nussbaum, "Nathan Hale", http://www.mrnussbaum.com/nathanhale.htm, (2006).

CHAPTER FIVE

WARRIORS IN HISTORY

Through history, to be a warrior has been to show oneself with a fearless heart. The embodiment of this was easily seen in the Masai Warriors of Africa. To be a warrior in that tribe was an honor bestowed only upon those who displayed true courage. A significant challenge in that process was to go out into the bush, alone and with only a spear, to kill a lion.[1] That would have been a remarkable feat for anyone. The kind of person even capable of doing that, especially considering that you had to take on the lion at around twelve years of age, could only have been one of immense bravery, incredible skill, and unquestionable fortitude. That was the Masai Warrior. He was remarkable in his ability to face danger and sacrifice all in the process.

Elitism

As we examine the traits of warriors in ancient cultures, the first one we look at it is elitism. One historical group that immediately stands out in this regard is the Samurai from Japan. These warriors held a place in society that was unparalleled and unquestionably revered. Who exactly are they; why are they thought of in this way; and how do they compare to modern warriors?

"The word 'samurai' signifies the military elite of old Japan, a knightly caste who commanded armies, and led followers into battle."[2] Though they rose in prestige, these warriors came from humble means. They initially were hired peasants and in some cases were family members of land owners who assumed the task of protecting areas from invasion. Japan had limited arable farm land and often one group would rise to take what another had. When this happened, local village chieftains would take the responsibility to form the protection needed by getting willing fighters from a community to repel advancing enemies.[3] As the urgency for protection grew, these fighters developed skill and proficiency and in time became elite warriors, experts in all forms of ancient combat.

While the samurai's prestige was tied to military prowess, it also went beyond that into civic leadership: "Their military and political skills eventually enabled them to control civilian governments."[4]

From this civil focus, as Samurai grew in prominence and capability, some founded their own smaller kingdoms, which became known as daimyos, and these groups held even more status in the warrior community. As one author states, "The samurai were the military elite of old Japan, and the daimyo, the 'Samurai Warlords', were the elite of the samurai."[5] Their role was to ensure the protection of all,[6] maintaining extraordinary influence and power in their areas of rule.[7]

Over time, even the daimyos were subjugated by their overall ruler, the emperor, to his appointed shoguns who became in the end the ones who were seen as the most elite warriors.[8]

What guided these samurai warriors was the Bushido. That word refers to "way of the warrior," and it might be understood as the embodiment of an ethic by which one lives.[9] This ethic took the form of a moral code. Yet as one scholar notes, "It is not a written code; at best it consists of a few maxims handed down from mouth to mouth or coming from the pen of some well-known warrior. More frequently it is a code unuttered and unwritten, possessing all the more powerful sanction of an actual deed, and of a law written on the tablets of the heart."[10]

Central to this code were duties like justice, courage, benevolence, truthfulness, honor, loyalty, wisdom, self-control, hara kiri (suicide for the sake of honor or devotion), and being one with the Sword.[11] It is all what enabled these warriors to become disciplined fighters who would die to stand by their beliefs, being fearless in battle and even seeing death as an honorable display of valor.[12]

What we find here with these samurai of ancient Japan is not at all unlike what is found with warriors today. Modern warriors too, rise up because they see a need and feel a calling to defend their beliefs. They train and fight, honing abilities and natural talents so as to excel over all others. Each, like the Samurai, wants to be the elite fighter.

For the samurai, this pecking order of greatness was determined not just by the position one had as discussed, but also by the battle role each samurai assumed. The cavalrymen, archers and spearmen were at the top of this list. Then, one went down to the foot soldiers who assumed a position of lesser regard, with the petty attendants and servants being at the bottom.[13]

As we know, this very same thing is true with modern warriors. A part of this for them has to do with the rank and position one holds, but it is also linked to the unit assignment one gets. It goes on and works its way to the status one has on a team, with the goal of course to become the "top dog."

With this kind of thing in play for both warrior groups, we see in the warrior psyche this requisite need to gain the authority and respect of peers and enemy forces. One samurai offered this to potential opponents: 'I am Yoshikiyo of the Minamoto clan, grandson of Tomokiyo, the former deputy governor of Musashi Province, and son of Yorikiyo, who distinguished himself in various battles in the northern territories. …So if any of you would like to test my strength of arms, come forth now.'"[14]

Modern warriors do the same kind of thing. In the Battle of Fallujah, it is reported that one Battalion Commander (BC) had the Marine Corps hymn played during the battle.[15] It was his way of showing his superiority, provoking the enemy and seeing if they wanted to test his superiority.[16]

Incidentally, the playing of sound tracks was only one of many kinds of challenges laid out during the battle of Fallujah. Another I saw was a message that one of our Marines in 3/5 left to the insurgents on a bridge in Fallujah, a bridge that spanned the Euphrates River. If you recall, the insurgents killed American Blackwater contractors near that bridge and then, hung their burned and mutilated corpses on its steel girders. Almost seven months after this time, our forces took over this area of Fallujah, and a 3/5 Marine involved in the effort left a message there for the insurgents. It definitely was a statement about justice, though crudely so, and it was also a way of taking pride in accomplishment and owning up to one's superior fighting skill. The message written on one of the steel spans of that bridge read quite simply: "This is for the Americans of Blackwater that were murdered here in 2004. Semper Fidelis. 3/5 P.S. Fuck You." What more can be said by way of showing the heart of an elite warrior? He is bold and secure in his abilities, and because he believes in his superior fighting skills, he will goad his enemy. If that enemy is affected by this message and wants to fight, it is all the better. That is what he is after anyway. It is all in keeping with the mindset that is a part of the elite warrior.

Invincible

When you think of invincibility in warriors of old, the army commanded by Alexander the Great is a definite fit. Under his command, this army is purported to have been undefeated in battle, and by his death, this army had conquered most of the known world.[17] That is amazing and by definition fits the word invincible.

What lay behind Alexander's success, besides having seemingly clairvoyant insight and being a master tactician in war, were the infantrymen.[18] These men, referred to as hoplite warriors, were drawn from all quarters of the Macedonian Empire. They were brought into the army at age eighteen, and thereafter, they bound their lives to each other and to their country through this oath:

I shall not dishonour these sacred arms, nor leave the man stationed beside me in the line. I will defend both the sacred and secular places and not hand over the fatherland smaller, but greater and mightier as far as I and all are able, and I shall listen to those in power at the time and the laws which have been drawn up and those that will be, and if anyone will abolish them I shall not give way to them as far as I and all are able, and I will honour the ancestral cults.[19]

Training in this army for the hoplite warriors took on various forms. Like modern day warriors, one thing these ancient warriors did was to go on long marches, thirty miles in a day with full armor: helmets, greaves (shin protectors), shields, sarissai (long wooden spears, up to twenty-four feet sometimes), and daily provisions.[20] They also, like modern warriors, practiced extensive drilling in formation. Yet for these ancient warriors, their drills related specifically to the coordination of close quarters movement in battle. Some of these movements were done while showing intimidating striking abilities of weapons in order to provoke fear in the enemy.[21] Overall, the strict and disciplined training these men received and their courage in battle enabled this group to achieve what no other army since had done.

As we venture even deeper into Alexander's army, though, we find another more distinct group of warriors whose belief in being unconquerable in battle was all the more legendary. These people were known as the Silver Shields or hypaspists; both names seemingly being used interchangeably.[22] This fighting group was "'distinguished by the brilliance of its arms and the bravery of its men'" and, at the great battle of Paraetecenein, their superiority as warriors became all the more widespread; "'undefeated troops, the fame of whose exploits caused much fear among the enemy'"[23] Overall, these warriors were widely regarded, and under the leadership of General Eumenes, they proved themselves to be invincible.[24]

To become a Silver Shield warrior was a matter of special selection.[25] Out of the vast Greek Army, these warriors were chosen exclusively on account of physical strength, valor and a resolute spirit to overcome challengers.[26]

One of their assignments was to be personal guard to Alexander the Great. This was a highly dangerous and challenging role as Alexander would take them on "special missions that involved speed and endurance, often fighting in rugged areas."[27] Yet, they excelled in their duty. The following story about one hypaspists called Philip shows the degree to which these warriors went in battle to keep fidelity to king and calling:

The King, frequently changing horses, pressed the retreating enemy relentlessly. The young noblemen who formed his usual retinue had given up the chase, all except Philip, the brother of Lysimachus, who was in the early stages of manhood and, as was readily apparent, was a person of rare qualities. Incredibly, Philip kept up with the King on foot although Alexander rode for over 500 stades ... Philip could not be induced to leave the King, even though he was wearing a cuirass and carrying weapons. On reaching a wood where the barbarians had hidden, this same young man put up a remarkable fight and gave protection to the King when engaged in hand-to-hand combat with the enemy.[28]

Here is a powerful example of this invincible spirit. This warrior refused to let anything overcome the obligation to keep honor and fulfill duty. He covered the distance of one thousand football fields while his commander was on horse, and he did this while carrying his body armor (cuirass) and weapons. Then, he went charging off into the woods, not even letting exhaustion stop his will to protect the King. After that, he had the fortitude and unassailable spirit to fight and kill the enemy. Amazing!

It is said about these indomitable warriors that "[t]he only thing they guarded more zealously than their king was their reputation."[29] It is, thus, no wonder that they garnered such a place in history as invincible warriors in an invincible army.

This relentless and unassailable will to fight is nothing short of what I saw in the warriors with whom I served. They too fought with a dogged spirit that would not back down. Army Staff Sergeant Bellavia, in the Battle of Fallujah, is a perfect example. Hear what Bellavia does, and be amazed at what invincible truly means.

We pick up with this story about Bellavia after he has already encountered enemy fire on several occasions and has killed a few insurgents.[30] Now, he is leading his men into a house filled with terrorists. He says, as he enters the house:

> My sudden appearance catches the enemy off guard. I expect the AKs to open up again as soon as I expose myself. But they don't. Instead, I squeeze the trigger and hold it down. Hellfire starts flying toward the enemy. ...The insurgents under the stairs react with discipline and speed. ...Bullets bash into the wall to my left. The door-frame splinters. Tracers hiss this way and that, bouncing off the bricks and ceiling. I'm in a firestorm, totally exposed. I'm amazed I haven't been hit.[31]

From here, Bellavia talks about how the battle rages and seconds seem like minutes. He tries to move toward the enemy, but he says his legs do not move in spite of repeated attempts. He just stands there, in the open, firing: "I push. I swear. My legs won't budge. The enemy remains unhurt, hiding behind the ripped-up barriers."[32]

Bellavia and his soldiers finally retreat from the house under heavy fire: "Bullets crack over my left shoulder and hit the outer wall in front of me. I keep running, my legs pumping furiously. And then I'm through the gate and with my men."[33] The chaos and confusion that continues in the on-going firefight prevent a calm planning session on the best way to approach this situation. Bullets are still whizzing past. Bellavia is taking cover as best he can. He is not done yet, though. With newfound resolve, Bellavia decides that he must reenter that house. Read what he says as he makes his decision:

My heart kicks into overdrive, pounding so hard I can hear the blood rushing through my ears. ...My breathing comes quick and shallow. I'm probably hyperventilating. ...I'm getting light-headed now. ...I hear noises all around me. I can't tell what is my imagination and what is real. Am I hallucinating? *Get a grip. Get a fucking grip.* I whack myself on the helmet. I'm still disoriented. It fails to clear my head. *Come on, you've got to get a hold of yourself.*[34]

It is so revealing to gain this candid look into the mental and emotional state of a warrior in massive conflict. Bellavia is driven by a clear mission to take out the enemy. He must go forward and he does: "In one sudden rush, I carry the fight to my enemy."[35] He goes into the house and clears one room after the next. He is brazen in one minute and controlling rising panic in the next. At this point, as he says, "I wait. Waves of fear rock me. I feel unsteady and totally vulnerable. *You've got to use the fear. Use it. Control it. Don't let it overwhelm you.*"[36] With these thoughts circling about his head, another insurgent pops out unexpectedly from a closet and shoots. In this firefight, Bellavia is hit in the arm, and the insurgent is hit in the leg, but they both keep firing. Eventually, Bellavia takes out this insurgent too, at which point, he regroups again. He knows now that he must either leave the house or carry the fight up the stairs. He makes his decision to keep going. As he moves up the steps, he slips in blood from one of the insurgents he killed. His slight falter saves his life as bullets from an AK-47 scream just above his head. He tosses up a grenade. After the explosion, he moves in to finish this guy off. He spots the insurgent lying out on the floor. He takes his M-16 and hits the insurgent hard on the head. The insurgent, still alive and somehow full of life, hits back with his AK, striking

Bellevia in the mouth and knocking out one of his teeth. From here, a full on, bloody, hand-to-hand fight ensues. Both Bellevia and the insurgent are clawing, beating, punching and gouging at each other. What follows next is a brawl that is right out of the pages of a batman comic book, except in this case it is real. It ends with Bellavia getting the upper hand and finally taking out the insurgent. Afterwards, beyond exhaustion, he leaves the room and sits on the stairs. Then, in his own words, "I pull out a Marlboro Red. My lips are distended and swollen. I don't care. I light the cigarette and take a long drag, and stare at the drying blood caked under my fingernails. I reach over and pull a chunk of the wardrobe's wood, no more than a supersized splinter, out of my arm above the elbow. *What a fucking day.*"[37]

The definition of invincibility is "incapable of being conquered, defeated, or subdued."[38] How else can one describe Bellavia? Equally as much, how else does one describe the hypaspist's warrior? Their will to surmount unbelievable physical circumstances and defeat the enemy is unremitting. When Bellavia says, *"I can't leave this fight," "This is what I am," "A warrior,"* there is no doubt that he is right.[39]

Warriors whether ancient or modern show themselves to be invincible. They seek to conquer their enemy no matter the obstacles. Without question, many die in this effort. Yet it is not without having shown a spirit of invincibility, an unwillingness to retreat. It is one of the many hallmark traits of the warrior.

Hard

"He who desires peace should prepare for war."[40] This is a maxim offered by the military writer Vegetius. He was speaking about Rome and what it took for them to maintain their dominance in the world for centuries.[41] A key element in this had to do with warriors. They possessed a steely constitution that remained firm no matter who the enemy was or how the battle unfolded. Let us look at this and see how closely those warriors resemble the warriors of today.

Being hard for Roman warriors, Centurions as they were called, was about superior mental and physical toughness. If fighters in training had these qualities and displayed them in war, they were accepted. If they failed to prove themselves in these regards, the tempering process began. The first step for those displaying weakness was to undergo physical torture to see if this would somehow harden their strength of will and stamina.[42] If this did not work, the process continued until these fighters became hard or died.[43] That is what being hard meant to these warriors.

This process of finding one's mettle began on day one for the Romans. When a recruit joined the service, he participated in a four month long grueling initiation to military service.[44] Involved in this and carrying forward into regular service were several disciplines, all of which tested determination and strength: 1) continuous synchronized marching; 2) twenty mile humps with forty-five pound packs and thirty pounds of armor to be completed in five hours; 3) endless practice in clearing obstacles, charging and breaking off combat, changing lines and relieving engaged units; 4) weapons and shield practice; 5) swimming; and 6) and the building of fortified camps.[45]

As is clear to see, this training steeled the Roman soldier. Those who endured filled the ranks of the Centurions and contributed to Rome's amazing legacy of triumph. One such notable victory came at the battle of Cynoscephalae, where a Macedonian army of eight-thousand was destroyed by a Roman army of seven hundred.[46] That is impressive by anyone's standard. It is no doubt linked to this quality in these warriors of unmatched mental and physical stamina. Weeding out the weak of constitution only made for a group of warriors who in the end could endure any and all hardships. As Vegetius says about these warriors and their success: "We see no other explanation of the conquest of the world by the

Roman People than their military training, camp discipline and practice in warfare."[47]

Certainly, what Vegetius mentions is not only that which contributed to Roman domination in its time, but further what enables the success of modern-day warriors. They too go through this process of pushing their bodies through harsh mental and physical challenges. It makes them hard. Marco Martinez, a former Marine 0311, a grunt, talks about this in a book he wrote called *Hard Corps: From Gangster to Marine Hero*. In this book, he offers numerous situations where "hardening" training was an aspect of everyday Marine life. In one account, he talks about a Marine friend who was as "hard" as they come. On a sub-zero freezing cold night in the deserts of 29 Palms while many Marines were complaining about the conditions, Martinez's friend said, "I love the pain."[48] It was a remark, Martinez said, that truly epitomized this Marine: "It wasn't macho bullshit: he seriously loved enduring maximum pain, including being frozen stiff in the damn arctic night air."[49]

Only those, like Martinez, who find pleasure in this punishing test of stamina and resolve will show themselves as warriors and remain in that elite group. Those who are not so hard will simply wash out, or as it was in ancient times, they died. It is an important part of weeding out true warriors from all others.

Yet, however harsh it might seem, it is critical. Front line fighters cannot quit, no matter what. They must prevail over the elements, the conditions and the enemy. They must have an impervious fortitude that outlasts, out-kills and simply out-wills the enemy. It is yet another critical element in the constitution of warriors and one that makes them both enjoy the process of war and the victory that inevitably comes because they simply cannot quit.

Self-Sacrificing

With this attribute of sacrificing for others, it is difficult to isolate one warrior community over another because this is a hallmark of warriors. By their very nature and position in war, they willingly commit themselves entirely to fight for others. However, in spite of this, there is a group that does have a very close association with the embodiment of self-sacrifice. It is the group composed of those known as the knights.

The roots of knighthood go back to Roman times when "…a roman soldier would attach himself to a superior officer, pledging his military service in return for the granting of a piece of land, which was known as a benefice."[50] Yet, the need for having knights continued well beyond the fall of the Roman Empire. In fact, one might argue that the collapse of the Roman Empire was the place of their greatest ascendancy. Once Rome fell apart, all regions descended into chaos and territories were rife for takeovers. Knights, therefore, were needed to give land-owners protection from invaders. Thus, to establish them "…local men began developing their own equestrian skills, and …[b]y the eighth century, knights began to emerge as the most important warriors on the battlefield."[51]

Some knights assumed their position by pledging their lives in service to a lord.[52] Their vow amounted to what was "…total obedience, performing a variety of duties, including fighting in the lord's army, guarding his castle, and acting as his messenger or ambassador. In fact, a knight's entire life could be defined by his relationship to his lord and master, who had the final say in whom he could marry, and also in the disposition of his estate upon his death."[53] This kind of unbounded sacrifice is remarkable, but that just speaks to the nature of this group. Whether it was to defend a lord, "to defend the weak, uphold his king's honor, [or] find glory in combat…. Knights lived and died for others, which was a glorious fate."[54] It is what set these fighters apart[55] and made them the sacrificial warriors that we remember to this day.

What knights are often remembered for, particularly those of the military orders, are the crusades where they were fearless fighters for faith. They fought for the Holy Land of Jerusalem and attacked other places where they believed paganism flourished. They committed themselves to these causes with abandon because they firmly believed that the promise of death for their God was superior to life itself.[56] They also determined that to take the life of one committed to injustice was honorable: "to kill a pagan is to win glory since it gives glory to Christ."[57] Their example was that of the fettered servant, following in the footsteps of their Lord, bound to a greater calling that found its ultimate reward in death for their savior.

One of the most famous knights of the Crusades, considered to be the most notable knight ever, was William Marshal. His beginnings, however, were quite inauspicious. Although his father was of some renown, he was forsaken by him. But if that was not bad enough, Marshal faced further hardship in that his King, for reasons that were not his fault, condemned him to be hanged.[58] It was a deplorable start to this young man's life. Yet out of this, Marshal rose in fame and societal position so that by the end of his life, he was privileged to have served five kings, to have displayed unparalleled skill in tournaments and combat, to have earned great wealth, to have become the 1st Earl of Pembroke, and to have distinguished himself as one of the most important figures in the history of medieval England.

What gave Marshal his edge and allowed him to become accomplished were his extraordinary abilities in horsemanship, use of weaponry, and sheer "brutish physicality that enabled him to deliver crushing blows" as well as receive them and continue on in the fight.[59] These assets he used often in knightly tournaments, otherwise known as Melees. The Melees were intended to be friendly competitions between knights to allow them to show battlefield skills. At these events, groups of knights from about twenty-five to one hundred would charge each other in a free-for-all without referees, trying to unhorse, impair or otherwise cause opponents to yield.[60] Although it was considered a sport and not war, and although testing and sharpening skill was the objective not killing, people died: "Sixty knights were killed in one French tournament, while in another a knight killed his own son."[61] Yet, the knights loved this kind of activity. It tested their bodies and skills to the max. It also allowed an unknown and untested knight in the making like Marshal to prove his superiority, and this Marshal did. He excelled in the tournaments, even amongst the best knights of his day. It brought him international success and considerable wealth.[62] Plus, it caused him to be sought after by several Kings in succession to be a member of their mesnie; i.e., a part of the "retinue of knights who gathered around a lord – the tightknit group of warriors serving as elite troops and trusted bodyguards."[63]

Marshal found his fame not only in tournaments, though, but also in war. In his first battle, he acquitted himself valiantly. He showed no signs of fear but rather charged boldly into the fray. He fought so viciously that he broke his lance and still refused to retreat. He rather drew out his sword and continued in the charge. In the end, with violent blows from a hardened frame, he cut a swath of death through opposing knights,[64] and those who observed him on this day considered him to be the finest warrior present in that battle.[65]

The valor and unmitigated brawn that Marshal showed in his first battle continued through every battle in which he fought. Even in his fifties, he distinguished himself. In one battle, as the tide had swung to the enemy's favor, Marshal rushed forward alone to take on the enemy, with sword in hand. He eventually climbed a ladder to a castle wall, jumped over the wall and dealt "so many blows right and left with the sword [that] those inside fell back".[66] The knights fighting with him were so stirred by his reckless valor that they charged after him, and eventually they defeated the enemy.[67]

Marshal showed in his life as a knight a sacrificial commitment to live and die both for what he believed and for those whom he served. It is the epitome of self-sacrifice that is found in a warrior.

A modern warrior who shows Marshal's same penchant for sacrificial service to his cause is Marine Corporal Dakota Myer, a Medal of Honor recipient. His story captures the sacrificial heart of one who joined the military after 9/11 because as he says, "I was more than willing to fight the bastards who had murdered three thousand Americans."[68]

Myer started his career as a Marine by deploying to Afghanistan. While there, he had several combat engagements. One led him into an area called the Ganjigal Valley. His actions in this area were notorious as evidenced by the Medal of Honor he was awarded.

On the day of his most spectacular engagement, Myer's unit was going to visit some officials in a village. From the start, Myer did not like the mission. First, it was because he was excluded from being with the team that was going into the village. That frustrated him because he felt like he knew this area well and would be an asset to the team. Beyond that though, he did not like the mission because he feared that with the location of this village, the enemy who was all around had the upper hand if they decided to attack.[69] For these reasons, Myer complained up his chain of command, expressing his concerns, but he was told to shut up. This he did, but with anger.

The mission as initially outlined went forward in the morning of 8 September, 2009, well before the break of dawn. Almost as soon as the lead team, Team Monti, made its way to the village, the sun started to rise and then, all hell broke loose. Rocket Propelled Grenades (RPGs), heavy machine gun fire and AK 47 rifle shots were coming at the team from various fronts.[70] Other nearby supporting teams on this mission also found themselves under heavy fire.

Myer, who was some distance away at this point and heard about what was happening, was desperate to help. He sought permission to move forward. His request was denied.

As the battle grew more and more fierce, there were frantic calls for the unit's Tactical Operation Center (TOC) to call in for air support. One such call was this: "The main element is being hit form the north, east, and south. All elements are engaged. I repeat, all elements are heavily engaged. We need fire missions now."[71]

140

These requests for support were continuously denied. But Myer, having heard all of this and sensing the desperation, decided to respond to the crisis with his own team, regardless of the order he received not to do so. He made this call: "Fox 7, this is 3-3. Sitting here is stupid. We're going in."[72] With this, his battle began.

The firefight into the valley for Myer was ferocious. He was up in the turret of a Humvee, firing all that he had, though his efforts did not seem to help much. Yet, he fought on with the sacrificial spirit of a warrior and moved further into the kill zone. As he did, he and his driver spotted what looked to be an Improvised Explosive Device (IED) in the road. It would have been wise for them to get out of their vehicle and check this out. The consequences of not doing that were potentially deadly. Yet, they realized as well that they simply did not have the time. Hence, they made the decision to drive on. It might have been a suicide mission, they decided, but so be it. Myer provided his thoughts on the moment as they drove forward: "I hung on to the turret, eyes squeezed shut. I waited to be flung into the sky and wondered if I could do a backflip in the air and land on my feet—not that it would make any difference. I'd be dead, but you have a few funny thoughts in the infinite split seconds of battle."[73] Fortunately for Myer and his driver, there were no IEDs.

Driving on, Myer and his driver faced intense fire. There were bullets buzzing all around. Unfazed, Myer continued to engage the enemy. Myer said about this moment: "Strange though it may seem, I wasn't scared or angry. I was beyond that. I didn't think I was going to die; I knew I was dead. There wasn't anything I could do about it."[74]

As Myer moved now to locate the team that went into the village, much to their joy, helicopter air support finally arrived, raining all kinds of firepower down from the sky upon the enemy. This gave Myer and his driver some needed cover. At this point, they were the only two still pressing toward the village. This mission was a certain death march though as Myer and his driver knew, but as

Myer said, "I'd promised to get them, and Rod and I had the only gun truck willing and able to go in."[75]

As this team pressed on, they did stop at points to help the Afghan friendly forces that they came across, racing around to aid the wounded, even under intense fire. At one point, Myer saw his closest Afghan friend. He was dead. He had been hit in the face. As Myer was next to his friend, one of the enemy forces came behind him and put the barrel of an AK 47 to the back of his head. This insurgent easily could have killed Myer. It was a mistake that he did not. The insurgent's hesitation cost him his life. Myer, reacting quickly in the situation, turned to the insurgent, got the upper hand, and took him to the ground, killing him in a knock down drag out hand to hand fight.[76] From there, his mission continued.

It was soon thereafter, with four hours of intense fighting having elapsed, that friendly reinforcements arrived. With this, the enemy evaporated. It was then that Myer and the others found the missing team. Myer was actually the first on scene. What he found was devastating: "The team was wiped out. Their bodies were stiff and cold."[77] It was the sad end to his heroic efforts to save this team.

A part of Myer's citation for the Medal of Honor reads as follows:

Disregarding intense enemy fire now concentrated on their lone vehicle, Corporal Meyer killed a number of enemy fighters with the mounted machine guns and his rifle, some at near point blank range, as he and his driver made three solo trips into the ambush area. During the first two trips, he and his driver evacuated two dozen Afghan soldiers, many of whom were wounded. When one machine gun became inoperable, he directed a return to the rally point to switch to another gun-truck for a third trip into the ambush area where his accurate fire directly supported the remaining U.S. personnel and Afghan soldiers fighting their way out of the ambush. Despite a shrapnel wound to his arm, Corporal Meyer made two more trips into the ambush area in a third gun-truck accompanied by four other Afghan vehicles to recover more wounded Afghan soldiers and search for the missing U.S. team members. Still under heavy enemy fire, he dismounted the vehicle on the fifth trip and moved on foot to locate and recover the bodies of his team members. Corporal Meyer's daring initiative and bold fighting spirit throughout the 6-hour battle significantly disrupted the enemy's attack and inspired the members of the combined force to fight on.[78]

To understand the warrior is to know that he is committed to sacrifice himself for the sake of others. His focus, as is the case for all warriors, is to get help to those in need. This warriors will do regardless of what might happen to them. It is astounding to consider and it is truly something beyond emulation for those who are not of this mindset.

In conclusion, it would be fitting as we close this comparison of the knights with modern warriors to look beyond their sacrificial comparison and see one more vital part of the warrior mindset. It has to do with the love that these warriors have for war itself. Listen to how one knight in the twelfth century describes this:

"...I love to see, amidst the fields, a spread of tents and pavilions; and it gives me great joy to see, drawn up on the fields, knights and horses in battle array. And it delights me when the scouts scatter people and herds in their path; and I love to see them followed by a great number of men-at-arms; and my heart is filled with gladness when I see strong castles besieged, and the walls broken and overwhelmed, and the knights on the bank...with a line of strong stakes, interlaced. Maces, swords, helms [helmets] of different hues, shields that will be driven and shattered as soon as the fight begins; and many knights struck down together; and the horses of the dead and wounded roving at random. And when the battle is joined, let all good men of lineage think of naught but the breaking of heads and arms; for it

143

is better to die than to be vanquished and live. I tell you, I find no such favor in food, or in wine, or in sleep, as in hearing the shout, 'On! On!' from both sides, and the neighing of steeds that have lost their riders, and the cries of 'Help! Help!'; in seeing men great and small go down on the grass…in seeing at last the dead, with the stumps of lances still in their sides."[79]

If ever you wanted an inner look at what modern day warriors think about war, these words from an ancient warrior express it perfectly. Many of the warriors with whom I went to war would accept these exact words as their own, only their terminology would change to fit their sense of battle. In fact, consider a modern-day example of the knight's words. They are provided by a soldier who had two tours in Iraq. He says this:

A few months ago, I found a Web site loaded with pictures and videos from Iraq, the sort that usually aren't seen on the news. I watched insurgent snipers shoot American soldiers and car bombs disintegrate markets, accompanied by tinny music and loud, rhythmic chanting, the soundtrack of the propaganda campaigns. Video cameras focused on empty stretches of road, building anticipation. Humvees rolled into view and the explosions brought mushroom clouds of dirt and smoke and chunks of metal spinning through the air. Other videos and pictures showed insurgents shot dead while planting roadside bombs or killed in firefights and the remains of suicide bombers, people how they're not meant to be seen, no longer whole. …I clicked through more frames, hungry for it. This must be what a shot of dope feels like after a long stretch of sobriety. Soothing and nauseating and colored by everything that has come before. My body tingled and my stomach ached, hollow. …I miss Iraq. I miss the war. I miss war. And I have a very hard time understanding why. …For those who know, this is the open secret: War is exciting. Sometimes I was in awe of this, and sometimes I felt low and mean for loving it, but I loved it still. Even in its quiet moments, war is brighter, louder, brasher, more fun, more tragic, more wasteful. More. More of everything. And even then, I knew I would someday miss it, this life so strange.[80]

What most never realize about the warrior is how intoxicating and enlivening war is. To be away from it is like having a limb severed, a part of you is gone, and you wish it were not so. Knights felt this way, and modern warriors do as well. General George S. Patton, a modern-day warrior, expressed this sentiment well. He talks about where a soldier truly belongs. He says, "There's only one proper way for a professional soldier to die: the last bullet of the last battle of the last war."[81] Where else would a warrior want to be or how else would he want to die?

Knights and modern warriors are one in kind. We did not even touch on yet another obvious comparison: the chivalrous code for knights and the core values of today, which dictate the behavior of modern warriors. Regardless, what we see in this analysis is that when it comes to being willing to sacrifice self for another, this is yet another trait that defines warriors throughout history.

Gusto Seekers

The love of adventure coupled with the will to defeat an enemy in battle describes not only warriors of today but also ancient fighters known as Vikings.[82] These Norseman were considered to be perhaps the bravest of early combatants and explorers.[83] Who could question it as they set off into the rough North Atlantic seas in a somewhat primitive sailing vessel called the knarr with a heavenly navigation system that "relied more on serendipity than on science":[84]

The rough, bearded men clutched at the sides of their long, wooden ship as foaming waves crashed and icy winds blew around them. The year was A.D. 986, and these brave sailors were caught in a fierce storm in the North Atlantic Ocean. For three days, the men were at the mercy of the sea. Their small open craft was pushed far off course to the south and west. At last, the storm abated, and the men on board could relax. But where were they? Even their leader, an experienced sailor named Bjarni Herjolfsson, was not sure.[85]

What was it that motivated these ancient warriors and made them such gusto seekers? There were several things. One was the pure joy of fighting for their gods, whom they believed watched over them in battle. Another was to fight for their families who they often brought with them. Still more, they fought for their leaders who were always out in front as the fighting raged.[86] Under the spell of these motivating factors, they were aggressive and ferocious in battle, fearlessly charging the enemy.

What helped these ancient Vikings become so dominant in their day were the special group of Viking warriors who fought amongst them: the Beserkers and the Ulfhedinn.[87] These unique warriors, set apart from other Vikings, were seen as crazed by the enemy because of the way that they acted in battle, seemingly charging forward with axes and spears in a psychotic bloodlust. They fought without regard for injury, often without shirts or protective gear, and were possessed by a frenetic spirit as they faced their opponent.[88] When these special warriors led the way into battle with other Vikings in trail, their ability to overcome the enemy proved almost insurmountable, and it definitely brought fear to all throughout the ancient world.

Overall, "The Viking's success in killing and oppressing everyone who stood in their way was no accident: The warrior mentality followed a Viking from birth until he proudly stepped into Valhalla."[89] Fighting was their way of life. From their earliest years, Norsemen trained for battle and eagerly sought the chance to earn their way into the Viking ranks and kill. For many, that transition began in their early teenage years but for all it would continue throughout their lives. It would only be death in battle that would stop them, but that too was still not the end. In death, Vikings believed that they were given the chance to be accepted into Odin's great warrior palace, Valhalla. That was what they really desired. For in Valhalla, warriors lived the warrior's dream; i.e., fighting all day long, being miraculously restored from their wounds to full health in the evening, and then, becoming part of the great warrior feast in the banquet hall at the end of the day.[90] This was every warrior's hopeful ending.

While perhaps modern warriors are not like their Viking counterparts in terms of being focused on the promise of Valhalla, they still have the same gusto and adventurous spirit moving them toward war. An instance of this can be seen in one Marine who was displeased with the fact that his men were not getting the chance to fight in battle, even though they travelled thousands of miles for the chance. That was unacceptable to him and he said as much:

> We weren't getting some. Others were. The truth is that a Marine, especially a grunt, can begin to feel really inadequate when he knows a unit other than his is engaged in combat. I know I felt that way. Being a grunt is really the only MOS (military occupational specialty) for which you train solely for what you might do as opposed to what you will do. But a grunt only gets to go through hell (combat) a few times—or sometimes never at all. He'll either stay in until he gets some or leave the Corps blue-balled and unfulfilled. It might sound strange, but this type of disappointment was the kind of thing that could stay with a guy for the rest of his life. Some of us were beginning to fear we might never get some.[91]

This Marine and all warriors alike have this adventurous and warlike spirit. They crave that moment of engaging in combat, overcoming any who stand in their way. They want the chance to get into the fight. Being denied this opportunity, depresses a natural part of their utter excitement to take on the enemy.

For the warriors with whom I served, I would likewise say that if there was no action to be had in a mission, there was no need to send Marines. Send some other group. This truth was echoed by the Marine Corps leader General James Conway at a point when the war in Iraq had tapered down. At this time, he talked to the Defense Secretary, Robert Gates, about drawing down his men from Iraq and sending them into the fight that was going on in Afghanistan. He told the Defense Secretary that he "would not object to the idea of a fairly strategic shift of focus of Marines from Iraq to Afghanistan."[92] He went on to say that as he saw it, "Marines could be put to better use fighting in Afghanistan than their current peacekeeping, nation-building mission in Iraq."[93]

As it was with the Vikings, so it is with all warrior groups today; they find adventure in chasing that new horizon and going to where the action is. Perhaps this spirit is best captured overall by Henry Kitchell Webster who wrote about the Vikings. In relaying the character of these warriors, he offers these words, which serve as the perfect summation of this point and could easily be used as the basis of any warrior's hymn:

Love of adventure and contempt for the quiet joys of home comes out in the description of Viking chiefs, who 'never sought refuge under a roof nor emptied their drinking-horns by a hearth.' An immense love of fighting breathes in the accounts of Viking warriors, 'who are glad when they have hopes of a battle; they will leap up in hot haste and ply the oars, snapping the oar-thongs and cracking the tholes.' The undaunted spirit of Viking sailors, braving the storms of the northern ocean, expresses itself in their sea songs: 'The force of the tempest assists the arms of our oarsman; the hurricane is our servant, it drives us whithersoever we wish to go.'[94]

Rigid Moral Code

A discussion of warriors in history would be incomplete without consideration of the Spartans. Their "society was carefully constructed around a strict moral code and sense of duty, and its people underwent extreme hardships and deprivation on their way to becoming accepted as full citizens."[95] Certainly, this life-style might appear rigid to most. Yet, it is undoubtedly for these reasons that Spartans were legendary in their exploits, and in one battle at Thermopylae, they showed the world that though an enemy, the Persians in this case, might win a battle, they will still lose the war.

What was it about these Spartan warriors that made them the most feared warriors in their time? Let us consider this as it will help us to see how these ancient warriors compare to modern warriors.

A Spartan warrior was defined by a code of honor to die for the common good of his people. It was a simple moral code, but one that was so entrenched in this society that it was not just the warrior who found nobility in this ideal, but even his own mother believed this kind of death to be glorious. "Come back with your shield - or on it" (Plutarch, Mor.241) was supposed to be the parting cry of mothers to their sons. Mothers whose sons died in battle openly rejoiced, mothers whose sons survived hung their heads in shame."[96] Clearly the warrior's code of honor held greater meaning than even the bonds of love.

Beyond this rigid code for the warrior was a life focused exclusively on the profession and execution of war. These warriors "...were forbidden any other trade, profession or business than war, and they acquired the reputation of being the Marines of the entire Greek world, a uniquely professional and motivated fighting force." [97] But to be in this group, you had to prove your worthiness. It started at birth. Those deemed unfit when born by virtue of physical deformity or simply by failing to react appropriately when dunked in a ritualistic bath of wine were killed.[98]

149

The next test started at the age of seven. Here boys were taken from households and placed under the tutelage of older boys, who themselves were preparing to be warriors.[99] If one got through that experience, then by the age of twelve, he was sent out to live off of the land, enduring the elements, hunger and wild animals. This was truly the Spartan existence.

Those who survived after one year were brought back for grueling war training: martial arts, physical fitness and various weapon system trainings. This too proved fatal for some, but even for those who made it through that, their test of fortitude was still not completed. "To toughen the young warriors and encourage their development as soldiers, instructors and older men would often instigate fights and arguments between trainees. The *agoge* was partially designed to help make the youths resistant to hardships like cold, hunger and pain, and boys who showed signs of cowardice or timidity were subject to teasing and violence by peers and superiors alike."[100]

At age twenty, the survivors of the Spartan training process were now allowed into the Army barracks and there they lived there for ten years, even if married. Finally, at the age of thirty, if they maintained faithfulness to the warrior code, they were made full citizens, true Spartans, and could live with their wives. From here, they remained as warriors until the age of sixty.

This development process for the Spartan warrior has no parallel in history, but its unique demands which weeded out the weak ensured that only a true warrior would survive. It further was an important method for developing the requisite skills which a Spartan would need for victory: steeling the body, mind and spirit for war. It is no surprise, thusly, that these warriors were so revered. When one fought a Spartan, he was fighting a true warrior, for only such a person was able to survive the grueling process of becoming that warrior.

Let us regard these warriors in action in the Battle at Thermopylae, one if their greatest triumphs, albeit even in death.

This battle occurred over a period of three days at a narrow pass with mountains on one side and the ocean on the other. Of great debate is the number of troops present on both sides. The Persian warriors were said to have numbered from the millions to a couple hundred thousand, and the Spartans were said to have had three hundred warriors present with an additional three to seven thousand Greek warriors by their side.[101] In terms of these raw numbers, the odds greatly favored the Persians.

The first day of the battle could not have been worse for the king of Persia, Xerxes, and his army: "...on three occasions, allegedly, Xerxes leapt up in horror from his specially constructed throne, appalled at the carnage and slaughter of some of his best men."[102] His response was to send better and better troops who only met the same fate as those before them—death at the hands of the Greek warriors with the Spartans out in front.

The second day fared no better than the first. In spite of Xerxes' use of his finest troops in battle, the Spartans continued to punish the Persians, piling up the losses. It was not until the end of the second day that Xerxes got a break. A Greek traitor came to Xerxes and revealed information on a way to attack the Greeks from their rear.[103] Xerxes used this information and prepared his men for a secret assault. This was to happen on day three. Let us consider this day.

The third day of this battle was even more impressive in terms of the numbers of Persians that the Greeks killed. It is said that on this day, "[w]ith their weapons gone or broken, the Greeks fought tooth and nail – literally, using their bare hands and their mouths."[104] They simply refused to surrender. However, with the traitor's information on the secret passage, the Persians were able to attack from the flank, eventually overtaking the Greeks and defeating them.[105] One only wonders what might have happened if Xerxes never did hear from this traitor. Perhaps even this merciless ruler would have withdrawn given his substantial losses at the hands of the Greeks and the Spartans.

Overall, the constitution of these ancient Spartan warriors who refused to dishonor their personal integrity was said to have shocked the King of Persia.[106] He felt like the Spartans were undeniably impressive in battle. Indeed, they were. That intractable belief in self and in a belief system that guided them as warriors[107] "… commanded them to stand firm always and to conquer or die."[108]

Knowing these things provides insight into why Xerxes was not able to bargain with these warriors before or during the battle. They did not care for money or position. It was not even their lives that they valued, but their principles, that rigid moral code which defined their existence. To stand resolute for that was considered nothing less than a "beautiful death."[109] Hence, in spite of their mounting losses, they simply told Xerxes that if he wanted their arms he would have to "[c]ome and take them."[110]

Poignantly their spirit is captured in a phrase that was written about these Spartans after they all died at this battle: "Go tell the Spartans, passerby, that here, obedient to their laws, we lie."[111] This is a powerful phrase that conveys to all the warrior ethos of this group; namely, you might take my life, but you cannot take away my resolute will to stand for what I believe. That, indeed, is what the Persians eventually learned, as they were ultimately driven by other Greek warriors out of Greece once and for all.

The fighting spirit of these Spartans is not at all unlike what I have seen in warriors today. When caught by surprise, when outnumbered, when in close quarters combat, when in need of rescuing a downed warrior, they are not about to surrender. They fight for what they hold dear: freedom, those whom they love, their country, their moral sense of honor, courage and commitment, and those by their side.

A compelling picture of this is found in the life and example of Marco Martinez. This Marine, the first Hispanic American since Vietnam to be awarded the Navy Cross, talks about an event on April of 2003 when his company was tasked to go to a town called Al Tarmiya, where there was a concentration of Fedayeen fighters.[112] These are the hard-core, drugged up, fighters whose goal beyond killing Americans is to die. During his mission, while moving through the area, Martinez's team leader gets hit by fire in an ambush. Martinez takes over the squad and begins a daring assault on the enemy who were positioned in a house. After his team made it to the house in a hail of bullets, the rest of the scene unfolded like this:

> The second we entered the house, we were in contact with enemy fighters. It was many of them versus only four of us. They were so close that when we shot them blood splattered the walls. ...Every room we entered on the first floor contained at least one terrorist. We were dropping body after body, often just a few feet away from us. Sweat soaked my sleeves. We crept up the stairs. 'Over there!" I heard Birdsong yell. We blasted the terrorist and cleared the room. After we busted into the next room and eliminated more enemy, I stopped to look down at the dead bodies....[113]

From here, once Martinez had cleared the inside of the house he went to check out the roof and once again was engaged in killing terrorists. By the time that engagement ended, his men had killed fifteen fighters, but the conflict was still not over. They left this house and charged yet another enemy position. In this fight, his men were immediately pinned down and one of his men fell wounded. At this, Martinez picked up an enemy RPG (Rocket Propelled Grenade) lying out on the ground, and after a few tries; he got it to fire, killing a few more insurgents. This action distracted the enemy and gave time for his fellow Marines to grab the downed Marine. Then, Martinez made a solo assault on the enemy. Firing his M16 and throwing grenades, he eventually finished off all attackers. At this point, one of his fellow Marines came up and said to him, "'Holy shit!'...'Did you see what you did to those guys?'"[114] To this,

Martinez did not remember responding because he said that he was overwhelmed by fatigue.

It is powerful to read this heroic account of harrowing conflict. Martinez offers some great words about this incident. Read these words and grasp what Martinez wants you to hear:

A grunt trains his whole life for battle. I'd had the privilege of experiencing it now—of playing a tiny role in the War on Terror. I knew guys who went all four years and never got the honor of experiencing combat. They'd reenlist and reenlist just for the chance to contribute—just for the chance to be baptized by fire. And here we were doing it in our first enlistment. ...But my Marine brothers and I carried weapons to defend our nation against its enemies. We, like the millions who came before us, used the awesome might of America's military power for liberation, not conquest. There's a profound moral difference between the two. Terrorists knowingly and intentionally target civilians, people who never signed up for battle or chose to enter a military conflict. But every ninja-pajama-wearing motherfucker who ambushed us that day had entered that battlefield with the full and complete knowledge of the consequences. When I hear the typical stronger college "genius" blather about how America is "just as evil as the terrorist," I think maybe he or she would do well to remember the distinction. In my past, I've used violence for evil. But I can tell you this much: My brother Marines and I never did. ...We weren't sick maniacs. We were Marines. We were the guys who were willing to do the shit that no civilian will do. Nobody who wears the uniform—Marine, sailor, airman, or soldier—does it for the pay. They do it because they love the nation that gives them and their family more than they could ever have dreamed of. People often ask me how my brothers and I did what we did that day. I always say the same thing: "if we didn't do it, who would?" Not everyone can or should wear a uniform. *But a person can't expect to live in the best damn country on earth and not be willing to fight and die for it. He or she can't be a freeloader of freedom.*[115]

Are you able to comprehend that this man is a warrior who relished the chance to do that for which he was created, standing to defend what he believed to be right? It was something that he felt privileged to do. He was willing to lay his life on the line for what he thought was true, and this he did many times over. He fought for his convictions and fought against those who desired to destroy the innocent. He knows what it is to be a warrior. He knows every facet of what that means. He understands the costs and knows what it is to sacrifice.

Like the Spartans, bound by their beliefs, he too knows what it is to put moral convictions and personal beliefs above self. He has done this. He has stood for what he believes. He is a warrior, a righteous warrior. One who goes to battle and confronts evil and destroys it. He is not unclear about what he is doing. He hears others back home talk about war as if it is unrighteous. Yet, he knows the difference. He clearly sees that it is his enemy who is truly unrighteous and needs to be silenced. Someone needs to stop them. For this, he volunteers. He does it out of duty. He does it out of obligation to country and freedom. He does it both because he has such a strong inner sense of what is right and an unremitting passion to defend it. That is the heart of a warrior.

Having a rigid moral code is living with an inner sense that there are some things that are right and worth defending. That creates an unassailable warrior as the Spartans knew well: "Through constant, daily reinforcement of their strict code of values, the Spartans ensured their survival against the enemies they had created by subjugating their neighbors."[116] The evidence of this was on full display at the Battle of Thermopylae. Martinez and his fellow Marines showed this same understanding in their fight. The Marines of 3/5 and many others showed it in the Battle for Fallujah.

Countless warriors through the ages have done the same. It is this for which they were born. They are the guardians of truth. They fight for what they believe. What a blessing it is to have those who will never surrender their convictions, even if it means they must die.

Conclusion

To fully know and engage with these inner impulses that send warriors off into danger and death is something that most will never be able to appreciate. Non-warriors simply are not wired that way. They have instincts and convictions that take them away from war. When they see danger, it is something to avoid. Their ideas of excitement are never death-defying events. They realize keenly that they are not impervious to injury or defeat. Their willingness to sacrifice is far less unyielding.

Because of these things, it is challenging for non-warriors to open up and explore the world of the warrior. That is unfortunate because the "expert advice" on developing, training and helping warriors, which by and large comes from non-warriors, ends up perplexing the very people it is designed to help.

At their core, warriors have a nature that moves them to be elite, invincible, hard, sacrificial, gusto seekers, sacrificial, and morally upright. These are qualities that have defined warriors through the ages. Other qualities could be mentioned too. Nonetheless, the traits offered are essential to what makes warriors and what makes them so important. Without them and that which defines their essence, we would not be effective in military engagements.

Endnotes

---

[1] "North African Masai Tribe",
https://northafricanmasaitribe.weebly.com/rites-of-passage.html,
(May, 2018).

[2] Stephen Turnball, Samurai Warfare, (New York: Sterling
Publishing Co., 1996), p. 10.

[3] Lyn GoldFarb, "Japan: Memories of a Secrets Empire, Samurai,"
http://www.pbs.org/empires/japan/enteredo_8.html, (2003).

[4] Ibid.

[5] Stephen Turnball, Samurai Warlords:The Book of the Daimyo,
London: Blandford Press, 1989), p. 9.

[6] H. Paul Varley, Samurai, (New York: Delacorte Press, 1970), pp.
94-95.

[7] Ibid. pp. 94-108.

[8] Ibid., pp. 69-108 and Historical Foundations of Japan's Military
Aggression, "Japan under the Shoguns 1185-1853,"
http://www.users.bigpond.com/battleforAustralia/foundationJapmila
ggro/Shogunate.html, (May 2009).

[9] Inazo Nitobe, Bushido: The Warrior's Code, (Santa Clara,
California: Ohara Publications, 1979), p.11.

[10] Ibid., p. 14.

[11] Ibid., pp. 23-86.

[12] Historical Foundations of Japan's Military Aggression, "Japan
under the Shoguns 1185-1853,"
http://www.users.bigpond.com/battleforAustralia/foundationJapmila
ggro/Shogunate.html, (May 2009).

[13] Oscar Ratti and Adele Westbrook, Secrets of the Samurai,
(Vermont: Charles E. Tuttle Company, 1973), pp. 84-86.

[14] Ibid., p. 23.

[15] Blackfive, "Marine Messages in Fallujah,"
http://www.blackfive.net/main/military_stuff/index.html, (November
15, 2004).

[16] Ibid.

[17] Joshua J. Mark, "Alexander the Great",
https://www.ancient.eu/Alexander_the_Great/, (14 November,
2013).

[18] C. M. Bowra, "Alexander The Great," Reports & Essays: Biography - Historical Figures, http://www.studyworld.com/newsite/ReportEssay/Biography/Historical Figures%5CAlexander_the_Great-323270.htm, (May 11, 2009).

[19] Nicholas Sekunda, Greek Hoplite, (Great Britian: Osprey, 2000), pp. 5-6.

[20] Waldemar Heckel & Ryan Jones, Macedonian Warrior: Alexander's elite infantryman, (Great Britain: Osprey Publishing, 2006), p. 12.

[21] Ibid, pp. 12-13.

[22] Weapons and Warfare ~ History and Hardware of Warfare, "Silver Shields", https://weaponsandwarfare.com/2015/12/31/silver-shields/, (2016, 6 May).

[23] Michael Park, The Silver Shields: Philip's and Alexander's Hypaspists, http://www.academia.edu/2397748/The_Silver_Shields_Philips_and_Alexanders_Hypaspists, (2016, 8 May).

[24] Elizabeth Carney, Daniel Ogden, Philip II and Alexander the Great: Father and Son, Lives and Afterlives, (New York: Oxford University Press, 2010), p. 102.

[25] "Membership was based on physical qualities as well as merit, but the demands were greater and life expectancy shorter. ...Their sense of belonging was based on having 'walked the walk,' both as a unit and as individuals." Waldemar Heckel & Ryan Jones, Macedonian Warrior: Alexander's elite infantryman, (Great Britain: Osprey Publishing, 2006), p. 52.

[26] Waldemar Heckel & Ryan Jones, Macedonian Warrior: Alexander's elite infantryman, p. 11 and Information About, "Hypaspist," http://www.informationdelight.info/encyclopedia/entry/Central_Busine...%20www.seattleluxury.com/encyclopedia/entry/Central_Business_District/hypaspist, (November 3, 2008).

[27] Heckel and Jones, p. 41.

[28] Ibid., p. 42.

[29] Ibid., p. 52.

[30] The details of this story, unless directly quoted, are summations of what Bellavia encounters as told in his memoirs, Staff Sergeant

David Bellavia, House to House: An Epic Memoir of War, (New York: Free Press, 2007).

[31] Ibid., p. 217.

[32] Ibid., p. 219.

[33] Ibid.

[34] Ibid., pp. 236-237.

[35] Ibid., p. 240.

[36] Ibid., p. 246.

[37] Ibid., p. 272.

[38] "invincible." Webster's Revised Unabridged Dictionary. MICRA, Inc., http://dictionary1.classic.reference.com/browse/infincible, (15 May. 2009).

[39] Ibid., p. 255.

[40] Moses Hadas, Imperial Rome, (New York: Time-Life Books, 1965), p. 89.

[41] Ibid.

[42] Ross Cowan, Roman Legionary, (Great Britain: Ospery Publishing, 2003), pp. 11, 22.

[43] Ibid.

[44] Vegetius, Epitome, 1.1 as cited by Cowan, p. 11.

[45] Ibid., pp. 11-12, 43.

[46] Hadas, p. 100.

[47] Cowan, p. 11.

[48] Marco Martinez, Hard Corps: From Gangster to Marine Hero, (New York: Random House, 2007), p. 71.

[49] Ibid.

[50] Alan Baker, "The Knight", Hoboken, (NJ: John Wiley & Sons, 2003), p. 8.

[51] James Barter, A Medieval Knight, (New York: Lucent Books, 2005), p. 9.

[52] Prestwich, p. 965.

[53] Baker., p. 9.

[54] Allen J. Frantzen, Bloody Good: Chivalry, Sacrifice, and the Great War, (Chicago: University of Chicago Press, 2004), p. 13.

[55] Ibid., pp. 13, 16.

[56] Desmond Seward, The Monks of War, Kindle ed., (London: Thistle Publishing, 1972), Loc., 97-98.

[57] Ibid., Loc., 288.

[58] Thomas Asbridge, The Greatest Knight, Kindle Ed., (Toronto, Canada: Harper Collins Publishers, 2014), p. 3.

[59] Ibid., pp. 49 and 122.

[60] Barter, p. 66.

[61] Ibid., pp. 66-67.

[62] Asbridge, p. 115.

[63] Ibid., p. 38.

[64] Ibid., p. 55.

[65] Ibid.

[66] Ibid., p. 250.

[67] Ibid.

[68] Dakota Meyer and Bing West, Into the Fire: A Firsthand Account of the Most Extraordinary Battle in the Afghan War, (New York, NY: Random House, 2012), pp. 25-26.

[69] Ibid, p. 83.

[70] Ibid. p. 91.

[71] Ibid, p. 102.

[72] Ibid, p. 107.

[73] Ibid., p. 122.

[74] Ibid, p. 129.

[75] Ibid, p. 138.

[76] Ibid, pp. 141-145.

[77] Ibid, pp. 155-158.

[78] Congressional Medal of Honor Society, "Meyer, Dakota", http://www.cmohs.org/recipient-detail/3480/meyer-dakota.php, (August, 2015).

[79] Ibid., p.45.

[80] Brian Mockenhaupt, "I Miss Iraq. I Miss My Gun. I Miss My War," http://www.esquire.com/features/ESQ0307ESSAY, (June 26, 2007).

[81] Inspiring Quotes, "George S. Patton," https://www.inspiringquotes.us/quotes/DqkE_o3wa7gvr, (10 May 2018).

[82] Mary Macgregor, "Stories of the Vikings", http://www.heritage-history.com/?c=read&author=macgregor&book=vikings&story=discoveries, (August, 2015).

[83] History Reference Center, Early Explorations. Everyday Life: Exploration & Discovery, http://0-web.ebscohost.com.dbpcosdcsgt.co.san-diego.ca.us/ehost/detail?vid=8&hid=115&sid=62ac5a90-fd1e-4dc2-a5df-3934873dc946%40sessionmgr102&bdata=JnNpdGU9ZWhvc3QtbG12ZQ%3d%3d#db=khh&AN=25262399, (2005).

[84] Tim Zimmermann, "Getting There First," U.S. News & World Report, (08/16/99-08/23/99, Vol. 127 Issue 7, p71), http://0-web.ebscohost.com.dbpcosdcsgt.co.san-diego.ca.us/ehost/detail?vid=11&hid=115&sid=62ac5a90-fd1e-4dc2-a5df-3934873dc946%40sessionmgr102&bdata=JnNpdGU9ZWhvc3QtbG12ZQ%3d%3d#db=khh&AN=2124008.

[85] Jim Gallagher, Viking Explorers, (New York: Chelsea House, 2000), p. 62, http://0-web.ebscohost.com.dbpcosdcsgt.co.san-diego.ca.us/ehost/detail?vid=18&hid=8&sid=77fdbe8d-43fc-41e5-88bd-b637fd5e0a5c%40sessionmgr108&bdata=JnNpdGU9ZWhvc3QtbG12ZQ%3d%3d#db=khh&AN=9210912.

[86] Njord Kane, The Vikings, The Story of a People, Ebook, (Spangenhelm Publishing, 2015), pp. 205-207.

[87] Ibid., p. 212.

[88] Ibid.

[89] Thor Lanesskog, "Viking Children Learned the Art of War", Thornews, https://thornews.com/2014/12/30/viking-children-learned-the-art-of-war/, (2014).

[90] Daniel McCoy, "Valhalla", Norse Mythology for Smart People, https://norse-mythology.org/cosmology/valhalla/, (2018).

[91] Marco Martinez, Hard Corps: From Gangster to Marine Hero, (New York: Random House, 2007), pp. 114-115.

[92] Brent Jones, "U.S. Marines will shift to Afghanistan," http://www.usatoday.com/news/washington/2008-12-08-marine-afghanistan_N.htm, (December 8, 2008).

[93] Ibid.

[94] Henry Kitchell Webster, Early European History, Forgotten Books.org, http://books.google.com/books/p/pub-4297897631756504?id=rXSqwPFMn3oC&printsec=frontcover&dq

=isbn:1606209353&source=gbs_summary_r&cad=0#PPA3,M1, (2008).

[95] Evan Andrews, "8 Reasons It Wasn't Easy Being Spartan," http://www.history.com/news/history-lists/8-reasons-it-wasnt-easy-being-spartan, (2013, 5 March).

[96] "Sparta: Famous quotes about Spartan life", https://www.pbs.org/empires/thegreeks/background/8c_p1.html, 12 October, 2017.

[97] Paul Cartledge, Thermopylae: The Battle That Changed The World, (New York: The Overlook Press, 2006), p. 29.

[98] Ibid., p. 80.

[99] The description of the warrior's training from age seven to sixty as described below is from Andrew Murphy, "Training warriors in ancient Sparta," http://www.helium.com/items/795298-training-warriors-in-ancient-sparta, (May 2009).

[100] Evan Andrews, "8 Reasons It Wasn't Easy Being Spartan."

[101] The British War Museum, "The Battle of Thermopylae: Spartans v. Persians," http://www.ancientgreece.co.uk/war/story/sto_set.html, (May, 2018).

[102] Cartledge, Thermopylae: The Battle That Changed The World, p. 145.

[103] Ibid., p. 146.

[104] Ibid., p. 150.

[105] Ibid.

[106] Ibid., p. 8.

[107] Cartledge, p. 9.

[108] David Frye, "Greco-Persian Wars: Battle of Thermopylae", http://www.historynet.com/greco-persian-wars-battle-of-thermopylae.htm, originally published in Military History Magazine, (January/February, 2006).

[109] Ibid. p. 81.

[110] Ancient Greek Battles, "Spartan Sayings," http://www.ancientgreekbattles.net/Pages/47931_Spartaquotes.htm, (May, 2018).

[111] The words of Simonides of Ceos as quoted by Cartledge, Thermopylae: The Battle That Changed The World, p. 153.

[112] The events as described below are those recounted by Martinez, Hard Corps: From Gangster to Marine Hero, pp. 185-201.

[113] Ibid., pp. 190-191.

[114] Ibid., p. 196.

[115] [Italicized added to emphasize moral desire to defend country and freedom], Ibid., pp. 199-200.

[116] Thomas R. Martin, "An Overview of Classical Greek History from Mycenae to Alexander,"
http://www.perseus.tufts.edu/hopper/text?doc=Perseus%3Atext%3A1999.04.0009%3Achapter%3D6, (2016, 6 May).

CHAPTER SIX

WARRIOR'S TRAITS AS WITNESSED IN THE BATTLE OF FALLUJAH

William Harvey Carney, born a slave, was the first African American to earn the Medal of Honor. He was a Union Soldier fighting in the 54th Massachusetts Volunteer Infantry. In 1863, he was a part of an assault on Fort Wagner. His all black regiment charged up a well-fortified embankment to the Fort, and it was an onslaught. Carney continued forward though as many around him fell wounded or dying. He noticed at one point that the flag bearer had been shot. As that man went down but before the flag could touch the ground, Carney grabbed the flag, lifted it up and led his troops in a spirited charge toward the enemy. It is challenging to think about what it must have been like to race up into a hail of bullets, as men around you were falling to their death, some screaming in pain, and to do this without directly engaging the enemy but with the sole purpose of bearing the flag. What possesses a person to act so courageously, believing that a flag is more important than one's life? By the time his unit withdrew, Carney had been shot twice. Yet, in spite of his wounds and failing health, he let everyone know, "The Old Flag never touched the ground!" That is commitment. It is commitment by one to a flag that unquestionably symbolizes the importance of standing for the belief that all men are created equal and endowed with the unalienable rights of life, liberty and the pursuit happiness. It is unyielding valor for the cause of justice. That is who warriors are. It is one of many things that defines their essence and makes them remarkable.[1]

This day was 8 November, in the early morning hours. 3/5 Battalion with five other Battalions to its eastern flank was starting the move into Fallujah. It was the first battle of its kind, an assault on a major city, rooting out the enemy building by building, house by house.

This moment for the warriors was something about which they had dreamed. They wanted to "get it on." It was a test of their skill and a fulfillment of character and natural impulses. To show this, let us go through some of my experiences and note the qualities of warriors as I witnessed them. I will place these qualities in bold letters as we come across them for ease of clarification.

The Battle of Fallujah: A Focused Recounting

I was back at our Forward Operation Base (FOB), just behind the train trestle, for this opening period of the war. Although occasional mortar rounds did come into the base, the threat was minimal.

In terms of my role as a chaplain, I felt like I was missing out. We had Marines on the front lines who were engaged in firefights, killing the enemy and seeing friends, not killed at this point, but wounded. Who was there to help them overcome guilt and doubt, and provide spiritual care and guidance? That was my role.

The position I did have for those who came back from the front injured was very unsatisfactory. This was because when injured Marines were brought back to our BAS (Battalion Aid Station), they were quickly surrounded by the surgical team. Those doctors performed immediate trauma care, stabilizing the wounds and injuries, and then, they bandaged the injured up for transport.

Before I had a chance to do any direct chaplain care, the injured were whisked away to a waiting helicopter to be evacuated to a safer location where a better equipped surgical team would treat them. I felt ineffectual. I questioned if being at the FOB was best. I believed that I should move forward, on the front lines, where I could have some direct impact. I went to our Battalion Commander and told him of my desires. He graciously allowed me to do what I felt I needed for the care of his Marines and that turned out to be a great decision. The warriors seemed to appreciate my presence with them. They knew that I did not have to be up front with them, but that fact alone had a deep impact, which is something that I discovered once I left this command.

Before we progress into the story of what happened, though, let me provide a visual of what this city looked like. Fallujah had about fifty thousand buildings at the start of the war.[2] It is estimated that about forty thousand of these structures were dwelling places, mostly single-family houses, but apartment buildings were also a part of this number.[3] Tight streets and alley ways ran haphazardly throughout the city and electrical wires dangled from one place to the next, across streets and passageways, precariously strung with an apparent disregard for aesthetics or safety. I remember at one point in the fight when a D9, huge bull-dozer, was brought down one of these tight alleyways. Because of its height, it had pulled along with it so many of these low hanging crisscrossing wires that the driver could not see out of the window; a black curtain of snapped wires obscured the entire view.

The houses, mainly one or two stories high, were generally grouped together in large blocks or grid squares. All homes were made of brick or cement block, and this material was usually covered with a mortar texturing. Most of the homes had privacy walls that surrounded them, with metal gates at the front to allow for entrance. Picture a block with lots divided by interconnecting brick walls, with a home in the center of each section. When you entered the gate to the homes, there were small open courtyard areas in the front, and generally tight passageways on both sides of the houses to the back where there were narrow strips of land that served as backyards.

The houses were modestly decorated inside, nothing fancy except in a few. There were usually about four rooms on the first floor and a cement stairwell to the second floor, which had about four rooms too. In addition, homes had a passage to the roofs which were flat with cement flooring; they were surrounded by privacy walls, four to five feet high, allowing for families to go to the rooftop during the summer months to sleep.

I entered hundreds of these homes during our time in Fallujah. Most were laid out similarly, but there were occasional surprises in the floor structures, making it difficult for the Marines to be certain of what to expect when they breached these homes in search of insurgents.

Besides the homes, there were numerous apartment type structures as mentioned, along with mosques, open air markets, cafes, stores, businesses, animal pens, schools and other assorted structures in the city. These structures were randomly dotted amongst the housing blocks. Occasionally, there were market areas where a concentration of shops could be found.

If anything mirrored American zoning laws, it was the fact that the heavy industrial areas were mostly kept away from the residential section. They were positioned to the southern-most end of the city. Also, just outside the city proper area was a hospital. It sat to the east, a hundred or so feet from Camp Baharia.

After I was given permission to go forward, I was able to get into the city immediately. On the afternoon of 9 November, a Gunnery Sergeant (Gunny) from one of our companies had come back to the FOB for supplies and was headed back to his Company out front. Of our three companies, his was positioned along the western edge of Fallujah, abutting the Euphrates River.

We hopped on board the rear of his Humvee, grabbed a seat on one of the two benches lining the bed and took off. As soon as we crossed the train trestle, the place where the battle began, an eerie feeling crept over me. At first, I saw the aftermath of combat; houses and shops showing obvious signs of war. It was odd to think that a week earlier this area was bustling with civilian life and traffic, but now it was uninhabitable, muted, and laced with a gloomy aura that was surreal. We travelled down the empty corridors of what was known as the Jolan district, the oldest and poorest section of Fallujah. I started to hear gunfire as we got closer to this company's forward position.

We were only about a few blocks into the city when we turned off one road and pulled down a tight lane. Then, we quickly stopped at a non-descript house. I went inside. It was my first home to enter and one to remember. As soon as I crossed the threshold, I saw a three foot high, two foot in circumference wicker cage filled with colorful chirping birds. There were at least fifty of them, mostly yellow and green. It seemed so odd. Why would someone have these birds and so many of them? Why would this person not release these birds when vacating the city? It was one of those incongruous moments of war when you see something so out of context, so unexpected; there were other times like this to come.

I went up to the roof of the house and greeted the Company Commander (CC) and those of his Headquarters Group. They were watching their three platoons move house to house just in front of them in search of the enemy. I looked over and saw where one platoon was positioned. They were in a firefight.

After about twenty minutes, I moved up cautiously to their position. When we got there, we entered the house from which they were fighting. It was on the northwest edge of what was called the Palm Grove. It was picturesque, if that is even a possible description that can be given to something during a firefight. It was an open grove with many palm trees, some tall grass, and it was nestled up against the banks of the Euphrates. In spite of its beauty, this area was a hot-bed of insurgent activity.

We went immediately from the ground floor to the roof where all of the Marines were positioned. Arriving on the landing, we saw a few of the Marines on the southwest edge of the roof. They were up against the privacy wall that encompassed the roof, firing their weapons toward the grove. Other Marines, not exposed to the enemy fire, were milling about behind the protection of the wall, acting light-hearted and casual as the battle was going on. This calmed me. If they were not alarmed, I should not be.

When these Marines saw us, they seemed delighted that we were there. A few inquired with puzzlement as to what we were doing in this area. I gave a rather generic answer. I wanted to seamlessly fit in—no questions, no bother, no one noticing me except any who might want to talk or need encouragement.

During the conversations that I was having, however, I remember thinking how odd it was to have friendly chatter with some Marines while others were over in the corner engaging insurgents in a gun fight. It was just one of those peculiar things about war; normalcy sometimes fits right in with chaos and danger. Eventually, I got up enough curiosity to go and look over the roof wall to see what the fight was all about. When I spied the places where the Marines were shooting, however, I did not see much but tall weeds; the enemy was invisible to me. I was told by one of the Marines that the problem I was having was the same our Marines were facing. The enemy was darting in and out of the nearby marsh grass, popping up to fire only to escape after a few spent rounds. It was not an easy fight.

Overall, I was amazed that here I was, at the front-most position of war, watching a real firefight. It certainly was something very strange, but I truly believed that coming forward to be with these Marines was right; this is where I was supposed to be. That belief was quickly justified. At one point in conversation, a general question arose as to whether killing was right. These Marines were killing the enemy and they had to know if it was the right thing to do. They needed the guidance of a chaplain to ensure that their sense of morality was not corrupted. They wrestled internally with what they were doing. They were **rigid moralists**. They were warriors. They wanted to make sure their kills were righteous, unlike the enemy. It is one thing to go into battle and have the desire to kill. It is another to do it and then, to wonder if that aligns with a sense of moral rightness. From my belief, nothing seemed clearer. These Marines were heroes, laying down their lives (**sacrificial**) for these oppressed Fallujans and killing an enemy that refused every attempt to surrender. I was grateful to be at this position to relay these words of assurance and I could visibly see how important it was to them to be assured of their actions. It is one thing to want to kill and entirely another to do it. The latter brings questions that need answers.

Dusk soon began to settle in. The plan was to use the advantage of the infrared night vision goggles, with which our Marines were equipped, to move into the Palm Grove and overtake the insurgents. The feeling was that in the cloak of darkness, the Marines could move in and eliminate them. Before that happened, however, there was a group going back to the company's headquarters position. We made the decision to head back with them. This would enable us hopefully to catch a ride on the nightly run back to the FOB. That run was something that every company did in the evening to discuss the day's events and get the orders for the next day. If we were at the Company's Headquarters in time, we could get this ride and then, we felt that we could always come back out the next day by getting another ride.

With this plan in place, we started on our way to the Company Headquarters' location. It turned out to be an eventful experience. Creeping darkness, along with a jumbled mish-mash of serpentine alley ways and narrow streets, torn up houses and structures, made it difficult for our Marines to figure out how to get back to the Company position. We went one way only to realize that we were moving into unknown territory. I was electrified. Insurgents could have been anywhere. They skillfully moved in and out of areas, popping up stealthily to gain advantage, and we were moving back and forth on ourselves, giving the enemy every chance to surprise us if they were there. We were apprehensive.

As we walked past one darkened house, passageway, or broken down wall after the next, I began to wonder if this mission to the Company position was ill-fated. I began to think that we were going to have to go back to the platoon and continue on with them through the Palm Grove assault. That thought was unsettling. Yet, so was our current situation where one wrong turn only led to another.

At one juncture, we came across an anti-aircraft machine gun. It was sitting there in an open lot, fully loaded, an ammunition belt extending from the weapon to a canister on the ground, unmanned, but fully tilted back on its tripod and prepared to fire. I wondered why, if our Company had already moved through this area, this weapon was not disabled in some way. Did that mean this was fresh territory I was traipsing about in? My disquietude grew.

At about this time, the team leader said that he would try one more alleyway, and if this did not lead us out, we would return to the platoon. I agreed; it seemed right, regardless of what it meant. As it ended up, this turn was the right one. We found our way back to the Company Headquarters' position and were able to catch a ride to the FOB.

The next morning, I went to the CP (command post) to check on how the battle was going. The news regarding the entire Battalion and their movement through the city was good, and that was wonderful to hear.

Beyond this, I found out that the mission through the Palm Grove went well too. The platoon that traversed this grove had no contact once they moved out. The insurgents apparently evaporated when these Marines moved toward them, likely working their way through the marshes over to the other side of the Euphrates.

At a later time, I was told a few other things about this movement through the grove. One Marine mentioned that his exciting moment in this assault came when he happened upon an insurgent who was lying in a ditch, not dead but dead asleep. The

Marine said he simply woke up the man, cuffed him and sent him back for interrogation. How the insurgent managed to nap at this time is telling. The impact of days without sleep, the depletion of adrenaline and drugs in his system likely made him crash hard. It turned out to be fortunate for him as it definitely saved his life.

Another thing I heard about the Palm Grove was that just on the other side of it, the Marines found one of the famed torture houses. A few of them were known to have existed. They were places that the insurgents used to terrorize, torment and kill foreigners and locals. The Marines entering it said it was a ghastly scene; blood on the walls, clear evidence of torture and murder, and there was one man chained up to a wall and he was miraculously still clinging to life. He was apparently abandoned by the insurgents as the Marines pushed their way in.

After having caught up on the news about our Marines, my RP and I waited for a ride to get back out into the city. As it happened, we landed upon a Gunny from a different Company and he was headed back to the front. This Gunny's Company was holding the middle section of our battle space. He let us get on board his Humvee, and out, once again we went. The mission I had in mind was again simple: to connect, be there, and find some way to support the Marines when and if opportunities availed themselves.

In about ten minutes of having travelled into the city, the Gunny signaled for us to get off the Humvee. He was letting us out so that we could move with the Company First Sergeant. The main body of this Company was still a few blocks forward, methodically moving through the buildings, clearing out insurgents.

The First Sergeant was behind them moving with about fifteen soldiers of the Iraqi Armed Forces; they were the friendly Iraqis fighting on our side. The specific mission of these Iraqi soldiers was to accompany the Americans through the city in order to go through the houses that had already been cleared, looking for any insurgent contraband or documents. The soldiers were obviously better able to know what might be an important find and where the insurgents might try to hide something. They did prove to be a valuable asset.

In the span of about an hour of moving with the First Sergeant, it was time to catch up to our troops on the front lines. They were just starting to move through a new set of houses on yet another block. When I got up close to where they were, I saw for myself the reason for this battle.

In the entryway to one house, on the front porch, a man was lying dead. His feet had been severed. Inside the house was a dead terrorist. In asking an Iraqi soldier about this man out front, we were told that he was likely a civilian that the insurgents had conscripted to fight. When the battle drew near, the insurgents feared he might flee. Hence, they cut off his feet, dooming him to die one way or another. I looked at the dead Iraqi while he was being examined. His body was being checked for hidden explosive devices, one of the terrorist's tricks. A Marine who deals with explosives (Explosive Ordnance Disposal Tech) was overseeing the situation. Eventually, he felt safe enough to move the body. I was right there as he did it and was grateful that he made the right call.

After this, we moved ever closer to the Marines on the front, hunting out the insurgents. I continued to see dead bodies as we caught up to their position. Finally, we arrived where these Marines were. This location held many stories for me, and it is worth providing a description of it.

The overall area, when looked at from above on a topographical map, was like a large rectangle that was sub-divided into four equal parts by two narrow streets. Picture a rectangular cake that is sliced one way down the middle and then, again sliced perpendicularly the other way, making four equal squares. The centermost point of the rectangle, where the two lines meet, became a center of activity for me.

Of a more detailed description regarding the area, as I stood facing south at the intersecting point of the two streets, to my left and behind me was one part of the rectangle, and on the corner of it there was a mosque. It was one of many mosques being used by the terrorists to stage assaults and to store weapons, even though this was prohibited by international military rules. The terrorists did not care about that, however, as Major General Richard Natonski, Commanding General of 1st Marine Division, stated:

> We respect the law of war, unlike our adversary who uses mosques. In almost every single mosque in Fallujah we have found an arms cache, we have found IED factories, we have found fortifications, and we have even found weapons repair facilities. We have been shot at by snipers from minarets, and we've also seen the use of schools for the storage of weapons. This is the enemy that we fight. It does not respect the religious mosques or the children's schools.[4]

To continue with the description, as I again stood at the intersection facing south, to my right and behind me there was another part of the rectangle, and on the corner of it was a large empty dirt lot. It was about a fifty by forty-foot area. At the far end of this lot and to the rear of it, the northern most part, there was an eight-foot high cinder block wall. Up against it and extending out toward the center was a lattice brick structure that was eight feet high and about fifteen feet long. When you peered inside of this structure, which you could do because of its design, you could see a large diesel water pump. Then, just outside of this brick pump house and attached to it was a four foot by four-foot cinder block well that held water which was about three feet deep. There was no covering for this well and the water was fetid and oily.

If we continue with the description of this area, going back to the intersecting point and facing south again, as I looked in front of me and to my right, there was the third part of the rectangle, and on the corner of it was an ice-cream store. It was a small concession-like brick structure that was attached to a house. What was odd about this ice-cream shop was that it had a huge painting of Mickey Mouse on one of its outside walls. Mickey was courteously waving with a big smile. When I saw it, I had another one of those moments where something seemed out-of-character to its surroundings. I wondered why Mickey was waving to anyone in the middle of Fallujah, right across from a Mosque that was being used to foment terrorist propaganda. I smiled.

Then, finalizing the description of this area, and again standing south at the intersection, to my left and in front of me was the fourth area, the last part of the rectangle. It contained a series of houses. They all abutted one another, each facing out as you went around this block, and all had the traditional privacy walls surrounding them. The homes on this block were all one or two story as I remember.

With this description then, not seconds after I entered this scene and began to take in these surroundings, a horrific firefight opened up. Unbeknownst to me at the time, it was taking place on that area of the rectangle where the houses were, the area just south of the mosque. I was standing right next to the mosque at the time. As soon as the mayhem began, all Marines standing in the area where I was, scrambled for cover. Here was a moment of true panic for me. I did not know where to go. None of us there had any idea from where this fire was coming or going.

Some Marines darted inside their Humvees to gain cover. I remember crouching there in the open, being jealous and peeved that I did not have a place to go like that. I started to feel like I was suffocating. It was a strange sensation. I felt completely helpless and my mind was racing with the thought that I would not get out of this. By this point, everyone that was around me was gone. Finally, I had the sense to gain cover myself. I ran into the courtyard of a house that we had just gone through, and my RP was next to me. The two of us were pretty much alone by this point. I cannot tell you how odd it was. At about this exact moment, the Gunny came around a corner yelling, gas-masks, gas-masks, don your masks. I started to scramble to pull mine out. We received training prior to coming over to Iraq on using this equipment in the event that the enemy used poisonous gases. Now my tension was sky-high. The threat of gas was present; the sound of gunfire was penetrating; what was I doing here, I thought to myself? Not long after calling for the masks, we were told to take them off. It was a false alarm. Then, I looked around the corner of the wall from where I was gaining cover, and I could see Marines in a house right above Mickey Mouse, firing down thousands of rounds onto the housing block area. I also saw at that intersection of these blocks a Humvee, and periodically, Marines were being loaded onto it, and they were then rushed out to our BAS. I marveled as I watched the **sacrificial courage** of these Marines running around in the firefight, rescuing the injured and getting them to safety.

One of the Marines injured in this time told me later the story of what happened to him during this firefight and it is worth recounting. Here is what he relayed, almost six months after it occurred.

He said that his squad was moving around the housing block area that sat just below the mosque where I was. As this group entered the courtyard of a house, mayhem broke out. This Marine, to whom I spoke, said he fell down injured from multiple bullet wounds while the other Marines with him quickly retreated, without realizing his fate. So he figured that was it. He was trapped, and because of his injuries, he could not get up and move. He expected the insurgents who were in the house, not more than ten feet from where he was lying, would come out any minute and finish him off.

Yet, suddenly, before that could happen, one of the Marines came rushing back into this nasty firefight to rescue him. However, and surprisingly, this injured Marine told me that he really did not want to be rescued. He did not want to risk the life of another to come and get him (**sacrificial**). Thus, he shouted to this other Marine as he was working to get him up, just to leave him alone.

In his mind, as he told me later, he figured that he was going to die of his injuries. There was no point, therefore, in risking another life for this. The other Marine, however, refused to heed those words, saying that either both of them would get out alive or they would both die right there (**sacrificial**). At this, both Marines got up, the injured deciding to receive the help. Quickly, they were able to exit the courtyard. They remained under fire in doing so, even when they were outside of the courtyard and in the street.

This fire ultimately caused both Marines in the scramble to fall down. There they laid, for what seemed like forever, as bullets from the insurgent traced just over the head of the **sacrificial** Marine who was now using his body as a shield for the wounded Marine. Is this not humbling to hear? Finally, the fire from the insurgent abated, and they both got up again and moved to the waiting Humvee.

From there, the injured Marine went off to get treatment for his injuries and was eventually sent back stateside because of the severity of his wounds. The other Marine went back to his squad, and never mentioned what he did and never received any credit for it as I was told. Why did he not make known this heroic deed? In my own opinion, it is because this Marine felt he was not doing anything of merit. He simply was doing what came naturally to him; i.e. being driven by an inner impulse to **sacrifice** for another. This is who warriors are, and it is what they do.

Coming back now to the moment of this firefight, here I was not far from all of this and witnessing the incredible action. At some point, I made the decision to go out from behind the wall in order to go to where the Marines were loading up the injured. I wanted to be there for these Marines and do what I could. I was not sure what my role would be, but I wanted to find one. My RP was upset with this decision, and understandably so, but I had to do it. What I ended up doing, inconspicuously and rapidly, was to lay my hands on and pray for those who were being loaded onto the Humvee. I felt like I was doing something, even though I was still feeling mostly stifled and frustrated about what my mission should and could be, in this position.

When the firefight ended, a somber moment confronted all of us. A Marine was being loaded on the back of the Humvee in a body bag. He was dead, our first casualty of war. I stood there watching him being taken away. The cost of freedom was made real. Fittingly or unfittingly, it was the Marine Corps Birthday, 10 November.

In short time, all the Marines were regrouping. That block where the fighting occurred was now secured. I stood there in the dirt lot and I was unsettled. Death, war, and chaos had a grip on me. The Gunny, who had carried most of the wounded and the dead Marine to the Humvee, and who naturally had lots of emotions and anger brimming, passed by me. He likely picked up on the uncertainty I was feeling. Rudely, he said something very close to this: "I guess you want to go back to the FOB now?" The way he said it, in a mocking tone, had the clear insinuation that I was too much of a pretend hero to be out there; I should go back to the safety of the FOB. Those words hurt. I am not sure quite why, but they did. Perhaps it was because his words only furthered my sense that my extreme efforts for the last five months to find my place in this Battalion really were to no effect.

All that time standing on ranges in the hot deserts of Twenty-Nine Palms, as one group after the next came through, the months on other ranges, the time spent out at other training sites, the effort to be involved with Marines in the humps and runs, the personal care given to many, and everything else that I did really did not seem to matter, or so it seemed at this moment. Assuredly, that was true for this Marine. It made me feel like I was still an outsider in spite of all the ways I tried to break into this unit. Regardless, I looked at this Gunny with anger for having the gall to say such a thing. I wanted to confront him, tell him my true thoughts, and let him know how off base his comment was. I did not, but I did look him squarely in the eyes, with self-assured words, and likely much to his surprise, said that I had no intention of going back to the base. My RP and I would be staying with this Company through the night. I told him that I wanted to be available for any who wanted to talk. Although my RP and I had not intended to stay out and did not bring any gear with which to do so, I could not figure out how in the world I could leave these Marines. This was not because of the interaction with the Gunny, but because of the other Marines. If ever there was a need for a chaplain, this seemed to be the time. Marines were seriously injured and one died. I thought for sure that I could at least find something that I could do to help.

After relaying my intentions to this Gunny to remain with the company, I waited around for the Marines who cleared the houses and were involved in the firefight to be available. Their current mission was to go back through the areas in which they had just fought. It was a re-clearing process to check and ensure that other insurgents had not snuck into the area and to make certain that those believed to be dead were killed.

As the main body of this Company did this, other Marines from the Company waited in the large dirt lot with the water pump on it. This area was again horizontally just across from the mosque, and it was catty-corner to the housing block area where most of the fighting just took place. I milled about in this area and had conversations where I could. Present in this area too, sitting down along the lattice looking brick wall that held the water pump, were our allied Iraqi Army Forces.

As discussions wore on, it started to get dark. The Marines had still not finished the re-clearing process. I, however, wanted to find the Company Commander (CC) to tell him that we would be staying with his Company with his approval. I got up to go find him. He was in a house with his leadership team, about twenty feet from where I was. I walked over to it. The moment I went inside this house, relayed my news to the CC, and settled in with them, the darkness outside lit up. Another firefight had erupted: flashes of gun fire mixed with grenade explosions abounded. I could not believe it. I was just out there. Realizing in the moment that I was inside and safe for this firefight, I admittedly drew a sigh of relief. But that comfort was soon to dissipate. The leadership team, highly confused as to what was going on outside, immediately grabbed their rifles, threw on their gear and raced out the door and into the line of fire. I was in complete shock. "What were they doing?"

As I know now, they were acting in accordance with that inner willingness to **sacrifice self** for the Marines. I was there on the front lines of war, witnessing the true heart of the warrior. It was humbling and astounding to see, even though it left me standing there once again with my RP, alone!

When it all quieted down, I went outside to find out what happened. Here is the report as it was told to me by the Marine who was at the center of all of this. An insurgent, unbeknownst to all, slipped out of the pump house. This happened as soon as I entered the house with the Command team. How did the insurgent get there? Perhaps, he had been there hiding the whole time. No one found him in the initial examination of this structure. Then, as darkness fell, he was hoping to escape the area by surreptitiously slipping past all. To do this, brazenly he walked right down a line of seated and relaxing Iraqi Forces. Fortunately for him, he remained undetected until he stumbled right over the outstretched legs of a Marine who was sitting next to the Iraqis on the ground. At this point, the Marine, not realizing who this was, started yelling at the guy, telling him to be careful. Then, one of the friendly Iraqi soldiers took notice of the situation and realized who this person was. He cried out to all that he was a terrorist. That frightening alert caused the insurgent to raise his AK 47 and fire. He sprayed bullets everywhere as all dove to the closest cover they could gain. Inconceivably, this terrorist was a bad shot and he missed everyone. Then, not seconds after the insurgent's initial burst, the Marines started to shoot back and throw grenades in the area of this insurgent. He was right next to the pump area and the water well that adjoined it. Here is the awakening moment for me of God's grace. Where this all went down, and where the terrorist ended up, was the exact spot that I had just been sitting, talking to Marines before I got up to come into this house. Amazing!

Now, back to the firefight, as Marines were returning fire in the direction of the insurgent, he somehow evaded all gun and grenade fire. Some thought that this insurgent had escaped, although that seemed hard to imagine with the high retaining wall at the rear of this area. Regardless, once the firing stopped, this Marine to whom I was talking and a few others went into the area where the insurgent was last seen. They expected to find a dead insurgent on the ground. Yet, they could not locate a body. The guy had incredibly vanished. Perhaps, the Marine thought, he had somehow jumped up on the well and then, scaled over the wall in the cover of darkness. However, the fact that he escaped amazed this Marine. Out of curiosity, though, the Marine said he turned on his barrel mounted flashlight, and looked into the well. There, to his complete surprise, was the insurgent. He was just below the water line in the brackish oily water, face up. He had been going up and down, submerging to gain cover and then, surfacing to get air. He had his AK 47 over his chest, ready to fire when the opportunity came. The Marine referred to this move as a Navy SEAL maneuver. Seeing this, the Marine instantly opened fire on the insurgent and killed him instantly. When he was telling me this, the two of us stood beside the well. I looked down in it and there was the insurgent, dead, and lying face down in the water, just below the water line.

After this incident, the Marines were gathering back in their platoons and organizing themselves for the night. I told the First Sergeant that I was available to meet and talk with anyone that needed it. I assumed that the losses we had experienced and the death of our Marine would impact our fighters. He passed the word, and it was a blessing to find that about two dozen Marines wanted to talk. I finally felt like I was where I should be. I believed that this is what it meant to be willing to go anywhere for a chance to be God's emissary. I was thrilled. I met with Marines in small groups, and I met with some alone. I counseled, prayed and loved them all. One Marine even became a convert to faith. He had been an atheist but this experience awakened his need for God. I was grateful to be there for him and the others.

After I met with everyone that wanted to get together, I went inside the house where the Headquarters Team for this Company had assembled. The Company leadership team was once again meeting on the first floor of this three story house, the one that I had previously entered when the firefight started. These Marines were talking about many things. Slowly, they assembled on the roof of this house. Like all rooftops, it was open air with a security wall all around. It was the perfect spot to gain cover from the ground and spy out the enemy. This was going to be the post for the night. Hence, since I was going to stay with these Marines, I found a spot on the roof to lie down and get some rest. My RP and I had nothing with which to bed down, so we just laid down on the concrete. It was cold, damp and the cement was hard. I found it difficult to get any rest. I was lying right next to an Army Staff Sergeant. He was the leader of the Psychological Operations (PSYOPS) team. As the two of us were talking, all of the sudden a mortar round from our enemy came screaming right over our heads. Everyone who was not already lying down hit the deck. The mortar exploded about twenty five yards away, on the ground. The Staff Sergeant looked at me and said with excited aggravation, "I'm getting too old for this. I'm done after this tour." I smiled. Fortunately, no other rounds came in.

The next morning, the mission was on again. The Marines were ready to move. We exited the house. Once on the ground, in the light of day, I was able to explore this overall area and see all that had transpired in the many firefights of the day before. There was the dead insurgent in the well. There were two more insurgents in the street right next to the Mosque. There was another dead insurgent not more than ten feet away from Mickey Mouse. Then too, in the block that contained the houses across from the Mosque, the scene was more macabre. More than twenty dead insurgents were scattered about. What a battle it had been.

While the three platoons of this Company went forward to continue the fight, I spent a good portion of this day with an element of the Headquarters Group as they went about rechecking everything in this area. For a time, I remained at the gated entrance of a house, talking with one of the news reporters covering the battle. I suggested to the reporter that he should write about how honorable and brave these Marines were in combat; something we both witnessed the day before. His response to me was that he did not want to take sides in this conflict since he was a reporter. He wanted to remain neutral, he said. I looked at him and told him that he was full of crap, just like that: "You're full of crap." I went on to reason with him by saying if someone went into your house and raped your wife, you would think that it was wrong and you would want to stop it. To his credit, he agreed. I continued, if someone then went on to abuse your children, you would again want to stop him at any cost, would you not? Again, he agreed. Then I said, these insurgents have been raping, pillaging, torturing, and killing these innocent people in Fallujah for the past year, and our Marines are the only ones in the world who are willing to stop their evil. They are marching through these streets, being wounded and dying trying to save people that they do not even know because it is right (**sacrificial and rigid moralists**). "They are heroes," I said to him, "write that!"

He looked at me in silence. I think my anger got the better part of me in the moment. I was not quite sure what he was thinking, but I didn't care; I was indignant. Ironically, less than ten minutes after this conversation, a few of the Marines and some of the Iraqi forces combing the area found an insurgent hiding in the exact location where this reporter and I had been talking, just behind us. There we were, completely unaware of the danger. How ironic it was that this discussion occurred right there! Somehow, I think that if this insurgent would have popped out firing, as the reporter was framing his ideological, "I am neutral" blatherskite, he would not have sought shelter in the arms of the insurgent, but would have screamed helplessly toward one of our Marines for cover. I wonder why? I think he had a better sense than he was letting on about who the true and noble warriors were.

Later that morning, I started to tour the houses that sat just south of the Mosque. It was the location of the massive firefight the day before. One house I investigated was filled with explosives. It was a command center for the insurgents before the war. When I toured the home, I saw inside, strung about on the walls, numerous insurgent fliers and banners. No doubt, it harbored those that the Marines just fought.

The Explosive Ordnance Disposal (EOD) Marines came in as I was walking around this house. Their mission was to blow this house up, with its massive cache of weapons. That was going to be quite an explosion. Once they had the house prepared, we all went to a house two blocks away to gain cover. We waited, and then, boom! When the explosion went off, it was massive. Even at our distance, debris from the exploded house fell down on the house we were in. It was raining dust and debris everywhere. Smoke filled the sky, and it decisively wafted its way into the house we were in.

After it all settled, we went outside. Surprisingly, an eight foot metal beam, from either the house blown up or one of those beside it, had flown up in the air and over a block of houses and then, arced sharply down in an alleyway to embed itself into the drive train of the First Sergeant's Humvee. It must have travelled up a hundred or so feet and then, over another hundred. We were amazed that this could have happened and surprised at the effect of the beam on the Humvee; the First Sergeant was pissed.

From here, I went further down the street toward the area of the explosion; the dust was still thick, making it hard to see. Finally, the air began to clear enough to look around. That was when I had another one of those completely incongruous moments of war. I was standing just about in front of Mickey Mouse, looking east down the street that had the mosque on one side and the house on the other side where the weapons cache had been. Peering through the haze, down in an easterly direction, I saw to my disbelief a cow staring right back at me. He was about twenty five feet away as I walked up to this scene. It seemed so surreal. Next to the cow was a goat. We all just stood there looking at one another, no doubt all three of us in certain confusion. I could only imagine what Gary Larson, of the Far Side comic strip, would have done with this. In my mind, I could not figure out how a cow and a goat got into the middle of this city. Who knows what the goat and cow were thinking?

I arrived at the area where the house had been demolished. All that was left was rubble. In fact, a good portion of that entire housing area was gone; only debris remained. The power of that explosion was unbelievable. It was nice to think that these weapons could not be used against us anymore.

This was only one of hundreds of stockpiles of explosives in this city, over fifty located in mosques as alluded to earlier.[5] When these stockpiles could be removed safely so that structures would not be destroyed, they were. At times, however, fearing or eyeing rigged explosive piles, the cache was blown up as was the case here.

Before we leave discussion of this particular area in Fallujah, there are two more stories to relay. The first is about a Marine who was awarded the Navy Cross: Private First Class Christopher Adlesperger. If you recall, at the moment when I first arrived in this area, a massive firefight had just begun. It was this Marine who was in the middle of that massive conflict.

It started as Adlesperger's squad was moving through the block of houses that was across the street from the mosque. At this point of the conflict, his fire-team was trying to get in a house directly behind the house with the weapons cache. Adlesperger was on point, lead man in the group, and he tried to move through the locked gate. He could not get it to open. Another Marine, Lance Corporal Hodges, came up to assist in getting through the gate, and then, they entered the courtyard. But as Hodges, who was now on point, did this, he was instantly killed. Numerous insurgents were inside this house and readied for an ambush of the Marines.

185

At this point, Adlesperger took over. He rushed through the gate, now opened, and into a vicious volley of machine gun fire. With grenades being thrown back and forth and firing his M16, he rescued two injured in his fire team. He got them to safety by moving them up to a rooftop, using an outdoor staircase. He did this while simultaneously fighting and killing insurgents. Then, once on the roof, Adlesperger continued to fight the insurgents; they were trying to storm his rooftop position. He fought them off, tossing back grenades thrown at him and shooting some of his own grenades from his grenade launcher. The insurgents were well positioned, and the fight carried on for more than thirty minutes. In spite of his personal wounds and utter exhaustion, Adlesperger continued to protect his men and kill the enemy. His heroics astounded us all, and what greater picture of **invincibility and sacrifice for others** does one find than this? In all, he is credited with at least eleven kills.

For his actions, Adlesperger was meritoriously promoted and put in for the Medal of Honor. As mentioned, though, he ended up being awarded the Navy Cross. Sadly, he died a little after this, taking point again on another house clearing. I was a few blocks away from that area at the time, moving with another Marine warrior who himself would soon be killed.

Adlesperger was an exceptional Marine. He showed not only the spirit of **invincibility** and a willingness to **sacrifice** self for others, but he showed too this natural penchant of the warrior to live by his **rigid moral code**. In his case, it was reflected in his display of loyalty to those with whom he fought and in his belief that honor, duty and care for others is worth fighting and dying for.

It is important again to grasp the full weight of Adlesperger's action. What possesses warriors to enable them to act like this? I walked later through the courtyard where this horrific battle had occurred. Dead insurgents were everywhere. Twenty six in all were killed at this one general location as I know because I came back with an Imam to collect the bodies. At that time, I walked the path that Adlesperger must have taken as he ran into this courtyard, grabbed the wounded, and ferried them up a back stairway to the roof of this house. As I made this trek, I passed insurgents that still lay dead. When I got to the roof, I stared down to the room where the enemy had set up their ambush. It was a room that had bars over large windows. This enemy was well concealed and heavily armored. In the stillness of this moment, I imagined what must have happened. It was hard to fathom all that Adlesperger went through as he traced these same steps, exposed to heavy machine gun fire and grenades, with the loss of his friend, trying to protect the wounded, and killing insurgents coming at him from all directions. The least one can say is that his actions were not those of a normal person. He unquestionably possessed the kind of *Uncommon Valor* that was lauded in the battle for Iwo Jima.

Yet, is this not the point we are after? Warriors are that unique. They do things that most would never want, fathom or be willing to do. They do these things simply because it is their nature. War is where this becomes visible. It is what makes them great and shows all that greatness. Here I was in Adlesperger's spot in history, the site of a warrior's heroism, and I stood in sobering silence, overcome in awe of who this person was. Of note, Adlesperger "would ... tell his fellow Marines that he thought he was going to die but if that was to be the case, he wanted to do a few things first: take care of his comrades and die with his finger on the trigger."[6] That says it all.

When all operations had ceased in this area, the Marines I was with moved up to join the other Marines from the company. They had just finished their operations for the day. It was time to bed down for the night. The Headquarters Group with whom I stayed picked a massive three story house in which to accommodate the Marines. It was highly ornate and had one gigantic benefit. It was filled with blankets. My RP and I, still without any gear, grabbed a few and got a good night's rest.

In the morning, I went down to the street level and did my chaplain thing: checking on people, striking up conversations and trying to support any in need. At one point, I was engaged in discussion with a Navy SEAL, one of several embedded with this company. In the middle of our conversation, he shifted his focus from me in an instant like a cat that suddenly spotted prey. As he stood staring down the street, I followed his eyes but could not see anything. Then, the object of his gaze became clear. An old man and woman came out of a lot that was cluttered with debris and trees and moved onto the street across our line of sight. The woman held up a stick with a white flag as they nonchalantly went on their way. It was yet another incongruous moment when you see something you never expect to see. What was this old couple doing? They knew that this was a war zone and the city was to be emptied of all except for insurgents who wanted to fight for their cause. Pamphlets indicating such things were strewn all about the city. I had a few. Regardless, here was this couple and immediately upon seeing them, the Navy SEAL raced into action to get them to safety.

On an aside, in spite of finding a few innocent Iraqis in this city at times, I never came across one dead Iraqi who was not a military aged male. In spite of what reports often relayed, I went into hundreds of homes and crossed this entire city and never did I see one dead child, old person or female. Also, even with military aged males, the ones assumed to be insurgents, what I also witnessed was that whenever we came across any who wanted to surrender, they were saved. The only ones killed, as I saw it, were those shooting back at us. That shows the extent to which our forces went to maintain their moral standards. They killed only the enemy and even then, only the enemy who was intractable in their desire to die for evil (**Rigid Moral Code**).

After this moment with the Navy SEAL, my RP and I readied ourselves to move on. Our desire was to move from this Company to the one with which we had not yet been. This shift was to take place before the morning battle rhythm started.

Soon the Company Gunny loaded us up in his Humvee, and off we went. We arrived in the area of the next Company, and the

Gunny dropped us off, pointing in the direction of this other group. We went to where he pointed. It was a residential block, surrounded of course, by walls and gates, and we were on a street just outside this row of homes. We walked to the edge of the block and tried to make our way into one of the homes. As it ended up, and without knowing it, we were running just in front of the houses where our troops were located; i.e., between them and the enemy.

When we found an opening in a gate, and after seeing our troops inside, we made our way in. Once in the courtyard, we moved our way to the roof. Our greeting was far less than gracious. The CC asked me something to the effect of "what the hell are you doing here, Chaps"? His tone was unfriendly. I asked him to clarify what he said because I was unsure why he was upset. His second greeting was less acidic and ended with the order to gain cover and quick. We did. Then, without much of a delay, minutes, a five-hundred pound bomb, one having been dropped by an F-16, exploded. The sound was deafening. "How close was that?", I wondered. Dirt and debris rained down on top of all of us. A metal fragment from the bomb actually hit one Marine next to me on his Kevlar Helmet. It was about a four inch by five inch piece. Thankfully, it just grazed his helmet. When everything cleared, we stood up and looked at the impact of this bomb. I then made my way over to the CC and he said to me something to the effect of, "that is why I wondered what the hell you were doing here? We had a bomb strike called in when you arrived." I understood well the gravity of the situation now. I told him that we were here because I wanted to spend some time with his Marines. He quickly said, "Well, it's great you are here. I have two guys over there you need to fix." With that said, he walked away.

I made my way over to these Marines needing support, but not before talking to the Fire Air Controller Officer (FACO). Each Company had one with them, and their job was to call in air strikes when needed. The FACOs were pilots themselves. I talked to this one about this last drop. He is the one who told me it was a five hundred pound bomb. I told him that it seemed like this explosion was a little too close. As it ended up, the bomb was a little bit off target he told me, landing in an empty lot just across the street. The place it landed was a fetid field with trash and what was likely sewage. We laughed about the fact that we all just had crap raining down upon us. It explained the pungent odor. In spite of the concerns I voiced about this bomb being too close, however, he retorted nonchalantly that it fell well within acceptable limits. He was okay with that. I thought to myself that our ideas of what acceptable was definitely differed.

The two Marines needing "fixing" were over in a corner of the roof. I spoke to them. They both had been through close-engagement fire-fights, and one had seen his Marine friend killed right in front of him. In our time together, one of these Marines just did not have it in him to go back to his squad. He was willing, however, to remain with the Headquarters Group on the front-lines. That, to be honest, was amazing. While moving with the squads was the highest level of danger, being with the Headquarters Group on the front lines was not without extreme risk. I was proud of this Marine for being willing to stay in the fight and do what he could. The other Marine, after we talked, did make the decision to rejoin his squad. It was also an unbelievable act of courage on his part. I was thankful to have helped him in this moment. Sadly, however, not long after getting back out, his squad again lost another Marine, and after that point, he was done. He too continued on with his Company on the front lines but never did rejoin his squad.

Of interest here is that what none of us realized at that point in time, and I believe the experts have made this clearer now, is that after combatants experience extreme trauma, some of them are going to need to be removed from the front lines, and some from the war zone altogether.[7] They need time to decompress and to work through their issues in an environment that is not still related to or continuing to add to their emotional breakdown. Then, it is only after they have decompressed and found personal resolve to continue with their war-fighting mission that they should be allowed to come back into the fight:

> Psychological first aid should be envisioned as the mental health correlate of physical first aid, with the goal being to "stop the bleeding." The patient should be removed from the traumatic situation. When the patient is in a safe situation the clinician should attempt to reassure the patient and encourage a feeling of safety. In their Disaster Mental Health Response Handbook (Raphael, 2000), a group of PTSD experts propose ... to protect survivors from further harm and from further exposure to traumatic stimuli. If possible, create a "shelter" or safe haven for them, even if it is symbolic. The fewer traumatic stimuli people see, hear, smell, taste, or feel, the better off they will be.[8]

After having spent time with these Marines, and others on site, I spoke with the CC about my desire to spend some time with one of his platoons. This particular platoon that I wanted to be with had been hit really hard. They lost two platoon officers in a short time, one killed. They also had a few of their enlisted Marines killed and many more lost to injury. I wanted to go with this platoon, walk with them as they pushed through the city and be available. This certainly was taking me to the very front of battle, but it just seemed right. I had made the decision to do this earlier in the day. At that time, a Marine from this platoon had been killed. I had the opportunity to meet with some of those who were with this Marine right after this incident. One Marine practically collapsed in my arms and asked if we could go off by ourselves and pray. These Marines were seeing heavy combat, facing trauma and in need of support; some deeply wanted prayer. I wanted, therefore, to be available in whatever place I could be most effective, and moving in some manner with this platoon seemed like a good opportunity. As it turned out, the CC for reasons he did not specify did not want me with that platoon. He placed me instead with another one. Since I in no way wanted to be a distraction, I was happy to do what he felt was right. It was his command, and I was just there to support. Thus, I readily agreed. It was a start and still an incredible opportunity. That night, my RP and I moved forward and spent time with this other platoon as they were bedding down and getting set for the next day.

The next morning, I woke up and got ready for the mission; namely, walking with a platoon through the streets of Fallujah as they hunted our enemy. It was conceivably dangerous, but I had complete peace within. It was an amazing moment of oneness with God. I was going to be with these Marines as they were facing the enemy for the day, and I truly was at rest about it. I was not being fatalistic or heroic in this moment. I just desired to serve God. Whatever that meant was what I felt the need to pursue. Hence, off we went, and I was very grateful to have this chance.

As we stepped off into unknown territory, I trailed the Marines, as this platoon, along with all other forces in Fallujah, went forward for the day. I watched in the courtyard of our first house as the Marines broke through the locked front door and as they went guardedly into the house. Once inside, their purpose was to check every inch of the house for the enemy, contraband or weapons. This process even continued onto the roof of the house as well. I followed in support, once the situation was cleared, talking to the Marines and helping out as I could.

While on the roof of one house, I got into an interesting conversation with a Marine. I noticed that he had a bandage around his wrist. I asked him how he got this injury. He told me that a few days ago, he cut himself on some glass as his squad tried to get through the front door of another house.

I showed sympathy for his wound at which time he remarked that it was not as bad as what happened last night. He was moving, he said, through a house and made his way onto the roof. As he did, he walked over to a corner of the roof to see if he could find anything there. It was pitch black and difficult to see much of anything. He looked anyway and as he moved closer to the edge of the roof, he eventually stepped right off, and was soon lying prostrate on the ground, having fallen two stories.

At this same time, his fellow Marines started to look for him and did not see him anywhere. Then, they got worried and called out for him. They finally realized what had happened and scrambled to help him.

When they came to him, they realized he was okay. Then they laughed about what happened. I laughed too as the story was recounted to me. This Marine then said to me that once he had recovered from the confusion and slight daze resulting from the fall, he just got up and pushed on. That is **hard**! It is pushing forward through all obstacles, whether cuts, bruises or gun-shot wounds to accomplish the mission. It is what separates warriors from others who sometimes look for excuses to get out of work. It was impressive to see.

Later that morning, we got to a house and the Marines labored excessively to get the front door open. They pried, pushed, banged and kicked. I was watching this scene unfold from outside the courtyard. But then, in their efforts to regroup and figure out how to get in, I walked up and said, "Let me try." I just wanted to be helpful. At my invitation, they stepped back and looked at me as if I was about to provide them some sort of entertainment. I stood about three feet from this door, and with all the muster and power I could invoke, I kicked the door right on the lock. Miraculously, the door exploded open. I was glad. The Marines looked at me with amazement and one shouted, "Wow, Battle Chaps, this is our Chaplain; he is now in our platoon." I laughed and was elated to make such a strong connection with these Marines. It is what I had been laboring for since I joined this Battalion.

With the door open, the Marines poured inside. As I always did in this process, I waited for the situation to be cleared, then went in the house and helped them check for hidden weapons or contraband.

The insurgents hid weapons in houses throughout the city. It was a part of their strategy. They knew that if they were out in the streets without a weapon, Americans would not fire upon them. Hence, the thought was to leave the weapons in one of the houses. That way, they could run around like they were innocent civilians caught in an unfortunate situation, and then, at the right time, they could grab their hidden AK's, and fire upon our troops.

After a morning of this movement through the city houses, we sat in a home that we had just cleared. The room we were in was a large area, and it had ample seating in a horseshoe like pattern. In short time, a conversation erupted, and I became the centerpiece of it. Marines peppered me with one question after another about the Ten Commandments and then, about faith. I was in awe. I do not know how to convey to you my sense of utter shock at what was happening.

I spent months with this Battalion and held numerous divine services and Bible studies, and through great effort managed to get only a small portion of this Battalion to engage. Yet now, here I was in the middle of a Muslim city in a Muslim house, and I was having the largest and most interesting Bible study that I had ever had with this Battalion. It was nothing short of a miracle to me. It made me realize that if I had not pushed forward to be here, this moment in time would not have happened. That would have been a great loss, for this was one of those rare moments in time when the heavens opened to me and I knew I was one with God. I was at complete rest in His will. It was a great experience.

When our discussion ended and lunch time was over, we pushed on. We continued with our movement through the city. We found many weapons and one sniper rifle. That latter discovery was a great find as a sniper had already taken out one officer from this company. Being able to locate this kind of weapon, therefore, was a great feeling. What we did not encounter, however, on this day, were any insurgents.

That night, we found a house that would be our resting place until dawn. After going in and securing my spot in the house to bed down, I went outside on the front porch to catch the remaining hours of sunlight. I sat on a chair and found myself looking through the broken down gate of this house to a wall across the street. That wall was severely pot-marked from mortar shrapnel. I saw some Arabic writing on the wall as well, graffiti that had been spray painted on it. I asked the Iraqi interpreter who was with this group what these words said. He told me that the top line said, "Allah Akbar," translated as God is great. The bottom line, he told me, said "Long live Al Zarkawi." Upon hearing that, I knew that these words were certainly written by one of the insurgents. Zarkawi, the famed leader of the terrorist cause, was in this city just prior to the war and had created quite a following. This writing reflected the zeal that his disciples felt for him. They might not have felt so enamored with this man if they would have known that he was going to depart the city prior to the war and leave them to do the fighting. Regardless, it was fascinating to see this graffiti, and it seemed fitting to see it right across from this area in Fallujah that Marines now controlled.

As I was seated on this porch, a Marine came out and sat beside me. The discussion I had with this platoon at lunch had deeply affected him. He declared that he wanted to become a Christian. We talked about this, and eventually, right there in the open, before others who were there, we prayed and he received Christ. Once again, I was floored. Being available and being willing to follow God's leading, opened up incredible ministry. In seeing this, I could not imagine being in any other place. As I often said during this time, being in the will of God is not just the right place to be, but it is the safest place to be, however antithetical to reason it might seem. I had it all in that moment.

After another day of pushing with this platoon, I made my way back to the Company Headquarters' position and eventually back to the FOB. I spent a few days there and then, went back out again. This time, I made my way back over to the Company I had been with the first time that we went out, the one pushing its way down the Euphrates.

By this time, they had lost one Marine, and it was good to be back with them. When I caught up with them, the Headquarters Company was staying in the most opulent house I had seen in Fallujah. It had gilded lattice work throughout the inside, nice textured fabric furniture, Persian rugs and many other opulent features. When the Fallujans left the city, they took their valuables, but that was not the case in this house. Perhaps this family was so rich that it did not matter. The house was incredible. Making it more spectacular was that it sat right up against the Euphrates River. It seemed like prime real estate in this city. Of additional importance about this house is that right down the street, not more than two-hundred feet away, was the bridge over the Euphrates where the Blackwater contractors' burned corpses were hung. This was an area of high insurgent activity prior to the war.

The mission of this Company was to go on foot patrols through the already cleared sectors to seek out other hidden weapons and caches. I volunteered to go on many of these missions as a way to be with the Marines as they did their work. It always turned out to be a great way to connect with everyone. Usually about eight Marines went out and you could have some good conversations along the way. Also, the sites of war and the city were always fascinating to me.

On one patrol, we spotted some trucks (MTVR 7's) bringing Marines through the city. I was not sure what the nature of their mission was. However, it was clear that these were not infantry Marines. That, of course, caused a stir. The Marines I was with were saying various derogatory comments about these other Marines. Why? As we know, these infantry marines considered themselves to be the **elite** Marines. For them, this judgment and feeling was likely more pronounced by the fact that they had just fought through the tough streets of Fallujah and that now, after the battle seemingly quieted, in came these other Marines. The timing was maybe unfortunate, but the scene conveyed clearly to me the sense that these infantry Marines had of being **elite** warriors.

After having been with this Company for a short stint, I continued to make my way around the Battalion. At one point, I travelled with a platoon of Marines as they were working their way through a sector of the city that was being checked to see if any insurgents remained. As we went from house to house, suddenly we heard shots in close proximity. We went to the roof of the house we were in at the time to see what was going on. As it I turned out, there was a firefight in the house just behind this one, literally about five feet away from the edge of the roof. When we got to the back of this house, up against the rooftop wall and looked over at the other house, the Staff Sergeant in charge with me called out to discover what was going on. He began a conversation with a Marine trapped on the second floor, in a room that was not more than four feet across and three feet down. Through the window of that room, the trapped Marine told us that he could not get out of the room without entering a hallway in the house and thereby, being directly exposed to an insurgent's cross-fire from an adjacent room. He was trapped. He further said that the Marines he was with initially had withdrawn, several of them having been injured.

Of note too is that as we were talking, the insurgent causing these problems was in the other back room of that house, on the same level, hearing the chatter through his window. Once we found this out, we were more cautious about peering over the wall of the house we were on.

As I stood there watching this scene unfold what struck me incredibly was the boldness and eagerness of these Marines (**sacrificial**) both to kill this insurgent and to rescue their trapped Marine (**rigid moralists**). It all happened so fast. When we first got on the roof and looked over, it appeared to me that we were the only ones there. Within what must have been minutes, Marines started appearing everywhere, on several neighboring rooftops and the roof of the house in question. Then, with precise and quick determination a plan was formulated to rescue the Marine, and it was put into action. The Marines who volunteered to storm the house and retrieve the trapped Marine were decided upon mainly by the speed at which they got into position. You would have thought someone had promised a million dollars to the first people to line up. Yet, what was really promised was a dangerous and deadly fire-fight, the chance to kill the enemy and retrieve a trapped Marine (**gusto seekers and elitism**). I was in awe. As this plan was being executed, suddenly another insurgent, one that was heretofore unknown, hiding on the roof perpendicular to us, jumped out from his position and started firing his AK 47, yelling out *Allahu Akbar*. As he went forward, screaming and shooting, not in our direction but toward Marines over in another area, his death came decisively. Fire rained down on him until he ceased to move. Then as that happened, this other insurgent was killed and the trapped Marine was rescued.

When the fighting was over, I jumped over to the other roof where the Marine had been held up; going from roof to roof like this was common practice. The houses were somewhat close and most jumps could be made with a little effort. Once on the other roof, I walked up next to the dead insurgent in this house and then, I went to the other roof and looked at that dead insurgent.

I had seen many dead insurgents by this point, but something about this situation struck me differently. Perhaps it was hearing the war call, *Allahu Akbar* [God is Great]. For whatever reason, I went up to them and stared. It seemed surreal. I also was engaging the Marines in this time, talking, comforting as I could, and witnessing their exuberance and raucous cheers for having defeated this enemy. It was something that they never doubted (**invincible**).

Overall, I encountered many other sights, sounds and experiences in combat. I also faced sadness as our Marines died and as we honored them in memorial services. In my time with these Marines, I did what I felt like I was called to do, and felt like I had at least, in my own way, found a place in war. In about a month's period overall of doing this, the Battle of Fallujah ended.

At this time, the mission changed. Our purpose now as a Battalion was to set up encampments around the perimeter of the city. Each Company would be given an area in which to patrol, and the goal was to keep the insurgents out and get the area ready to bring the citizens back in. Naturally, I breathed a sigh of relief. I figured the worst was over, and now the Marines could settle in for a quiet and uneventful phase. What I soon realized was that these Marines were not entirely content with that mission. They were unsettled. These Marines, like all infantry warriors, want excitement; a good fight is at the top of the list (**gusto seekers**). That is why they are in the Corps. The fact that the insurgents were now dead was disappointing to them. There was not anyone left to kill. Intelligence reports also indicated that no insurgents were coming back. The chatter indicated that they wanted to stay away from Fallujah. It was too dangerous. Hence, the streets were quiet. The Marines were restless. Something more was needed.

What finally got some of the Marines revved up again was a new mission. There was word that maybe the insurgents had slipped up to a different city, Saqlawiyah. It was time to seek out the enemy once more. However, that city, unlike Fallujah during the war, was fully populated. To ferret out insurgents in that area was going to be a dicey mission. Yet, the Marines were more than up for the challenge. It certainly beat out the other option: guarding an empty city. So off went a company of Marines. I moved up with them. Again, I wanted to be there for support.

While this mission kept these Marines busy for a time, it ended up that there were no insurgents to be found. Likely, these terrorists got word that the Marines were coming and left or decided to blend in with those in this city. Either way, the lack of a fight proved to be a disappointment to many of these Marines. Most dreaded what came next; i.e., a return to Fallujah to join up with the others for daily patrols on quiet streets.

Truthfully, though, in spite of the lack of combat, these Marines did still have a lot of diversity in their daily missions. They set up and ran check points, reintegrated the people of Fallujah into the city, provided support in the Iraqi elections, and did humanitarian work. These were all complex missions. Yet, they did not involve killing, and so the Marines honestly were not as enthused. They nonetheless executed every mission well, but by the time it was all over, the Marines were happy to go home. They were bored; the war had ended. Without the promise of what they considered true adventure, these Marines had a hard time existing from day to day. They were **gusto seekers**, and without war, there was no gusto to be had.

Conclusion

I will finish this story about being with the Marines in Fallujah by offering a one word description of what I witnessed about them in this time: **invincibility.** When it came to this battle, there was absolute certainty in the minds of all these Marines that they would kill every insurgent and liberate this city. It was simply impossible for them to consider otherwise. This battle for them was no different than any of the other storied Marine Corps Battles in history. The odds might be against them. The enemy might be well entrenched and fortified so as to guarantee the great loss of life. Yet, the circumstances do not matter. They know, regardless of the situation, that they will conquer and kill any who stand in their way. They will also, in fact, enjoy the process. That is just who they are. That is, without question, what I witnessed. Warriors come alive in war. It is for this kind of experience that they are made. They love every part of it. When people are able to find that place where their nature is given the chance to experience all that it is created to be, it is electric. There is a current of excitement and enjoyment in the air, and there is a true focus and zeal to carry out the needs of the day. It is what life should be for all people. That is what war is for the warrior.

There have always been warriors, and there always will be. They have set the course of history and will continue to do so. Strangely, though, their greatest threat does not come from those they fight, but rather from those for whom they fight who do not rightly understand them and, thereby, fail to support them. This, however, we can change.

Endnotes

[1] American Civil War Facts, "William Harvey Carney Facts", http://www.civil-war-facts.com/Black-Civil-War-Soldiers-Facts/William-Harvey-Carney-Facts.html, (May, 2018).

[2] Sophia Barbarani, "Fixing Fallujah: City tests Iraq's ability to bounce back", https://www.irinnews.org/feature/2017/10/02/fixing-fallujah-city-tests-iraq-s-ability-bounce-back, (2 October, 2017).

[3] Ibid.

[4] U.S. Department of State, 2004 Press Releases: "Terrorists using mosques and schools as weapons caches, U.S. reports", http://iraq.usembassy.gov/iraq/041111_fallujah_briefing.html, (November 11, 2004).

[5] Diggersrealm, Fallujah Investigation - Evidence Of Atrocities, IED's and Weapons Caches [Pics And Images], http://www.diggersrealm.com/mt/archives/000452.html, (June 6, 2009).

[6] Vik Jolly, "Saluting a Marine's bravery: LCpl Christopher Adlesperger", http://www.leatherneck.com/forums/showthread.php?71820-LCpl-Christopher-Adlesperger, (14 April, 2007).

[7] "Acute catastrophic stress reactions are characterized by panic reactions, cognitive disorganization, disorientation, dissociation, severe insomnia, tics and other movement disorders, paranoid reactions, and incapacity to manage even basic self care, work, and interpersonal functions (52). Treatment includes immediate support, removal from the scene of the trauma, use of anxiolytic medication for immediate relief of anxiety and insomnia, and brief, supportive, aggressive, dynamic psychotherapy provided in the context of crisis intervention." Matthew Friedman, "Post-Traumatic Stress Disorder", https://www.acnp.org/g4/GN401000111/CH109.html, (2000).

[8] Department of Veterans Affairs Department of Defense, " VA/DoD Clinical Practice Guideline for the Management of Post-Traumatic Stress," http://www.healthquality.va.gov/ptsd/ptsd_full.pdf, (2004, January).

CHAPTER SEVEN

WARRIOR'S VIEW OF KILLING

Taking on a human being in war and killing that person is a passion for those of the warrior mentality. It is something more obvious with infantrymen because it is there that impulse to kill is clearly visible. Yet, the warriors of the sky, the airmen, also share in this hope to kill. Max Hastings, one who wrote about these warriors during the early years of flying, said that these pilots would undergo great risk just for the chance to get someone in their crosshairs and pull the trigger; "they were killers."[1] He went on to say that "the objective of the air fighter throughout the twentieth century was to descend upon an enemy from behind and shoot him in the back. Ideally, an attacker inflicted mortal injury before the victim glimpsed his nemesis. The business of a successful fighter pilot was unpleasant and indeed brutal."[2]

There is one more aspect of the warrior's nature that needs development. It has to do with his desire to kill. This is what warriors hope to get the chance to do. It is one reason they sign up for military service. That understandably sounds bizarre to most. That someone sets out to kill another human being is judged by most to be psychopathic or sociopathic.[3] Certainly, this is true in part. There are disturbed people who are callous emotionally or depraved of mind and they do set out to kill.

Warriors, however, are different. While they share in this desire to take life, it is attached at its best to an inner sense that there is a just need to kill. That alone can propel them forward with great zeal in conflict:

> Some of the guys really enjoyed this part of the job—teenagers who found their true nature in the jungle, who discovered that they were born for the warrior life. ...They went after the Japanese with a competence and enthusiasm that made them almost as frightening to their officers as they must have been to their enemies. "It was just amazing..., how could you take kids like this and put them out into the jungle, and in just a few weeks they'd be great at jungle warfare. ...They'd come back from patrol and you'd hear them talk. ...'How many did you kill?' And they'd brag, 'Well, I killed two, I killed four.'"[4]

To see more of this and to become familiar with this part of the warrior mentality, let us look at some material.

Studies on Warriors and Killing

Finding support for the uniqueness of the warrior begins by looking to a signature work on war by S. L. A. Marshall, *Men Against Fire*. In this work, which provides an extensive analysis of firing rates amongst veterans during World War II, Marshall offers a clear dividing line between the group we are after, warriors, and those who often serve with them. The former group, as Marshall makes clear, will fire in combat while others with them seemingly will not. Marshall says this:

> A revealing light is thrown on this subject through the studies by Medical Corps psychiatrists of the combat fatigue case in the European Theater. They found that fear of killing, rather than fear of being killed, was the most common cause of battle failure in the individual, and that fear of failure ran a strong second.

It is therefore reasonable to believe that the average and normally healthy individual—the man who can endure mental and physical stresses of combat—still has such an inner and usually unrealized resistance toward killing a fellow man that he will not of his own volition take life if it is possible to turn away from that responsibility. ...At the vital point, he becomes a conscientious objector, unknowing.[5]

This information certainly shows that some get thrown into the combat environment and it is psychologically debilitating for them. They find themselves, as Marshall goes on to say, being incapable of engaging the enemy: "...not more than 15 per cent of the men had actually fired at the enemy positions or personnel with rifles, carbines, grenades, bazookas, BARs, or machine guns during the course of an entire engagement."[6] That news would be disturbing to any combatant commander. He counts on his troops to kill when given the opportunity. Yet, what makes this statistic even more astonishing is that these men, according to Marshall, had seen combat in such a way "...where it would have been possible for at least 80 percent of the men to fire, and where nearly all hands, at one time or another, were operating within satisfactory firing distance of enemy works."[7]

This is amazing as what Marshall is showing is a strong refusal to shoot at the enemy, even when they are in close proximity, and the need to fire is pressing, the enemy is upon them. However, Marshall does not even stop with this but goes beyond to say that these combatants would not fire to their own peril, allowing themselves to be defeated: "There were some men in the positions directly under attack who did not fire at all or attempt to use a weapon even when the position was being overrun."[8] This is all surprising. Some in combat would rather die than kill, or so it appears: "...they would not fire though they were in situations where firing was their prime responsibility and where nothing else could be as helpful to the company."[9]

This is all strong evidence supporting the idea that some will not engage the enemy. That is vital to recognize. But do not miss what Marshall also says clearly above. It is that there were some, about 15 percent of those on the front lines, who did shoot to kill. In another place, Marshall puts the figure of this group up to around the 30 percent mark.[10] These people in my estimation are of the warrior community. They fire even if others will not. They might be small in number as the percentage shows, but they are there. This much Marshall makes clear, and since it is such a thorough study on the topic it is good to find the information here.

Niall Ferguson in his book *The Pity of War* also develops in a forceful way the overlooked truth that there is joy in the violence of war for some: "There is another possibility which has received too little attention in the historiography of the First World War, for the simple reason that it is not very palatable. That is the thesis that men kept fighting because they wanted to."[11] There were some, Ferguson says, who just enjoyed it: "…many men simply took pleasure in killing."[12] He records the testimony of one soldier who was excited when he talked about a kill that took place at very close range: "I saw his teeth glisten against my foresight, and I pulled the trigger very steady. He just gave a grunt and crumpled up."[13] Others Ferguson mentioned "…took pride in their skill as snipers and with the bayonet, partly to 'get even' but partly just to do the job 'beautifully.'"[14] In sum, Ferguson says,

But the crucial point is that men fought because they did not mind fighting. …For most soldiers, to kill and risk being killed was much less intolerable than we today generally assume. …even the most famous war writers provide evidence that murder and death were not the things soldiers disliked about the war. Killing aroused little revulsion…. For some, revenge was a motivation. Others undoubtedly relished killing for its own sake: to those intoxicated by violence, it really could seem 'a lovely war.'[15]

These people who Ferguson describes are certainly warriors. The atmosphere of war is not one for them to avoid. It is rather a place that brings fulfillment in its own unique way.

Another writer providing substantive proof that the desire to kill motivated front line warriors is Joanna Bourke. Her book *An Intimate History of Killing*, which is a definite read in understanding the impact of killing on a warrior, takes on the issue of killing from many unique angles. In one place, she talks about the awkwardness the warrior feels when he comes home from war and spends time with those who are not of his warrior community. In these situations, Bourke mentions that the warrior is unsure how to interact with civilians since he believes they would be repulsed to know his true feelings about war and killing:

> [V]eterans' reunions were awkward occasions precisely because the joyous aspects of slaughter were difficult to confess in all circumstances. To describe combat as enjoyable was like admitting to being a bloodthirsty brute: to acknowledge that the decisive cease-fire caused as much anguish as losing a great lover could only inspire shame. ...Killing had a spiritual resonance and an aesthetic poignancy. Slaughter was 'an affair of great and seductive beauty'. ...The experience seemed to resemble spiritual enlightenment or sexual eroticism: indeed, slaughter could be likened to an orgasmic, charismatic experience. However you looked at it, war was a 'turn on'.[16]

What Bourke rightly exposes is the all too common situation that exists when a warrior returns home. He feels strange and out of place because he has just had the greatest thrill of his life in killing the enemy. Now his trophy kills, the wondrous stories of adventure, and the conquests need to be withheld because they sound so barbaric to those on the outside. Thus, the warrior says little to nothing, creating all kinds of confusion and misunderstanding. But what choice does he have? How does he admit that killing is fun when he feels those around him will consider him to be sociopathic or psychopathic? The experts on the subject unwittingly contribute to this problem by wrongfully heralding that killing is unnatural and undesired for all humans. Consider the words of Dave Grossman on this. He writes in his book *On Killing*:

> [A]uthors have examined the general mechanics and nature of war, but even with all of this scholarship, no one has looked into the specific nature of the act of killing: the intimacy and psychological impact of the act, the states of the act, the social and psychological implications and repercussions of the act, and the resultant disorders (including impotence and obsession). *On Killing* is a humble attempt to rectify this. And in doing so, it draws a novel and reassuring conclusion about the nature of man: despite an unbroken tradition of violence and war, **man is not by nature a killer**.[17]

This assessment is both wrong and tragic for warriors. They have just been through the pinnacle experience of life and now they feel that they need to bury all of the glory because experts and non-warrior friends and family do not seem to understand. It is the opposite of what needs to take place and is a critical piece of emasculating warriors. It undercuts them at the heart of who they are and robs them of the profound celebration that should be taking place. These people are war heroes, just having returned from the front with wondrous tales of bravery, cunning tactics, shrewd maneuvers and honorific duty. Giving them a chance to relay it all and feel proud of what they have done should be the order of the day. But the message that "the combatant who loves to kill must be psycho" is commonly accepted, and so the distance between warriors and all others remains.

Bourke provides insight to break the false image that exists about warriors. She gives testimony from warriors wherein they talk about specific acts in combat and how they reveled in the experience. For these people that she cites, what is relayed is a true love for fighting and killing. In one example, a warrior comments: "One day...I secured a direct hit on an enemy encampment, saw bodies or parts of bodies go up in the air, and heard the desperate yelling of the wounded or the runaways. I had to confess to myself that it was one of the happiest moments of my life."[18] As you can see from this anecdote, there is nothing that shows self-disparagement for killing. Another warrior offers this:

Killing was intrinsically 'glamorous'. It was like 'getting screwed the first time' and gave men 'an ache as profound as the ache of orgasm'. In the words of a Black Muslim Marine, 'I enjoyed the shooting and the killing. I was literally turned on....'[19]

What Bourke is recording here is what I have had infantry warriors tell me. They talk about what they have done and find the experiences to be a dream come true. Even pilots, as Bourke shows, gain great satisfaction from eradicating the enemy on behalf of their fellow combatants on the ground: "After a kill, pilots admitted that they 'all felt much better' and there would be 'a good deal of smacking on the back and screaming in delight.' Although the mutilated and dead Germans staining the rear cockpit of their planes might be described as 'sad and beastly,' airmen admitted that they had felt 'elated then.'"[20]

Bourke continues to affirm this kind of pilot satisfaction through yet another testimony: "I opened fire, the bullets roared out over the noise of the engine. They don't rattle like an ordinary Army Vickers gun. No, sir! When the 8 Browning opens fire – what a thrill! The smoke whips back into the cockpit and sends a thrill running down your spine."[21]

This testimony can also be found in other literature on combat pilots. Edward Rickenbacker, nicknamed 'The Killer' since he was the most successful scout pilot of World War I, offers these

209

words in reflection of his first kill: "It was one of the great moments…I experienced the greatest elation of my life. I had no regrets over killing a fellow human being."[22]

To those not of the warrior culture, it definitely sounds abnormal that killing or the attempt to do so could somehow be described as wonderful or a 'spine-tingling' sensation. It is true, though, as Bourke relates from her studies. She says further that "[t]roops were only happy when they've had a "kill"…."[23] In fact, as she pushes the issue even more, she mentions that warriors needed not just to talk about what they did, but many were prone to exaggeration of conquest and some even collected mementos from kills. With respect to the latter, Bourke records one veteran as saying: "In Vietnam, Harold 'Light Bulb' Bryant testified that soldiers took ears to 'confirm that they had a kill. And to put some notches on their gun'."[24] Others took skulls as trophies.[25]

What Bourke and others point out here is that for some in war, it is not enough to kill. There needs to be some physical marker of it, a way to relive the experience and connect with it intimately. Though clearly such behavior is not right, defaming a corpse is not justice, it is important to uncover such behavior. It shows how closely warriors want to be associated with what they have done in battle. In one incident, I heard a Marine talk about killing two insurgents. His buddies nearby recounted this event too from their own perspectives. They were all thrilled to be talking about this incident. The excitement in their voices, the pride in their warrior buddy who made the kill, their desires to experience the same were all a part of that warrior's life.

This similar scene is repeated in an account of a soldier who got his first kill in Afghanistan. His name is Jerome. As the story is told, he is sitting amongst his friends at an evening fire. We read, "Jerome is enjoying the notoriety he's received for his confirmed kill on this very mission…. He's rewarding himself with a celebratory gallop around the campfire while he is cheered on for his confirmed kill, to which the conversation repeatedly returns."[26] During this celebration, another soldier, who has not had his first kill, gets upset. He says, "I just want to fucking kill something!"[27] After his comment, the talk goes back to the actual kill: "You should have seen him go down! Pop! Bam! ...Don't run from us, or I'll kill you."[28] This conversation ends with "...general agreement and laughter all around the fire."[29]

Bourke's material on a warrior's view of killing makes it clear that some do enjoy the kill. However surprising or unorthodox this comes across, this is what warriors think, and it is a subject of their conversation. Most never hear this jovial banter because the topic is only discussed amongst warriors and a rare few who have been given their trust. However, it is a subject of great delight to warriors. Bourke does a good job of pointing this out. It is information that uncovers the complexity of the warrior's life where nature, nurture, cohesion, justice and other elements like this become inextricably linked to war and killing. To ask them at some point to deny any aspect of this is emasculating warriors by undermining their purpose for being.

Martin van Creveld is another researcher who believes there is evidence to support the fact that there are those who are quite comfortable with killing. He is the author of eighteen books and is considered a leading expert on war. In his most recent work, *The Culture of War*, he acknowledges that "[s]ome researchers have argued that killing does not come naturally to man. To make it possible, they say, it is first necessary to brutalize one's own side and dehumanize the enemy."[30] Contrarily, Van Creveld says, "This seems to fly straight into the face of everything we know about war as it has been waged from the Stone Age on."[31] From the beginning of time, Van Creveld contends, men have been involved in killing and have found it satisfying. He offers a reason for this. "One reason why killing is, or at any rate can be fun, is because it involves overcoming resistance."[32] A person is forced and enabled through killing to know that feeling of gratification that comes with success, achieving something not without intense and real struggle. A

211

personal challenge of the greatest order, loss of life, has been placed before him and to kill rather than be killed is to know a feeling of winning like no other:

War...far from being merely a means, has very often been considered an end—a highly attractive activity for which no other can provide an adequate substitute... War alone presents man with the opportunity of employing all his faculties, putting everything at risk, and testing his ultimate worth against an opponent as strong as himself... However unpalatable the fact, the real reason why we have wars is that men like fighting.[33]

Obviously, for one to be possessed of this line of thinking, the risk of death is high. Yet oddly, for the warrior this is only another facet in the fascination of war. To overcome what has the greatest potential to destroy one's existence has the ultimate consequence of engendering the ultimate sense of achievement. It is as Van Creveld offers: "Probably one reason why people so often enjoy killing is because it enables those who commit the act and watch it to come face-to-face with their fears. Since we must all face death in the end, inflicting it and seeing it inflicted could almost be called a form of psychotherapy."[34]

There are other reasons that Van Creveld offers as to why men enjoy killing: innate desire to destroy, hatred, revenge, heart-felt causes, the sake of fellow-warriors, cohesion as developed through flags, banners, standards, music, and close order drilling.[35] These things inspire the warrior, enabling him to kill willfully and making the overall process of war fun. Given this, it is no surprise to hear that many prominent leaders of war, Robert E. Lee, Winston Churchill, Ariel Sharon, General Patton, Theodore Roosevelt and "countless others" as Van Creveld offers, all "confirm how enjoyable war can be, and often is."[36] To categorically say otherwise is unsupportable. This is certainly what Van Creveld elucidates.

Having examined what leading researchers have found regarding the view of killing by warriors, we find conclusive proof that there are those who are quite comfortable with taking life in battle. Let us look from here at personal testimony of how warriors view killing.

Marine Corps Warriors and Killing

When exiting 29 Palms Marine Corps Base, there is one marker after the next, and each lists a storied Marine Corps Battle. It is moving to drive past them. It is a reminder of a special group of men and women who have signed up to go forward and fight our country's battles. Their service embodies that prototypical warrior image. These are the ones who made it over six hundred miles of Libyan Desert to rescue hostages at the shores of Tripoli; who faced such fierce opposition at the Halls of Montezuma that 'blood stripes' were added to the uniforms to commemorate the ninety percent of the leadership who died in the fight; who fought so viciously and seemingly without regard for life at Belleau Wood that the only apt description as given by their enemy was *Teufelhunden—Devil Dogs*; who boldly charged into an endless rain of deadly fire at Tarawa, and by defeating the enemy in three days did what the Japanese Commanding Admiral said would take "a million men and a hundred years" to accomplish;[37] who went ashore onto the black and bloody sands of Iwo Jima and showed irrefutably in the history of war uncommon valor to be a common virtue; who repelled a well-fortified North Korean force at Inchon through the most spectacular amphibious assault of all time; who pulled off the most astounding ever recapturing of a city, Fallujah, and gave it back to its people a free and democratic state; and who continue to be first in every major fight of America.

These are the Marines, guided forward in battle by those front line warriors. When looking to its past, what has been the essence of that call? "In 1907, when Army posters said, "Join the

Army and Learn a Trade," and Navy posters said, "Join the Navy and See the World," the Marine posters came to the point with disarming simplicity, "First to Fight."[38] Being on the front lines, first to get the chance to kill, this is the call of the Marine warrior. Gunnery Sergeant Walter Holzworth said it this way, "They tell me we are headed for war. If it comes to a fight I want to be in at the start. That's where the Marines belong."[39] James Hebron, a Marine scout-sniper, offers this: "That sense of power, of looking down the barrel of a rifle at somebody and saying, 'Wow, I can drill this guy.' Doing it is something else too. You don't necessarily feel bad; you feel proud, especially if it's one on one, he has a chance. It's the throw of the hat. It's the thrill of the hunt."[40] James Brady, Marine and author of *Why Marines Fight*, gave this account of his connection to this passion for fighting: "The stunning surprise, to me as to those who knew me, was my immediate reaction to hostile fire, a sense almost of exhilaration. Not quavering fear, no shock of nerve, no urge to flee…, [but] sheer, manic excitement and an odd sense of happiness that I was here, a Marine. I was one of the guys. I was, to my astonishment, actually in war." [41]

John Chaffee provides his own startling look at this pull of the Marines Corps which gave him a chance to fight. As a Yale student, from a prominent and wealthy Rhode Island family, he could have done anything. Yet, he made a decision that was confounding to those who did not share his passion in life. He rejected every high societal, privileged educational and well-connected economical pursuit and chose not just to join the Marine Corps but to put aside officer candidate opportunities in order to enlist because he wanted to ensure he got to the fight as quickly as possible.[42]

Joe Owen, awardee of the Silver Star and author of *Colder than Hell*, an account of the battle at Chosin Reservoir, says this about that chance to fight that the Marine Corps afforded him: "All of us shitbirds had joined the Corps because we wanted to fight and Marines offered the surest way to battle. …We're fighters. That's why we became Marines. ...'First to fight, every clime and place, where we could take a gun.' We're all front line fighters."[43]

Jacklyn Lucas provides an interesting glimpse into the unrelenting will to fight.[44] At the age of fourteen, he fooled the Marine Corps into giving him an enlistment. He received orders to Hawaii as a truck driver. This frustrated him since "he wanted to fight."[45] He, therefore, "stowed away on a transport out of Honolulu, surviving on food passed along to him by sympathetic leathernecks on board. He landed on D-Day [Battle of Iwo Jima] without a rifle. He grabbed one lying on the beach and fought his way inland."[46] [specific battle added] His battle ended when he jumped on a live grenade to save his fellow Marines. Miraculously, he survived and after twenty-one reconstructive surgeries became the only high-school freshman to receive the Medal of Honor.

Continuing on, in the book *Generation Kill* about a Marine Recon unit as it worked its way up to Bagdad in Desert Storm, there are also numerous anecdotes that speak about warriors and killing. Here are a few: 1) a Marine, waiting for his chance to kill finally gets the opportunity and afterwards yells, 'I got one' and later says about another kill, 'Hajji in the alley, zipped him low, I seen his knee explode!'; 2) a Marine in a firefight says, 'Gotta love this shit!'; 3) the Battalion Executive Officer of a Marine unit is frustrated since his job keeps him from shooting, but then he does come under fire and thinks it is 'cool' to shoot, killing one Iraqi and seeing him disappear in a 'big cloud of pink' and then shooting another saying with satisfaction, 'My aim is good'; and 4) a Navy Corpsman working with this unit gets his own kills and says, '...I couldn't give a fuck about those guys I just killed...It's like you're supposed to feel fucked-up after killing people...I don't.'[47]

With one last picture of this zeal to fight, we look at a Marine who talks about killing terrorists and says, "Shit, these punk-ass motherfuckers think they can fuck with my country and I'm going to just let that shit ride? Fuck that! I'm getting me some 'get back.' If I die, I die."[48] His reasoning for feeling this way is quite simple to him: "Because I'm a MOTHERFUCKING UNITED STATES MARINE! ...I want to go toe-to-toe with these fucking cocksuckers."[49] This Marine goes on to say, "I wanted to go to Iraq. Most of us did. Hell, we were grunts. This is what we joined the Corps for—to serve and see combat."[50]

This is a sufficient profile of Marine warriors and there is not a picture here of people who want to avoid killing, retreat in the face of fire, or allow themselves or their fellow warriors to be killed rather than kill. The portrait is instead of those who sense a calling to charge recklessly into combat, without hesitation, killing the enemy and feeling good about it. If any more proof is needed to depict this mentality and conviction, let the Battle at Tarawa provide the final evidence.

In graphic and clear detail, it shows the farcical belief of those who say men will cower and avoid fighting. To show this, consider first, not the Marines in this war, but their opposition, the Japanese warriors. A profile of these warriors alone, with their commitment to fight to the death, is powerful to see. They, following the Samurai Warrior tradition and their own version of the Bushido code, were unabashedly killers.[51] They fought for their Emperor and were willing to kill all who were not of their kind. They died recklessly in battle, refusing to surrender, wanting first to kill the enemy and second to die a noble death in battle. This is the warrior spirit for which many fail to account. It itself overturns any idea that all men by nature refuse to kill or will surrender in war. Yet, it does not stop there. Consider now the counterpart to the Japanese warrior, the Marines. They met face to face at Tarawa. In this engagement, these Marines did not retreat, surrender, fire aimlessly, or lack the desire to kill. For the Marines, the mission statement was simple: seek out, close with and destroy the enemy. Read to discover the resolve these specific Marines possessed in combat as described by James Bradley in his book, *Flags of our Fathers*. We pick up the fight as Marines are hung up on reefs in their landing crafts, far out from shore:

The actions of these Marines trapped on the reef would determine the outcome of the battle for Tarawa. If they hesitated or turned back, their buddies ashore would be decimated. But they didn't hesitate. They were Marines. They jumped from their stranded landing crafts into chest-deep water holding their arms and ammunition above their heads. In one of the bravest scenes in the history of warfare, these Marines slogged through the deep water into sheets of machine-gun bullets. There was nowhere to hide, as Japanese gunners raked the Marines at will. And the Marines, almost wholly submerged and their hands full of equipment, could not defend themselves. But they kept coming. Bullets ripped through their ranks, sending flesh and blood flying as screams pierced the air. Japanese steel killed over 300 Marines in those long minutes as they struggled to the shore. As the survivors stumbled breathlessly onto shore their boots splashed in water that had turned bright red with blood. This type of determination and valor among individual Marines overcame seemingly hopeless odds and in three days of hellish fighting Tarawa was captured. The Marines suffered a shocking 4,400 casualties in just seventy-two hours of fighting as they wiped out the entire Japanese garrison of 5,000.[52]

Without debate, warriors on both sides of this battle fought for their convictions and willingly killed their enemy or died in the effort. They were doing what came naturally, and not even the risk of losing life or the taking of another's life could subvert this. To somehow believe that men do everything possible to avoid conflict and killing after reading about this battle or reading any accounts of the storied Marine history is impossible to understand.

Navy Warriors and Killing

It is not just about the Marine Corps, as we know, when discussing the heart of warriors and the desire to kill. In the Navy, when seeking out those who qualify as modern day warriors, one group that makes every list is Navy SEALs. They are an impressive group. There is no question too that they are killers. That is their job. Let us look at how this plays out in the SEAL community.

One book that is done as a research project on the SEALs is *Never Fight Fair!* by Orr Kelly. He offers a few descriptions of these warriors. One is of their unrelenting push to challenge and overcome death: "They really, really, really want to go into life-threatening, extremely dangerous situations. They want to go up to Father Death and look him right square in the face and give him a knockout punch in the eye." [53]

Still another aspect of this warrior that Kelly profiles and that we would expect to find from our studies on this group is that of a killer, a person who wants combat and seeks the chance to kill. Kelly talks about this quality:

SEALs are gunslingers. That's what we do. SEALs are trained to hurt folks and blow things up. That's what we do. And if you don't like guns, what the Sam Hill are you doing in a SEAL team? ...If you can't accept the responsibility for taking a human life, if you've got to kneel down and pray on it—you've got to get all that done way before. I pray. I pray to the Lord to protect me and I pray that every time I fire a shot I kill something. If he would just bless me with those two things—which he has so far.[54]

This focus is unquestionably that which drives SEALs and it has been there from the start. One of the leading figures in the formation and development of SEAL teams was Richard Marcinko. He is a controversial figure in and outside of the SEAL community. He pushed the edges in every possible way. In spite of himself, i.e. his acerbic and uncompromising ways, he excelled as a SEAL and overcame not just the enemy, but perhaps more impressively many senior officers who deplored his style, leadership and existence. He

218

definitely fits the description of the title of what I consider to be his best book: *Rogue Warrior*. In that book, he lays out how the SEALs evolved, his role in it, and how they fought. They were unconventional warriors. One point that he makes clear is the SEAL's ardent wish to kill:

A decade and a half ago, in Vietnam, I'd learned firsthand what SEALs did best: hunt men and kill them. ...SEALs are tactical. We want to be sent on missions. We wanted to shoot and loot, hop and pop—do all the wonderful, deadly things that SEALs are supposed to do. ...War, after all, is not Nintendo. War is not about technology or toys. War is about killing.[55]

How much clearer does it get? These warriors go with the intention of killing as it is an important part of their mission. This they do without remorse. It is their job and they go about it aggressively:

A point should be made here about the way Americans tend to regard the act of killing. Like most of my generation, I grew up on Western movies where the hero—Hopalong or Roy or Gene—chivalrously tosses his gun aside after the black-hatted villain runs out of bullets and subdues the bad guy with his bare fists. That may work on celluloid, but not in real life. In real life you shoot the motherfucker and you kill him dead—whether or not he is armed; whether or not he is going for his gun; whether he looks dangerous or appears benign. That way, you stay alive and your men stay alive. ...So, my philosophy in battle has always been to kill my enemy before he has the chance to kill me and to use whatever it takes. Never did I give Charlie an even break. I shot from ambush. I used superior fire-power. I never engaged in hand-to-hand combat unless there was absolutely no alternative—to me, the combat knife should be a tool, not a weapon. ...So the fact that seven of us had just made bloody hamburger out of five undernourished, unsuspecting, unarmed Vietnamese didn't strike me as ruthless, immoral, or unfair. All my SEALs were still alive; and there were five fewer of the enemy. [56]

When you read about Marcinko and the cryptic world of SEAL warriors, one sees that there is no hesitancy to kill. These people are killers who love every aspect of getting that kill. It is assuredly a message that does not sit well with most, but it is, nonetheless, what warriors think.

What Marcinko offers by way of insight into his culture of warriors is echoed by another SEAL, Chuck Pfarrer. His book, *Warrior Soul*, provides yet another fascinating glimpse into this highly demanding life. Notable in Pfarrer's career was being on the Military base in Beirut on the morning when the bomb exploded just outside the Marine Corp Barracks. He was on a six month deployment, conducting sniper operations. Although he survived that moment physically unscathed, he did suffer from guilt, dealing with the common question that survivors ask, "Why did I live when so many good men died?" [57] But notice what he says overall about his experience in war:

There were things that I struggled to put aside: oddly, others did not trouble me at all. I do not know exactly what this says about me, but I felt no grief for the people we killed. Their faces do not haunt me and never have. Some I remember as motionless lumps face-down in the street, legs crossed oddly, hands open, and weapons lying where they had fallen. I remember returning days later to one place we had contact, to find the bodies swollen and black with sun. In the street, trash blew around the corpses. I felt as little then as I feel now. I did not care that they were dead, and it seemed fitting to think that no one on earth had bothered to even drag them from the road. ...I was aware then, and am aware now, that I took human life. This will sound flippant, perhaps even nonchalantly cruel, but there are some people who need to go to hell and stay there.[58]

Pfarrer's spirit here of having killed without compunction, and even disdain toward the enemy, is one many warriors share. It is an attitude expressed well by perhaps one of the most famous SEALs of today: Chris Kyle. He is credited with the most kills by a Navy SEAL, over 150 sniper kills, the most in U.S. military history. The ones he killed he typed as savages, and when asked in an interview with Bill O'Reilly if he had any issues related to those kills, his reply seemed unexpected, and that is because it was a response that few would understand: "None of my problems come from the people I killed."[59] For Kyle, killing those he felt needed to die did not create any inner turmoil, and in fact, he went back to the war zone four times to execute this mission with perfection. He appears to have enjoyed what he was doing, and it again shows the heart of a true warrior. It is an experience in life that only the warrior would seek and relish.

That is just the warrior spirit. It is one born, in part, out of the nature of warriors and in accordance with their inner moral sense of justice. They seek this calling, face it when it comes, and afterwards, are thrilled to have lived in accordance with their sense of purpose in life. To deny this aspect of their being or to say that these impulses are wrong is to fail in understanding the nature of a true warrior and to bring confusion to those who are doing what comes naturally to them.

Army Warriors and Killing

John Keegan, a prolific war historian, supports well the thesis that there are some who will readily kill in battle. In his book *The Face of Battle*, he talks about the Battle at Waterloo and says that "[w]ithin a space of about two square miles of open, waterless, treeless and almost uninhabited countryside, which had been covered at early morning by standing crops, lay by nightfall the bodies of forty thousand human beings and ten thousand horses, many of them alive and suffering dreadfully."[60] This shows the ferocity with which men fought to kill. On this Keegan says, "[w]e must take account of the undoubted willingness of some men at all times to risk, even apparently to enjoy, extreme danger and arbitrary cruelty."[61]

One such person Keegan mentions is from later warfare, Corporal Lofty King. He says of him, "[h]e was a hard fellow in many ways and very hard with his men; he didn't give a damn if he knocked a man down. ...He genuinely enjoyed fighting and looked happiest, indeed inspired, in battle. In the field, he was kinder to his men, as if the fighting were a kind of release for him."[62]

Another person mentioned by Keegan is Julian Grenfell, a World War I British veteran of the Battle of Somme. He was said to have enjoyed killing Germans and even had a special sniping rifle made to do so.[63] These people obviously found killing not just something they were willing to do, but also what they loved doing.

Continuing with Keegan, but this time using information from a different book, *Soldiers: A History of Men in Battle*, he says about fighters and their experience of war: "...killing may even be pleasurable, either because sheer satisfaction of hitting a difficult target or outwitting a cunning adversary, or because of hatred for an enemy whose death gratifies the desire for revenge."[64] In support of this, Keegan offers testimonies. Let us look at some of them. First, Keegan cites a Green Beret, a Vietnam veteran, who said, "'it's an accomplishment, more or less stalking a person, stalking something alive, just like going hunting for deer.'"[65] Next, he offers Staff Sergeant William Deaton, an Iraqi veteran. This man too shows delight for killing: "I enjoy killing Iraqis."[66] Still another Iraqi veteran soldier Keegan mentions is Staff Sergeant Robert McBride who says after killing some Iraqis: "It did not bother me at all to see those bodies up close. I'm a warrior."[67] Those stories show that there are for some no mental reservations about killing.

What Keegan offers here about soldiers is found in other examinations of those who fight in wars. Consider these words from a soldier who fought in Vietnam:

> Well-intentioned souls now offer me their sympathy and tell me how horrible it all must have been. The fact is, it was fun. Granted, I was lucky enough to come back in one piece. And granted, I was young, dumb, and wilder than a buck Indian.... *But it was great fun* [Anderson's emphasis]. It was so great I even went back for a second helping. ...I lived on life's edge and did the most manly thing in the world: I was a warrior in war.[68]

Yet another anecdote about the thrill of the kill comes from a book by Johnny Rico. The book is called *Blood Makes the Grass Grow Green*. In the book, we hear words from an Army company commander. He is in the midst of inspiring his troops for battle, and he says, "...[W]e're fucking goddamn infantry killers!"[69] After having stated this to his men, a soldier speaks up and says, "...We're gonna kill some motherfuckers today! Finally! Let's fucking kill someone!"[70]

Most convincing of all when it comes to showing an inner hunger to engage in combat and kill is the example of Audie Murphy. This soldier is said to have had no hesitation "...about killing his fellow man."[71] To read his memoir, *To Hell and Back*, is to be amazed by one story after the next where this soldier looked for ways to kill the Germans: "Murphy sought the front constantly, and became well-known for his enthusiasm for seeking out the enemy alone, stalking and killing Germans wherever he could find them."[72] He is reported to have killed over two hundred and forty men while wounding and capturing others.[73] For his efforts, he earned a meritorious promotion and an officer's commission, three purples hearts; every distinguished medal for valor offered, some more than once, including the Medal of Honor and five foreign awards.[74] In the fight for which he earned his Medal of Honor, he was facing six German tanks and hundreds of German soldiers. In seeing this, he realized that he and his men were going to lose this fight, and thus, he ordered his men to retreat. Then, he took on the incoming enemy by himself. He manned a broken down tank with a machine gun that was loaded and ready to fire, then he called in mortar strikes; and fired continuously, all while being injured. Finally, after an hour of battle, being too weak to continue he left the field of Battle. When he got back to his men, he collapsed from exhaustion, undoubtedly to the amazement of all.[75] This man was possessed by the warrior spirit. His memoir is worth reading to see just how driven he was to engage in battle. Never did he retreat, surrender or refuse to kill the enemy. His actions were everything opposite of that. He alone reveals a spirit to fight that discounts any notion that by nature people have an aversion to killing.

Before we move away from this examination of soldiers, it is important to gain a picture of the overall commitment to fighting that these brave warriors possess. A battle that rises to the top of any discussion in the glorious history of the Army is the battle at Normandy, specifically for our purposes what took place at Omaha Beach.

German Field Marshal Erwin Rommel, in charge of defenses at Normandy, placed extra fortifications on this beach to halt an invasion: iron crosses covered with limpet mines to stop heavy transport, waist level stakes with mines set atop to explode when bumped into by infantry, concrete barriers, barbed wire, and thousands of randomly scattered underwater mines and land mines.[76] That should have caused an Army to retreat, and if any were faint of heart, they certainly would not have tried an assault of such impregnable defenses. Soldiers, however, did. They came ashore in waves, one being decimated after the other: "'We were cut to pieces', said Sales, the sole survivor of the 30 men in his boat."[77] "Everywhere men lay with severe head and stomach wounds. The limbless died quickly from blood loss… Intestines and internal organs had to be pushed back into men struck dumb by terror. There were so many wounded, so many severe cases of trauma...."[78] It was not until after four hours of unimpeded butchery that infantrymen started to make their way up the hundred foot cliffs that jutted up from the sandy beaches. By that time, there were over two-thousand casualties, and numerous wrecked vehicles, landing crafts and ships littering the shore lines.[79] "Some infantry units had lost most of their soldiers."[80] There were thousands of bodies about: "You could walk on bodies, as far as you could see along the beach, without touching ground. Parts of bodies—heads, legs and arms—floated in the sea."[81] It is no wonder that this beach earned the name 'Bloody Omaha'.[82]

The heroism in this battle cannot be denied. As one soldier in the fight stated: "Every man was a hero, [I] never saw a coward...."[83] One such soldier was Colonel Charles Canham. He set foot onto the beach, got shot through the hand, denied medical attention though blood was pouring from his wound, refused as well an order to be evacuated to safety, then carried a colt-45 pistol in his good hand and charged to the bluffs with men in tow trying to find a way to scale the cliffs.[84] Another leader refusing to back away from fighting, though none would have expected him to be on the front lines, was Brigadier General Norman Cota. Acting impervious to danger, this General "...strode about defiantly, back straight, chewing his unlit cigar, mumbling ditties to himself when he wasn't cursing the Germans."[85] Then, he continued his charge through gaps in concertina wire and up the bluffs and eventually, to the place where he could lead men on direct assaults of machine gun positions.[86] The courage of this man alone, who did not bow though many told him to gain cover, inspired men who saw him to get up, organize and advance.[87]

There were other leaders as well on this beach whose fighting spirit rose to the level of heroic as they organized men, some while being wounded, and charged the enemy.[88] First Lieutenant Jimmie Monteith, a posthumous Medal of Honor recipient at Omaha, was yet another important example. Leading an assault on a German

Machine gun position, Monteith's group was surrounded by the enemy. The Germans, knowing they had the upper hand, called out for Monteith and his men to surrender. This Lieutenant did not answer but instead crawled silently toward the voices of the Germans and took out their position single-handedly. He continued this relentless assault, one place after the next until he was killed.[89] Overall, the situation in this assault on Omaha Beach was as Major Sidney Bingham said of the D-Day invasion:

> Everything that was done was done by small groups led by the real heroes of any war. Most of them were killed, and very, very few were decorated chiefly because no one was left to tell about what they did. The minefields behind the beach were strewn with these guys. They were lying around the hedgerows on top of the bluffs and, of course, they were piled—literally—on the beach proper.[90]

What this Major reveals is that there were numerous gallant soldiers who died unheralded. Some stood out and led the charge, being exposed to death. I believe many of these people are the warriors who do rise up when others do not. They cannot help themselves as it is an integral part of their nature that no amount of incoming fire can deaden.

Conclusion

This examination has been vital in showing that there are those in all branches of service, including the Air Force which was referred to in a few places, who will rise up and kill. They do not feel bad about it and most often are overjoyed by the experience. They are warriors. It is what warriors do. War sates them in a way that nothing else does. Everything about this setting makes them feel alive, and having the chance to kill is the pinnacle moment. This all explains why warriors love war as one more quote shows:

The Jungian analyst James Hillman sees 'a terrible love of war' as central to the human psyche. ...Part of war's intoxication comes from the difficult but undeniable fact that there is pleasure in it. Some people can come to enjoy killing. It gives them a buzz of pleasure and power. Many describe it as erotic.[91]

The sooner we gain this truth, the better we will be at knowing how to employ warriors and support them.

Endnotes

[1] Max Hastings, <u>Warriors: Portraits From the Battlefield</u>, (New York: Alfred A. Knopf, 2005), pp. 156-157.

[2] Ibid., p. 157.

[3] In the DSM-V, both the psychopath and sociopath are listed in the same category, Antisocial Personality Disorder, and share common traits like no remorse or guilt for behavior, emotionally deprived, callous when harming others, violent in pursuing desires and have a general disregard for rules. Some, however, do draw a distinction between the two. The psychopath is believed to act this way as a result of nature, being born with this predisposition. Additionally, the psychopath will likely be interactive with others, able to appear normal and connected emotionally though it is a learned skill of mirroring emotional states, and usually this person is educated and can be well liked. The sociopath, however, will develop this state of being as a result of nurturing, growing up in hostile and abusive environments. This leads the sociopath to be more prone to rage, isolation and withdrawal from others, unpredictable in behavior and even less educated. Both can serve in the military and the psychopath can be highly effective in this environment, being better able to follow rules and charm others to gain important goals. American Psychiatric Association. Diagnostic and Statistical Manual of Mental Disorders, Fourth Edition. (Washington, D.C.: American Psychiatric Association, 1994).

[4] Lt. Col. Dean Ladd, and Steven Weingartner, Faithful Warriors: A Combat Marine Remembers the Pacific War, (Annapolis Maryland: Naval Institute Press, 2009), pp. 197-198.

[5] Marshall, S. L. A., <u>Men Against Fire</u>, (Gloucester, Massachusetts: Peter Smith Publisher, 1975), pp., 78-79.

[6] Ibid., p. 54.

[7] Ibid.

[8] Ibid., p. 56.

[9] Ibid., p. 59.

[10] Ibid., p. 56.

[11] Niall Ferguson, The Pity of War, (New York: Basic Books, 1999), p. 357.

[12] Ibid., p. 363.

[13] Ibid.

[14] Ibid.

[15] Ibid., p. 447.

[16] Joanna Bourke, An Intimate History Of Killing, (New York: Basic Books, 1999), pp. 2-3.

[17] [boldness added for emphasis] Dave Grossman, On Killing: The Psychological Cost of Learning to Kill in War and Society, (New York, NY: Little, Brown and Company, 1995), pp. xiii-xiv.

[18] Bourke, An Intimate History Of Killing, p. 19.

[19] Ibid., p. 20.

[20] Ibid., p. 21.

[21] Ibid., p. 21.

[22] Hastings, pp. 158 and 167.

[23] Ibid., p. 22.

[24] Ibid., p. 27.

[25] Paul Fussell, Wartime: Understanding and Behavior in the Second World War, (New York: Oxford Press, 1989), p. 120.

[26] Johnny Rico, Blood Makes the Grass Grow Green, (New York: Presidio Press, 2007), p. 296.

[27] Ibid., p. 296.

[28] Ibid., p. 297.

[29] Ibid.

[30] Martin van Creveld, The Culture of War, (New York: Presidio Press, 2008), p. 110.

[31] Ibid.

[32] Ibid.

[33] Van Creveld in the Transformation of War as quoted by Niall Ferguson, The Pity of War, p. 360.

[34] Van Creveld, The Culture of War, p. 111.

[35] Ibid., pp. 106-128.

[36] Ibid., p. 108 and Martin van Creveld, The Transformation of War, (New York, The Free Press, 1991), p. 162.

[37] I. C. B. DEAR and M. R. D. FOOT. "Tarawa, capture of." The Oxford Companion to World War II. Oxford University Press. 2001. Encyclopedia.com. 24 Jul. 2009 <http://www.encyclopedia.com>.

[38] Ibid., p. 176.

[39] Krulak, Victor, First To Fight, p. 175.

[40] Bourke., p. 20.

[41] James Brady, Why Marines Fight, (New York: Thomas Dunne Books, 2007), p. 30.

[42] Ibid.

[43] Ibid., pp. 214-215, 220.

[44] What follows is a story relayed by James Bradley in Flags of our Fathers, (New York: Bantam Books, 2006), p. 175ff.

[45] Ibid.

[46] Ibid.

[47] What follows is a story relayed by James Bradley in Flags of our Fathers, (New York: Bantam Books, 2006), pp. 4, 95, 110, 116-117, and 253.

[48] Ibid., p. 111.

[49] Ibid.

[50] Ibid.

[51] Bradley makes the point made by others that "The Japanese fighting man believed he was fighting in the proud tradition of ancient samurai. But this was not the case." He talks about the perversion of the Samurai tradition and the Bushido code. Bradley, Flags of our Fathers, pp. 66-67.

[52] Bradley, p. 96.

[53] Orr Kelly, Never Fight Fair!, (Navato, California: Presidio Press, 1995), pp. 2-3.

[54] Ibid. p. 7.

[55] Richard Marcinko, Rogue Warrior, (New York: Pocket books, 1992), p. 12.

[56] Ibid.,pp. 100-101.

[57] Chuck Pfarrer, Warrior Soul, (New York: Presidio Press, 2004), p. 287.

[58] Ibid., p. 287.

[59] YouTube. (Mar 10, 2012). 2-10-12 The O'Reilly Factor: Chris Kyle 'American Sniper'. https://www.youtube.com/watch?v=tDyAT1TVQ9Q.

[60] John Keegan, The Face of Battle, (England: Penguin Books, 1976), p. 199.

[61] Ibid., p. 331.

[62] Ibid., p. 332.

[63] Ibid. p. 280.

[64] John Keegan and Richard Holmes, Soldiers: A History of Men in Battle, (New York: Konecky & Konecky, 1985), p. 267.
[65] Ibid.
[66] Charles Duhigg, "Soldiers trained to kill, not to cope," http://seattletimes.nwsource.com/html/nationworld/2001984566_combat21.html, (July 21, 2004).
[67] Ibid.
[68] Grossman, On Killing, p. 236.
[69] Johnny Rico, Blood Makes the Grass Grow Green, (New York: Presidio Press, 2007), p. 128.
[70] Ibid.
[71] Hastings, p. 222.
[72] Ibid.
[73] Ibid., p. 11.
[74] Richard Rodgers, "Audie Leon Murphy: Memorial Web-Site," http://www.audiemurphy.com/welcome.htm, (August 18, 2009).
[75] Murphy, 238-242.
[76] Alex Kershaw, The Bedford Boys, (Cambridge, Massachusetts: Da Capo Press, 2003), pp. 103-104.
[77] Ibid., pp. 51-52.
[78] Kershaw, p. 151.
[79] Drez., p. 52.
[80] Ibid.
[81] Kershaw, p. 161.
[82] Drez., p. 52.
[83] Kershaw, p. 153.
[84] Ibid., pp. 152-153.
[85] Ibid., p. 155.
[86] Ibid., pp. 156-157.
[87] Ibid., p. 155.
[88] Ibid., pp. 199, 244-245, 247, 253, 294.
[89] Ibid., pp. 292-293,
[90] Ibid., p. 347.
[91] Hugo Slim, Killing Civilians: Method, Madness, and Morality in War, (New York: Columbia University Press, 2008), p. 233.

CHAPTER EIGHT

SEPARATING WARRIORS
FROM NON-WARRIORS

It was challenging to see those who did not want to be on the front lines when I served with warriors in the Battle of Fallujah. Their reticence to engage the enemy or outright refusal made them suffer. There is little doubt that to this day, some of these Marines and Sailors feel devalued because they believe that they could not measure up and overcome their fears in or objections to combat. That is a travesty. Not everyone belongs on the front lines as we will see, and this says nothing about their worth, importance in military service or value as a human being. They are only different, and that difference needs to be noted, appreciated and aligned with the war effort. At times though, it is not. Army Medic Agustin Aguayo found this out. He completed one successful combat tour and was highly respected for his work; and this even though he would not load his weapon in combat because of his convictions not to take a life. Then, things began to unravel for Aguayo. On the eve of his second tour, he faced the realization that he could not return with his unit to war. His anti-war and anti-killing convictions were too strong by this point to even be around combat. He struggled internally with what to do because he knew that his beliefs were not going to be received well. He communicated them anyway to his command and applied for conscientious objector status. At the conclusion of the reviewing process, his request was denied. Once again he was confronted with the fact of having to go to war. Ultimately, he held to his beliefs and acted by failing to report when his unit deployed. That got him arrested, tried for desertion, convicted and sent to the stockade. Overall, he did not care because as he said, "I tried to obey the rules, but in the end [the problem] was at the very core of my being. ...How do you correct a person's mind?"[1] Aguayo's story shows that not everyone is made for combat. Some do not have the nature for it and others have inner beliefs against it. Not seeing this becomes detrimental to people and to the war effort. It is time to start recognizing war-types and how that makes a difference in combat.

Warriors are made for war as David Smith shows in his book *The Most Dangerous Animal*. He says, "The naturalness of war lies in its role as an innate, biologically based potential: something that nature has built us to be capable of."[2] This inherent aptitude becomes even more evident by the fact that those who fit this warrior profile not only gravitate to the military for a chance to get into combat, but they come alive in that setting where chaos and mayhem abound. J. Glen Gray, author of *The Warriors: Reflections on Men in Battle*, speaks to this. He says, "Anyone who has watched men on the battlefield at work with artillery, or looked into the eyes of veteran killers fresh from slaughter, or studied the descriptions of bombardiers' feelings while smashing their targets, finds it hard to escape the conclusion that there is a delight in destruction."[3] Great satisfaction comes for warriors in war and the aftermath of it. Gray makes this even clearer by saying:

Most men would never admit that they enjoy killing, and there are a great many who do not. On the other hand thousands of youths who never suspected the presence of such an impulse in themselves have learned in military life the mad excitement of destroying...the delight in destruction slumbering in most of us. When soldiers step over the line that separates self-defense from fighting for its own sake, as it is so easy for them to do, they experience something that stirs deep chords in their being.[4]

Obviously, combat is rhapsodic for warriors, and it is so in ways that only they get. For what person but a warrior who is emotionally charged in the execution of heavy combat would be able to appreciate this soldier's testimony: "As he watched pieces of men's bodies fly up into the air and listened to the screams of the wounded..." he 'wept with joy' at what he considered to be an extreme pleasure?[5] I cannot think of one. Yet, that is the point? For warriors and for them alone, war is that place where they are consumed by the moment and intoxicated in delight: "The monstrous desire for annihilation, which hovered over the battlefield, thickened the brains of the men and submerged them in a red fog. ...A neutral observer might have perhaps believed that we were seized by an excess of happiness."[6]

Recognizing that people have different desires, personalities, abilities, natures and ideologies is important. As much as we would not expect a warrior to understand how a librarian can find pleasure in the tranquil existence of that setting, so we should not expect non-warriors to revel in extreme combat. People are diverse, but in seeing this we must begin to acknowledge it with regards to those we send to war. Failure hangs in the balance. Getting that right person on the front lines can be the difference between life and death, victory and defeat. Hence, let us take what we have learned about the uniqueness of warriors and sort out, in the broadest possible sense, those who should and should not be in war. We must go through the process of determining what war-types there are? Then, we should apply these understandings to see what a difference this all makes in the lives of those who serve.

Warriors and War

Literature on the topic of war conflates the term warrior, using it to say that any person who goes to war is a warrior.[7] This is wrong. Warriors are a select group. When Marshall says that about fifteen to thirty percent of people in battle were willing to kill, that figure is likely reflective of some who were warriors. It is a small group, but they are nonetheless clearly visible in battle. They are natural killers. They are at ease and even giddy about doing what others see as abnormal. War is their home.

A warrior, par excellence, is Franklin Miller. He wrote about his time in Vietnam in a book called *Reflections of a Warrior*. He was awarded the Medal of Honor, Silver Star, two Bronze Stars and the Air Medal for heroism in battle as well as six Purple Hearts for injuries. Some of these injuries were severe enough that they could have enabled him to be sent back stateside, ending his time in Vietnam. Yet, when the opportunities came to go home, this warrior not only turned them down but in a few instances cajoled army friends in the administration department to issue him orders that would reroute him back into the fight in Vietnam.

As a result of his persistent effort to remain in the fight, he amassed six tours in Vietnam. They were all front-line, hard-corps infantry combat tours. Why would anyone in their right mind do that? Miller answers this question in a few different ways, but in the end, it all amounts to the same thing: "...'Nam was where my heart longed to be."[8] Obviously, jungle warfare was this warrior's home and so true was this that when Miller realized the war was going to end, it frightened him: "...I began to get scared. Really scared. The war was winding down, and I could see my way of life coming to an end. I didn't want it to end. Ever."[9]

When it came to the role of a killer, Miller, being the warrior that he was, found this to be one of his strengths, and this should come as no surprise to us by now since we understand warriors. It is something for which they show extreme adeptness. Miller says it this way: "...most of us had a talent, a very special talent. We gathered intelligence and killed human beings under extremely hazardous and adverse conditions."[10] Miller goes on,

Killing someone is a unique ability all by itself. Not everyone can lay a weapon's sights on a fellow human being and crank off a round. The Army has been keeping data on soldier's killing abilities ever since World War II. The data supports the conclusion that out of an entire platoon of soldiers, you have perhaps two men who qualify as genuine killers. Men who actually see enemy troops, put the front sight blade on them, and blow them away. ...Genuine killers are not to be confused with guys who simply spray an area and happen to hit and kill someone. There is nothing wrong with that method, of course. ...But you'll find that most guys who kill people in that fashion can't perform a calculated kill. A there-he-is-line-him-up-put-him-down kill. It takes a certain something not found in everybody.[11]

Miller here in discussing this penchant for killing that warriors possess also offers something else we are after. It is the comparison between warriors and those with them on the front lines who avoid killing. This distinction is salient to him. He is not passing judgment, yet it is remarkable. How could people in war, not want to kill, he must wonder? This is what he wants. It happens to be what others in one squad he is assigned to want as well. This becomes evident one day when this unit is out on patrol and they spot an enemy combatant:

Immediately everybody wanted to take him under fire. ...We had been very successful in killing just about everybody we encountered, so we wanted to shoot all the time. As soon as we saw the enemy troop my M-79 (40mm grenade launcher) man spoke up. He started complaining, 'Shit man, Lemme shoot him.

I never get to shoot like the rest of you fuckers with your M-16's. C'mon, man, lemme do it.'[12]

This shows that inner craving. It is the hope and prayer that events in combat will afford warriors a chance to kill. When that opportunity arises, warriors come alive. Albert Jacka, an Australia soldier, revealed this attitude in his time on the front lines. He has been considered by one military historian, C.E.W. Bean, as "Australia's greatest fighting soldier."[13] It is said about him that "[h]e thrived on the spectacle of war; he excelled at soldiering...; he proved extraordinarily skilled at destroying Turks and Germans; and he relished the thrill of danger."[14] This all certainly describes the warrior. That picture gets even clearer when you read about his heroic tales in war. During one encounter at a place called Pozieres Ridge, we read, "Jacka was hit seven times leading a counterattack through a hail of bullets on a German position. He killed a dozen Germans with revolver and bayonet and captured 50 more."[15] The people who witnessed this on that day were gawking in astonishment, and how could they not as his fighting was believed to be "'the most dramatic and effective act of individual audacity in the history of the AIF' [Australian Imperial Force]."[16]

These are the warriors. War befits them like no other atmosphere. It makes them burst with exhilaration. As J. Glenn Gray writes, there is something in war that simply appeals to this group in the spectacle of it all, in the comradeship, in the delight of destruction and danger, and in the complete intoxication of the battle.[17] They are indeed incredible assets to any nation in need of defense.

Protectors and War

There is another class of people who end up in war, and I would call them protectors. They join the fight because they have an inner impulse to serve and stand for truth which arises from both nature and their principles of duty to country or cause. Warriors share this same inner core, only for them another part of their nature likes fighting just because. They fight because it is who they are. Protectors, contrarily, fight solely because they sense obligation to something vital. Hence, they will kill under the right circumstances, but it is not something in itself that motivates them. Seeking the chance to kill is not fundamental to their psyche or being. They are not charged by the action in the way of a warrior.

Theodore Nadelson in his book, *Trained to Kill*, touches on the Protectors. He says, "Most men possess the capacity to kill, and it can be kindled by training and war. Few Vietnam combatants, however, thought of themselves as "born killers," very few started training for combat in Asia with a single passion for inflicting mortal harm. The number of "killers" among soldiers in World War II, those who sought out opportunities to kill because they liked it, was about 2 percent."[18]

Nadelson's comments align with what the literature on war supports. This includes Marshall and others who note that there are those who will kill given the right training, but it is something they do by way of faithfulness to duty rather than compelling desire.[19] Nadelson brings more clarity to this point by offering this:

The ordinary loving men who discover their attachment to war (Broyles 1984) are not killers "bred in the bone" who find war somehow and couple with it. "Natural-born killers" are rare, different from other soldiers. It is as if they have been waiting for the hammer and heat of combat to shape them fully; it is as if they have been programmed in their genes to kill (Herr 1977). Those men easily become one with war's force and are reluctant to leave it.[20]

A soldier that Nadelson cites in his book, Fred Downs, who himself is an author of books on combat, talks about this protector group in this way: "…war was prosecuted mostly by men who were drafted into service but were 'professionals' because of the way they managed their responsibility and their lives in combat. They were 'dependable men who knew what they were there for, learned the tough job, and did it' (F. Downs, interview). They were not there for heroics, but they gave all they had."[21]

These are indeed the protectors. They join because their country calls upon them. They perform their jobs and do find great meaning in standing for justice, but they are not hungering for the front-line combat opportunity to kill.

Another writer on war who notes this same kind of distinction between what we are identifying as warriors and protectors is Lieutenant Colonel Dean Ladd. He makes the following clear in a book called *Faithful Warriors, A Combat Marine Remembers the Pacific War*: "But if some of the men truly relished battle—embraced and enjoyed killing, the brutality, the horror, all of it—it is important to establish that, on the continuum of brutal human behavior, the rest of us were not that far removed from them and we tended to move closer as the war went on."[22] Here Ladd in a more subtle ways identifies a difference between two groups in war: one that easily kills and the other that must be nurtured to that place. Both groups, Ladd offers, will be able to kill, but a difference does exist.

Going back to Miller from the beginning, I believe that he too illustrates this point we are after. In one example he provides, he discusses two distinct fighting groups in Vietnam, the warrior group of which he was a part and what I consider to be the protector group, a group he calls in this anecdote RT Vermont. Notice what he says:

RT Vermont had excellent soldiers who were ass-kickers, but they were slightly hesitant when it came to hosing down the bad guys. I guess it was a matter of attitude. ...[W]e constantly took enemy troops under fire. We'd engage them immediately even if we were a small element, just to see how many of them we could shoot. ...Folks in RT Vermont were more...passive. They'd see the bad guys out in the woods and it was like, Hey. There are some enemy troops. Let's not fuck with them. Let's leave them alone. It wasn't because they couldn't deal with them. ...It's just that they were more laid-back, more casual.[23]

As we see from Miller and others, warriors and protectors are distinguishable on the battlefield and they are in this sense we are addressing here by virtue of how they approach killing. Protectors become in this setting, using Nadelson terminology and identification, "Good soldiers," those who "...do not start out as takers of life; [but] they kill because they must. They are attached to their fellows, to some of their commanders, and to the purpose of the nation and because of that, essential to it, they try not to shirk from killing the enemy."[24] Yet, it is not something we see that always and necessarily drives them to kill. That is something unique about the warriors. But for both, while there is nothing wrong with how each approaches war, that there is a difference is critical to realize because it has implications that should be addressed in training, combat and support post combat.

Patriots and War

As a chaplain serving with Marines in combat, I was afforded many experiences. At one point after the initial battle for Fallujah had ended, I was with a group of Marines who was given a chance to re-clear areas in the city. These Marines were not a part of the initial assault because they had Marine Occupational Specialties that did not put them on the front lines of combat. But now was there chance to engage the enemy, and clear out the insurgents who were missed in the first movement through the city. What struck me with many of these Marines as I moved with them was just how out of place they seemed. A few were hesitant to move into structures. Some hung back and allowed others to go on while they maintained security. They wanted to be there or else they would not have volunteered.

But their approach to this mission as against the others I had travelled with in the first part of the war was remarkably different. The zeal, enthusiasm, assuredness, hunger to engage and other such things were gone in several of these Marines. Why?

I now realize that the reason is related to the very idea that Marshall observed in his study: "It is therefore reasonable to believe that the average and normally healthy individual—the man who can endure mental and physical stresses of combat—still has such an inner and usually unrealized resistance toward killing a fellow man that he will not of his own volition take life if it is possible to turn away from that responsibility."[25]

These people are Patriots. They join the military out of love for nation and desire to serve and even sacrifice for what they believe. They are not helpless like sheep but they are also not desirous of having to kill in combat. They want to support the effort. They are willing to be exposed to danger to do so, but that role has its limitations. There is nothing wrong with this. It is meritorious in every respect. They are happy to let others go charge off and fight enemies while they do all that they can to support that effort. Vicki Haddock who wrote *The Science of Creating Killers* offers this:

In World War II, when U.S. soldiers got a clear shot at the enemy, only about 1 in 5 actually fired, according to sensational and controversial research by Army historian Brig. Gen. S.L.A. Marshall. It wasn't that they were cowards: On the contrary, they performed other perilous feats, including running onto the battlefield to rescue fellow soldiers, and sometimes they even placed themselves in greater personal danger by refusing to fire. And yet at the moment of truth, they just couldn't kill.[26]

Lieutenant Colonel Dean Ladd, the Marine who wrote *Faithful Warriors*, also talks about this dynamic. He says that as his Marines pushed through the fight in the Pacific during WWII, the unit would occasionally get new Marines to fill the ranks. However, some of these Marines clearly did not belong in this kind of forward fighting position as "they couldn't hack combat."[27] What this meant for Ladd was that these people could not find their place in hunting down the enemy, killing them or just being in this kind of environment where they might be killed. That marked difference was noticed. The other Marines, the true front line warriors, made fun of these people, calling them cowardly or yellow bellied. Ladd did not let the negative atmosphere take over, however. He fought back saying, "'Now, wait just a minute. This guy is *not* yellow. He *tried* to do the job. But he just could *not* do it. It's not that he is saying, 'I won't do it, I'm not going there.' He tried, there's a difference."[28]

What Ladd shows here is that people, who join the military to serve their country, can clearly end up in the wrong place. That serves no purpose. It brings up questions of self-value as misfits wonder why they cannot measure up. Miller speaks to this as well:

I ran across many really good, squared-away individuals who just weren't killers. These guys would go out on missions and gather outstanding intelligence, but the fact that they couldn't bring themselves to shoot the enemy caused them grief. It wore on them. It was a heavy load. …They'd take any job in the camp that prevented them from going out again.[29]

For Miller, this failing of putting people in the right combat role has consequence. Since infantrymen are sent forward to kill the enemy, their refusal to engage in this mission must cause feelings of ineptitude. A simple fix is in order. Recognize patriots for their unique calling and abilities to serve and provide them with missions commensurate with natural inclinations so that they can be as honorable as any other group.

An outstanding example of such a patriot is Desmond Doss. He enlisted in the Army during WWII. "Doss was a patriotic American who wanted to serve his country."[30] What was curious to all about Doss, however, was that regardless of his sense of duty to nation which inspired his military service, he did not want to use fire arms, even carry one, and he refused to kill anyone. His religious convictions prevented him from these kinds of things. As you might imagine, however, this stance did not go over well. His commanding officer actually tried to get him kicked out of the army under a section 8, i.e., rejected for being mentally unfit for service.[31] It did not work, and Doss was allowed to serve.

Doss became a medic and ended up in the Battle of Okinawa in 1945. At one point in the battle, as his Army unit pushed up an escarpment to engage the Japanese, the soldiers faced hellacious opposition. They ended up suffering numerous casualties. This gave Doss plenty of work to do and that he did. He raced around the battle field without a weapon, charging numerous times out into open fire, rescuing the injured and dying. He was credited with having saved 75 men in this way. One of those he saved was a fellow soldier who had earlier threatened to kill him because of his odd convictions.[32] Later in that battle, Doss was injured himself but continued to attend to others. For his unusual way of serving, but for undeniable gallantry, Doss received the Medal of Honor. Years later he said of his service, "I felt like it was an honor to serve God and country ...I didn't want to be known as a draft dodger, but I sure didn't know what I was getting into."[33] Never could there be a better picture of a patriot, one desirous of serving his nation in the military, though without a desire to kill!

Pacifists and War

Still another group that needs mentioning is made of those who are by inner conviction pacifists. For many in this group, there is a belief system that trumps all other considerations. It is built on the notion that one should never act out to harm another or be involved in some effort where that will occur. This means sacrificing personal rights to uphold peace no matter what.[34] One might ask why this group should be covered. The answer is that people with this conviction do end up in the military. Their belief system is typically not formed upon enlistment. But at some point, often through the engagement of war, their faith becomes established and determinative. Thus, they need to be recognized and addressed.

Camilo Mejia is a great example of the pacifist who comes to these convictions while in military service.[35] When he joined the Army his singular reason was to establish a life for himself. He had to drop out of college for lack of funds. He also could not find a job that paid well. The military promised both financial stability and college benefits.[36] Thus, it seemed like a good option. Interestingly, his parents were against the choice because they felt he was not "the warrior type."[37] Mejia joined anyway. Then, after he had given eight years of his life to the military, including reserve and active duty time, he was ready to move out of the service. However, before his separation could occur, 9/11 happened. At that point, Congress passed a stop-loss-order which prevented all active and reserve military forces from leaving the service. Mejia was stuck. He was forced to continue on in the military. This was highly disappointing to him, but he could do nothing about it. So he refocused on the mission that his unit had, which was to go forward and be involved in this war on terror. We will look at some of this time that Mejia had, but we will do so with a special focus on those things that seemed to bring within him a growing inner conviction for pacifism.

What I see in Mejia's military story, which seems to be a pattern for those who become pacifists while serving in the military, is a growing disillusionment with the military mission. The ideals of standing for truth from one's perspective begin to collide against a rising inner agitation that war is not the answer to resolving conflict.

Mejia was unquestionably finding this. It started with his belief that this war he was in, the Iraqi war, was really about oil and not about finding weapons of mass destruction.[38] This belief conjoined with other considerations: the negative experiences of being in war, poor and abusive leadership toward troops, illegal treatment of prisoners at a POW camp in which his unit served, and abusive treatment of innocent Iraqis in and around Ar Ramadi.[39] All of this, for Mejia, created a fundamental change within:

> The truth as I see it now is that in war, the bad is often measured against what's even worse, and that, in turn, makes a lot of deplorable things seem permissible. When that happens, the imaginary line between right and wrong starts to vanish in a heavy fog, until it disappears completely and decisions are weighed on a scale of values that is profoundly corrupt.[40]

Here we find the burgeoning conviction for Mejia that being in military service is wrong. It leads him eventually to the place of not being able to find any redeeming purpose in violence. Mejia says it this way:

> It can be claimed that a particular war is justified politically, or that it has the support of the international community and the blessing of international law. But these arguments can never convey the images, the sounds, the smells, or anything that remotely depicts the full horror of war. Escaping those arguments is the irreversible damage war always inflicts upon humanity, and upon everything worth loving on earth. War, ultimately, is the destruction of life.[41]

Mejia's experience is like that of many who get into the military but at some point become incapable of assimilating that mission into a crystalizing pacifistic belief system. In time, after the non-violent beliefs begin to shape and concretize, life becomes difficult. People like Mejia find themselves incapable of living the lie. They also begin to feel trapped, incapable of severing this commitment or resolving the tension. Those who do manage to speak up and act on their convictions can find themselves, like Mejia, quickly ostracized and eventually headed for punishment of some kind. When it got to this point for Mejia, he went AWOL (absent without leave). Eventually, he decided to turn himself in. This led to a court martial, and he did end up in the stockade for a period of time. He has now moved on with his life.

When we speak of pacifism in the military an interesting book about this during the Vietnam era is by James Tollefson. It is called *The Strength Not to Fight—An Oral History of Conscientious Objectors of the Vietnam War*.[42] One story in it is about a soldier like Mejia who becomes a pacifist after enlistment and thereafter, decides that he will not fight in war. This naturally leads to punishment and time in prison. This is what that soldier said about all of this:

> One thing I learned, though, is that it's not that hard to be a pacifist in prison. I found I could take a beating with the best of them. It's not any worse to be beaten up in prison than it is to be beaten up in high school. In fact, for pacifists, in some ways it's easier, because at least your head is clear. ...If you know what you're standing for and you're consistent, you can create a kind of moral authority in prison that people will respect.[43]

These words are powerful in that they reveal the heart and conscience of a person who knows both what he believes and what he is willing to stand for, no matter what. That kind of inner conviction is no different in its essence than what we find in any other group that is mentioned in this book. Certainly a differing ideology underlies it, a refusal to act out in violence, but the absolute devotion to belief remains. That must be considered noble.

All should be likewise fixed on convictions of truth no matter where they take us. Obviously, the caution is to be continuously willing to challenge what is believed to see if it is indeed aligned with truth. However, with reasoned conviction to stand, we should stand. For it is at that point that we have the strength of our belief to guide. It is here that we become whole to the extent that our conscience holds to what is justifiable. This is true whether we end up in agreement with the warrior, protector, patriot or pacifist.

Tollefson's book offers many stories about what pacifists endured during Vietnam. What they reveal collectively is an important picture of (a) what it is like to have the conviction that military force is not the answer, (b) the challenges involved in holding to this, and (c) the often bitter consequences that follow from standing for conviction. As he further states,

> In interviews across the United States, I found that there is no single truth of the conscientious objectors' story during America's war in Vietnam. But perhaps this book holds part of the truth the part that includes the struggles between sons and their parents—especially their fathers, who fought in World War II—and between young Americans and their country.[44]

These words are striking. To believe that war is wrong is to face the tearing apart of family and nationality. That is a huge price to pay for one's convictions. Regardless, for this group, once the convictions for pacifism become awakened and hardened, there is a belief system that cannot and should not be denied. A pacifistic statement that captures this poignantly is the following: "If my survival caused another to perish, then death would be sweeter and more beloved."[45] That definitely shows the utter commitment there is for the pacifist to live so as not ever to harm another. It is a commitment to die for what is believed that is no different than the warriors though focused differently.

The central point here is that there are pacifists who end up in the military, and to force them in some way to violate their convictions is to their detriment and to that of all others. If they are on the front lines with these convictions, they will not fire at the enemy or they will fire aimlessly into the air and will be ineffective and ultimately dangerous to all. Hence, we should raise our awareness about this type and allow them to find their place in the military or outside of it.

Psychopaths and War

When it comes to this war-type there have been studies done to identify those who fit a psychopathic profile and who have had military service. One 2001 study claims that at any given time, the military has about 7% of its people who fit the classification of a psychopath.[46] That is a small percentage overall but definitely shows that these people are present in the military and therefore, can become a part of front line combat.[47]

Even more to consider on this is another study that looked into the connection between those who were in the military but who later displayed signs of psychosis by virtue of the fact that they were mass murderers.[48] There were hundreds of people listed in this study. Obviously not all of them qualified as psychopaths, but some did fit this clinical profile. Here are a few of their names: David Berkowitz - The Son of Sam; Gary Ridgway - The Green River Killer; Jeffrey Dahmer – The Infamous Cannibal Killer; Dean Corll – The Candy Man; Randy Kraft – The Freeway Killer; and Dennis Rader - The BTK Killer.

As one can see, psychopaths do get into the military, and once in they become skilled in the art of killing and some even rise to positions of great leadership. That becomes devastating as these most infamous psychopaths show: Adolph Hitler, Josef Mengele, Sadaam Hussein, Joseph Stalin, Ivan the Terrible and Vlad the Impaler.

Given that psychopaths do get into the military, what we want to address now is what that profile looks like. As we do so, we will consider them against another group which they can appear to be like; the warrior group. The two do at times look alike in combat. Yet, that appearance is foundationally deceiving.

In terms of similarities, psychopaths and warriors both show aggressiveness in attacking and killing the enemy. Also, each will kill the enemy without remorse or regret. Even more, both groups gain a true sense of satisfaction from having taken on the enemy and having killed them. Undoubtedly to focus on these things alone, one might say that these two groups are one. But that is not the case. Psychopaths display personality traits which typically make them challenging to have in the military and particularly in the combat environment: paranoia, eccentric behavior, lack of social interaction or close friends, social anxiety that does not abate in time, aggression toward animals and people, destruction of property, inflated sense of self, deceitfulness or theft, serious violation of rules, irresponsibility, impulsivity, and lack of remorse, which is often rationalized or the blame shifted to a victim.[49] These traits alone make it clear why psychopaths in no way compare to warriors or belong in war. They disrupt and create friction in the combat mission.

Additionally, when looking at psychopaths, they unlike warriors kill solely for egoistic motivations. Hence, they do not take a life for the sake of others in need, for higher principles of truth, for duty, country or loved ones. They do it because they want to kill to pursue internal gratification, or to satisfy a morbid desire to take life.

With this limited profile of the psychopath, let us now consider what makes the warrior different from the psychopath?

First, if a warrior kills someone who ends up being a non-combatant, or even an enemy soldier killed without warrant, he will feel tremendous guilt. This is a very strong indicator of the difference. Psychopaths will have no regret in situations like this.

Secondly, when considering warriors, we know too that they have an inner sense of being elite, invincible, hard, self-sacrificing, gusto seekers and holding to a rigid moral code.

This then offers some comparison between psychopaths and warriors. While it does show some similarities between these groups, it critically offers striking dissimilarities too. Considering this, it is disturbing to have some like Dave Grossman conjoin these groups: "Whether called sociopaths, sheepdogs, warriors, or heroes, they are there, they are a distinct minority, and in times of danger a nation needs them desperately."[50]

These two groups should not be thought of in the same way. Psychopaths or sociopaths, included together as Anti-Social Personality Disorder in the Diagnostic Statistic Manual 5, are mentally unstable, fundamentally unlike warriors, and never should they be as suggested placed on the front lines. They are not "desperately" needed to save a nation. They need treatment and should be as far away from war as is possible. They will kill wantonly with disregard for rules of engagement. They will motivate others to do the same and thus, can create an atmosphere of malfeasance. It is best in every regard to notice this war-type and to remove them from military service.

All Classifications and War

Now that we have identified five war-types we will return to Gray's *Warriors: Reflections on Men in Battle*. Gray offers his own appraisal of differences in people when it comes to the combat experience of killing. These descriptions are closely aligned with the war-types as offered in this book.

Gray starts in his profiling of soldiers by talking about one group that when confronting death in combat appears to have an air of nonchalance. He says that for this group, "Death is an impersonal force that can rob other men of their motion and their powers, but for them it has no body or substance at all."[51] What I find Gray saying here is that there are some who seem detached from the experience of war, devoid of the passion that is normal in the battlefield experience. This emotional deadness is remarkable. How can someone not react in some way, positively or negatively, to the experience of war? It is odd. Yet, these people are there. They exist, as Gray goes on to say, without anxiety, immune to what is happening to others around, and with a lack of emotional connection even in the face of death.[52] Gray adds that these people seem to live in some "…childish illusion that they are the center of the world and are therefore immortal."[53]

From Gray's overall description here, one can easily evaluate that this group would not be one to have in war. Their myopic attitude, and even selfish disregard toward death and dying, promotes reckless behavior. It is an attitude that will likely cause as many deaths as it exacts from the enemy. This group sounds like those I would type as psychopaths.

A second group Gray discusses is one that is similar in thinking to the first group in that death in war is not controlling for them. However, for this group, the reason why death holds no ultimate power is not because of emotional detachment but because of an indomitable belief that death cannot overtake them; this group sees itself as invincible, holding to a "fanatic faith in their destiny which is only strengthened by narrow escapes."[54] This group thusly has the utter conviction that it will conquer all; nothing can stop them. They live with confidence in war and experience a sense of ecstasy in warfare.

Gray states it this way, "In philosophical terms, such soldiers are affirming human finiteness and limitation as a morally desirable fact. Just as the bliss of erotic love is conditioned by its transiency, so life is sweet because of the threats of death that envelop it and in the end swallow it up. Men of this sort are usually in love with life and avid for experience of every sort."[55] In other words, death for this group is about the possibility of finding the most lively and supreme form of existence, going out in battle and testing their mettle to overcome the greatest of all foes. That challenge, makes battle all the better. "What they desire is experience, and the fuller and more intense that experience is, the more content they are. War offers them something that peace cannot: the opportunity to telescope much experience into short compass. If death be the issue, they are normally fatalists by instinct and can accept it more calmly

251

than the prospect of a boring, empty period in their lives."[56] For this kind of soldier, "War is a game for him, exciting and dangerous because a man may strike out or foul out at any time. Such possibilities make both life and war worth the effort expended."[57]

Certainly, this group must be typed as the warriors we have identified: feelings of invincibility against the enemy, loving the dangers of death that lurk around every moment, and wanting take on life in such a way that it will explode with meaning. Gray even goes on to say something more about this group: "They are commonly leaders and win recognition as fearless **warriors** whose iron nerves and will to victory are out of all proportion to those of other men."[58] Most definitely, these are the people you want on the front lines of battle.

Another group that Gray offers is one that enters war for deep convictions of truth that need to be upheld. Defending those truths become more important than life itself. Gray says it this way regarding this kind of fighter: "He has not thought much or at all about what it is like to be dead or what dying signifies, because he is overcome by enthusiasm for some living ideal or person sufficient to render his own independent existence of lesser value."[59] This group is charged with "love for his country or for a glorified leader or for an ideal,"[60] and thus, is able to lay thoughts of death aside. "Duty is, for this professional, the highest value, and courage in performance of his duty is a shining ideal. Death must not be shunned if the interests of duty and honor require it, however unpleasant dying may be."[61]

Clearly here we are identifying the protector; the one who goes to battle only for what he believes and is willing to do what he must to maintain fidelity to those beliefs. This without question means a willingness to be on the front lines to engage the enemy and kill when justice is clear.

Still a different group of people in battle for Gray are those who willingly "...endure every hardship and humiliation of military life without flinching, yet cannot face personal danger with any composure at all. Such soldiers feel that all bullets are intended for them and every shell likely to land on that particular spot they have selected as temporary shelter. Insatiable death lurks everywhere ready to pounce upon them, and every one of his victims they see makes them more certain they will be the next one."[62] These soldiers, as Gray sees it, "are quickly found out in combat and become the butt of their comrades' ridicule and contempt."[63] They are spirited and have a place in helping, but recoil from danger so that their credibility suffers.

How can this group not be our patriots: the ones who gratefully serve their nation but do not particularly want to be on the firing lines in doing so?

Finally, Gray talks about soldiers who have religious or spiritual convictions that create within them a contradiction when it comes to death in war. For one in this group Gray says, "He is conscious of the pacifistic injunctions of his faith and has not been able, in all likelihood, to make the easy distinctions between destroying life in peace and in war that governments insist upon. Even though he may have privately determined that no one shall fall by his hand, his conscience seldom leaves him in peace."[64] With those in this group, it is certain that the reality of death itself is damnable. It is not so because of what death means to them but because of what it means to be involved in bringing this about. In the end, one in this group just should not have fought in war. Those in this group are certainly pacifists.

This outline of the various kinds of people in combat by Gray is refreshing to find. His experience from being in war has allowed him both to witness first hand and thereafter, to identify in his book the very groups that we have labored to outline. This obviously shows that the experience of war differs with respect to what we call war-types. Finding out the importance of honoring this difference is of significance next.

War-Types and Why it Matters

Now that we are aware of war-types, we should go a little further to realize just how much this matters. Let us take a singular war experience and consider how many different ways it can be understood, depending upon the war-type of the person. This will be revelatory in that it will show why those who go to war can be so misunderstood and so confused by our counsel when we assume that they all are alike in their approach to war. An interesting incident to review is one found in Dave Grossman's book *On Killing*. This book provides strong evidence for the case that to kill in combat creates deep personal suffering. Here are a few of his quotes on this:

> The soldier in combat is trapped within this tragic Catch—22. If he overcomes his resistance to killing and kills an enemy soldier in close combat, he will be forever burdened with blood guilt, and if he elects not to kill, then the blood guilt of his fallen comrades and the shame of his profession, nation, and cause lie upon him. He is damned if he does, and damned if he doesn't.[65]

> Looking another human being in the eye, making an independent decision to kill him, and watching as he dies due to your action combine to form the single most basic, important, primal, and potentially traumatic occurrence of war. If we understand this, then we understand the magnitude of the horror of killing in combat.[66]

This kind of mindset that a person can be crippled by taking a life in combat is not an uncommon assumption though we see from this study that it is not categorically true. We want to regard it though, as it feeds into this anecdote from Grossman we want to review, and as it will prove in this analysis to be a central problem if, and when all war-types are counseled with the same foundational conviction about killing. The anecdote to consider is about a soldier who comes to Grossman and confesses his struggles with having killed a person in combat. What troubles the soldier particularly is that the killing he did happened at close range.[67] This information is enough to lead Grossman to conclude that "[w]ith very few exceptions, everyone associated with killing in combat reaps a bitter harvest of guilt."[68] In fact, Grossman goes on to say, "[t]he burden of killing is so great that most men try not to admit that they have killed. They deny it to others, and they try to deny it to themselves. …Killing is what war is all about, and killing in combat, by its very nature, causes deep wounds of pain and guilt."[69] While Grossman's overall understanding and even counsel here is likely right for those we call patriots and pacifists, this is not true for other war-types. Let us walk through the process of showing why. For ease of reference when we refer to this experience, we will refer to this soldier as Mark.

First, let us look at this scenario as if Mark is a warrior. Let us say too, that we have talked to Mark on many occasions and we know that he has been in many firefights and has killed many enemy soldiers. Mark has even bragged about these other kills. But then, let us say as well that Mark comes one day and expresses deep anguish for having killed someone at close range. What might this mean for a warrior? It likely does not mean that "killing in combat reaps a bitter harvest of guilt." The warrior enjoys killing in combat. What is going on then? Perhaps, what we discover is that Mark shot someone who he later determined to be a non-combatant. The person caught him by surprise, popped out of hiding, and was killed. Mark knew instantly, however, that this person was a non-combatant since he was killed up close. This, then, is what bothered Mark and it is easy to understand why. But if we are going to help Mark with this, it is important to connect the confession with the true cause of remorse. It is not the killing, but the killing of an innocent person. If we cannot see this because we do not recognize the nature of a warrior or that Mark is one, we will go in the direction of providing counsel that will only bring confusion.

For the sake of making this point clearer, we could go on with Mark as a warrior and imagine that the up close killing was a child planting an IED. That Mark, in accordance with Rules of Engagement (ROEs) and given his limited choices in this situation, killed this child, a conscript from a demented enemy that uses this tactic often,[70] is still something that haunts him. This we understand. Who wants to shoot a child, particularly a warrior who tries to protect children? But once again, what we find importantly is that it was still not the killing per se that created the problem but an aspect of the killing. The difference is of paramount importance in understanding and helping warriors.

Next, what do we say about Mark as a protector? First, we do know that if he kills someone in combat, he is willing to do so, even though he does not relish the chance like the warrior. We also know that for Mark as a protector in this case while he will kill it is regardless an act for which he requires a definite just cause; he does not want to kill just because he can. It must be the last resort. Thus, with this knowledge in mind, we can move to counsel Mark and ask him questions to discern what it is about the kill that is causing guilt.

Let us say that what we find is that Mark is tormented because he was feeling pressure from others to kill. His war buddies were harassing him because he had not killed anyone yet, and they were goading him to get his first kill. Therefore, when the next combat situation came up where he was able to kill, he bowed under the pressure and shot immediately. He was within the ROE's to do so, but he struggled anyway, wondering if he really needed to kill this person.

That he was up close in this situation only compounds his remorse because he sees the man's face and thinks about him, about his possible family, and wishes all the more that he would have acted first to give this man a chance to surrender. This is what generates Mark's crisis of being, and if so, we see once more that it is not killing another that is bothersome but the question of if this killing was the right option.

Hence, in counseling Mark, it would understandably cause Mark confusion if we said the reason for his guilt is related to the fact that killing is wrong and not in keeping with the human nature. That is not true for the protector.

Moving quickly forward, what about the patriot? If Mark is a patriot, we know that the kill is going to create issues. He desperately hopes to avoid this kind of thing. But then one day, let us say he finds himself on the front lines of combat in a massive firefight and he feels that he has no choice but to shoot. So he fires his weapon, but he does so aimlessly and harmlessly away from enemy combatants, preferring to die rather than kill.

But his plan does not work out as expected. Let us suppose in his case that one of his random shots "accidentally" kills an enemy combatant. He fires, he shoots away from the enemy, but he happens to hit one who pops out of nowhere. At that moment, when he sees what he has done, he is paralyzed. His buddies are not conflicted about this kill, though, as everyone is cheering him on. They cannot believe he had the keen insight to make this kill in an area right next to them where no one else saw the enemy. He becomes a hero to his unit because of his "quick thinking that saved them all and his great skill in hunting down the enemy." How ironic it would be, and the more he hears about his heroics, the more he cringes within. We can see why; it is because deep down inside he does not want to kill a human being. In truth, he never thought it would come to this, but then it did.

Counseling Mark in this situation will take on other issues. He feels guilty for having taken a human life. This is true for the patriot and follows in line perfectly with what Grossman offers. Thus, counseling Mark will be different than before with the warrior and protector. Here it will be about guilt for having killed a person.

All manner of trying to convince Mark with notions of patriotic fervor, or messages about the greater good will miss the point. You must deal with the underlying issue.

Let us move now to our next category, the pacifist. If Mark is of this war type, the issue of killing will go against his belief system and certainly bring about a major psychological and/or spiritual struggle. To face such a possibility would be to abandon core convictions which mandate peace not war. An identity crisis is sure to follow. Thus, in this case, if we say that Mark as a pacifist kills someone, irrespective of the proximity, the reason for the guilt will be apparent.

Also, consider that this pang of conscience can even be true for Mark if he never fired a weapon but was involved supporting the effort to kill. In either of these situations, Mark struggles because he feels like his direct or indirect efforts on the front lines contributed to killing. These kinds of things go against his inner ideological or spiritual convictions. Focusing on that, therefore, is what Mark needs. It is not a matter of counsel directed to the idea that people do not want to kill others because it is not in their nature. It is rather about focusing on inner convictions of truth that ground identity, faith and being.

Finally, let us finish all of this by looking at our last war-type: psychopath. As we know, psychopaths do get in war as well and can be highly efficient killers. Hence, let us say that in this case, Mark fits the profile of a psychopath and he comes one day saying that he is extremely agitated for having killed someone at close range in war. What we might initially assume in this case, if we know that Mark has this personality disorder, is that his emotional state as connected to killing is likely not real, particularly if we hear Mark talking about having guilt in this situation. Psychopaths would not react in this way. So we are left to decide what is really going on. One interpretation is that Mark's story of pain or even guilt for having killed is not truly about what he feels but about what he is wanting out of his time with you as the counselor. Psychopaths are manipulative. They understand that others feel emotional states, and they know too that these feelings can be used to achieve certain ends. Thus, a counselor would have to watch out for this and not spend time focusing on issues of how unnatural killing is. Other issues altogether are obviously present.

Overall, the point in this examination of war types is that when it comes to killing in combat it is vital to consider one's nature, spiritual conviction, and mental condition in order to know how to interpret the struggles one has.

Making a universal assessment about killing and saying that "[k]illing is what war is all about, and killing in combat, by its very nature, causes deep wounds of pain and guilt"[71] would be wrong. Warriors, hearing this will wonder what is wrong with them since they take pride in killing and enjoy it; are they psychopaths?

Protectors will question their deficiencies as well since they are more than willing to kill, though they might not gain the inner satisfaction that a warrior does.

Patriots may draw comfort and understanding in knowing this about killing, but they might still be confused. The reason is because they will not be able to explain why, if killing is so unnatural, it appears to be so easy for those whom they admire and trust, those who are out there by their side fighting for truth, the warriors and protectors. Those people do not seem to have a problem with killing. Can killing really be wrong, therefore, they might still wonder?

What, then, do we say about pacifists? For them to hear some proclamation that killing brings guilt because it is not natural will be to no avail. The real issue for them rests with core ideological or spiritual convictions. Failing to address this, will leave them in crisis.

Then, there are the psychopaths. They certainly will have no internal struggles with killing, and so messages about killing bringing guilt will be empty chatter to them. Different than the others, what this group really needs is to be identified for their mental condition and taken out of the battle altogether. In sum, what needs to happen for all is for awareness of types to be regarded, identified and then, addressed appropriately.

Conclusion

In view of this chapter, we see readily how failing just to recognize war-types leads to ineffectiveness in carrying out the mission. Miller makes this point for us one last time in a story where he talks about being with a patrol group and trying to get them to see how they can use the enemies' very tracks to hunt them down. As he found, no amount of attention to this knowledge and the skill involved in the hunt influenced this other group. They just seemed disinterested. As Miller later realized, "I eventually concluded that they simply didn't want to find any signs of the enemy. If they'd had proof that the enemy was in their area, they'd have had to do something about it, and I don't believe they were willing to do anything that involved direct contact with the enemy. I'm not implying that they were afraid; I just feel they didn't want to make an effort to engage the enemy."[72]

That kind of disparity between war-types has to be seen and honored. The consequence of doing otherwise brings corrosion to cohesion and mission success. Miller finds this to be true for himself when he is with this very patrol group. They eventually got tired of his zeal to engage the enemy, and tried to get rid of him by accusing him falsely of killing a civilian.[73] The tactic does not work, but it shows how failing to regard war-types engenders unit friction.

Given this, as much as it would prove arduous and extremely challenging to begin a process of sorting out military members by placing them in appropriate groupings and assigning them functions that fit them best in accordance with type, it is something that needs to be done. The mental, physical and spiritual health of those who serve in the military lies in the balance.

Endnotes

[1] Mary Wiltenburg, "When a US Soldier in Iraq refuses to kill", https://www.alternet.org/story/59733/when_a_u.s._soldier_in_iraq_r efuses_to_kill/, (August 15, 2007).

[2] David Smith, The Most Dangerous Animal, (New York: St. Martin's Press, 2007), p. 36.

[3] J. Glenn Gray, The Warriors: Reflections on Men in Battle, (New York: Harper Torchbook, 1970), p. 51.

[4] Ibid., pp. 52-53.

[5] Smith, p. 214.

[6] Ibid., p. 52.

[7] Grossman, On Combat, p. 138.

[8] Franklin Miller, Reflections of a Warrior, (Novato, California: Presidio Press, 1991), p. 180.

[9] Ibid., p. 194.

[10] Ibid., p. 74.

[11] Ibid., pp. 74-75.

[12] Ibid., p. 46.

[13] Michael Evans and Alan Ryan. The Human Face of Warfare: Killing, Fear and Chaos in Battle. St. Leonards, NSW: Allen & Unwin, 2000. eBook Collection (EBSCOhost), EBSCOhost (accessed August 26, 2015), p. 42.

[14] Michael Rowland, "Albert Jacka: the 'Australian Achilles' whose bravery saw him awarded the country's first Victoria Cross of the war", http://www.abc.net.au/news/2015-04-23/albert-jacka-the-australian-achilles/6360196, (22 April 2015).

[15] Ibid, p. 43.

[16] Ibid, parenthesis added for clarification.

[17] Ibid, p. 44.

[18] Theodore Nadelson, Trained to Kill, (Baltimore, Maryland: The Johns Hopkins University Press, 2005), p. 55.

[19] Marshall, S. L. A., Men Against Fire, (Gloucester, Massachusetts: Peter Smith Publisher, 1975), pp., 36-37, and 78-79.

[20] Nadelson, p. 56.

[21] Ibid., p. 55.

[22] Lt. Col. Dean Ladd and Steven Weingartner, Faithful Warriors, A Combat Marine Remembers the Pacific War, (Annapolis, Maryland: Naval Institute Press, 2007), p. 205.

[23] [clarification added] Miller, p. 72.

[24] Nadelson, p. 72.

[25] Marshall, S. L. A., Men Against Fire, (Gloucester, Massachusetts: Peter Smith Publisher, 1975), pp., 78-79.

[26] Vicki Haddock, "The Science of Creating Killers/ Human reluctance to take a life can be reversed through training in the method known as killology", http://www.sfgate.com/science/article/THE-SCIENCE-OF-CREATING-KILLERS-Human-2514123.php, (13 August, 2006).

[27] Lt. Col. Dean Ladd and Steven Weingartner, Faithful Warriors, A Combat Marine Remembers the Pacific War, (Annapolis, Maryland: Naval Institute Press, 2007), pp. 206-207.

[28] Ibid, p. 207.

[29] Ibid., p. 75.

[30] James Joyner, "Desmond Doss, Pacifist Medal of Honor Recipient, Dies at 87", http://www.outsidethebeltway.com/desmond_doss_pacifist_medal_o f_honor_recipient_dies_at_87/, (24 March, 2006).

[31] J.F. Sargent and Dustin Koski, "The 6 Most Aggressively Badass Things Done by Pacifists", http://www.cracked.com/article_20157_the-6-most-aggressively-badass-things-done-by-pacifists.html, (23 December, 2012).

[32] Ibid.

[33] Adam Bernstein, Lauded Conscientious Objector Desmond T. Doss Sr., http://www.washingtonpost.com/wp-dyn/content/article/2006/03/25/AR2006032501181.html, (March 26, 2006).

[34] Mark Allman, Who Would Jesus Kill?, (Winona, MN: Anselm Academics, 2008), pp. 63-69. Allman notes that there are some who identify as pacifist and believe that while it is important to approach conflict with the desire to bring peace without hostility, that conviction might change if the initial approaches to seeking justice fail. In the event of the latter, war would be justified. For our purposes, we will focus on the first group where the conviction is

never to rise in war. Peace is always the objective, and acting to achieve it through non-aggression is right.

[35] What follows comes from Mejia's autobiography, Camilo Mejia, Road from Ar Ramadi, (New York: The New Press, 2007).

[36] Ibid, p. 15.

[37] Ibid, pp. 15-16.

[38] Ibid, pp. 22-24, 299.

[39] Ibid., pp. 26ff, 40ff, 117.

[40] Ibid, p. 126.

[41] Ibid, p. 299.

[42] James Tollefson, The Strength Not to Fight—An Oral History of Conscientious Objectors of the Vietnam War, (Boston: Little, Brown and Company, 1993).

[43] Ibid, pp. 88-89.

[44] Ibid, pp. 5-6.

[45] Alexander Moseley, Pacifism, Internet Encyclopedia of Philosophy, http://www.iep.utm.edu/pacifism/, (April 19, 2005).

[46] James Alan Fox and Jack Levin, Extreme Killing: Understanding Serial and Mass Murder, (Sage Publishing: Thousand Oaks, CA), p. 34.

[47] Under the general heading of Antisocial Personality Disorder, sociopaths are classified with psychopaths in the Diagnostic and Statistical Manual of Mental Disorders V (DSM V) since they share overall similarities, specifically in this discussion, a lack of empathy, no moral regard and a willingness to kill without concern. Some do distinguish between the two, going beyond what is offered in the DSM V, and see the psychopath as one who is better able to get along with people, follow social protocol, develop a sense of emotional relation, and manipulate others; all these things they can do in order to achieve ultimate goals. This kind of person could work his way through the military and actually find success. Hence, we will refer in this discussion to those of this profile as psychopaths. This does not mean that sociopaths could not also make it in the military but their strong anger states seem to make them more likely to fail in military service. Kara Mayer Robinson as reviewed by Joseph Goldberg, MD, "Sociopath vs. Psychopath: What's the Difference?" http://www.webmd.com/mental-health/features/sociopath-psychopath-difference, (2005-2015).

⁴⁸ J.T.O., "Murderers who have served in the U.S. Military: A Database", https://ajaor.wordpress.com/2012/12/05/murderers-who-have-served-in-the-u-s-military-a-database/, (05 December, 2012). This study is included in AJAOR: American Journal of Arcane and Obscure Research, "about AJAOR", https://ajaor.wordpress.com/about/, (August, 2015).

⁴⁹ Ibid., pp. 659-663.

⁵⁰Dave Grossman, On Killing: The Psychological Cost of Learning to Kill in War and Society, (New York, NY: Little, Brown and Company, 1995), p. 185.

⁵¹ Glenn Gray, The Warriors, p. 106.

⁵² Ibid, pp. 106-107.

⁵³ Ibid.

⁵⁴ Ibid, p. 109.

⁵⁵ Ibid, p. 122.

⁵⁶ Ibid, p. 123.

⁵⁷ Ibid, p. 124.

⁵⁸ Ibid, [boldness added for emphasis].

⁵⁹ Ibid, pp. 116-117.

⁶⁰ Ibid, p. 116.

⁶¹ Ibid, p. 125.

⁶² Ibid, p. 111.

⁶³ Ibid.

⁶⁴ Ibid, p. 120.

⁶⁵ Grossman, On Killing, p. 87.

⁶⁶ Ibid., pp. 30-31.

⁶⁷ Ibid., p. 89.

⁶⁸ Ibid.

⁶⁹ Ibid., pp. 92-93.

⁷⁰ Fred W. Baker III, "Al Qaeda Recruits Children, Women for Terror Missions, American Forces Press Service," http://www.defenselink.mil/news/newsarticle.aspx?id=48885, (6 February, 2008); and Now, "Over 50 ISIS child soldiers killed in 2015", https://now.mmedia.me/lb/en/NewsReports/565591-over-50-isis-child-soldiers-killed-in-2015, (20 July, 2015).

⁷¹ Ibid., p. 93.

⁷² Miller, p. 137.

⁷³ Ibid., p. 142.

Section III

Establishing a Moral Compass for War

Chapter Nine
Basis for Morality in War

Chapter Ten
Just War: What is it for Combatants?

Chapter Eleven
Moral Injury: Consequence of Missing or Misaligned Morality

CHAPTER NINE

BASIS FOR MORALITY IN WAR

There are some things we know that are true but we cannot show why; they are self-evident. Laws of logic are that way. Take the law of excluded middle. I know that a proposition, or statement regarding some fact, is either true or false; this is a motorcycle or it is not. That same kind of awareness about truth is apparent to us as well for considerations regarding moral good. I know that love and not evil is right and I know this ultimately for no other reason than I know it. Justice as well as another aspect of the moral law is something that I likewise know is proper to uphold, and for combatants, because of their nature, they will rise to ensure that this justice is upheld. Yet, as we all know combatants, like the rest of us, can fail at times in knowing the application of what is just in situations. Thus, it is vital to do all we can to ensure that combatants have a very clear picture of how justice relates to them in war. Emasculating combatants is failing in this regard.

From the issue of war-types, we consider the topic of morality. To know why combatants should go to war and kill has to be answered. To take a life without moral justification is murder. It might not seem this way to combatants whose focus in the moment is duty to an oath and nation. But that simple resolve will not sustain them post combat. At that point, they question what it meant to kill, and without any just cause behind that action, veterans face a crisis of conscience and being. This has to be avoided. We want just combatants in just battles for just wars. That requires knowing a moral cause for war, and it requires ultimately knowing what moral goodness is in the first place. What, then, is it? This will be our focus.

In his sardonic and brutally honest assessment of war, Johnny Rico in *Blood Makes the Grass Grow Green* provides insight which for him shows that war is wholly nonsensical. It is not a testimony that compares with what I saw, heard or continue to find in my counsel and work with those in the military. Yet, I have no doubt that his central antiwar observations and beliefs are shared by others. What makes his work valuable, though, notwithstanding your position on war, is the frankness with which he presents his views, even if he might be perceived as sacrilegious, crass or seemingly un-American. Also of value is that he shares his thoughts on topics that few are willing to discuss. Let us consider what he offers.

In one dialogue, Rico forces the reader to consider the issue of why soldiers fight. He says,

I have become fascinated with the responses to the question of what motivated people to join the Army. For most soldiers it was an afterthought, because they failed in their first or second choices and retreated with their tails between their legs to the U.S. Army. For others it was the call of adventure and the opportunity that just maybe they'd get to kill somebody, a perennial favorite of testosterone-laden teenagers with no outlet for aggression or for testing themselves in a safety-conscious, politically correct society.[1]

Rico's summation here of why people join the Army is something that most would likely see as devoid of nobility in itself. Rather than these responses, the idealistic hopes for enlistment are related to service of country, protection of rights, and prevention of worldly injustice. These responses endear us to those in the service. Rico's words, thusly, are unsettling. Fortunately, it does get better.

In one case, as Rico goes on ferreting out causes for enlistment, he finds a soldier, Sergeant Derrens, whose ambitions to join the Army are honorable. Derrens says that he came into the service *to protect Americans* and because as he says, *this is his country*.[2] Finally, we have an answer that is admirable, and even Rico when he hears the words is humbled. He says, "I'm suddenly ashamed of my own selfish motivation for joining. I pretend that protecting people, my fellow Americans, also factored into my decision. Sergeant Derrens blows me away with his innate all-around goodness."[3]

Rico's reaction is understandable. Nobility, as a quality, stands out, and those who possess it and genuinely guide their decisions by it leave us in awe. But in this case, before Rico becomes overly enamored by this Sergeant's response, he returns and offers an interesting challenge. He says,

Sergeant, if the only justification for your devotion to country is that this one is yours, then so what? This one is yours, and that one is his, and that one over there is hers. If everybody is just responding to their environments and adopting that as what they fight for, then what's the difference between anybody's point of view? Where's the external validity for one person's idea over another? Don't you think it's important to have external validity? I mean, you're willing to die for America, aren't you? If you're willing to die for America and her ideas, shouldn't your faith in her have external validity, some ultimate truth, something more than just that this is where you were born? ...By this rationale, if you were Palestinian, then you'd fight for Palestine because that's where you were born. You'd fight for Afghanistan because that's where you were born. There has to be an external validity to an idea, a justification for one side that's so apparent that it's obvious to external observers who is right and who is wrong. Don't you see? Your own justification for American nationalism is, in itself, an argument against American patriotism![4]

This is a wonderful observation and Rico is to be lauded for raising it. It is an issue that no one confronts, but why not? Every person owns the responsibility to know why he fights, and the basis for that justification needs to be something that convinces him that his cause rises above his enemy's. A person needs to know that he fights for the sake of truth, and nothing else, and that his enemy does not. That is the only way to justify the need to kill that enemy. No one wants to kill for reasons that are not founded in justice. To fight and kill others just because they have been born elsewhere is murder. It is no wonder then, given what Rico shows about all of this, that he further says, "My mind reels with the enormity of the number of soldiers I imagine dying throughout the course of civilization for causes that they would've fought against and died for had they simply fought for the home turf. ...It was all absurd. The whole damn world was absurd."[5]

I really like what Rico has to say. War is insanity if it is waged solely for the sake of national and clannish identity, the establishment through power of one people over another, and while this might not be noticed by combatants during war, it will become apparent to most after war. When they return home, they will then think about what they have done. If those acts lack sound justification, they will be bothered. What will make their inner turmoil worse will be those who come up to them in their confusion and say things like "that war was not just." "It was wrong to invade that country." These kinds of statements, right or wrong, will mess with their minds. Warriors and others will soon seriously wonder if what they did was right and if those whom they killed were actually murdered. It will bring about the devitalization and debilitation of all combatants.

An obvious question is now before us: How does one know when he stands for what is just while the enemy stands in unrighteousness? Getting to this answer will involve a few steps. Let us start with what we can say about the human condition when it comes to morality. This is a challenging step as it involves discussion about foundations of moral truth. Yet, we will be involved in this discussion briefly and only with enough detail to provide that essential grounding which motivates combatants in war. From there, we will turn to consider how all of this applies to the issues regarding a just basis for war.

Central to the idea of morality is that people have some inner sense of rightness or goodness. They have an awareness of what is good as has been proposed by philosophers throughout the ages, most notably by Aristotle in the earliest of times. He stated this: "Every art or applied science and every systematic investigation, and similarly every action and choice, seem to aim at some good; the good, therefore, has been well defined as that at which all things aim."[6]

This belief about goodness, a realization of what morality involves, is not something in its essence that comes from a practical or useful observation about a way to live (e.g., do not lie because you do not want people to lie to you). It is rather a truth that is simply known. In this sense, what we are talking about with the belief of goodness is what can be called a first principle.

A first principle is a self-evident truth that is believed for no other reason than it is known to be right. It is accepted solely because it reveals itself as such. It is "a basic, foundational proposition or assumption that cannot be deduced from any other proposition or assumption. In mathematics, first principles are referred to as axioms or postulates."[7] These kinds of truths once revealed are immediately evident. They have no justification and do not need one as they are obvious once known.[8]

Consider something in math like the transitive axiom which states that if $a = b$ and $b = c$ then $a = c$. In this case, I know for certain that whatever "a" is it is equal to "c". I know this because it is apparent to me. Thus, I do not need to go through a process, for instance, of determining whether this axiom works in every instance, substituting different things for the values represented by the letters to see if the axiom upholds. I know that it will. The truth of the

272

matter is self-evident. In fact, I am also fully aware that there really is no way to disprove what I know about this axiom anyway as there is no place to go for verification of it. It is simply what I know to be true. Likely, I will need to teach what I know about this truth to a person until that proverbial light goes on for him. But after that, that person too just gets it.

John Finnis in his book about morality, *Natural Law and Natural Rights*, speaks about the nature of these kinds of truths. He says, "In every field there is and must be, at some point or points, an end to derivation and inference. At that point or points we find ourselves in face of the self-evident, which makes possible all subsequent inferences in that field."[9] There are simply some things that we know by virtue of the fact that they are self-evident. Finnis lists quite a few of these self-evident principles of truths,[10] but his overall point is that these principles of "theoretical rationality are not demonstrable, for they are presupposed."[11] This says nothing, however, about their objective reality. For "anyone who has experience of inquiry into matters of fact or of theoretical (including historical and philosophical) judgment [knows that] …they do not stand in need of demonstration."[12] At some point, you realize with foundational judgments of truth that they simply exist and it is impossible to go beyond that. C. S. Lewis brings this point to great clarity by saying:

You cannot go on explaining away forever, or you will find that you have explained explanation itself away. You cannot go on 'seeing through' things forever. The whole point of seeing through something is to see something through it. It is good that you can see through a window, because the garden beyond is opaque. But if you see through everything, then everything is transparent, and a wholly transparent world is an invisible world. So to 'see through' all things is the same as not to see.[13]

What we are getting at so far is that some knowledge depends ultimately on an intuitional basis which offers truth that just is.[14] One facet of that knowledge, as proposed, is a self-evident moral goodness. It is knowing what is morally good with nothing other to ground it. G. E. Moore in his landmark book on ethics, *Principia Ethica*, provides an insightful description of this kind of self-evident knowing in terms of the principles of the moral good. He says,

The expression 'self-evident' means properly that the proposition so called is evident or true, by itself alone; that it is not an inference from some proposition other than itself. The expression does not mean that the proposition is true, because it is evident to you or me or all mankind, because in other words it appears to us to be true. That a proposition appears to be true can never be a valid argument that it really is. By saying that a proposition is self-evident, we mean emphatically that its appearing so to us, is not the reason why it is true: for we mean that it has absolutely no reason. It would not be a self-evident proposition, if we could say of it: I cannot think otherwise and therefore it is true. For then its evidence or proof would not lie in itself, but in something else, namely our conviction of it. That it appears true to us may indeed be the cause of our asserting it, or the reason why we think and say that it is true: but a reason in this sense is something utterly different from a logical reason, or reason why something is true.[15]

This is a tremendous explanation of what is meant when talking about self-evident epistemic foundations. The critical issue is that what one knows in this way is known simply. One can offer nothing else. It is just the nature of this kind of knowing.

Importantly though, while this determination of the moral good is self-evident and thus, not knowledge as some would claim which is based on human nature (e.g., emotivism) or the experience of it (e.g., utilitarianism), this in itself does not disconnect it from revealing what is experientially good for humanity. For example, take the matter of the sanctity of human life. My knowing that it is morally right to honor the integrity of a person is something that I know apart from any experience or practical consideration of it. Yet, in saying that, it does not then follow that that I cannot see in practical situations of life what it means rationally or practically to honor life. Of course, I can. I can know both things and this is true as well when it comes to any awareness I have about the moral good. What I know by virtue alone of its appearing to me as right is still something that can be evident to me in my experience of and decisions for life.

Robert George speaks about this in his book *In Defense of the Natural Law*. He says about activity regarding the moral good that "[o]ur knowledge of the most fundamental principles of human well-being and fulfillment may be underived—because these principles are self-evident practical truths—yet remain knowledge of human well-being and fulfillment."[16] For this reason, we can say that the activity we know we should pursue to bring about the moral good though perfectly suited to nurture human nature is not known because it is judged to be good for humanity. It is rather the case as George goes on to explain about these acts of the moral good:

They are known in non-inferential acts of understanding in which we grasp possible ends or purposes as worthwhile for their own sakes. The most basic reasons for action are those reasons whose intelligibility does not depend on deeper or still more fundamental reasons. As *basic* reasons, they cannot be derived; for there is nothing more fundamental that could serve as a premise for a logical derivation. Therefore, they must be self-evident. [17]

In the end, morality is simply what we know is right and it has truth in itself, not as a means to some end. Yet, all of that does not prevent us from forming understanding about how the moral good aligns with human activity.

Something further to offer in knowing the moral good is that as we go through life realizing all that is involved in it, we find that the activity of goodness itself is purposed to enable life to flourish. Mortimer Adler offers this as the first precept of the natural law, along with avoiding evil.[18] For him, the true goodness of humanity is to realize in life all things which allow that life to be lived to its fullness. However, this is not something ever attained in a moment, as he says, but something toward which a life constantly moves: "The human good, the good for man as man, is a whole life made good by the possession of all the real goods toward which the common human nature of each individual tends for the satisfaction of its inherent needs."[19] He goes further to offer this:

The common-sense view of what is involved in making a good life for one's self can appeal to the truth of two basic propositions—both self-evidently true, both intuitively known. The first is that the good is desirable. The second is that one ought to desire or seek that which is really good for one's self and only that which is really good. In the light of these two propositions, common sense can see that one ought to make a good life for one's self, but only if a good life is conceived as consisting of things that are really good—the things that a man needs, not just those that he may want whether he needs them or not.[20]

Central here is that the moral good is about wholeness of being. It is to exist in that perfect state of being in which one is created to be. It is realizing in life everything that is needed to flourish to the extent that those things lead to genuine happiness, not just in a temporary state but for the larger purpose of one's life. This is a foundational aspect of moral goodness.

Given this, as Adler goes on to express: "And the moral obligation that each man has to make a good life for himself—to achieve this *totum bonum* in his individual life—is not only a categorical ought; it is also one that is universally binding on all men in the same way."[21] Thus, as much as we all share in humanity, we personally and communally share both in knowing what goodness is and what enables that condition of being for all.

Before moving on, let us do a quick review. First, when it comes to the principle of a self-evident moral goodness, what we discussed was how it is known simply, without any proof than that we know it.

A second important piece of this discussion is that regardless of the fact that moral goodness is known to us not as a result of experience in life, we still are able to gain comprehension about what it is to experience and do the morally good.

Still another important part of this about the moral good is that all aspects of what it can be, everything that the moral good is, is what enables an ideal state of existence to be. The moral good, therefore, becomes that means by which one is able to live the 'good life'; a life completed in knowing every good possible in so far as it enables one's life to flourish in its most pure state. This means seeking real goods; goods which do not temporarily offer satiety or completeness, but which always help to gain one's fullest potential. These goods would be the things that continuously ensure life, the liberty to have that life, and the freedom to have completeness in that life.

Further, it is obvious that we are not focused on a list of rules in saying all of this, but on a principle in the broadest sense that captures what morality should be: wholeness of being in its perfect and most complete state. The persuasiveness in this is that we will easily find universal agreement to what is offered when we consider the essence of it. Who would argue against a morality that enables the fullest existence of life and the true liberty to pursue real goodness to its fullness? No one of clear mind, I assume, as it is self-evident. Hence, let us use this as the starting place. From here, we can offer a more practical view of what the moral good reveals by considering a moral truth for goodness upon which all seem to agree. What we will talk about here is rape.

When it comes to goodness, we clearly sense that an aspect of it is to act toward all by regarding real needs for wholeness, maintaining the integrity or purity of everyone. This is just something that we know. In comprehending this, though, as we connect it to an act like rape, we can easily see that this kind of activity cannot be defended. For as much as goodness is about enabling life to flourish to its proper end, we see that this is an act that in no way contributes to that. Even as a means for the rapist in imposing control or sating a sexual urge, rape cannot be defended. For in this case, rape is self-defeating to the extent that it misappropriates the essence of what goodness is with respect to sexuality and involvement in it (e.g. a misuse of power). Therefore, it never has the potential of realizing its purpose. Rape, thusly, is devoid of goodness. It is evil. It does not lead to wholeness for the one abused. It is further a reflection of the lack of wholeness and being in the rapist. That is why, regarding the rapist, this person needs rehabilitation. He needs to face justice through punishment with the goal of bringing back a rational state of mind that realizes what it is to achieve goodness in its most complete form.

But again, these things we know. We know them simply, self-evidently, and we see the force of them clearly elucidated in this example where the corruption of goodness is clear.[22] Those who without question become most deeply aware of this are victims of rape. For them, it is "a form of violence that causes destructive consequences to both the physical and spiritual health of women [and men]."[23] This is true even for children who likely do not even understand what the event is about. All that they know is that a violation has occurred, and it is one that cannot be dismissed simply after their body heals:

278

Child survivors feel numb and lost. Cast adrift in a horrifying world, they sense that a part of them has died. They wander through each day feeling as if they exist in a hollow shell. And then the terror returns and the pain is so great that they are plunged into what can only be described as a living hell. All these feelings persist, even if they are repressing the memories of abuse. Is it any wonder that abused children feel like they are dead? Or wish they had died? And yet these children live. They cling to life as if that action alone can defeat their attackers.[24]

Given these observations, we now see how goodness informs us in practical activities of life in terms of what it is to have existence in its most complete sense. In this case, we talk about rape and we see that goodness as related to self in its perfect order is not found in this activity. That much should be blatant.

Moving slightly forward, then, we can say as well that what we find to be true about rape as a practice that fails to establish goodness is something that could be shown in many aspects of how a person knows goodness in connection to self. For the core elements of what goodness establishes remain the same irrespective of the activity: namely, preservation of self, ordering the existence of self, and doing this in a way that brings about one's most complete state, *totum bonum*.

Since this much is intuitive to all, it is not surprising to see these very elements captured dynamically as well in the Preamble to the Constitution of the United States: "We hold these truths to be self-evident, that all men are created equal, that they are endowed by their Creator with certain inalienable rights, that among these are life, liberty and the pursuit of happiness."[25] Also, since these foundational truths are not just something particular to those in this country but are fundamental to all being, we are not shocked to see them guiding all nations as evidenced in the United Nations Universal Declaration of Human Rights. In that document we read,

(Article 1) All human beings are born free and equal in dignity and rights. They are endowed with reason and conscience and should act towards one another in a spirit of brotherhood. (Article 2) Everyone is entitled to all the rights and freedoms set forth in this Declaration, without distinction of any kind, such as race, colour, sex, language, religion, political or other opinion, national or social origin, property, birth or other status. Furthermore, no distinction shall be made on the basis of the political, jurisdictional or international status of the country or territory to which a person belongs, whether it be independent, trust, non-self-governing or under any other limitation of sovereignty. (Article 3) Everyone has the right to life, liberty and security of person.[26]

This perfectly shows how the revelation of goodness can be captured in practical rights.[27] It shows too how we cannot dismiss what we have spent time defending, the reality of a self-evident moral goodness that guides humans to what has been called their *totum bonum* and that the keeping of that just seems right.[28]

In having laid out how we know what moral goodness is and what it looks like in practice, we are almost ready to apply this to combatants and war. However, before that step is taken, there a few other issues that should be discussed. One issue is that when we speak of self-evident goodness that guides the activity of existence to its proper end, it is possible that confusion can arise about how to act in goodness. Humans can err in understanding and activity as related to the moral good. They can be immoral as we considered with rapists. They can even be convinced, again as with rapists, that this corruption of existence is somehow right. This is not a statement against the reality of a self-evident goodness, but a realization that people can be deficient both in their ability to know goodness and in their exercising of it. We experience this constantly when emotions, desires, illness, corruption, urges or the like create such a pull to abuse the self or others to gain what we want in the moment that we dismiss and even deaden ourselves to what we otherwise would know to be right. Sometimes and mercifully we are able to see the corruption later, but at times the immoral practice empowers our decadence. Americans segregated races until a true appraisal of moral goodness was realized. During this process, it was not moral goodness that changed but people in understanding what it was and how it applied. In the end, every example of corruption in knowing goodness does show the need to be ever aware of what might obscure morality. Yet, this does not mean that goodness itself as a self-evident principle does not exist.

A second matter to address about a self-evident principle of moral goodness is that if we really do not believe in it, then there is no such thing as moral transformation toward the good. Yet, we know that moral progress exists in as much as we know that when misogyny, pedophilia, wanton cruelty, slavery, genocide and the like are overturned that it is good. Something lost was gained, restored, and enabled with respect to goodness such that a more perfect state of understanding the good and living it out was permitted.

A final thing to say on this, although much more could be offered, is that whenever people proclaim that there is no such thing as a moral goodness or that it is only subjective in nature, that argument holds up only until the goodness of those people is put in question. At that point, these people will proclaim violation of rights which they want restored. But how can they appeal to a standard for rights when as far as they state all are allowed to act as they see fit? They really cannot. In truth, their protest and assertion of rights shows that they truly do uphold in some manner a universal self-evident truth of goodness. It is hard to deny this. People just seem to have a common basis for understanding what is morally right.

In having given these clarifications, it is fair to say that challenges could be offered to them but then as well, detailed counter arguments could be provided. Such explicit debate would, however, detract from our purpose. Hence, we must leave that for now. But what is here at the least becomes critical in giving a basis for moral goodness and this will enable us to see how it applies to combatants. So let us begin to do that.

We start by taking what we learned and going back to the dilemma that Rico placed before us. Remember that for him, fighting an enemy strictly for the sake of country and brethren is something that while being honorable is still not right. For as he shows, those reasons for killing another when it is the basis for war become empty when considering that the enemy is fighting for the same thing. So how do we address this now? There are several things to say.

First, a clear answer to Rico is provided in the self-evident principle of goodness. Warriors and all should not fight because they are from a different place or race than others. If they fight, it is because they believe that they are upholding in some way this self-evident understanding of what it is to realize universal goodness. To fight is to maintain and uphold one's sense of what is good, of what enables one's own integrity and that of all others. This grounds a combatant's purpose, orders his world, and enables him to know that he is not arbitrarily, vainly, or egoistically killing another. He acts in an ultimate sense for the universal ordering of morality, a self-evident revelation of what is right and good for the utmost integrity of all. If a combatant follows this, standing for what is universally morally right, he cannot also then fight for what is morally wrong.

Considering this, it can be stated that when a country is actively violating goodness, the rights of people, that is a cause for war by a righteous nation. Let that righteous nation rise, therefore, to execute justice on behalf of the oppressed. That is good. At that point, you have a right for war that rises above the enemy's right. This is what Rico fails to see.

However, that is not all that we should say. In fairness to Rico, it is still not enough to state that combatants should fight and kill because they believe that they fight for the moral good when their enemy fails to recognize and honor this. The reason is because while one side in a war might say this, it only brings up another question; What should happen in those situations when the enemy believes the same thing, when two warring parties both believe that their cause is based exclusively on the fundamental goodness and rights of its people? Now we posit two opposing camps that fight because they both believe that they stand for the moral truth of goodness. In this scenario, who has the ultimate right? Who is the real enemy of goodness? There are several things to state about this.

One response is to say that it is possible that a nation could be convinced that they are right about something and fight for it and be wholly wrong. Personal or collective conviction does not establish moral truth. Moral truth in fullness can be established only if one sees and executes it rightly, and here we are talking about truth in the sense of some belief that remains justifiably true; that is, a moral truth for goodness that consistently fails to be overturned in examination of it.[29]

Hence, when it comes to this question of war, if one side in battle errs in standing for moral goodness, then it is only the nation that stands for that moral truth which has the legitimate cause to fight, and thus, they alone are the ones who rightly stand to stop injustice. The nation in error may never see this, but that is their miscalculation. People do as noted misjudge moral truth and suffer the consequences: e.g., fighting for the cause of ethnic or racial segregation only later to realize the immorality of such a practice, and thereafter, to suffer incredible loss and the extended ramifications that come from misguided moral reasoning.

What this means overall and specifically in regards to Rico's question is that even if two nations oppose each other in battle and then fight for perceived moral truth, this does not make war insane if one nation indeed stands for the ultimate moral truth. That just nation is honorable in action and displays a noble cause to fight. The question will always be whether one nation in a battle can make this claim. On this, all need to be ever certain about their convictions for moral truth and to fight for them only as they remain firm in the knowledge and need to bring about that perceived justice.

Looking further into this question of two nations at war for what each perceives to be moral uprightness, though, another way to look at this dilemma is to say that it is possible for two opposing nations, each with their own convictions, to be convinced that they must go to war for moral goodness, but then, for each to be wrong. In this case, different than the last, neither nation upholds the moral high-ground. Certainly here, one might consider it nonsense for these nations to battle. In truth, it would be. Both nations should have done a better job in discerning true justice; i.e., what it is to bring about moral goodness for all. That neither did and that both fight for unjust causes will sadly lead to their demise. This does make war about madness as Rico would say. It also shows even more how vital it is for a nation, not just some in that nation but for all, to labor to know the moral cause for war. Failing to gain moral truth and where it applies brings great and senseless destruction.

But this point brings us to a final and certainly a critical response to offer to Rico. It is this. Let us say that in pursuing war two opposing nations do all that they can do to discern, prior to fighting, that they do stand for moral goodness. And then, once they have gone through this, they still decide that they must fight. On this, how can we say that these nations should not fight to stand and defend what they believe to be morally right? Unquestionably, one or both might be in error. But that does not mean that they should not rise to defend what they truly believe is morally right. I truly see no other way to resolve this. It sounds like a peculiar answer, but it is nonetheless true.

If a nation and its people see gross injustice being committed and they have questioned themselves to determine the moral rightness of their belief, and have thereby, become convinced of the need to act for those whose moral goodness is being slaughtered, then unquestionably they must act. People must go forward and make a stand for moral truth when they believe unequivocally that the fight is about standing against an intractable, repugnant evil that is ruinous to all sense of life, liberty and goodness, and which cannot be silenced in any other way than war. For the sake of goodness, for the sake of the integrity of a just nation who sees evil and knows that it must act, let that nation rise in battle as they feel compelled to do so. Moral truth must be defended for the sake of goodness. If anything, what this truly shows is that utter caution needs to be had when it comes to declaring war, and that there is a need for extreme certainty of what moral truth is. But ultimately, it too shows that to rise in honest defense of people whose rights are perceived to be abysmally disregarded in scandalous evil must be done.

What is often overlooked in this discussion is the fact that what is offered here as an explanation as to why two sides must fight is something that goes to the heart of our approach not only to moral truth but to all truth. What option do we have but to stand for what we believe? This is what Rico misses. He chides combatants for fighting when their justifications are the same. On this, I agree, but only when it comes to the things akin to what he listed: nationality, race, benefits, orders, loved ones, those by my side.... These are not in and of themselves ultimate reasons to go to war.

War has to be about foundational moral principles of truth as they are known to the deepest core of being, and only then, when this is known in such a way that not addressing these rights will destroy all potential for goodness. When a nation reaches this place, what other option does it have but to stand for justice? If you truly believe something, you will and must act in accordance with it. You do not jump off of tall buildings because you believe that there is this mysterious force called gravity, a force that you cannot see or that anyone has ever seen. Regardless, you act every day in accordance with this perceived force in mind because you believe it is real and it defines your life. You do this as well with many kinds of perceived truths. We act on what we know and believe to be true. If we did not, we would suffer and die.

But then too, that we act this way in a moral sense is no different. Hence, with our moral sense always open to consider what might have been overlooked, we should go about doing what we can to ensure goodness for all to the best of our ability.

For a nation, it means martialing its resources to make a stand for what is right. For those in the military, it means owning your part in the battle to the extent that it fits with war-type. For others, it might mean protest of some kind because there is a feeling that this war or any war is not right. Yet, wherever people fall out, acting on moral truth is always essential. Stand for your convictions. If you do not, then you are the one who refuses to do what you believe to be right. You are the one who fails to live for life, liberty and goodness as you perceive it. You are the one who is truly mad. Inactivity in the face of knowing what we ought to do is worthless and does not lead to well-being. If you perceive that a train is coming, get off the track. If it is only an illusion, you will have to deal with that and find out why you missed truth. But to act in either case was paramount and the only way to try your best to find wholeness in being.

To not live by what we believe to be true, especially in a moral sense, is to reject self-integrity and to lose one's sense of self-identity. Thus, in answer to Rico, if truth for a combatant is found in fighting for some ultimate moral cause, he compromises his well-being if he chooses not to fight because it is theoretically conceivable that he is wrong.

We need to be, at the end of the day, truth seekers in morality and in all matters of truth. We should be people who continuously examine the critical issues of our lives with a fervent desire to know what is right. This conviction should be derived from studies and revelation about what is right, with a desire to uphold these rights, but always with humility to be challenged.

Conclusion

The kind of challenge offered here is good for those who fight in war. It is recognition about the realities of their lives. Since the moral right is what is good for them, fighting is not just to stand for moral truth; it is to realize self-integrity by protecting goodness. In this sense, healthy combatants fight for three interrelated reasons: 1) because they fundamentally believe to know what is morally right; 2) because they want to protect that; and 3) because in protecting that right, they are realizing their completeness in justice. To help them in this quest, therefore, let going to war be about preparing combatants to establish and maintain that integrity in being. This we have to get right. Otherwise, we do find Rico to be right that war is insanity.

What has been offered should be a starting place for all to explore the foundations of moral truth. For if we are going to rise to kill, we must know why and have that inner moral sense aligned with that reason. Let us then discuss the ethical process by which we know goodness as it relates to rights of life and liberty (metaethics), gain clarity as well about how this this connects to values like courage or honor (normative ethics), and dialogue about how this translates into action (practical ethics). These conversations have to happen for the sake of combatants. To send them to war not knowing moral truth and all that surrounds it is to cripple their conscience and moral being. That would be to our shame. We must ensure ethical training for war. Going into more depth in this consideration is our next focus, seeking a just cause for a just battle in a just war. Nothing less should be the foundation for war.

Endnotes

---

[1] Johnny Rico, Blood Makes then Grass Grow Green, p. 120.

[2] Ibid., pp. 120-121.

[3] Ibid., p. 121.

[4] Ibid., pp. 121-122.

[5] Ibid., p. 123.

[6] Aristotle, Nicomachean Ethics, (New York: The Bobbs-Merrill Company, 1962), p. 3.

[7] Ellis Washington, "On Euclid, Archimedes and first principles," "http://www.renewamerica.com/columns/washington/140531, (May 31, 2014).

[8] Francis Beckwith and Gregory Koukl, Relativism: Feet Firmly Planted in Mid-Air, (Michigan: Baker Books, 1998), p. 59.

[9] John Finnis, Natural Law and Natural Rights, (Oxford: Clarendon Press, 1980), p. 70.

[10] Ibid., p. 69, Here are seven such principles Finnis lists: One such principle is that the principles of logic, for example the forms of deductive inference, are to be used and adhered to in all one's thinking, even though no non-circular proof of their validity is possible (since any proof would employ them). Another is that an adequate reason why anything is so rather than otherwise is to be expected, unless one has reason not to expect such a reason.... A third is that self-defeating theses are to be abandoned.... A fourth is that phenomena are to be regarded as real unless there is some reason to distinguish between appearance and reality. A fifth is that a full description of data is to be preferred to partial descriptions, and that an account or explanation of phenomena is not to be accepted if it requires or postulates something inconsistent with the data for which it is supposed to account. A sixth is that a method of interpretation which is successful is to be relied upon in further similar cases until contrary reason appears. A seventh is that theoretical accounts which are simple, predictively successful, and explanatorily powerful are to be accepted in preference to other accounts.

[11] Ibid.

[12] Ibid.

[13] C. S. Lewis, The Abolition of Man, (San Francisco, California: Harper Collins, 2001), p. 91.

[14] Consider the example as well of one person being taller than another. You do not need to know anything about the people involved to be able to understand what this means. "'You need only whatever experience is necessary to understand the concepts involved, such as 'being taller than.' To believe this proposition a priori [without prior sense experience], one need only consider it. No particular experience—perceptual, testimonial, memorial, or introspective—is necessary.' Intuitional truth doesn't require a defense—a justification of the steps that brought one to this knowledge---because this kind of truth does not result from reasoning by steps to a conclusion. It's a truth that's obvious upon consideration." Francis Beckwith and Gregory Koukl, Relativism: Feet Firmly Planted in Mid-Air, (Michigan: Baker Books, 1998), p. 56.

[15] G. E. Moore, Principia Ethica, (Cambridge: University Press, 2002), p. 193.

[16] Robert George, In Defense of Natural Law, (Oxford, Oxford University Press, 1999), p. 87.

[17] Ibid., p. 85.

[18] Mortimer Adler, "The Nature of Natural Law", http://www.faculty.umb.edu/gary_zabel/Courses/Morals%20and%20Law/M+L/adler_naturallaw.html, (28 January, 2016).

[19] Mortimer Adler, The Time of Our Lives, (New York: Fordham University Press, 1996), p. 111.

[20] Ibid., p. 98.

[21] Ibid., p. 111.

[22] There are examples where rape is used as a tactic in warfare. This does not disprove rape as morally wrong in the eyes of those who abuse their enemy in this way. One reason is because those who do this would at the same time quickly say that raping their own people is wrong. Hence, to them rape is wrong. Why then do they rape? The reason is because they disregard facts that would make rape morally wrong with their enemy. That is to say, when it comes to their enemy they claim that these people are prizes, less than human, property or the like. Changing the facts about who these people are excuses them in that they can sexually molest these "objects"

without violating what they know to be true about sexual practices. Rape is not rape for them as long as those they act against are not human or do not deserve rights for some reason. This same train of illogic is used by some religious groups where women are not considered human because they have no soul (e.g., Alawites). With these people, there can be no rape of women since they are objects to be used at a man's discretion. Still more, another reason people can rape without moral conviction is because like all of us they find justification in the moment to make what they otherwise would see as a wrong a right. We all do this. In this case, the justification is that the enemy needs to be punished, the victor has a right to use the enemy as they desire, their sexual need in the moment trumps other considerations, the person deserved it or really wanted it, etc.... Regardless, try to rape these same perpetrators later or those that they love and they will object because they too realize that rape is wrong.
[23] Gina Messina-Dysert, "Rape and Spiritual Death", Feminist Theology. vol. 20 (2) 120-132. (January 2012). [Emphasis on men added.]
[24] Elizabeth Adams, Understanding the Trauma of Childhood Psycho-Sexual Abuse, (Bedford, Massachusetts: Mills & Sanderson, 1994), p. 6.
[25] "Declaration of Independence (Preamble)," http://users.wfu.edu/zulick/340/Declaration.html, (31 October, 2017).
[26] The Universal Declaration of Human Rights, http://www.un.org/en/documents/udhr/, (10 September, 2009).
[27] "Almost all countries have now ratified a later document, the International Bill of Rights, which consists of the Universal Declaration of Human Rights (1948), the International Covenant on Civil and Political Rights (1966), and the International Covenant on Economic, Social and Cultural Rights (1966). Although the process of international ratification makes these legal rights in international law, human rights constitute the foundation, which is distinctively moral in nature." Anthony Hartle, Moral Issues in Military Decision Making, (Lawrence, Kansas: University Press of Kansas, 2004), p. 87.

[28] C. S. Lewis cites many examples of timeless universal moral norms as well: 1) the law of general beneficence; 2) the law of special beneficence; 3) duties to parents, elders and ancestors; 4) duties to children and posterity; 5) laws of justice; 6) laws of good faith and veracity; 7) laws of mercy; and 8) laws of magnanimity, C. S. Lewis, The Abolition of Man, (San Francisco, California: Harper Collins, 2001), pp. 83-101.

[29] There is a discussion in philosophy about whether one can ever know truth to the extent that it is justified true belief. I will refer you to an excellent discussion on that rather than offer it myself. For now, I simply say that for one to have a belief that is true, it must be true, it must have justification that makes it true, it must be a true belief that the person has, and it for me, must always be scrutinized to ensure it remains a justifiable true belief as far as the person is capable of knowing it. For more, read J. P. Moreland and William Lane Craig, Philosophical Foundations For A Christian Worldview, (Downers Grove, Illinois: Intervarsity Press, 2003), pp. 71-85.

CHAPTER TEN

JUST WAR: WHAT IS IT FOR COMBATANTS?

What it means to fight a just war has been debated for millennia. Some have said it is about politics, power, resources or revenge. While we will consider these responses, we will ground our basis for war in justice, the protection of goodness. We will do this with a continual focus on how this connects to the fighter. This will make this chapter a practical guide for those who fight in terms of finding a way for them to know with certainty how to be just combatants in a just war. Yet, the chapter is not just for the combatant. It is also directed to a nation to know as well when and if war is just. For at the end of the day, war is about a nation and all of its resources being used for the sake of justice.

King David of the Hebrew writings is a warrior par excellence. As a boy he was a shepherd. This was arduous duty as it involved hard living in sparse terrain and at times the endurance of particularly harsh weather conditions. It also was a job that was very dangerous. Sheep and goats were tempting targets for thieves, and a shepherd was the only protection. Of greater peril still were the animal predators. David once killed both a lion and bear as they tried to take sheep from his care, and who knows how many other wild animals like hyenas and jackals he fought off? The critical point is that only the most steeled, courageous and dedicated person would do this kind of work with integrity as it essentially involved risking life and limb. But that was David; one who displayed even in his youth, the heart of the warrior—bound resolutely to sacrifice for belief.

To see the fullness of these characteristics in the life of David, one can regard the story of his encounter with Goliath (I Samuel 17). As the story is told, David is instructed by his father to take food to his three brothers who are on the battle lines: Israel versus Philistia. For forty days, this line was drawn, and twice each day a giant named Goliath from the Philistine Army, a man measuring over nine feet tall and clad with impressive armor and weaponry, would step out and dare anyone to fight. In the process, he defamed the Israelites and their God. Yet in spite of these things, no one would confront him.

Think about how ironic this is. Thousands of Israeli "warriors" stood on line across from their enemy and received eighty challenges to come and fight. Every time it happened, their integrity and identity were being called into question. Yet, no one would rise to fight. That is what warriors do. Particularly it is what they do when injustice confronts them. That aspect of this confrontation could not have been clearer. Goliath was of a nation that embodied moral depravity, as far as the Israelites believed. The fact that not one "warrior" would rise for the sake of their God and for justice is astonishing. But it happened: "On hearing the Philistine's words, Saul [the Israeli King] and all the Israelites were dismayed and terrified."[1]

Then one day, a boy comes along, by this time a teenager: David. He hears this giant **one time**, and that is it. He cannot and will not let this man defile truth as he knows it. He is by nature and conviction a guardian of what is right and true. In keeping with this, he knows he must kill this evil giant. This determination truly is astounding; a boy going up against a hardened war giant. The physical odds of victory are incontestably not in his favor. Yet, David seems not just willing to fight, but he is also convinced that he will be the victor. Is it impetuous youthful thinking that leads David forward? Is he too blind to see the improbability of conquest? I do not think that any of this is true. What we witness is a warrior on the lines of battle. Listen to his invincible resolve as he expresses it to his king:

David said to Saul, "Let no one lose heart on account of this Philistine; your servant will go and fight him." Saul replied, "You are not able to go out against this Philistine and fight him; you are only a boy, and he has been a fighting man from his youth." But David said to Saul, "Your servant has been keeping his father's sheep. When a lion or a bear came and carried off a sheep from the flock, I went after it, struck it and rescued the sheep from its mouth. When it turned on me, I seized it by its hair, struck it, and killed it. Your servant has killed both the lion and the bear; this uncircumcised Philistine will be like one of them, because he has defied the armies of the living God. The Lord who delivered me from the paw of the lion and the paw of the bear will deliver me from the hand of this Philistine."[2]

In warrior fashion, David finds his calling and fulfills it. With one rock thrown from a sling, the giant is struck and falls to his death. Upon seeing this, the dispirited Israelite Army found its courage. Behind this warrior, they discovered their will, and attacked, killing the entire Philistine Army.

This story of David exemplifies clearly that the warrior has a strong internal sense of what is right and must fight for it. He cannot and will not compromise truth. When someone cares to challenge him, no matter how imposing, he will attack.

Interesting to point out as well is that Goliath was no different than David. Both were warriors. They each knew what they believed, were certain of it, had intractable confidence in an ability to defeat the enemy, and had no good choice but to go and be faithful to their integrity and identity as warriors. That is who warriors are, and what they do. Read about the actual confrontation between these two men:

Then he [David] took his staff in his hand, chose five smooth stones from the stream, put them in the pouch of his shepherd's bag and, with his sling in his hand, approached the Philistine. Meanwhile, the Philistine, with his shield bearer in front of him, kept coming closer to David. He looked David over and saw that he was only a boy, ruddy and handsome, and he despised him. He said to David, "Am I a dog that you come at me with sticks?" And the Philistine cursed David by his gods. "Come here," he said, "and I'll give your flesh to the birds of the air and the beasts of the field!" David said to the Philistine, "You come against me with sword and spear and javelin, but I come against you in the name of the Lord Almighty, the God of the armies of Israel, whom you have defied. This day the Lord will hand you over to me, and I'll strike you down and cut off your head. Today I will give the carcasses of the Philistine army to the birds of the air and the beasts of the earth, and the whole world will know that there is a God in Israel. All those gathered here will know that it is not by sword or spear that the Lord saves; for the battle is the Lord's, and he will give all of you into our hands." As the Philistine moved closer to attack him, David ran quickly toward the battle line to meet him. Reaching into his bag and taking out a stone, he slung it and struck the Philistine on the forehead. The stone sank into his forehead, and he fell face down on the ground. So David triumphed over the Philistine with a sling and a stone; without a sword in his hand he struck down the Philistine and killed him.[3]

The value of this story for our instruction is to see what it looks like when a warrior finds his identity and seeks to actualize every aspect of goodness in his life. For both of these warriors, that process is about standing for what is believed without death being a

295

controlling factor. In this case too, it is about rising up in battle with two alternate views of reality. But which one is right? David wins the battle but that does not ensure his rightness. Moral truth is determined not by victory but only as it aligns with goodness.

Given this, what is incumbent now is for us to provide some means by which the combatant can be certain that what he believes is in fact that ultimate goodness. What haunts combatants who desire to uphold truth is unjust killing. This might not be the case in battle, but in the end, if that cause for taking a life is not justified in their moral convictions, they can easily be destroyed. For this reason, the discussion we are about to have is requisite. All going to the front lines of battle should be convinced, like David, that what they are doing is not simply following orders to kill, but rather defending the ultimate good as far as they can know it. To remove this standard is to emasculate those who defend truth. For the sake of combatants, therefore, let us not go down this path. Let us find a way to orient all for war so as to maintain moral goodness in every aspect of being and action. To achieve this, we will start by offering an explanation of justice itself. From there, we can move to see how justice becomes central in knowing if war is needed.

Step 1: What is Justice?

We begin with a preliminary discussion on justice. What is it? In a simple statement justice is the enabling of the moral good to be realized by all. In one part, that involves power and punishment both to break the will of those misaligned toward goodness and to provide the conditions wherein one is afforded the chance to recognize goodness for what it truly is. But then again, in another part, it involves restoration of being when the goodness of a person has been violated. Yet in either situation, for justice to be justice it involves knowing the self-evident truth about goodness and the protection of its viability for all.

In the course of history, the process by which this is carried out has shifted on the whole from that of a sovereign leader controlling the masses through grave punishment to a kind of democracy wherein all are equally empowered to know freedom and fulfillment.[4] Central always, however, no matter how or through whom justice is executed is the need to maintain a standard for behavior and the means by which to re-attain that standard when it is not honored.

Likely the most popular way that people think justice is to be grounded is through a social contract. Gloucon, in Plato's *Republic*, is a first to voice such a thought. He says the following:

And now for my first heading, the nature and origin of justice. What they say is that it is according to nature a good thing to inflict wrong or injury, and a bad thing to suffer it, but that the disadvantages of suffering it exceed the advantages of inflicting it; after a taste of both, therefore, men decide that, as they can't evade the one and achieve the other, it will pay to make a compact with each other by which they forgo both. They accordingly proceed to make laws and mutual agreements, and what the law lays down they call lawful and right. This is the origin and nature of justice. It lies between what is most desirable, to do wrong and avoid punishment, and what is most undesirable, to suffer wrong without being able to get redress; justice lies between the two and is accepted not as being good in itself, but has having a relative value due to our inability to do wrong.[5]

Justice in this formulation arises by awareness that mutual sacrifice for the common good is the best way to achieve personal fulfillment. This philosophy has captured the attention of many influential social theorists (Thomas Hobbes, John Locke, and Jeremy Bentham). Of most recent note is John Rawls.[6] In his influential work, *A Theory of Justice*, he frames justice upon the basis of a society where one accepts generalized principles of moral goodness in order that all will have a fair chance at acquiring needs.[7] This does not mean that all will have the same things. There will be people who are more motivated to achieve than others and they will gain more, and there will those too who have different desires, tastes, interests and talents and that will move them in different directions.[8] Yet, regardless for Rawls, his central point is that what benefits all when it comes to justice is a cooperative schema where fairness and equity overturn temptations for exclusion centered on prejudice or unfair advantage.[9]

Irrespective of what Rawls and others have popularized, however, as far as the notion of justice is concerned, what we will use as a basis for justice is what we found in the previous chapter; the pursuit of the self-evident moral goodness by all which is protected so that people can pursue that goodness to its ultimate end, the *totum bonum*. While this realization of justice does not permit, as some might want, a definitive list of rules or principles, there are clearly things which are universally known to be in line with human flourishing and likewise to be a clear misappropriation of goodness in every way. On this, Robert George offers some clarification: "[t]he most basic practical principles refer to ends or purposes which provide non-instrumental reasons for acting. These principles identify intrinsic human goods (such as knowledge, friendship and health) as ends to be pursued, promoted and protected, and their opposites (ignorance, animosity, illness) as evils to be avoided or overcome."[10]

With these considerations in hand now, we should move to see how all of this impacts those in combat. What constitutes for them justice in war? This will be vital to answer. They are the ones, in the end, who are tasked to uphold justice. Thus, they of all people need to know what a just war is. It is a critical part of protecting their goodness.

Step 2: Justice for Combatants

Guidelines that help to know if war is needed are found in what is called the Just War Theory. It is a theory that stretches back in its origin to ancient philosophy and it still has force today as reflected by the fact its principles ground the United Nations Peace Keeping efforts when it comes to worldly conflict.[11] The theory is established around three principles: 1) *Jus Ad Bellum*, the idea if a nation goes to war; 2) *Jus In Bello*, the notion of how a war is to be conducted; and 3) *Jus Post Bellum,* the determination of how a war is resolved for the best interests of all parties.

Significant for our purposes are the first two considerations. The goal is to help combatants align their inner sense of rightness with a practical moral framework for war from which they can be informed as to when and how they should be in war.

Jus Ad Bellum

When deciding whether there is a moral cause for justice that would lead to war, Jus Ad Bellum, there are several issues to consider.[12] We will regard them all and offer the application of these considerations to combatants.

Issue 1 – Cause (what grounds my belief that war and killing is just)

There must be some legitimate reason to use force against an opposing group. What receives broad support is when a sovereign state's rights are violated to the extent that its existence is being impacted or its existence has already suffered severely. At what point, though, is it clear to say that a state's existence is impaired enough or is in true jeopardy so as to go to war? Is it one physical act of aggression or several? Is it a question of political, social, economic or existence itself?

299

These questions are difficult to answer as there will never be an exacting formula by which to determine the matter. That does not make the issue unanswerable though. What became clear for America in terms of this was the attack on 9/11. In one sense, the overall loss and impact to America was not such that it threatened existence. Regardless, a cause for war seemed fully justified: the extreme violation of sovereign rights, the loss of life, infrastructure, and the fact that current and future resources used to sustain the goodness of Americans were compromised. Additionally, since the resolve of Al Qaeda and Osama Bin Laden was not to surrender, but to maintain an attitude toward the further desecration of goodness with deadly acts, that meant that war needed to occur. These people needed to face justice.

Going one more step, however, and exploring this issue of a cause for war further, it is believed too that a cause for war can be found not just when a nation's rights have been attacked, but also when a nation sees the need to intervene on behalf of others. For instance, there are times when the rights of a nation's citizens under a tyrannical regime are being violated. At that point, it is thought that nations not directly impacted can rise to support the oppressed. For in that situation, rogue leadership for a state is deemed to have forfeited its sovereign rights on behalf of its people. Thus, foreign nations can and should rise against degenerate leaders on behalf of the citizens.

Adding even more to this discussion and similar from what is just provided, a just cause for war is said to be found as well if a nation wants to assist another nation in its defense against some external aggressor. In that case, two or more friendly nations, uniting for the purpose of justice, are said to have a cause for war in helping to stop a foreign incursion on an innocent state. This clearly was the case with Nazi Germany during WWII. It was also the foundation for the first Gulf War, aka Operation Desert Shield, where many nations rose up to defend the rights of Kuwaitis who had suffered the invasion and destruction of their country by Iraq. In this time,

President George H. W. Bush made this statement about the just cause for war:

> In the life of a nation, we're called upon to define who we are and what we believe. Sometimes these choices are not easy. But today as President, I ask for your support in a decision I've made to stand up for what's right and condemn what's wrong, all in the cause of peace. Less than a week ago, in the early morning hours of August 2d, Iraqi Armed Forces, without provocation or warning, invaded a peaceful Kuwait. ...There is no justification whatsoever for this outrageous and brutal act of aggression. A puppet regime imposed from the outside is unacceptable. The acquisition of territory by force is unacceptable. No one, friend or foe, should doubt our desire for peace; and no one should underestimate our determination to confront aggression. We succeeded in the struggle for freedom in Europe because we and our allies remain stalwart. Keeping the peace in the Middle East will require no less. We're beginning a new era. This new era can be full of promise, an age of freedom, a time of peace for all peoples. But if history teaches us anything, it is that we must resist aggression or it will destroy our freedoms. Appeasement does not work. ...Standing up for our principle is an American tradition. As it has so many times before, it may take time and tremendous effort, but most of all, it will take unity of purpose. As I've witnessed throughout my life in both war and peace, America has never wavered when her purpose is driven by principle. And in this August day, at home and abroad, I know she will do no less.[13]

That is the essence of a just cause. In this case, it is defending the rights of the innocent by developing a coalition of just nations to overturn an egregious invasion.

Aside from defending the rights of one's own people after attack or those of another nation undergoing suffering, still another scenario where people see a just cause for war is when there is an *imminent* threat of destruction by some outside nation. In this case, the threat must be about the destruction of a peaceful nation where it is unprovoked, and most critically, certain to come. Why wait for a rogue nation to attack, it is believed. A preemptive strike is better and definitely forms the basis of a cause for war since it will silence the pending affront to the rights of the citizens. Let us take a moment to think about this. It is controversial.

President George W. Bush once spoke about the need for nations to be able to conduct preemptive strikes. He said, "Some have said we must not act until the threat is imminent. Since when have terrorists and tyrants announced their intentions, politely putting us on notice before they strike? If this threat is permitted to fully and suddenly emerge, all actions, all words and all recriminations would come too late."[14]

In this view, if there is a credible threat that has been issued by a rogue nation, and the means of addressing this conflict through peaceful means are exhausted, then as Bush states, it is not a matter of waiting for anything but of deciding upon what is the best time to attack. Goodness hangs in the balance. Not wanting for evil to destroy what is right and good means that war should occur. Supporting this notion, once again, is President Bush in a Commencement Address at West Point:

"We cannot defend America and our friends by hoping for the best. We cannot put our faith in the words of tyrants, who solemnly sign nonproliferation treaties, and then systemically break them. If we wait for threats to fully materialize, we will have waited too long. …And our security will require all Americans to be forward-looking and resolute, to be ready for preemptive action when necessary to defend our liberty and to defend our lives."[15]

As should be apparent, there are those who disagree with this view. They object by saying, "The mere *threat* of war, and the presence of mutual disdain between political communities, does not suffice as indicators of war. The conflict of arms must be *actual*, and not merely latent, for it to count as war."[16]

Without question, this challenge is valuable. What if one nation acts on what is bad intelligence; how can that be justified? All of this shows the difficultly involved when a cause for war is not established by clear unassailable evidence, a devastating attack being the most obvious proof.

Recognizing both sides of this dilemma, a good overall caution should be regarded. It comes by way of an excellent discussion on "The Justice of Preemption and Preventative War Doctrines" by Neta Crawford. She says this:

Preemption can be justified if it is undertaken under immediate threat, where there is no time for diplomacy to be attempted, and where the preemptive action is limited to reducing the immediate threat. There is great temptation, however, to slide over the line from preemption to preventive war, because that line can be vague in the world of asymmetric war and weapons of mass destruction and because the stress of living under the threat of terrorist attack or war is great. But the temptation of preventative war should be avoided. The stress of living in fear should be assuaged by true prevention: arms control, disarmament, negotiations, confidence-building measures, and the development of international law.[17]

By way of an example where preemption formed the basis for war, we can consider the American led invasion of Iraq in 2003. Here the goal was to oust the Iraqi leader, Saddam Hussein, because he supposedly had weapons of mass destruction and was making various threats to destroy America.[18] Donald Rumsfeld, Secretary of

303

Defense of the United States at the time, stated this regarding those threats:

Saddam Hussein possesses chemical and biological weapons. Iraq poses a threat to the security of our people and to the stability of the world that is distinct from any other. It's a danger to its neighbors, to the United States, to the Middle East and to the international peace and stability. It's a danger we cannot ignore. Iraq and North Korea are both repressive dictatorships to be sure and both pose threats. But Iraq is unique. In both word and deed, Iraq has demonstrated that it is seeking the means to strike the United States and our friends and allies with weapons of mass destruction.[19]

Not everyone, however, believed in this cause for that war. That dissatisfaction grew stronger in time since the evidence for the large scale production and possession of weapons for mass destruction seemed lacking. Military members too, the ones fighting that war, began to struggle with this as well. A famous case in the news was that of Army First Lieutenant Ehren Watada. Let us regard his story.

Watada, at first, was for the Iraqi war. This conviction slowly waned. The reason was because as he started to prepare to go overseas and fight in this war, he could not find in his research a cause that justified going and killing Iraqis. This was vital to him. He felt he had to align this mission with his own internal moral sense of rightness, and he needed to be able to have this answer for those he led as well. Yet, the more he looked into it, the more he started to feel that there was not a just cause for war. "The books and articles I read would change my views forever. They exposed in detail the president's deliberate manipulation to initiate this war. Recent reports show us that this war is a debacle of enormous proportions and that there never was any **just cause**. I felt as though our lives were being wasted for nothing."[20]

This information led to a crisis of being for Watada. Should he go to war without an inner conviction of the just cause? He said of that time, "Never in my life did I ever imagine I would have to disobey my President. But I have come to the conclusion that participation in this war is not only immoral but a breach of American and international law."[21]

This is an interesting dilemma that needs our fullest consideration. Many are critical of those in the military who decide when and where they will fight, and rightly so. One who obligates to serve his country ought to fight for the country. But contrary to that general point, would we not all agree that a person should kill only when that conviction to do so is founded in his conscience on a just cause? Certainly, we would not advocate shooting others arbitrarily or solely because it is an order. We would not encourage combatants to take lives without believing that the duty is founded in justice. Also, would it not be better to keep people off of the front lines of war if they are unwilling to fulfill their mission because they are greatly conflicted about a cause for justice or because they do not share in the cause of justice? That seems reasonable. Consequently, perhaps the right solution is to start training about just causes for war with military recruits, teaching them when it is right to kill and how that right is inextricably tied to a just cause. In this way, we develop combatants who are formidable on the front lines, having no inner disturbance about seeking justice.

If some, however, in the face of a war remain in doubt about the cause, let them be challenged. If in the end they refuse to fight for the cause of war, let their cases be processed. If it is determined that they are dishonorably trying to avoid the duty for which they swore an oath to uphold, prosecute them and send them to the brig or stockade. If it is determined that their convictions are genuine, put them in another military assignment that does not involve direct combat. You do not want them on the front lines of battle anyway; they will not aid in developing the cohesion and unity of spirit that is needed in that milieu. They will also lessen the strength of the

305

fighting force if they are forced to be where they do not belong. In the end, deal with these people as we should deal with all, aligning their efforts to their convictions about a just cause for war. How can we want anything less?

Finding a just cause for war is stabilizing to the effort of war. It becomes the fuel that moves combatants to action. It becomes the confirmation after battle for why combatants needed to rise and kill. Hence, it must make sense to ensure that all have this inner conviction for justice.

There is a fascinating story in the Hebrew canon on this. It is in the book of Judges. Therein we find the story of Gideon who is amassing an army to fight against the Midianites. He starts with thirty thousand fighters. He is told to get the number down by announcing this to the army: "Anyone who trembles with fear may turn back and leave Mount Gilead."[22] Many do leave at this point, but the winnowing process continues until he gets his army down in size to three hundred and it is with this small group that Gideon defeats an enemy that massively outnumbered his army.

But that is what is important to see. For what a commander needs are those who resolutely stand for truth. That is what wins battles. That is what won this battle. It did so because the Midianites fled. Their strength was their numbers and that strength evaporated in the face of valiant resolve for justice. Fear, lack of conviction or any other weakness in the mind of a combatant is deadly to the cause for justice. Thus, we should not fear assembling only combatants who will fight to die for what is believed. That is what wins the war for justice. Hence, do what is needed to help combatants understand the cause for justice so that they can know why they fight and find that inner moral justification to fight without any inner confliction for truth.

I am aware that this proposal is likely to be criticized. Some consider it wrong to suggest that combatants should question their orders at all. They should not, as it is considered, spend time thinking about just causes for war or for that matter think about any jus ad bellum issue. That is not needed, these people say. Combatants simply need to go to war in support of their nation.

My question to this line of reasoning is how can it be possible to suggest that combatants should not know the cause for war, the reasoning for why they must go and kill? To kill someone without righteous justification as the motive is murder. On that, I think we would all agree. Why then would we advocate that combatants should suspend thought on this matter and blindly follow orders when they will be the ones taking those lives? Giving them the just cause, therefore, is vital since it removes every opportunity for them to question if what they are doing is in keeping with justice. Additionally of note, if the just cause is the reason for battle, then the one who will be most inspired to know this and act on it is the combatant who wants to rise and defend for this very reason.

In spite of what is offered, some will continue in this discussion and say that combatants need not worry about justification for war because they have immunity when it comes to killing the enemy. It is recognized, so many aver, that combatants are only following the orders of their leaders and thus, they should not and are not to be held accountable for their actions in war. Let them just follow orders, then, these people say again.

One might ask from where this line of reasoning arises? One answer likely goes back to Augustine when he raised the idea that a fighter is only standing to defend his King, regardless of the rightfulness of the ruler and therefore, is only doing his duty to kill when ordered:

"[A] righteous man...under an ungodly king, may do the duty belonging to his position in the state in fighting by the order of his sovereign—for in some cases it is plainly the will of God that he should fight, and in others, where this is not so plain, it may be an unrighteous command on the part of the king, while the soldier is innocent, because his position makes obedience a duty."[23]

Here Augustine offers justification for the combatant to kill the enemy, even if he fights in an unjust war. The reason is because he is just a pawn in the effort, one incapable of exercising will other than to follow the orders of a sovereign. While this defense to me is not persuasive, it carries on today anyway under the terminology of the "moral equality of combatants". The idea is that those who fight the war, while accountable for how they fight in war (jus in bello), are not to be punished whether or not there is a legitimate cause for war (jus ad bellum). Hence, let them kill in war, following the rules of war, but clear of responsibility as to whether they should kill in the first place.

My challenge to this should be clear just from applying the material on justice. Combatants should not only be concerned about how they fight in war but about whether that fighting is aligned with the preservation of the good. If injustice is the basis for war, if a nation declares war without just warrant, every act of aggression against another is furtherance of that injustice. It is murder in every classification.

Is this not what was determined about 9/11 when Al-Qaeda unjustly attacked the United States? It was not just Osama Bin Laden who needed punishment but all involved with him who set about to destroy goodness. All were morally wrong in their actions, culpable and in need of being held accountable for the injustice. This only makes sense as having accountability for taking the life of a human being who has inalienable rights to that life is something we know is right.

Consider on this too the fact that when it came to the German combatants who followed Hitler's propaganda, they were not righteous combatants, and this even though they might have been faithful to follow jus in bello rules of war. They were criminals because they murdered millions of just combatants from other nations, millions of civilians caught in the crossfire, and they did all of this in the national effort to eradicate a race of people and conquer the sovereign territories of other nations. How can they possibly, therefore, not share culpability with their leaders for such vile behavior? To kill another in war solely because someone or some nation told you to do so cannot be justified and does not deserve impunity if the initiating cause for the war is unjust. If my nation wants me to kill, I need to be enlightened as to why.

This discussion is more critical for combatants who have this rigid internal moral code that needs to be aligned with their behavior. To refuse to help them find that just cause for battle is to emasculate them. They might not suffer at the time of the kill and might temporarily feel justified for following orders in war, but that can change instantly when they return from war. At that time, they will begin to reflect upon what they did, taking the life of a human being. The self-evident truth of goodness will impinge upon their conscience. They will then wonder if they had a just cause for their actions. If they cannot find one, and if a nation later grows tired with the war and says that there was no justification for going to that war, it will all come crashing down on combatants (Vietnam, Iraq). They will begin to think that what they did was murder because they cannot provide any moral right for going to another country in order to kill people just because it was their duty. While this might not be evident to those not directly involved in the fight, realize that it will be an issue for combatants.

I am encouraged to find one ethicist, Jeff McMahan, who supports what appears to be so apparent. He has an excellent article where he lays out his position. He says,

The principal lesson I believe we should draw is that we must reject the complacent view of the orthodox theory of the just war that combatants do nothing wrong by fighting in a war with an unjust cause, or indeed in any unjust war. We should stop telling combatants that they needn't concern themselves with whether their war is just and that they will be doing all that's required of them if they simply obey orders and conduct themselves honorably on the battlefield. We ought instead to encourage moral reflection, even among active duty military personnel, and not only about what is permissible to do during war but also about when it's permissible to participate in war at all.[24]

I could not agree more with McMahan as has been seen throughout the treatment of justice as a part of moral goodness. War and killing requires accountability from all in the military. We must educate those who fight about this. We should be able to provide just causes for battle. This will give those killing, the peace of mind about what they are doing. There are many examples that show failing in this regard. One confused soldier went to his senior Staff Non-Commissioned Officer (NCO) to overcome his sense that there was something wrong with fighting in the Iraqi war. He was in need of some justification for killing. Rather than what he was hoping to get, his superior Staff NCO told him that they were going to fight not "for the right reasons but for money."[25] After this, the Staff NCO stated "that he didn't want to deceive them [his subordinates] with ideas and information that he thought were inaccurate or untrue because he owed them the truth, and he wanted them to fight with their eyes wide open. They would see battle and had to fight, but when they returned to the United States and were free of the situation, they would have a better understanding of why war was wrong." [Clarification added].[26] This answer is dismaying. A soldier wanted justification for war, but what he got undoubtedly failed to help him reconcile his inner sense of justice with his nation's call to action.

Overall, it is paramount that combatants believe in the cause for war and fully support their authorities in executing that mission. It becomes the empowerment that moves combatants to action, and it becomes the confirmation after battle for why they needed to rise and kill. To go to war without having a grasp of what a cause for war is and whether one exists fails everyone in the just war effort.

Issue 2 – a war is to be declared publicly and by a proper authority

A second issue regarding jus ad bellum is about the need for war to be *declared publicly* and *by a proper authority*. As to the first concern, *public declaration*, war should only be conducted after an offending party has been informed that war is imminent if the contested issues are not resolved. This does not mean announcing the timing. It simply is about giving the enemy certainty that staying on the present course of dispute will bring war. The reason for this is obviously to avoid war if possible. That is always the best way to resolve a dispute for the protection of all. Perhaps this changes nothing in the overall situation, but at least the opportunity for a peaceful resolution was offered.

Regarding the second part of this rule, *declaration of war by proper authority*, it is held that a determination to go to war is ultimately a decision that is made by a sovereign entity on behalf of its people. It is believed that justice is to be carried out not by some individual or infiltrating groups like Al Qaeda, but at its final point by representative bodies. The most likely answer for why this is considered right is tied to the Treaty which established the Peace of Westphalia, 1648. That period in Europe involved decades of war. To resolve the constant disputes, the ruling bodies of Europe decided to grant sovereignty to states, regions at the time, and to allow these areas to be self-governed so as to stop the continued interference from outsiders.[27] That concept became the basis for the states' rights we know today. It is codified in the *Charter of the United Nations and Statute of the International Court of Justice*: "All Members shall refrain in their international relations from the threat or use of force against the territorial integrity or political independence of any state, or in any other manner inconsistent with the Purposes of the United Nations."[28] Thus, it is now believed to be appropriate only for sovereign states to work out their own internal disputes with the assistance but not direct interference of others. The additional right flowing out of this is that it is only proper for the ruling body to make that declaration for war on behalf of its people.

The impact for combatants when it comes to the need for war to be *declared publicly* and *by a proper authority* is great. For instance, when it comes to a public declaration for war, one of the most troubling issues for those in war is the deaths of those other than the enemy. In the combatant's eyes, those who are not actively engaged in opposition to them should be protected at all costs. To kill someone in this category, thusly, is devastating. Hence, make a public declaration for war since it has the potential to minimize casualties as it gives those who are not hostages a chance to leave a war zone, particularly if they do not believe in the moral stance of their nation or its leaders anyway. The sooner this can be done the better, as freedom of movement by all, is easier without warring parties in place.

On the second part of this rule, *proper authority*, a nation's representatives are ultimately that right authority to make the final decision for war, and military members by the fact that they are in military service have already made a decision to be aligned with that authority. When a just war is declared, therefore, those combatants become the arm of that authority by which war is executed. There should not be much of an issue here for combatants then as long as they have been trained all along in the principles and issues of a just war. However, if and when issues of dispute about war arise for those in the military, these things can be addressed. It will not stop the war effort. If war is genuinely about a righteous cause, combatants will line up to serve. They are hungry for that chance. That is what history shows. Hence, let us not be afraid to confront this as we need to help all understand the reason for war.

Issue 3 – right intention (assuring that the war is about the just cause and not something other)

A third issue for Jus Ad Bellum is *right intention*. Upholding this, is to know that a nation has a just cause for war, and that cause is the reason for war and not some other furtive agenda: taking resources, gaining land, disliking leaders or other such things. On this then, a cause needs clear identification, and that cause alone must be the motivation for going to war. Then, when the cause is accomplished it, when justice is restored, the intention for fighting in war must not change to some other thing; e.g., reciprocity, recouping losses.... This will bring confusion to the war effort.

For the combatant, there is little to add in this regard except to say that since the just cause is the reason for the war, it is that intention which needs to drive his own movement in war. He too, is not seeking personal agendas along the way, but is connected to the larger national cause for war. In keeping with this, it would be good for him to be continuously instructed to maintain this right intention as his focus. Otherwise, he too might be tempted on a smaller scale to act wrongly against a foe. A combatant gets excited by a just cause and finds enthusiasm about the opportunity to go and execute the mission. This is sound. However, if a combatant sees his buddies go down and starts to kill for them, he can think that this is the cause for war: kill the enemy because he is killing my military members. When that becomes the sole cause, when the larger just cause gets lost, when emotions cloud reasoning as we discussed earlier, when anger begins to allow that trigger finger to get edgy, devastation can result. Hence, maintaining the right intention for war always needs to be paramount.

Issue 4 – last resort (all means other than war should be pursued before any fighting begins)

A fourth rule for Jus Ad Bellum is *last resort*. It raises the issue if the action to go to war in support of the just cause is the only remaining way to pursue justice. Has a nation exhausted every other means to rectify the injustice? Here we consider things like the following: economic pressure, having other nations provide diplomatic support to diffuse the tension, providing clear threats of intention to restore justice so a wayward group can count the cost of their unjust positioning, and blockades. Once these means and others have been exhausted but no change is forthcoming, it becomes obvious that a just war is the only remaining way to establish goodness.

This rule is a critical issue for combatants. There are moments post-war that they will question their actions. It is comforting in this time to know that there was no other choice but war. All else was tried. Nothing succeeded. War was the only option. Hence, take the time to walk a combatant through the process whereby war has become the last resort. Those justifications will be the very things that come back to him if after the war he struggles. He will then know that he was executing his duties faithfully, and if he had not acted, justice would not have been established.

Issue 5 – conviction to act (finding that inner certainty that one must fight in war)

A final rule offered for *Jus Ad Bellum* is *conviction to act.*[29] This is a personal addition to the issues normally involved with *Jus Ad Bellum*, and it stands against two issues that are traditionally held: *proportionality* and *probability of success*. Let us consider all of this.

Proportionality is the idea that a group should do a cost analysis of the war; do the benefits outweigh the losses? Will going

314

to war lesson the evil or generate only more hardship and suffering? The other issue, probability of success, calls into question whether acting on behalf of a just cause will in the end be triumphant at least to some degree. If a nation does not feel like success is possible, it should not proceed with war.

Those issues, proportionality and probability of success, are wrongful determinations of the will to act against injustice because when it comes to war, goodness and the need to establish it against evil are the reasons for fighting. Determining the level of sacrifice involved or the certainty of victory are not the goals. To make them considerations is to miss the point entirely of what a just cause is. When a nation and its combatants rise to fight, it has to be done because people's rights are being severely trampled upon. To see this is to understand that this effort might well bring suffering of various kinds. It is to know as well that victory might not come. Yet, in spite of those things, what remains in view is not whether standing for what is right meets some threshold that makes a war worth it, but the dire need for justice to be established. That is what a nation and its combatant need to be certain of.

Stepping away, then, from proportionality and probability of success, the real issue in deciding for war is to determine if a just cause is something a particular nation and its combatants are being called to defend. Is there, in other words, *a conviction to act* on a matter of justice? Evil abounds all over this world. There will always be the destruction of goodness as people constantly reject what they know to be right for personal gain. That creates endless suffering. Yet, not every instance of it necessitates action on the part of a nation and its combatants. That much seems obvious. Hence, to separate what battle belongs to whom allows for a conviction to act to become a central point in deciding upon war.

A good question to ask is how does a nation and its combatants know if they have a conviction to act against some injustice? The process is easy for combatants. In this case, as long as justice is served, the decision is made for combatants when their

315

nation moves to war. That is because the obligation to serve one's nation involves honor to oath. That is where their conviction to be in war lies. Combatants must then move toward justice as their nation calls. Finding that conviction to act on the part of a nation, however, will involve additionally the certainty and utter conviction of the people and its leaders that justice can and only will be fulfilled through their intervention. This brings their conviction to act.

That conviction was seen all over America after the attack on Pearl Harbor. From the President, to Congress, to the citizens either joining the military or doing everything possible for the war effort, there was an unparalleled determination that war needed to happen. The destruction of goodness was visible in all corners of the land. A patriotic fervor to restore goodness was evident to everyone. It was an electric feeling that pulsated throughout the land and energized the call for justice. That is the conviction to act.

Summation on *Jus Ad Bellum*

In Just War Theory, this principle provides a framework by which to determine if a war is just. It should become a part of all military training. Combatants will rise for justice because it is a part of who they are. Helping them to understand this part of themselves is vital. They need to know that they kill because justice hangs in the balance and that their involvement is central to upholding goodness. For the sake of truth, therefore, let the call to war be sounded and answered by those who know that what they will do is what enables justice in every aspect of their being, and what singularly establishes justice for others as well.

Jus In Bello

Fighting for goodness means upholding what is right for all and destroying only that which is actively involved with injustice. Thus, once the decision for war is made (Jus Ad Bellum), there is also a need to ensure that the application of arms is only directed to those things fueling immorality. This is the matter for *Jus In Bello*. As we consider the issues involved here, there will again be offered an application of how those issues relate to combatants. Making this connection is just as important as it was with *Jus Ad Bellum*. For when combatants' actions in war become disconnected from justice, they can start killing without knowing why and without caring.

To get a picture of this, consider the words of one Marine, Sergeant Jason Lemieux. He talks about the standard combat Rules of Engagement (ROE's) and how they lost their meaning to those in his unit: "With no way to identify their attackers, and no clear mission worth dying for, marines viewed the Rules of Engagement as either a joke or a technicality to be worked around so that they could bring each other home alive."[30]

That kind of activity and thinking is wrong. The outcome of it is not good, and it was in fact not for Lemieux and his unit. They quickly lost sight of justice as Lemieux goes on to show:

Something else we were encouraged to do, almost with a wink and nudge, was to carry drop weapons, or by my third tour, drop shovels. We would carry these weapons or shovels with us because if we accidentally shot a civilian, we could just toss the weapon on the body, and make them look like an insurgent. By my third tour, we were told that if they carried a shovel or heavy bag, or if they were seen digging anywhere, especially near roads, that we could shoot them. So we carried these tools and weapons in our vehicles in case we accidentally shot an innocent civilian. We could just toss it on there and be like, "Well, he was digging. I was within the Rules of Engagement." This was commonly encouraged, but only behind closed doors. There obviously wasn't a public announcement, but it was pretty common.[31]

I can say that I never detected this attitude and it was certainly not the practice with the Marines with whom I served. Yet, this callous nonchalance toward ROE's existed and there are several examples of it as one can find by searching the news.

The reason for our concern here is to prepare combatants against this mindset. Without it, what might seem right at one point could well bring internal angst later on. Robert Meagher in his book *Killing From the Inside Out: Moral injury and Just War*, makes this point as well by saying, "[s]oldiers who one day have no questions or qualms about their duties, can the next day find themselves frozen stiff by a command or situation, once familiar but now quite foreign and paralyzing. Some call this the 'crystallization of conscience.' Others call it a damned nuisance. Whatever we call it or however we understand it, such a moment of moral crisis is all too real."[32] This issue is also addressed by an ex-Marine Captain and Iraqi war veteran, Tyler Boudreau. He says, "...desensitization doesn't eliminate morality from the consciousness. It merely postpones cogitation. Sooner or later, when a man's had a chance to think things over, he will find himself standing in judgment before his own conscience."[33]

With complete agreement that those in war can lose sight of their true purpose in serving justice and can thereby be a force for injustice, let us take time now to look at what it means for the combatant to be in war.

Issue 1 – obey all international laws on weapons prohibition

The first rule is to *obey all international laws on weapons prohibition*. One aspect of this law focuses on chemical and biological weapons. As has been widely accepted but not always followed, these kinds of weapons are not to be used in war: "The 1972 Biological Weapons Convention and the 1993 Chemical Weapons Convention are the most recent international agreements prohibiting these types of weapons. Both have been signed by many countries."[34]

Syria, under the leadership of Bashar al-Assad, is the most recent nation to violate this ban. The results, as any can imagine, are devastating and certainly reveal the injustice of both that leadership and the use of these weapons.

Beyond the goal to cease the employment of these chemical weapons, there is also strong opposition regarding the use of nuclear weapons in war. One question to ask at this point, though, is why take away any advantage or means available that can be used against the enemy? The best answer goes right back to what is fundamental about justice as it relates to moral goodness. Weapons are employed to bring about justice. But justice needs to be pursued in the right way or it is not justice. That right way is to stop all that is bound to corruption, destroying its potential to exist. This can be on a more limited scale measures that bring correction to the wayward: economic sanctions, blockades or other punitive techniques. But if these things do not work and war is needed, justice moves forward with lethal weapon systems. Yet here, the goal is never to bring revenge or wholesale destruction. The goal is always to do only what must be done to stop injustice. This might mean killing the enemy. However, this does not involve intentionally maiming the enemy for no purpose but to create undo or extended suffering. To confront evil is always for the purpose of restoring full goodness. So what the enemy does not need is to be tortured, indiscriminately defaced or left in agony just because that is possible. This is why these kinds of weapon systems should be banned. They do not accomplish the purpose of silencing evil but only of bringing about long-term vengeful torment. This fails in the pursuit of justice.

As we focus now on combatants with regards to all of this, it is important for them to grasp these issues as well. Questions drawing this out should be asked. What weapons do they possess, and what is the proper use of them? What constitutes an improper use? What kinds of situations might they find themselves in where a weapon might be used improperly?

A challenge for this last point was raised in the Battle of Fallujah. Articles reported that white phosphorous was used in this battle. That point is accurate but of note is that it was used only to obscure field of vision, illumination, destruction of the enemy's structures and weapons.[35] These are approved uses for that weapon system as outlined in Geneva Protocol III.

Unfortunately, though, some reported that the Americans were using these weapons for other purposes; namely, to target civilians. Yet, both in my research of this, and in my extensive movement throughout that city, I never found any proof for this. Yet, the issue itself does show the need to make certain that combatants have clear understanding and guidelines to ensure that all weapon systems are used properly.

Issue 2 – discrimination and non-combatant immunity

A second rule for *Jus In Bello* is *discrimination and non-combatant immunity*. On this, let it be noted that the combatants' task today is complex. They must not just be the best prepared and equipped for combat, but additionally, while holding onto this demand, they must execute every duty with absolute precision. This is because when it comes to combat, they do not want to kill any but those upholding injustice. Yet, identifying and targeting the enemy when they often hide amongst civilians is a daunting task. It has to be done with great care, but this is what discrimination and non-combatant immunity is all about.

On this point of non-combatant immunity though, it is worth noting that some non-combatants willfully decide to stay in a war zone. Perhaps they are aligned with the enemy or profiting from their presence in some way. While that still does not make these people a target of fire, it might make them subject to fire:

...although it is illegitimate to directly target noncombatants, this certainly does not mean that every attack which causes harm to noncombatants is an illegitimate one, for non-combatants may be harmed, even killed, as a result of an attack against a legitimate military target. Equally important, noncombatants only retain their immunity from direct attack as long as they retain their status as noncombatants, so if a noncombatant actively engages in any form of combatant activity, then they will lose their immunity and may be directly targeted.[36]

This entire discussion shows again the need for a proper military campaign where all in a country to be attacked are notified about an on-coming war and the responsibility that they have to leave an area of battle if they do want to be aligned with the enemy. This is what the public declaration for war is. People must be alerted about what will happen if they choose the side of injustice. At that point, they have at least six options:

1. Denounce citizenship and go to a place that stands for what they believe.
2. For pacifistic reasons denounce war and be prepared to suffer whatever fate comes.
3. Remain a citizen, denounce war, and work within the legal and political system to end the perceived injustice that brings about a war.
4. Work within, but also outside of one's country, to overcome the ruling party's injustice.
5. Decide to remain in a war zone because of perceived advantage or alliance with the enemy.
6. Be uncertain or indifferent about what is right, remain in the country anyway, uninvolved in the war effort, but then understanding of what that decision might bring.

All options are available and all must choose their fate. Yet, choosing is critical because a war zone is a dangerous place for anyone and those who decide to remain subject themselves to the consequences of that decision.

In this examination, we see that what is prioritized as a target in war is that which unquestionably directs, sustains and carries forward the enemy's survival. In this sense, authorities of a nation, combatants who fight for it, and all that which clearly fuels their existence are the primary targets. For these elements are not just aligned with the injustice but ensure its viability. Hence, the woman who works at the bomb factory needs to know that she places herself in greater proximity to the enemy's cause than the subsistence farmer. If that factory is bombed, therefore, that woman needs to realize that she made the decision by working in this setting to side with injustice and thereby, she exposed herself to this fate. The more we do to support evil, the greater our potential to be hurt. The less we follow error and side with it, the more minimal our suffering.

This brings us to one more important point to make on behalf of combatants in this discussion. It is about the need to establish a means by which they can after war, find reconciliation of mind and spirit from failings. Mistakes occur in war. Non-combatants do get killed. When it happens, combatants confront the imperfect reality of pursuing justice. A grievous internal strife is created. It is something from which combatants need to find relief. Interestingly, all through history, examples of purification rituals to address these kinds of things can be found. Jonathan Shay in his book *Odysseus in America* brings this issue to the forefront. He says,

Most warrior societies, as well as many not dominated by warfare, have historically had communal rites of purification of the returning fighter after battle… The ancient Athenians had a distinctive therapy of purification, healing, and reintegration of returning soldiers that was undertaken as a whole political community. …The early Romans had a ceremony of purification

322

for returning armies, the details of which we know little. It apparently involved passing under a beam erected across a street, with head covered, as well as other ceremonies, purifications, and sacrifices.[37]

Shay's insight here about what armies of old did in returning from war is lost today. That is something that should change. Purification rituals should be reenacted and offered to those who feel the need. It would thereby become the means by which inner atonement could be found if one feels like his involvement in war violated his relationship to moral goodness and justice. It is not something that all will need or want. But for many, it might be the key to inner peace.

Issue 3 – proportionality (do only what is necessary to stop injustice)

Moving forward, a third issue provided for *Jus In Bello* is *proportionality*. The idea here is only to use the level of force needed to accomplish the mission. This just makes sense and is always a part of any tactical mission. You do not want to drop a thermite bomb on a village just because insurgents are there. You engage the enemy for the purpose of and only to the level of destroying their will to live. Spitefully wrecking villages, blowing up crops, killing civilians as a part of killing insurgents is overkill and unjust. Target only what brings injustice and only to the extent that it is needed to stop the injustice.

For combatants, this point is a great overall caution in the war effort. To realize that justice is best served by limiting those killed and destroying only what furthers immorality is important.

Issue 4 – benevolent treatment of prisoners of war

A fourth issue in *Jus In Bello* is *benevolent treatment of prisoners of war*. Essential here is that one who gives up his will to stand for immorality is no longer a threat to goodness and thus, is not a target. Surrendering is relinquishing one's will to stand and fight for injustice. When this happens, people should be treated humanely and safely. You do not want to destroy those who have the ability to be restored, and you do not want to compromise justice by maltreatment of those detained. This is what made the Abu Ghraib prison scandal so egregious. It stood against all that America claimed to be doing as a nation and all that was involved in protecting goodness. It is no wonder that American credibility was in part lost through this incident. This needs to be protected in the future.

For the sake of combatants, training should be given on what the justice process is for captives and how that ties into goodness. This allows those involved in the effort to avoid what only has the potential in the future to be mentally crippling.

Issue 5 – mala in se (evil in itself)

Another issue for *Jus en Bello* is the prohibition against any activity in war that is *mala in se*, evil in itself. Traditionally, this has included the following things: "…mass rape campaigns; genocide or ethnic cleansing; using poison or treachery (like disguising soldiers to look like the Red Cross); forcing captured soldiers to fight against their own side; and using weapons whose effects cannot be controlled, like biological agents."[38] Certainly, from all that has been said thus far, acting in these ways is patently wrong. Any activity bad in itself is a clear violation of goodness and thus, the involvement in it defeats justice from the start.

For combatants, it is always good to question the moral uprightness of an action. At one point, it might seem right to put a gun to the head of an enemy soldier with the desire to gain information. However, this is not right as it fails to recognize the status of a detainee and errs in knowing what it means to be just. Instilling fear or wanton cruelty is to no person's advantage or to his pursuit of goodness. It might be tempting, but it is not right. The activity is *malum in se* and has no place in war. Thinking through this kind of thing prior to war will help to avoid creating headlines that simply distract from the effort to defeat the enemy and bring justice.

Issue 6 – vengeance

A final issue in this section is the order for one *not to act in revenge*. The point here is so obvious now because it all flows seamlessly together. You do not act in vengeance because vengeance is not your motivation to fight. Vengeance is about trying to equal or maximize the suffering of your enemy because of what he has done. That is a miscarriage of justice.

For combatants, it is paramount as they walk through the emotional cycles of war, the painful loss of friends, and the bitterness that can grow toward the enemy, that justice remains the focus of every activity. It is tempting to maim, kill, torture or abuse the enemy in response to their callous march toward evil. It cannot be done, however. Justice always remains movement toward bringing about what is good. Since vengeance is not founded in goodness, it does not move toward it and cannot ultimately bring it; it simply has no place in war.

Summation *on Jus in Bello*

This section in the Just War Theory has vital connection to combatants since it is all about how one acts in war. While these issues are typically the focus of training with respect to Rules of Engagement, what is missing is the more important consideration of what underlies these rules. That discussion, I would argue, is equally as important, if not more so. To know why you act in accordance with rules enables you to define those rules when difficult situations arise and the clarity of what should happen is lacking. Additionally, to know why you follow rules in war has value to the extent that it ensures that one never loses sight of his ultimate purpose which is to be a just warrior in a just battle for a just cause. That is the truest sense of what justice demands, what this discussion allows and what fuels the combatant in war.

Jus Post Bellum

This is the third principle involved in declaring and maintaining a just war. The essence of this issue is to outline how a victorious nation is able to restore true justice in those defeated. There are many steps or rules that guide this process. For our purposes, we will not address them since our focus remains on the execution of war itself. Peace keeping efforts ideally involve non-hostile efforts. Hence, we will move past this discussion by simply affirming that true goodness in war cannot occur without a victorious nation bringing in the right personnel and resources to reconstitute a defeated nation to allow it to find the fullness of goodness for itself and in its relationship to other nations.

Conclusion

It is said by some that "war is evil."[39] Consequently, as this thinking goes, "In war, however just the cause, no one emerges with clean hands."[40] If this is true, then all that is considered so far is pointless. If war is evil, it should not occur for any reason. But as you can see by now, this is not true. There are times when war is needed because underlying it is the pure and right desire to maintain goodness. It is not about evil, therefore, but solely about the hope to arrest injustice and prevent it from the unabated destruction of goodness. It is, thusly, a right thing to pursue when carried out strictly for the sake of justice.

This, of course, does not imply that evil is not a part of war. It has to be in one sense, as an aspect of the enemy's agenda, or war is not just. Further, one could say too that evil exists in war because imperfect beings fail to carry out justice perfectly. Neither of these two things, however, means that war should not be. Evil must be stopped. If the process is not perfect, right the wrong, restore the lost goodness, and move again toward what is right. Do this through a just war process. But failing to do this, allowing evil to flourish, is what would truly be evil. It would be seeing the destruction of life and goodness but in apathy or indifference, standing by to watch it occur. Fortunately, combatants will not let this happen. They will rise to defend justice.

From the explication of what has been provided on these principles and the issues involved, a definition for just war should be apparent: It is the final act to restore every aspect of goodness through the rightful execution of lethal power and for the ultimate realization of humanity existing in its proper interrelationships. That, and that alone, is the reason to kill. Yet, to move in that direction requires a clear sense of moral goodness and a faithful application of it. For when war is conducted improperly, we emasculate warriors and all who serve with them. For that reason, we should all do our collective parts to ensure a just war is the only war in which we engage. That is what ensures that combatants fight for moral goodness.

Endnotes

[1] [identifier added] The Holy Bible: New International Version. Grand Rapids : Zondervan, 1996, c1984, S. 1 Sa 17:11.

[2] The Holy Bible : New International Version. Grand Rapids: Zondervan, 1996, c1984, S. 1 Sa 17:32.

[3] [Identifier of David added]The Holy Bible : New International Version. Grand Rapids: Zondervan, 1996, c1984, S. 1 Sa 17:40.

[4] David Johnston, A Brief History of Justice, (West Sussex, United Kingdom: Wiley-Blackwell, 2011), p. 15.

[5] Plato, The Republic, as translated by Desmond Lee, (London: Penguin Classics, 2007), p. 42.

[6] John Rawls, Justice is Fairness, (London, England: Belknap Press of Harvard University Press, 1971), pp. 132-135.

[7] Ibid., p. 12, 17-22, and 136ff.

[8] Ibid., pp. 60, 118-120, and 126-127

[9] Ibid., pp. 14-15.

[10] Robert George, In Defense of Natural Law, (Oxford, Oxford University Press, 1999), p. 102.

[11] It is not the purpose here to show the idea of the Just War Theory from Plato, Cicero, Augustine and forward to today. A few solid overviews of this for those interested are the following: Bill Rhodes, An Introductory to Military Ethics, pp. 26-44 and Mark Allman, Who Would Jesus Kill?, (Winona, MN: Christian Brothers Publications, 2008, pp. 158-255.

[12] What follows are personal reflections from reading articles and books on Just War. Two articles particularly helpful in understanding what is involved and which directed personal thinking on this topic are the following: Brian Orend, "War," http://plato.stanford.edu/entries/war/, (July 28, 2005) and Alexander Moseley, "Just War Theory," Internet Encyclopedia of Philosophy, http://www.iep.utm.edu/justwar/, (February 10, 2009). Books that are helpful are these: Jean Elshtain, Just War Against Terror; Mark Allman, Who would Jesus Kill?, and Martin Cook, The Moral Warrior.

[13] George H. W. Bush, "Address on Iraq's Invasion of Kuwait (August 8, 1990)",

http://millercenter.org/president/bush/speeches/speech-5529, (2016, 6 June).

[14] Mark Allman, Who Would Jesus Kill?, (Winona, MN: Christian Brothers Publications, 2008), p. 213.

[15] Ibid., p. 217.

[16] Orend, "War."

[17] Neta Crawford, "The Justice of Preemption and Preventive War Doctrines". In Mark Evans, Just War Theory: A Reappraisal, (Great Britain: Palgrave MacMillan, 2005), pp. 47-48.

[18] Quotes from Saddam and Iraq's regime-controlled media, "Saddam Hussein: In His Own Words", http://www.au.af.mil/au/awc/awcgate/iraq/sadquots.htm, (2002, 18 October).

[19] Center for American Progress, "In Their Own Words: Iraq's 'Imminent' Threat", https://www.americanprogress.org/issues/security/news/2004/01/29/459/in-their-own-words-iraqs-imminent-threat/, (January 29, 2004).

[20] [boldness added for effect] Michael Wong, The Truth Set Him Free: Ehren Watada vs. the U.S. Army, http://www.inthemindfield.com/2011/03/25/the-truth-set-him-free-ehren-watada-vs-the-u-s-army/, (March 25, 2011).

[21] Ibid.

[22] Judges 7, The Holy Bible, New International Version, (Colorado Springs, CO: International Bible Society, 1973), p. 215.

[23] Bill Rhodes, An Introduction to Military Ethics, (Santa Barbara, CA: ABC-CLIO, 2009), p. 28.

[24] Jeff McMahan, "On the Moral Equality of Combatants", The Journal of Political Philosophy: Volume 14, Number 4, 2006, pp. 377–393, Web. 18 January, 2016.

[25] Rita Nakashima Brock and Gabriella Lettini, Soul Repair: Recovering from Moral Injury after War, (Boston: Beacon Press, 2013), p. 28.

[26] Ibid.

[27] Stephen Coleman, Military Ethics: An Introduction with Case Studies, (New York: Oxford University Press, 2013), p. 67.

[28] Charter of the United Nations and Statute of the International Court of Justice, Chapter 1, Purposes and Principles, Article 1 (4),

https://treaties.un.org/doc/publication/ctc/uncharter.pdf, (2016, 6 June).

[29] Note that there is not an agreed upon list of Jus Ad Bellum rules. I have focused on those which I believe to be central to the discussion.

[30] Robert Meagher, Killing from the Inside Out: Moral injury and Just War, (Eugene, Oregon: Cascade Books, 2014), p. 134.

[31] Ibid., p. 135.

[32] Ibid., p. 137.

[33] Ibid., p. 136.

[34] Microsoft Encarta Online Encyclopedia 2009, "Chemical and Biological Warfare," http://encarta.msn.com/encyclopedia_761558349_4/Chemical_and_Biological_Warfare.html#howtocite, (1997-2009).

[35] International Humanitarian Law - Treaties & Documents, "Protocol on Prohibitions or Restrictions on the Use of Incendiary Weapons (Protocol III). Geneva, 10 October 1980," http://www.icrc.org/ihl.nsf/FULL/515?OpenDocument, (October 21, 2009).

[36] Stephen Coleman, Military Ethics: An Introduction with Case Studies, (New York: Oxford University Press, 2013), p. 151.

[37] Jonathan Shay, Odysseus in America, (New York: Scribner, 2002), pp. 152-153.

[38] Brian Orend, "War".

[39] Andrew Rigby, "Forgiveness and Reconciliation in Jus Post Bellum," Mark Evans, Just War Theory, p. 177.

[40] Ibid., p. 178.

CHAPTER ELEVEN

MORAL INJURY: CONSEQUENCE OF MISSING OR MISALIGNED MORALS

Major Jeffrey Hall was an infantry officer who was a warrior in every respect, wanting whenever possible the chance to engage and destroy the enemy.[1] Having had two combat tours in Iraq, therefore, should have fulfilled him as a warrior. It did not though. There were many things that contributed to this, but one incident in particular caused him to break down entirely.[2] It was the time he was ordered, against his will, to go to a grieving family who had lost relatives during a cross-fire between Americans and the enemy in order to return the corpses of their loved ones; corpses which by this time had rotted from being unenbalmed and left out in the sun. That created a moral crisis for Hall, but it did not end there. He was further commanded to hand over to this family death certificates which were erroneously stamped, ENEMY, in bold red letters.[3] It was a humiliation and lie that damaged every understanding that he had of himself as a warrior in war. Justice for him evaporated as he said, "You have to understand. My PTSD had everything to do with moral injury. It was not from killing, or seeing bodies severed or blown up. It was from betrayal, from moral betrayal."[4]

War is an experience where people see, do and hear things that live explosively in their minds. For some, these memories are paralyzing, leaving them in a state of horror and depression. No matter what they do to escape the plague of conscience, they feel trapped. A Marine who served in the Vietnam War, Camillo "Mac" Bica, shows clearly how frustrating finding peace can be.

Upon return from his tour of duty, he sought healing through the Veteran's Administration (VA) Hospital. What he saw and experienced in this process proved to be both damaging and misguided. He witnessed veterans who were spaced out on the drugs that they were given to silence pain.[5] He also saw veterans having to fight for care and even to meet in secrecy to strategize about how to get needed issues resolved.

He too had failings with his own medical care as he was misdiagnosed with a personality disorder.[6] Through it all, Mac resigned himself to the belief that war trauma was something that could not be addressed. It was a condition from which no one ever fully recovered or so he stated:

> Though physical wounds may heal, the psychological, emotional, and moral injuries of war linger and fester. Vietnam forever pervades my existence, condemning me to continually relive and question the past. 'Did I do enough?' 'Could I have done better?' 'Did I make the correct decisions?' Inevitable concerns of those who must take life and whose decisions cause others to die. Despite the urging of well-meaning friends and loved ones, I can never forget Vietnam nor put it behind me. No one truly 'recovers' from war. No one is ever made whole again. The best that can be hoped, I think, is to achieve a degree of benign acceptance. To that end, I strive each day to forgive and absolve myself of guilt, and to live with the wounds of war that will never heal.[7]

In this admission, Mac shows where many veterans can end up, somewhat dispirited and resigned to accept a life without the wholeness once known. But this state, in my estimation, is not something that veterans should accept. There are ways to find healing. Yet to get there, we have to be willing to acknowledge the impact that morality has in war. Not being aware of this, thinking that the motivation for war is exclusively about unit cohesion or nationality, can easily cause one to be mired in moral conviction as Mac shows.

To reveal the extent of this problem and the issues involved is what will be explored in this chapter. We will uncover how moral conflict and suffering play out in war and post war. Typically, this discussion happens under the topic of moral injury. It is a condition as most say where one feels guilt for witnessing, associating with, committing either directly or indirectly, or failing to prevent transgressions of moral norms.

While we will accept this understanding of moral injury, we will also broaden it to cover situations where one in fact upheld the moral right but still suffers. The latter consideration might seem strange in this discussion, and in one way it is. To do what is morally right on the battlefield as we have addressed brings great moments of elation where the righteous becomes one with self and purpose as a defender of justice. Yet, in spite of that, upholding morality can also bring intense internal strife. That is because there can be a real cost to doing what is morally right in situations.

Let us consider all of this. We will do so first by using several case studies wherein we look at the lives of veterans and see how each uniquely reveals a different aspect of moral injury. From there, we will consider some overall thoughts on moral injury, and then finally, suggestions will be made about how to bring greater awareness and healing. It will all aid in exposing the depth of complexity that exists when it comes to war.

HM1 Marcus Luttrell, SEAL

Marcus Luttrell did an interview on *The Today Show* with Matt Lauer in 2007. He was the only surviving SEAL Team member of a mission in Afghanistan that went bad after it was compromised by three goat herders. In the interview, the question arose about the goat herders and whether the team made the wrong decision in letting them go. Should they have killed them instead? The decision to release them led to the Taliban being alerted as to their presence in the area, the ensuing firefight, and the death of all but Luttrell. In response to Lauer, Luttrell said that he second guesses his decision to let them go every day, and he adds that it would be worth "doing the time in prison if my buddies were still alive."[8]

This similar kind of statement is also made clear In *Lone Survivor*. In the book, Luttrell lays out the scene where this incident happened with the herders. The reader is allowed to see the spirited debate between the SEALs that took place. It covered many issues, including the topics of whether killing these people would bring about jail time and if this would constitute murder.[9] After some discussion, which intensely played out over valuable time that these warriors did not have, the team finally made their decision and it was to let these Afghans go.

Yet, right after having stated this, Luttrell relays to the reader an aside: "It was the stupidest, most southern-fried, lame brained decision I ever made in my life. I must have been out of my mind. I'd turned into a fucking liberal, a half-assed, no-logic nitwit, all heart, no brain, and the judgment of a jackrabbit. At least, that's how I look back on those moments now. Probably not then, but for nearly every waking hour of my life since."[10]

From this remark, it seems again like Luttrell does have regret about not having killed these herders and this, even though in most of his on-line interviews since the time of the book, he clearly says that the team made the right decision to let the herders go.

Why is this important? The answer must be obvious. It is because of moral injury. Warriors fight by moral codes. They suffer and die because their kills have to be unquestionably just.

Imagine the restraint and turmoil that accompanies this desire to uphold true justice in certain situations. That is why these herders were released. That is why three warriors died. This is all why

Luttrell suffers. He experiences the high cost of being an ethical warrior, watching just warriors die to preserve goodness and being confronted perpetually by the memory of that time. As he says, "I live through that every day in my head, from the time I lay down in bed through the night, up in the morning. There's not a moment that goes by that I don't think about it."[11] That is moral injury. It can live in those who do what is right. It is the cost at times of moral justice.

War is not always about the disaffected selection of option A or B. It can rather be about the need to make an all-consuming, intense, conflicting choice that rends the soul. This is something to realize. We have to become aware of the complexity of war. It can be a situation where one is abruptly awakened to what moral injury is all about. Luttrell offers us but one picture of this through his story, where he both draws comfort in knowing he did the right thing and sadness in knowing he did the right thing. It is the latter that can become dangerous as it makes one wish that he would have done otherwise. Yet, that choice certainly would have been worse. For Luttrell, it would have meant that he killed three people who did not pose a threat at the time. It would have meant as well that he would have been conflicted later in a different way, struggling with a darkening of the soul and with a mind spiraling down toward self-destruction. Both sides of this injury are possible and present a provocative and enlightening picture of how morality can play out on the battlefield.

Overall, this discussion shows how challenging it is to remain true to the just cause. So many factors arise that weigh in on a decision to kill: rigid moral code, fatigue, emotion of the moment, ROE's that do not seem to apply, personal interpretations of ROEs that are vague, lack of better options, downed communications which do not allow for senior leadership input, interaction with those captured and seeing disdain in their eyes, knowledge of possible mission failure to members who refuse accepting failure, the constant ticking of the clock, fear that making the wrong decision will bring scrutiny to a brotherhood of warriors, fear that making a wrong decision will bring jail time, fear that all back home will hear about this and somehow think that they could have done better, and countless other things.

An intense conflict can arise between what is expedient and what is morally right. Decisions of this kind can be excruciating. If warriors were not bound to a moral code if there was no moral truth for them, then that challenge would vanish. They could do what they wanted. Yet, that is not what happens. They go into the war zone guided by their mission and directed as well by moral principles. Luttrell even talks about this. He says,

> Dead ahead, in Afghanistan, awaited an ancient battleground where we could match our enemy, strength for strength, stealth for stealth, steel for steel. This might be, perhaps, a little daunting for regular soldiers. But not for SEALs. And I can state with absolute certainty that all ... of us were excited by the prospect, looking forward to doing our job out there in the open, confident of our ultimate success, sure of our training, experience, and judgment. You see, we're **invincible**. That's what they taught us. That's what we believe. It's written right there in black and white in the official philosophy of the U.S. Navy SEAL, 'We train for war and fight to win. I stand ready to bring the full spectrum of combat power to bear in order to achieve my mission and the goals established by my country. The execution of my duties will be swift and violent when required, yet **guided by the very principles** I serve to defend.[12]

Warriors live by principles of moral truth. That directs them as much as the mission, and in fact, for just warriors that is the mission. Hence, though Luttrell could have opted to kill these men, he knew it was not right: "Something kept whispering in the back of my mind, it would be wrong to execute these unarmed men in cold blood."[13] Undoubtedly, Luttrell's moral impulse here is right. While such an act might have saved the lives of the SEALs and allowed the mission to go forward, another part of him would have died. He would have lost fidelity to who he is as a SEAL.

Yet, realize something more here. That moral truth does go to the core of the warriors' being, and that they will angst and take valuable time to determine how to execute justice faithfully shows that they need options made available to them when it comes to morally injurious situations. For instance, with the goat herders, why were these warriors not equipped with other gear to address this conflict? They could have been given non-lethal means to incapacitate people; i.e., a dart gun with sedatives, vials with Xanax, chloroform, GHB, or any such drug to render people unconscious for a period of time. Duct tape too could have been used to detain these people and cover their mouths. Other creative and harmless things could have been provided as well. But that nothing was provided, that no equipment or training about the possibility of this kind of thing happening was given, meant that three warriors died and that one lives with the struggle of this every day.

What makes it more egregious is the fact that this was not the first instance where something like this had occurred.[14] Other Special Forces had been previously compromised in this exact kind of way. We are emasculating warriors by not taking seriously the ethical conflicts that can arise in battle, but in this case it is not because of immoral activity but because of the high cost involved in upholding goodness.

Lieutenant Colonel Bill Russell, Army Special Forces

Lieutenant Colonel Bill Russell was in the Army. His story is captured in the book: *god is not here: A soldier's struggle with Torture, Trauma and the Moral Injuries of War*.[15] What we see in this story is a soldier who fights just to keep his moral self from rupturing and being brought to the precipice of moral insanity. How does all of this happen?

Russell works in an Iraqi compound with Iraqi interrogators. His job takes him on dangerous missions out in a volatile region of Iraq to grab insurgents. These people are then brought back to the base for questioning where Russell is tasked to observe the process, ensuring that those captured are treated justly. What bothers Russell in this work is neither the dangerous and emotionally draining job of snatching the enemy, nor the unsettling nature of working on a compound that is occasionally under fire. It is, instead, the process of observing interrogations where he sees firsthand the villainous nature of this enemy. It is something he witnessed time and again, and the decadence of those captured appalls and disgusts him.

On one occasion, Russell observes the interrogation of some locals who are found to be accepting money from the insurgents for the purpose of torturing and killing innocent people. It makes no sense to him. Why would these people do this to innocent people who just want to be left alone? How can these men be so base, he wonders? As Russell says, "...these men confound me with their details, with their various acts of inhumanity. I try to stop my slide into their darkness, and so far I've succeeded, barely; but tonight is different. Tonight, when Shoeib, a detainee, wails for some higher power's assistance, I feel a fracture slide down the center of my chest. Tonight, for the first time in my life, I passionately, fervently want to kill another human being."[16]

This is the moral battle that goes on in Russell's mind. The complexity and intensity of the situation is hard to fully fathom. Surely a part of what complicates the desire to remain stolid in the moment, is an additional plea that a detainee makes to the interrogators: it is a cry for God to rescue him. Russell must wonder how God is somehow connected to his depravity. His words at this moment are profound, "...from only a few feet away I feel the shimmers of evil come off his man, this same man who dares to sit here and plead for God's help. Well, God is not here."[17]

This honest reflection by Russell shows how close he is to rending at the seams of his moral being. The intransigent evil of his enemy is overwhelming. How is it even possible, we might ask, for Russell or any other combatant to confront this kind of evil and still maintain moral bearing? How do combatants in these situations manage not to become like those whom they fight? The temptation must be alluring. The sheer willpower to maintain the moral right has to be the greatest battle on the field of battle. These combatants want justice to reign. Their lives are sacrificed for it. To stand by idly in the face of abominable injustice, day after day, implodes the soul. Russell, at one point, allows us to appreciate this. He says,

> God, I want to hurt, to kill, this man who takes innocent life and then pleads for our mercy. God, I desperately want to give in, to forget about such things as wrong and right. In Iraq, on these streets and in these cells, such clear distinctions have taken flight. Past rules of the civilized seem childish, completely irrelevant to this new life. Now I just wander without any guiding light and so I close my eyes. I give in, and, in give I. I become a man I no longer recognize. I've lost myself.[18]

I truly do not think that we can appreciate these words enough. This is a glimpse into the moral soul of a warrior who conducts war with those who live in the epitome of decadence. It unquestionably leads to this place of moral injury. The process can be slow but certain. Watch it play out, scene by scene, in Russell's life. It starts by the observance of and personal disturbance in seeing wicked men who wantonly violate rights of the innocent. As Russell shares, "I have been here, listening, watching, and participating in these interrogations for what seems years, and night after night these men confound me with their details, with their various acts of inhumanity. I try to stop my slide into their darkness, and so far I've succeeded, barely...."[19]

This brings Russell to the desire to find justice for those harmed. It is a desire that grows ever determined, and at one point, Russell lets it slip fatefully into action: "...I reach out and wrap my fingers around his [detainee's] neck: he deserves the justice a raped and dead girl cannot give him. I begin to squeeze and I feel the heart beat, faster, as my grip becomes tighter, and eventually the struggling, breathing, and then thinking slows, and quietly the world becomes one person-less better. I actually sense the shift, which is not a good thing-in-itself. I just know the scales have changed, for a balanced equation is a moral obligation. It feels good, this doing something."[20] Russell is stopped in this process before he kills the detainee but the scene is palpable as it expresses the passion in Russell to do something to restore goodness. He is feeling helpless in this process, though, even as he tries to right himself, and this moves Russell down to the next stage in this real life drama. He evaluates his role in war, the overall conduct of this war, the initial hope of bringing change to these people but of not feeling that this is happening, and it is then that he realizes that his efforts, all that he has done and all that America is doing, is really ineffectual. This conclusion inspires a feeling of impotence:

I am overwhelmed by the atrocity and the inhumanity of these killers and here, in these cells, I have the power to stop them. And I'm morally wrong when I do, and when I don't. I now realize that I am just trying to use logic to convince myself that Saedi the Iraqi interrogator, is right, that I am right, that these prisoners are guilty horrible people who don't deserve any sympathy or mercy, that they have information that could save a life, that they deserve justice. It would be so easy to say that I don't have the luxury of civility that a confession would put them behind bars, and that torture would stop them from killing again. But I also realize that my arguments exert on me a relentless pull to continually lower my bar. …But where am I willing to stop? There is no logical end to this reasoning! I will always be able to convince myself that I am right, that this killer is guilty and in "this case" torture is necessary, and that it is justified. But God damn it! I know that this is such bullshit,

340

because I've seen and I know how torture is always the immoral choice. This understanding is not hypothetical: it is empirical. I daily witness these mental gymnastics, and I constantly force myself to stand in the way of my own, and of others', descent into a moral abyss. And some days I lose these arguments. I'm afraid of where I'll go, and that I've lost myself.[21]

Russell is powerfully in the grips of uncertainty about himself and his role as a warrior in war. It is provocative to read this very struggle as it plays out. We are able on the outside looking in to see the intensity of emotion and the thoughts that drive his state of being. He offers more, though, that enables further understanding. He says,

We catch killers, we interrogate them for a few days, and if we have enough information, mostly which depends on a confession, we turn them over to the Iraqi police. Then they enter the "system." If there is not confession or overwhelming evidence— an impossible thing in a counterinsurgency—they are then released back to the streets, to kill again. Some prisoners that Saedi and I release even end up right back here, in our jail, to start the cycle all over again. It's all fucking bullshit. And because of this, I know the single most important topic that now consumes almost every minute of every big meeting I have with Iraqis is the lack of strong procedures [torture] necessary to convict, imprison, and punish terrorists. And by "strong procedures," they also mean the latitude to use hard interrogation methods, for me to stop saying "no," because from their perspective this inability—my rules, my boundaries—means an insurgent will quickly return to the street and neighborhood with little to no punishment. The longer I am here, the more I realize this disease infects us all. When terrorists are released, it causes anger, fear, and complacency within the populace, which then allows the insurgency to grow. This insurgency is a never-ending cycle; it's beyond frustrating; these killers are literally always within arm's reach and there is nothing I can fucking do![22]

These words reveal that Russell's internal disturbance is awaiting its final eruption. The quest for justice goes in circles, a revolving door of lunacy and a complete affront to goodness. Nothing changes. Russell becomes the victim, trapped by the justice he desires to enact. He moves on to a final stage in his moral injury from here. He starts to feel a "crisis of being." He has come to grips with the fact, as far as he can see it, that he is incapable of making change. As he stated earlier, "I've lost myself." He does not know who he is anymore; he is facing the complete collapse of self. Being in this state, one will struggle to resolve the moral dissonance. It can be a process that along the way engenders dark thoughts. This is where we find Russell. By this point, he is out of the war zone, back home. Racing in his mind are disturbing ruminations about his life and being. At one point, Russell enters therapy. He is trying to hold on, but he is having suicidal thoughts, and he needs help. Yet, when he comes to the therapist, he refuses to share these intimate thoughts. He says,

But these words are trapped and my surface stays silent. …It's obvious he doesn't hear me shouting. Because lately, I've started to imagine doing something really, really stupid, like jumping off a cliff or driving the car off the side of the road … there I am, hands on the wheel, and I see a tight corner approaching. My speed stays constant and my hands stay locked on the 10 and 2. I close my eyes and I imagine myself floating. I am smiling. There is no fear, and I feel a … release, a weight lifting, and well, I just feel. It's a satisfying feeling and it reminds me of how I felt in Iraq, how it felt to stand up in the turret, with my head exposed, with death all around. Does he realize that dying is addictive? But no, of course he can't understand me, so I don't tell him about these ideations. I barely even whisper them to myself.[23]

Now you have another picture of moral injury. It is a multifaceted inner conflict that exists singularly because we are a moral people with a moral conscience. We are directed in the purity of our being by a self-evident goodness that invades our understanding of existence. For the warrior in war, this moral truth is the driving force for being. To lose sight of it, to fail in upholding it, to be restrained in the use of it, or to be untrained in the application of it, all has the potential to bring about the emasculation of the warrior.

Unbelievably, this topic does not consume our training time and discussion on war. This is something without question that has to change. If it does not, we will continue to lead people like Russell down the path to insanity. He collapsed under the inability to maintain justice. For him, it was clearly related to the failure in being able to uphold justice, seeing those with guilt go through a revolving door of injustice. Nothing could be more injurious to a warrior. It fights against every aspect of being. For Russell, it left him feeling impotent and brought about an existential crisis where he struggled to understand who he was in war and in this world. That too is moral injury.

The Soldiers of 1st Tank Battalion 68th Armor Regiment (1–68 Armor)

Still another picture of moral injury is related to what happens in war when one acts grievously outside the scope of justice. A great picture of this comes from a book entitled *None of Us Were Like This Before*.[24] It is another book, like Lieutenant Colonel Bill Russell's, which talks about detainee operations. Yet, opposite of that one, these soldiers become entirely ignoble by participating willingly in torture. At times, they cannot see it because they offer what they consider to be "righteous" justification for their sordid deeds.[25] But as we know, this justification is empty. Justice

343

can only be realized in goodness. That is what these soldiers failed to understand. Let us look into this situation.

1st Tank Battalion 68th Armor Regiment (1–68 Armor) participated in the 2003 invasion of Iraq during Operation Iraqi Freedom. Months into the war, it established itself in the city of Balad, Iraq at what became known as Forward Operation Base Lion.

The mission of the Battalion was varied, doing things like patrols, raids, and traffic control checkpoints. One unique mission for the Battalion was one that would haunt the unit well after the time of their return to the States. It had to do with their management of the base detention center. Suspected terrorists were captured from raids in the local areas, brought back to this center, and interrogated. Sadly and despicably, what these soldiers supposedly did to these captives could be defined as nothing short of torture. The story regarding this is recorded in the work of investigative journalist Joshua Phillips. He lays out what he discovered from years of seeking out personal testimonies of military members who served in the Balad detention center. The entire testimony is alarming. Let us take a look.

The book begins by chronicling the story of Adam Gray. He was one of the tankers from 1–68 Armor who was tasked to be a guard in the detention center. It was a mission that would change his life forever. This became evident once Adam's deployment was up and he returned home. At that time, his step-father recalled about Adam that he "'...was aggressive. His mood swings were horrible. ...You could sometimes hear him screaming in his sleep and not being able to talk about anything."[26]

His mother, Cindy, also noticed the metamorphosis. When she spoke to him about this, what she uncovered horrified her. Adam relayed the dark inner secrets that were tormenting him. He talked about what that tour in Iraq entailed and what his time in the prison was like. He talked frankly about abusing prisoners where he worked: "So then we tie their hands up and then tie them to the highest rung on the [jail] bars. And then they'd have to hang there for a couple of days and they're not allowed to sleep, drink, and eat."[27] Adam went on from here to say that he and his cohorts would blast deafening music all night long at the detainees, and they would subject them to frightening situations where blood would be splashed up on the walls to scare them, causing them to think that they would soon be tortured. It worked well, Adam told his mother. The detainees would see the evidence of extreme cruelty and implode with fear, shrieking in horror.[28] At this point, Adam explained the detainees would be so scared, hungry and tired that they would answer any questions asked.[29]

When Adam's mother heard these stories, her reaction was absolute horror. She said to her son: "I'd rather be shot in the head than have to torture somebody like that. …They're people, they're human beings. …It doesn't make any difference who you are, just because they live in a different environment. Those mothers still love their children," she said.[30]

What impact these words had on Adam is not known. Soon afterward, he went on to his next duty station and did not talk about this again. That was an unfortunate turn of events. If ever Adam needed someone to talk to about his time in Iraq, this was it. His readjustment back to the States continued to be overwhelming. He struggled to live with his memories. His conscience was plagued with guilt. It left him without the ability to sleep or eat well. He suffered physically and was highly emotional. Often, he was violent, at one point holding a knife to the throat of another soldier and almost being processed out of the military. He also struggled with suicidal ideations and had one failed suicidal attempt. He further misused alcohol and drugs. In fact, it was that very approach to dealing with his problems that ultimately brought about his demise. He was found dead in his room one day after inhaling Dust-off with a plastic bag around his head.[31]

Why did all of this happen? It was undoubtedly connected to the self-induced moral injury. Adam simply could not get rid of the thoughts of what he did to the prisoners. The memories overwhelmed him with a guilt that tortured his mind. Adam's mother, in fact, found this to be true about others in Adam's unit. They all exhibited the same tortured behavior that Adam displayed, living out the same self-destructive disposition, "frequently getting drunk and getting into fights. They had difficulty focusing on their work and maintaining lasting relationships."[32] In seeing all of this, she realized that "[t]his is not just about Adam. This is about all of these kids that are in serious trouble."[33] They all suffer, she believed, from what they did in Iraq.

To see this more, let us look at the life of Daniel Keller, another member of 1-68 Armor. His abuse of detainees in this time was horrific. It is shocking to think that he could act in this way and that no one would step in and stop the abuse.

Regarding Keller, he says that he took part in the abuse of the detainees simply as a means to overcome boredom: "And the only thing that really does excite you is when you get to ... torture somebody. ... Honestly, a lot of the things that were done to the detainees were...just someone's idea of a good time."[34] What did that look like for Keller? He "described how he dragged detainees through concertina wire that was lying on the floor. At times he just used zip ties to force detainees into painful positions for hours—sometimes days. 'I once left a person zip-tied to a cell door for two and a half days, suspended on his own weight.'"[35] There were times too when Keller would try out inventive techniques of torture because as he says, "I just wanted to hurt [a prisoner]."[36] This kind of thing for Keller and a few other victimizers became routine. They used various macabre practices to induce torture: water-boarding, refusing to let prisoners use the restroom, and even tricking them into thinking that they would die if they asked to use the restroom. As far as Keller saw it, "we thought it was fun as hell."[37]

What Keller could not anticipate, however, would be how all of this would affect his life once he returned to the States. What he found was that he, like Adam, could not let go of the guilt and pain that accompanied his memories. Additionally, he, like Adam, lived

346

with an intense anger that seemed to control his life, and he said, "I drank a hell of a lot, absurd amounts... That's the self-medication I was doing—when you actually try to drink yourself to death."[38] He goes on from here to say, "There's a lot of stuff that you're not supposed to do that you do over there and...of course it raises the morality issues.... A lot of your emotional ramifications come from these feelings of guilt."[39]

Those feelings ran deep for Keller, unrelenting in their control. You see the substance of this displayed in a comment he made while painfully trying to get through college:

If I hadn't actually hurt anybody, I'd be sitting pretty—I'd be happy as could be.... I wouldn't have any problems. I wouldn't be on fucking medication. I wouldn't be sitting here doing an interview because I wouldn't know anything, and I would be fucking living life out there. I would be done with fucking school because I wouldn't have had three fucking years where I self-medicated, fucking drinking myself to death over this dumb shit until I realized that it was okay to get help because I'm not an asshole... My violence robbed me. ...The terrible things that I did ... and I'm still paying the price for it.[40]

Keller's story reveals the weight that morality holds over the soul. In this case, what makes that impact greater has to be the wonton disregard for goodness that he showed. It is one thing to make a mistake, to learn, and change. It is another to show abject disregard for human life and goodness. That is the trauma which Keller endures daily. That is moral injury.

Before we leave the discussion on this unit, however, let us consider one more story. It regards Jonathan Millantz. He was yet another soldier in the prison system with Gray and Keller.

Millantz was a combat medic, one ironically in the prison to take care of the detainees. That he did not do. What he did, instead, was observe and participate in prison hazing rituals. He stood by and watched on one occasion as a prisoner's wrist broke from extreme exercise.[41] He also participated in torture for fun, breaking bones, "mind fucking prisoners," and doing other such things.[42] Millantz even admits knowing "it was bad deep down inside, …[e]specially if you have twelve soldiers from a different country yelling at you, screaming at you, pointing guns at you and having stuff done [to you]. I can only imagine how traumatizing that would be to someone."[43]

How could such moral disregard not later evoke moral conflict? We know that it must, and not surprisingly as it did with Gray and Keller, so it did for Millantz. When he returned home, he ended up receiving a discharge from the Army, one related to PTSD and other physical problems.[44]

But, being away from the military did not relieve his mental challenges. He continued on with his struggles in civilian life, battling the memories and trying to quiet them with drugs, both illegal and prescribed pain-killers. "He said he was wracked with guilt and often agonized over those experiences. 'I was contemplating suicide—I couldn't believe what I did …It's very tough when you have a conscience that is filled with atrocities [and] you know what you did to people. I went to confession, I went to counseling. I still can't forgive myself for what I did to those poor people.'"[45] That crisis of conscience never did stop for Milantz, no matter what he tried. In short time, after one failed suicidal attempt, he finally died of a drug overdose.[46]

Moral injury plagued Millantz; moral injury killed him; and in death, moral injury becomes a testimony to all of the need to recognize the reality of upholding moral goodness. It is a potent force over the human soul toward goodness. Those who disregard it do so to their own peril. Justice will be exacted. As another member of this very unit assessed, "We lost more guys in my unit after we got back from Iraq than we lost in Iraq as a result of suicide, reckless behavior, ODs, whatever else. And those guys didn't die in honor of their service. They didn't die as patriots and defenders of freedom.

Those guys died because they were trying to drown out and hide from the reality that the war had dug into their hearts."[47]

Captain Timothy Kudo, Marine Infantry Officer

Moving on, let us consider something else that is often linked to the topic of moral injury, killing another human being in war. This is a complicated issue. In one sense, understanding it involves knowing what we have already discussed about one's natural disposition toward executing war and justice. That relates to what we have called war-type. Now we add this other factor, morality, which is certainly tied in with it but considers as well how these things come together for the sake of justice. Let us look into this.

Captain Timothy Kudo received momentary notoriety by anti-war activists for being a Marine Officer to speak out against killing in war. He had been to the conflict in Afghanistan, and though he never directly fired and killed someone, as an Officer in Charge, he directed others to kill. Even this impacted him and contributed to his own sense of being morally injured. He "thinks of himself as a killer - and he carries the guilt every day"[48] and consequently, as he says, "I can't forgive myself."[49]

Kudo clearly is unable to get past his experience of war. It relates to him having been involved in killing. This generated his confusion: "I held two seemingly contradictory beliefs: Killing is always wrong, but in war, it is necessary. How could something be both immoral and necessary?"[50]

This is indeed an interesting position. If Kudo is correct in what he offers, killing is wrong but necessary, I understand his moral confusion. I get too why it is so difficult for him post war to find healing from moral injury. How can you ever feel good about acting contrary to what you know is morally right, particularly when it involves something so monumental as taking another person's life? I think it would be challenging. Yet, the right question to ask is if Kudo is right in what he proposes; is killing wrong but necessary?

349

Obviously from what we have seen in the discussion about morality, he is not.

First of all, this is because, contrary to Kudo, immorality is never necessary. It is never right to torture a person for fun because it brings pleasure, for instance. We just witnessed the truth of this with 1st Tank Battalion 68th Armor Regiment. Doing something that is wrong, violating goodness, is never necessary. It fails to maintain goodness of being in self and others.

Yet beyond that, what about the issue of killing? Here again, different from what Kudo says, to take the life of someone is not necessarily wrong. To kill a murderer, that person actively involved in taking life in a way that corrupts his own well-being and that of another, is not immoral. It is rather good. That is what justice is. It is the activity to bring all to what is good.

We know this in so many ways. If people act against goodness out of insanity, we forcibly detain them with the hope of their restoration and for the protection of others. If people act criminally against goodness with sanity, we again forcibly detain them with the hope of their restoration and for the protection of others. In either case, the goal is to arrest the will of these people to go against goodness because we know that goodness is what needs to be protected for all. On this, we all agree.

It is the same idea with war and killing. When an enemy combatant is determined to destroy goodness with lethality and will not relent in this pursuit, the moral good is to stop that person. It requires lethal force in many situations because that is what is being used to attack what is good. If it was less than lethal force being used or even with lethal force if there was some way to stop the person short of death, you would not kill the person but apply less than lethal methods to arrest the will and power of this wayward person. That is justice.

Some might interject at this point and rebut what is offered by saying that if goodness "for all" is the focus, what about the person who is killed? That cannot be for his goodness. But do you see the problem here? This argument is once again as confused as the one Kudo offers. The reason is because in this argument, the focus is solely about the life of the person without recognition that life as we intuitively know it to be must be ordered to what is ultimately in keeping with its own well-being and that of others. All things to be good appear to be about what enables them to flourish not in the moment but toward their true purpose for being. Think back to what has been provided with respect to goodness. Goodness as a moral truth is not about some material, human or utilitarian calculation. What is good is not good because it appears to be beneficial. It is good simply; something known as a self-evident truth about existence. When it comes to the person killed then, you do not weigh goodness in the matter by looking at the life taken. You do so rather by knowing what goodness is and gaining that inner conviction about what it is in life to ensure that goodness unto its greatest end. In this sense, that a murderer is killed is a reflection of goodness in as much as it is a part of ordering life and liberty in strict accordance with intuition of what is good. It certainly would have been good if this person did not pursue wrongfulness with lethality because then he could have been detained and hopefully restored to ultimate goodness. Yet, his choice to destroy goodness with lethality became his choice to have his will arrested by the same means. This is all what Kudo fails to see.

A fundamental issue here is that when it comes to goodness in terms of what we know about it and how it appears to us there seems to be real consequence to rejecting it. To violate what is good clearly moves us toward our own demise. Gluttony, addiction, lying, cheating, stealing, abuse, illicit sexuality, denial of rights, enslavement and a raft of other vices and misbehaviors, are not in keeping with what goodness is and they each have deleterious consequences for those who practice them. In fact, every step taken in one of these ways brings suffering, and the greater the activity to destroy personal well-being or that of another, the greater it appears the potential for corruption. To be temperate, contrarily, and to seek only those goods which are real goods to the extent that they enable life to flourish toward its ultimate purpose is what simply seems right.

That we know and see these things is to understand too why all which is intractable in its activity to corrupt goodness by nature or choice is something we should expect to be prevented (i.e., a lion hunting humans or a serial killer). It follows in our recognition of what goodness is and how it orders existence. Thusly, we see why combatants rise to stop and kill if necessary those who are irredeemably fixed on the destruction of their own goodness and that of others. It is because the self-evident truth regarding goodness appears to direct all things in a way that does not make life itself the primary thing, but life as ordered perfectly toward real goodness, the summum bonum. Taking the life of a murderer, then, when it is the last resort, seems right both intuitively (for warriors, protectors and patriots) and in terms of how the good orders existence.

A second thing to consider now has to do with Kudo and his war-type. It seems apparent that irrespective of what might be good and how one preserves this, Kudo is likely coming at this issue with pacifist convictions. What this means is that there is a deeper conviction still which forbids doing anything that involves aggression regardless of how goodness is being corrupted or of how it might be protected. One, as a pacifist, never acts to harm another. If goodness is lost in the process, it is acceptable. More fundamental is being non-violent. This is not to say that goodness is unimportant. It is rather to say that for the pacifist achieving what is good for all never is believed to be realized through external force in this view. Given this, it is perfectly understandable that Kudo would say:

> War makes us killers. We must confront this horror directly if we're to be honest about the true costs of war. I didn't return from Afghanistan as the same person. My personality is the same, or at least close enough, but I'm no longer the "good" person I once thought I was.[51]

352

How could we think otherwise for Kudo if he genuinely comes at this issue of war as a pacifist? That is just what he believes. He sees life from a perspective that is unique and that needs to be honored.

If anything, what this all shows is why we have spent so much time addressing war-types and recognizing that people have different inner convictions which further complicates the matter. Add to this that we have not in military training recognized these dynamics appropriately, but have treated all the same when it comes to preparation for war, and you gain the picture of why we emasculate warriors and all who serve with them.

It is no wonder given this discussion that so many veterans suffer from their actions in war. Consider what one study provides specifically about involvement in killing: "Killing, regardless of role, is a better predictor of chronic PTSD symptoms than other indices of combat, mirroring some of the results on atrocities."[52] This same study goes on to say, "killing was a significant predictor of PTSD symptoms, dissociation, functional impairment, and violent behaviors, after controlling for general combat exposure (Maguen, Metzler, et al., in press). Also, after controlling for combat exposure, taking another life was a significant predictor of PTSD symptoms, alcohol abuse, anger, and relationship problems among Iraq War veterans."[53] How would we ever expect otherwise if we subject people to the experience of killing who either do not understand the moral basis for their actions, who are not the right war-type to be engaged in that activity or both? We must do what we can to address what it means to take a life in combat, ensuring that people are in the right place for that experience and that they are morally equipped to face the battles.[54] This would have been the thing that would have helped Kudo to avoid his moral crisis and confusion.

Conclusion

We have considered moral injury from several perspectives. What we looked at, however, was not the full extent of how moral injury comes about in the lives of those who go to war. There are other ways.[55] But even from what we did examine, we find that moral injury creates a crisis of being. This is what studies on the matter report:

> If individuals are unable to assimilate or accommodate (integrate) the event [in war] within existing self- and relational-schemas, they will experience guilt, shame, and anxiety about potential dire personal consequences (e.g., ostracization). Poor integration leads to lingering psychological distress, due to frequent intrusions, and avoidance behaviors tend to thwart successful accommodation. ...The more time passes, the more service members will be convinced and confident that not only their actions, but they are unforgiveable. In other words, service members and veterans with moral injury will fail to see a path toward renewal and reconciliation; they will fail to forgive themselves and experience self-condemnation.[56]

Recognizing the truth in all of this, we have to do better. That means accepting the reality of moral injury. This condition is not something fictional or a product of human creation. It is a genuine experience that happens as a result of war as studies are now showing: "Service members are confronted with numerous moral and ethical challenges in war. They may act in ways that transgress deeply held moral beliefs or they may experience conflict about the unethical behaviors of others."[57]

Without question, this is true because there is a self-evident moral goodness that when violated, brings about a mental dissonance that disturbingly raises questions of justice. Avoidance of this conscience conviction does no good. The effects will take hold:

"Chronic collateral manifestations of moral injury may include: self-harming behaviors, such as poor self-care, alcohol and drug abuse, severe recklessness, and para-suicidal behavior, self-handicapping behaviors, such as retreating in the face of success or good feelings, and demoralization, which may entail confusion, bewilderment, futility, hopelessness, and self-loathing. Most damaging is the possibility of enduring changes in self and other beliefs that reflect regressive over-accommodation of moral violation, culpability, or expectations of injustice."[58]

We must start to appreciate moral injury for what it is, especially when it comes to the impact that it has on those who fight and kill.[59] The long term diagnosis for those left untreated is poor: "A small but growing body of evidence suggests that, in addition to general combat experiences that veteran's experience, committing acts of war, such as killing enemy combatants, may be particularly traumatic and lead to suicidal behaviors."[60]

There is a lot of work yet to do, though, as other research on moral injury shows: "There has been very little attention paid to the lasting impact of moral conflict-colored psychological trauma among war veterans in the clinical science community. A possible reason for the scant attention is that clinicians and researchers who work with service members and veterans focus most of their attention on the impact of life-threatening trauma, failing to pay sufficient attention to the impact of events with moral and ethical implications; events that provoke shame and guilt may not be assessed or targeted sufficiently."[61] This is unfortunate, but it is not the end of the story. There are some who see the need and are pushing for more research: "Whatever the reasons for the scant attention paid to moral and ethical conflicts (after DSM-III), we argue that serious exploration is indicated because, in our experience, service members and veterans can suffer long-term scars that are not well captured by the current conceptualizations of PTSD or other adjustment difficulties."[62] Let us hope this challenge comes to fruition.

A promising movement in the exploration of moral injury is offered by Alan Fontana and Robert Rosenheck, two researchers calling for the investigation of a different approach in healing moral injury, one that sees potential value in addressing the spiritual side of a person. In their article, *The Role of Loss of Meaning in the Pursuit of Treatment for Posttraumatic Stress Disorder*, they show work from having examined veterans who found critical help in overcoming their crisis by turning to the clergy.[63]

While these researchers in the results of their study were not willing to conclude that religion was the answer, they did determine that what religion offered appeared to be helpful. Other scholars have agreed with these findings and are pushing for more research into this area: "…development of intervention studies that branch out from the traditional fear-based models of war-zone exposure and focus on guilt- or shame-based injuries that directly target moral injury are … important. …Research involving larger systems that can facilitate recovery from moral injury is also needed, particularly across disciplines that integrate leaders from faith-based and spiritual communities…."[64]

We are well past the point of accepting the possibility that morality plays a role in war. In truth, it is ignorance in this regard that has created so much confusion in preparing people for war and in helping them heal afterwards. Hence, let all areas of exploration into the impact of moral injury become central in dealing with veterans. We have to get this right. It is just as important as any other aspect of training and going to war. That we have missed this has not been good, but that can change. We can revamp military recruiting and training to reflect these important truths. As a nation, we can also consider war differently in terms of what happens and why. From there, we can each do our part to make changes when and where needed. In the end, while moral injury is not something that will ever be completely removed from the experience of war, it can be greatly minimized, and there is no reason why we should not apply every effort to do so.

Endnotes

[1] Sherman N. Recovering lost goodness: Shame, guilt, and self-empathy. Psychoanalytic Psychology [serial online]. April 2014; 31(2):217-235. Available from: PsycARTICLES, Ipswich, MA. Accessed March 4, 2016.

[2] Ibid.

[3] Ibid.

[4] Ibid.

[5] Consider one of several references on the matter, Jamie Reno, "Medicating Our Troops Into Oblivion": Prescription Drugs Said To Be Endangering U.S. Soldiers", http://www.ibtimes.com/medicating-our-troops-oblivion-prescription-drugs-said-be-endangering-us-soldiers-1572217, (2014, April 19).

[6] Rita Nakashima Brock and Gabriella Lettini, Soul Repair: Recovering from Moral Injury after War, (Boston: Beacon Press, 2013), p. 72.

[7] Ibid., p. 75.

[8] Marcus Luttrell Interview, (2007, August 9). Marcus Luttrell, author of "Lone Survivor", interviewed by Matt Lauer on The Today Show on June 12, 2007. https://www.youtube.com/watch?v=irC4K7Q4JCo

[9] Marcus Luttrell and Patrick Robinson, Lone Survivor, (New York: Little, Brown and Company, 2007), pp. 200-207.

[10] Ibid., p. 206.

[11] Ibid.

[12] [Boldness added for affect] Ibid., p. 15.

[13] Luttrell and Robinson, Lone Survivor, p. 205.

[14] Lone Survivor: A Conversation, History vs Hollywood, (2016, March 10), Marcus Luttrell Responds to Controversy over Freeing the Goatherds, http://www.historyvshollywood.com/video/lone-survivor-controversy/.

[15] Lieutenant Colonel Bill Russell, god is not here: A soldier's struggle with Torture, Trauma and the Moral Injuries of War, (New York: Pegasus, 2015).

[16] [clarification added], Ibid., p. 27.

[17] Ibid.

[18] Ibid., p. 28.

[19] Russell, god is not here: A soldier's struggle with Torture, Trauma and the Moral Injuries of War, p. 27.

[20] [clarification added], Ibid., p. 144.

[21] Ibid., pp. 251-252.

[22] [clarification added], Ibid., pp. 194-195.

[23] Ibid., pp. 31-32.

[24] Joshua Philipps, None of Us Were like this Before: American Soldiers and Torture, (New York: Verso, 2012).

[25] Ibid., pp. 62, 66. For example, one soldier stated, "'I was consumed by hate, and that's the best way I can describe it…. I was pissed off, and [wondered], what the hell are we doing here? What's our purpose? Innocent people were getting killed—poor soldiers, poor mothers have to … see their kid in a body bag.' …We weren't in the CIA—we were soldiers'. He added that it was reckless 'to give that much power and responsibility to a bunch of guys who were full of hate and resentment—getting shot at and watching their friends get killed … seeing people decapitated [in videos]—and then putting those guys in direct control of the people who did these things.'" (p. 66),

[26] Ibid., p. 6.

[27] Ibid., p. 7.

[28] Ibid., pp. 7-8.

[29] Ibid., p. 8.

[30] Ibid.

[31] Ibid., p. 12.

[32] Ibid., p. 13.

[33] Ibid,, pp. 13-14.

[34] Ibid., p. 64.

[35] Ibid.

[36] Ibid.

[37] Ibid., p. 65.

[38] Ibid., p. 130.

[39] Ibid., p. 135.

[40] Ibid., pp. 135-136.

[41] Ibid., p. 59.

[42] Ibid., p. 195.

[43] Ibid.

[44] Ibid., p. 188.

[45] Ibid., p. 191.

[46] Ibid., pp. 196 and 198.

[47] Ibid., p. 202.

[48] The Associated Press, "'I can't forgive myself': U.S. veterans suffering alone in guilt over wartime events", (2013, February 22), http://www.cbsnews.com/news/i-cant-forgive-myself-us-veterans-suffering-alone-in-guilt-over-wartime-events/.

[49] Ibid.

[50] Timothy Kudo, "I killed people in Afghanistan, Was I right or wrong?", (2013, January 25), https://www.washingtonpost.com/opinions/i-killed-people-in-afghanistan-was-i-right-or-wrong/2013/01/25/c0b0d5a6-60ff-11e2-b05a-605528f6b712_story.html.

[51] Ibid.

[52] Brett T. Litz, Nathan Stein, Eileen Delaney, Leslie Lebowitz, William P. Nash, Caroline Silva, and Shira Maguen, "Moral injury and moral repair in war veterans: A preliminary model and intervention strategy", Clinical Psychology Review, Volume 29, Issue 8, (2009 December), Pages 695–706.

[53] Ibid.

[54] Please note again that PTSD can be associated closely with moral injury in that both share similar symptomology and both can be present from the same experience. The distinguishing mark for moral injury is connection to an event where the issue of morality is a significant factor for a person.

[55] Shira Maguen and Brett Litz, "Moral Injury in Veterans of War", National Center for PTSD, "PTSD Research Quarterly", (2012), Volume 23/No.1, ISSN, 1050 -1835, http://www.ptsd.va.gov/professional/newsletters/research-quarterly/v23n1.pdf.

[56] [Clarification Added], Ibid.

[57] Brett T. Litz, Nathan Stein, Eileen Delaney, Leslie Lebowitz, William P. Nash, Caroline Silva, and Shira Maguen, "Moral injury and moral repair in war veterans: A preliminary model and intervention strategy", Clinical Psychology Review, Volume 29, Issue 8, (2009 December), Pages 695–706.

[58] Ibid.

[59] Shira Maguen, Barbara Lucenko, Charles Marmar, Brett Litz, Karen Seal, Sara Knight, Mark Reger, Gregory Gahm, "The impact of reported direct and indirect killing on mental health symptoms in Iraq war veterans." Journal Of Traumatic Stress [serial online]. February 2010;23(1):86-90 5p. Available from: CINAHL Complete, Ipswich, MA. Accessed March 4, 2016.

[60] Jessica Tripp, Meghan McDevitt-Murphy, Aisling Henschel, "Firing a Weapon and Killing in Combat Are Associated With Suicidal Ideation in OEF/OIF Veterans". Psychological Trauma: Theory, Research, Practice, And Policy [serial online]. October 12, 2015; Available from: PsycARTICLES, Ipswich, MA. Accessed March 4, 2016.

[61] Brett T. Litz, Nathan Stein, Eileen Delaney, Leslie Lebowitz, William P. Nash, Caroline Silva, and Shira Maguen, "Moral injury and moral repair in war veterans: A preliminary model and intervention strategy", Clinical Psychology Review, Volume 29, Issue 8, (2009 December), Pages 695–706.

[62] Ibid.

[63] Alan Fontana, and Robert Rosenheck, "Trauma, change in strength of religious faith, and mental health service use among veterans treated for PTSD", Journal of Nervous Mental Disease, Volume 192, Issue 9, (2004, September), pp. 579-584.

[64] Shira Maguen and Brett Litz, "Moral Injury in Veterans of War", National Center for PTSD, "PTSD Research Quarterly", (2012), Volume 23/No.1, ISSN, 1050 -1835, http://www.ptsd.va.gov/professional/newsletters/research-quarterly/v23n1.pdf.

Section IV

War is a National Effort

Chapter Twelve

A Nation Owning its Part in the Battle for Goodness

CHAPTER TWELVE

A NATION OWNING
ITS PART IN THE
BATTLE FOR GOODNESS

A military unit in combat is tightly webbed together in its various functions which all work seamlessly to bring justice. This unity has many interconnected parts: command element, fighters, logistics, and air. They each must do their part to enable success. What is missing here, however, and what is usually not a part of the discussion is the role that a country, its people, its politicians and its resources play in war. If anyone of those things is significantly misaligned to the cause, the front-line war effort will suffer. The greater the disconnection is, the greater the potential for the mission to fail. War is afterall a collective effort by all the people of a nation to stand for justice.

That there are combatants who can stare down their enemy and gladly kill them is difficult for most to fathom. So challenging is it that some claim the opposite:

There is ample indication of the existence of the resistance to killing and that it appears to have existed at least since the black-powder era. This lack of enthusiasm for killing the enemy causes many soldiers to posture, submit, or flee, rather than fight; it represents a powerful psychological force on the battlefield; and it is a force that is discernible throughout the history of man.[1]

In spite of what is said here, however, and regardless of how counter intuitive it might seem, there are people who will kill as guardians of truth. This we need to accept. I have been with those who rush to kill the enemy in spite of death. We have seen this resolve as well throughout the material in this study. There are clearly combatants who cannot and will not bow down in the face of injustice. They cannot and will not live in a world that compromises what they know to be true. It is their honor to rise and kill in these situations.

See this very truth come to life in the Civil War Battle at Little Round Top. At Gettysburg, July 2, 1863, Joshua Chamberlain, Colonel in the Union Army and the leader of the 20th Maine, was in a terrible predicament. The Confederates were advancing on his position. "Had it fallen, the flank of the Union position, rolling away along Cemetery Ridge, would have been turned: the battle would be lost, and with it the campaign and even the war."[2] Does it get direr, or does the need to fight and kill for what one believes become more urgent? It is hard to imagine how. So what happens? With clear conviction about standing for what was believed, these men under Chamberlain expended all of their rounds, hoping to kill their enemy. Yet, those efforts failed. To their frustration, the enemy still advanced, coming in for the final kill. Given this, what was the best thing for these soldiers to do: retreat, surrender, and give up the cause for truth? They had no more ammunition and were certain to be overcome. This is what Chamberlain did in his own words:

I saw the faces of my men, one after another, when they had fired their last cartridge, turn anxiously towards mine for a moment; then square to the front again. To the front for them lay death; to the rear what they would die to save. …Not a moment was about to be lost! Five minutes more of such a defensive, and the last roll-call would sound for us! Desperate as the chances were, there was nothing for it, but to take the offensive. I stepped to the colors. Then men turned towards me. One word was enough,—"BAYONET!"—It caught like a fire, and swept along the ranks. ... It was vain to order "Forward." No mortal could have heard it in the mighty hosanna that was winging in the sky. Nor would it wait to hear. ...The grating clash of steel in fixing bayonets told its own story; the color rose in front; the whole line quivered for the start; ...down into the face of a half a thousand! Two hundred men![3]

To witness conviction in the heart of combatants that drives them to stand and fight for truth in war regardless of consequences is inspiring. Listen again to the words: "To the front for them lay death; to the rear what they would die to save." This is the heart of goodness as steeled in the lives of those who cannot abandon convictions for truth. Death might be my fate, but I cannot turn back. Surrender is not my option. I will rise to kill or be killed. This same spirit was captured throughout the fighters in the Civil War.

At Gettysburg, there were an estimated 51,000 casualties with another 5000 mules and horses killed.[4] The deadliness and sheer intensity of this engagement shows that people can be resolute to stand for what is believed. In fact, among the corpses found there were two women.[5] They both had disguised their gender to come alongside their male counterparts to fight. They did not have to do so but they could not stop themselves as they too were rising to defend what they believed. How does all of this not show the unrelenting willingness that people have to face evil as they see it and die for what is believed to be right?

This passion was equally visible at other Civil War engagements: e.g., at Antietam there were 22,000 killed or wounded in less than twelve hours, and at Chancellorsville the figure was 30,000 in four days.[6] In fact, numerous Civil War studies reveal that it was not a lack of will to take the life of the enemy that prevented more killing in battle, but factors like the following: 1) extreme exhaustion from long marches to the battle with heavy packs; 2) sleep deprivation that caused many to sleep during battle; 3) rabid hunger; 4) succumbing to the elements;[7] 5) ill-preparedness for battle conditions[8]; 6) with a desire to get as many rounds off as possible, and considering the lengthy process of reloading, hasty and inaccurate shooting was the norm[9]; and 7) the lines or formations, in which men shot, called for them to shoot up, and not straight ahead.[10] These are the things that stood in the way of killing, and thus, it cannot be attributed to a lack of conviction to kill. In sum, there are those who will rise to defend justice and will kill to do it.

Given all of this and all that we know from this study, we can easily say that the spirit to kill the enemy is something combatants possess. However, as we additionally know, a willingness to kill the enemy is not enough. It has to be founded in a noble cause that enables goodness for all. Otherwise, people might kill for what they believe but it will not be for justice. That needs to be guarded against. To kill for an immoral cause is unjust. Even to kill for a cause that is solely about national identity or loved ones, easily can bring about the emasculation of combatants when and if that cause is later examined and seen to be ignoble. This we must address. We have to ensure that those who rise for justice indeed rise for justice. We must equip them for the just cause that grounds their purpose in a truth that rises above that of the enemy. That is what moral goodness demands and that is the only way for moral goodness to be realized.

Evil abounds. There are threats and actual violations of moral goodness in all places. People around the world are dying, facing death or in deep grief because their rights are being butchered by regimes or terrorist groups who are intent on destroying every vestige of humanity and civility.

In large portions of Syria, ISIS has brutalized people. The United Nations has listed the following atrocities: "[m]assacres, beheading boys as young as 15, and amputations and lashings in public squares that residents -- including children -- are forced to watch figure on the list of crimes, as does the widespread use of child soldiers, stoning women to death for suspected adultery."[11]

Women of this country have also been kidnapped and sold into sexual bondage, having been forced to undergo abortions so as to be subjected to the on-going sexual whims of their captors, and many are then killed as well when their value is lost to the captors. Keep in mind too that these women are actually children, usually around twelve years of age.

The injustice continues too beyond Syria. In Afghanistan, a man's eyes were gouged out, he was skinned alive, and then thrown off a cliff. In Nigeria, over two hundred young girls were kidnapped to be used as sex slaves. How many other places in this world do we know of where basic human rights are discarded as people are decapitated, burned alive, used for harvesting organs, thrown off of buildings, buried alive, and undergo countless other atrocities? It is appalling to hear about such clear violations of fundamental rights. As Americans we cannot imagine living in such an existence. But consider for a moment what this would be like. What if you did not have patriots, protectors and warriors rising up to defend your rights? What would happen if we removed the very combatants who enable this nation to know the richest expression of freedom that any country has ever known? What if the terrorists took over, as they would like to do, and denied you all freedoms of speech, assembly, religion, gender equality, and the like? How different your life would be then. It is frightening to even ponder. Granted, it will never come to that. Of that we can be assured. There will always be American women and men on the front lines of battle with undying resolve to fight for moral goodness for the sake of all humanity. That is our blessing and responsibility.

We began this book by looking at veterans who suffer from war. We will end by doing the same. We must keep their stories from living in the shadows of everyday existence. It is our duty to be awakened to their plight and to support those who stand up for our goodness. To motivate you to this end, regard the story of Douglas Barber.

Barber served in the Army as a reservist and was activated for a seven month tour in Iraq. That was all it took for him to have undeniable brain changes, not from blunt force trauma, but from emotional trauma. Consequently, when he returned home, his emotional and mental states were wrecked. He was paranoid, withdrawn, incapable of keeping his eleven year marriage together, not able to even walk down the street without worrying that someone would blow him up. What happened to this man?

Barber served as a truck driver in Iraq, on edge daily from traveling up and down roads strewn with IEDs, aware that every moment could be his last. Further, "[h]e was haunted by the deaths of his colleagues and by the fear and desperation he saw in the faces of Iraqis."[12] He stated, "It was really bad - death was all around you, all the time. You couldn't escape it. Everybody in Iraq was going through suicide counseling because the stress was so high. It was at such a magnitude, such a high level, that it was unthinkable for anyone to imagine. You cannot even imagine it."[13]

Even Barber's minister noticed the change that one short tour in war brought to him. He remarked, "He was a really good guy, pretty level-headed ... He liked to have fun. But when he came back from Iraq the difference in him was so sad."[14]

What explanation is there that accounts for Barber's changed emotional state and attitude post war? Barber himself stated that PTSD was the culprit behind his suffering:

> All is not OK or right for those of us who return home alive and supposedly well. What looks like normalcy and readjustment is only an illusion to be revealed by time and torment. Some soldiers come home missing limbs and other parts of their bodies. Still others will live with permanent scars from horrific events that no one other than those who served will ever understand. We come home from war trying to put our lives back together but some cannot stand the memories and decide that death is better. We kill ourselves because we are so haunted by

seeing children killed and whole families wiped out. PTSD comes in many forms not understood by many: but yet if a soldier has it, America thinks the soldiers are crazy. PTSD comes in the form of depression, anger, regret, being confrontational, anxiety, chronic pain, compulsion, delusions, grief, guilt, dependence, loneliness, sleep disorders, suspiciousness/paranoia, low self-esteem and so many other things. We are easily startled with a loud bang or noise and can be found ducking for cover when we get panicked. This is a result of artillery rounds going off in a combat zone, or an improvised explosive device blowing up. I myself have trouble coping with an everyday routine that often causes me to have a short fuse. A lot of soldiers lose jobs just because they are trained to be killers and they have lived in an environment that is conducive to that. We are always on guard for our safety and that of our comrades. When you go to bed at night you wonder will you be sent home in a flag-draped coffin because a mortar round went off on your sleeping area. It is something that drives soldiers over the edge and causes them to withdraw from society. As Americans, we turn our nose down at them wondering why they act the way they do. Who cares about them, why should we help them?[15]

As Barber says, war changes a person, and confusion can abound for those who have gone through it and those who witness it. But how can this not be the case? With respect to the combatant, the daily grind of a never ending mission that always has the body primed with fear, anxiety and anger goes on and on with the haunting thought that every second of the day could bring about one's violent death. There is no rest in this. This is war for many; it is war on the battlefield and it is war back home. Regarding the latter, this is where Barber found himself. He could not silence the cacophonous sounds of battle. His life was now an enduring nightmare of agonizing memories. No one who sent him to war seemed to care or understand his plight. In a state of desperation, unable to silence the piercing noises in his head, he went out on his front porch one day with a shotgun. A call was made to 911, alerting the police of the situation. When they arrived Barber appeared to be trying to get the cops to shoot him, "suicide by cop." He longed for death. When it became clear that the cops would not kill him his response was quick. He turned from the policemen, put the gun to his head, and pulled the trigger. That was it, another veteran gone!

We love our freedom. We assert our rights every day. But there is a serious problem for many who defend this freedom and it needs national scrutiny. We send people to war who are not prepared for it, who in cases should not go, and who are not equipped in many ways to deal with it. Naturally, they come home with severe problems. When will we see what lies in the shadows? The proof is plentiful:

> The mental and physical health of veterans returning from war zone deployment is of substantial concern to the public as well as military leaders and civilian policymakers. …Recent research on the Gulf War and Operation Enduring Freedom/Operation Iraqi Freedom (OEF/OIF) veterans confirmed increased risk for mental health problems, including posttraumatic stress disorder (PTSD), depression, suicidality, neuropsychological deficits, and alcohol and drug use. These disorders have implications for individual and unit readiness; physical, social, and emotional health of veterans and their families.…[16]

We need to make changes as a nation in terms of how we go to war. That is our job, and this book offers suggestions and insights on how to bring that change for defenders of justice. The most essential pieces are the following:

1) Recognize the incredibly high cost of not understanding all who fight in war;

2) See that just as there are differing personalities in people so too there are differing constitutions when it comes to how people approach and defend justice;

3) Mandate an entry test for military service that allows individuals to determine if they are willing to take the life of another;

4) Educate and train military members uniquely in accordance with how they view killing and war;

5) Recognize the driving engine of moral goodness and develop training that honors how each person will engage experience and encounter war;

6) Faithfully train on how combatants find a just cause for war and how that ties into combat;

7) Provide therapy to people respecting their war-type;

8) Offer healing rituals for veterans when they return from war so as to deal with any spiritual and moral issues;

9) Ensure that veterans of war are cared for in every way when they come home from defending your rights; and,

10) Celebrate warriors and those who fight with them for all that they have accomplished.

These are just broad outlines from what has been given in this book. May each of us find the resolve to do our part, preparing Just Warriors, Protectors and Patriots with a Just Cause for a Just Battle in a Just War. If we will not do this, stop sending combatants to defend justice and be willing to live with the consequences!

Endnotes

---

[1] Dave Grossman, On Killing: The Psychological Cost of Learning to Kill in War and Society, (New York, NY: Little, Brown and Company, 1995), p. 28.

[2] John Keegan and Richard Holmes, Soldiers: A History of Men in Battle, (New York: Elisabeth Sifton Books, 1986), p. 39.

[3] Joshua Chamberlain, "Bayonet! Forward", (Gettysburg, Pennsylvania: Stan Clark Military Books, 1994), pp. 32-33.

[4] History.net, "Gettysburg Casualties (Battle Deaths at Gettysburg)", http://www.historynet.com/gettysburg-casualties, (1 July, 2018).

[5] Ibid.

[6] Paddy Griffith, Battle Tactics of The Civil War, (New Haven: Yale University Press, 1989), p. 19.

[7] Numbers 1-4 are from Keegan, pp. 134-143.

[8] Richard Holmes, Acts of War: The Behavior of Men in Battle, (New York: The Free Press, 1985) pp. 167-175.

[9] Ardant Du Picq, Battle Studies: Ancient and Modern Battle, (Harrisburg Pennsylvania: The Military Publishing Company, 1958), pp. 231-237.

[10] For even more reasons why men did not kill in battle according to du Picq but none related to a fundamental refusal to kill a human regard the following, Ibid., pp. 231-271 (fear), pp. 44-45 (self-preservation), pp. 45-46 (kinship with enemy, they "...recognized each other as brothers, and rather than spill fraternal blood, they extricated themselves from combat as if it were a crime.", and pp. 20-21, 51, 69, 94-95, 110, 121, 122, 128, and 154 (discipline in the ranks, lack of devotion to a cause, morality, leaders, the worthiness of a cause, the question of unity and cohesion amongst troops, organization, and self-esteem).

[11] Staff writer, "ISIS accused of crimes against humanity," Al Arabiya News, http://english.alarabiya.net/en/News/middle-east/2014/11/14/ISIS-commits-crimes-against-humanity-in-Syria.html, (14, November 2014),

[12] Andrew Buncombe, "The life and death of an Iraq veteran who could take no more",

http://www.theinsider.org/news/article.asp?id=1819, (25 January 2006).

[13] Ibid.

[14] Ibid.

[15] Ibid.

[16] Susan V. Eisen, Mark R. Schultz, Dawne Vogt, Mark E. Glickman, A. Rani Elwy, Mari-Lynn Drainoni, Princess E. Osei-Bonsu, and James Martin, "Mental and Physical Health Status and Alcohol and Drug Use Following Return From Deployment to Iraq or Afghanistan", http://www.ncbi.nlm.nih.gov/pmc/articles/PMC3496463/, (March, 2012).

BIBLIOGRAPHY

ABC News, "Abu Ghraib Prison Soldier Admits Guilt," http://abcnews.go.com/GMA/Story?id=127625&page=1, (August 26, 2004).

Adams, Elizabeth. Understanding the Trauma of Childhood Psycho-Sexual Abuse. Bedford, Massachusetts: Mills & Sanderson, 1994.

Adler, Mortimer. "The Nature of Natural Law", http://www.faculty.umb.edu/gary_zabel/Courses/Morals%20and%20Law/M+L/adler_naturallaw.html, (28 January, 2016).

_____. The Time of Our Lives. New York: Fordham University Press, 1996.

Allison, Julie., Wrightsman, Lawrence. Rape: The Misunderstood Crime. Newbury Park, California: Sage Publications, 1993.

Allman, Mark. Who Would Jesus Kill?. Winona, MN: Anselm Academics, 2008.

Amen, Daniel. Change Your Brain. Change Your Life. New York: Three Rivers Press, 1988.

American Psychiatric Association. Diagnostic and Statistical Manual of Mental Disorders, Fourth Edition. Washington, D.C.: American Psychiatric Association, 1994.

Andrews, Evan. "8 Reasons It Wasn't Easy Being Spartan," http://www.history.com/news/history-lists/8-reasons-it-wasnt-easy-being-spartan, (2013, 5 March).

Aquinas, Thomas. Treatise on Law: (Summa Theologica, Questions 90-97). Washington, D.C.: Regnery Publishing, 1956.

_____. ST I. Q. 78, A. 4. obj. 4, ST I. Q. 78. out. 1. Summa Theologica, II IntraText Edition CT, 2002. http://www.intratext.com/IXT/ENG0023/_INDEXHTM. (9 January, 2004).

Aristotle, Nicomachean Ethics, New York: The Bobbs-Merrill Company, 1962.

Armstrong, R. Primary and Secondary Precepts in Thomistic Natural Law Teaching. Hague, Netherlands: Martinus Nijhoff, 1966.

Associated Press, "Vietnam veteran wins insanity-defense case", https://news.google.com/newspapers?nid=1310&dat=19811011&id= d7RQAAAAIBAJ&sjid=VOIDAAAAIBAJ&pg=5727,2820890&hl =en, (October 11, 1981).

Audi, Robert. Epistemology. New York: Routledge, 2003.

_____. Moral Knowledge and Ethical Character. Oxford: Oxford University Press, 1977.
Alexander, Joseph. The Three Days of Tarawa: Utmost Savagery. Annapolis, Maryland: Naval Institute Press, 1995.

Ardant Du Picq, Battle Studies: Ancient and Modern Battle. Harrisburg Pennsylvania: The Military Publishing Company, 1958.

Axinn, Sidney. A Moral Military. Philadelphia, Pennsylvania: Temple University Press, 1989.

Balkoski, Joseph. Omaha Beach: D-Day. Pennsylvania: Stackpole Books, 2004.

Baker, Alan. "The Knight", Hoboken, NJ: John Wiley & Sons, 2003.

Baker, Fred. W. III, "Al Qaeda Recruits Children," Women for Terror Missions, American Forces Press Service, http://www.defenselink.mil/news/newsarticle.aspx?id=48885, (6 February, 2008).

Baron, Larry and Straus, Murray. Four Theories of Rape in American Society. New Haven: Yale University Press, 1989.

Barr, Jennifer. Within a Dark Wood: The Personal Story of a Rape Victim. Garden City, New York: Doubleday & Company, Inc., 1979.

Barter, James. A Medieval Knight. New York: Lucent Books, 2005.

Beckwith, Francis and Koukl, Gregory. Relativism: Feet Firmly Planted in Mid-Air. Grand Rapids, Michigan: Baker Books, 1998.

Bellavia, David. House to House: An Epic Memoir of War. New York: Free Press, 2007.

Benjamin, Mark, Olmsted, Dan. "Exclusive: Green Beret's strange suicide", http://www.upi.com/Business_News/Security-Industry/2004/05/11/Exclusive-Green-Berets-strange-suicide/71431084296160/, (May 11, 2004).

Bennett, William. Why We Fight. New York: Doubleday, 2002.

Bernstein, Adam. Lauded Conscientious Objector Desmond T. Doss Sr., http://www.washingtonpost.com/wp-dyn/content/article/2006/03/25/AR2006032501181.html, (March 26, 2006).

Bethke, Elshtain and Popenoe, David. Council on Families in America, Institute for American Values, 1995.

Blackburn, Simon. Being Good. Oxford: Oxford University Press, 2001.

Blackfive, "Marine Messages in Fallujah," http://www.blackfive.net/main/military_stuff/index.html, (November 15, 2004).

Blestman, Szandor. Ron Paul Revolution: We Have Not Yet Begun to Fight, http://www.americanchronicle.com/articles/view/42524, (November 09, 2007).

Bloom, Harold. The American Religion, New York: Simon & Schuster, 1992.

Bosco, Peter and Bosco, Antoinette. rev. World War I. New York: Facts on File, 2003.

Bowra, C. M. "Alexander The Great," Reports & Essays: Biography - Historical Figures, http://www.studyworld.com/newsite/ReportEssay/Biography/Histori calFigures%5CAlexander_the_Great-323270.htm, (May 11, 2009).

Bourke, Joanna. An Intimate History of Killing. New York: Basic Books, 1999.

Brady, James. Why Marines Fight. New York: Thomas Dunne Books, 2007.

Bradley, James. Flags of our Fathers. New York: Bantam Books, 2006.

Bremner, Douglas J., Elzinga, Bernet. Schmahl, Christian, Vermetten, Eric. Structural and functional plasticity of the human brain in posttraumatic stress disorder, http://www.ncbi.nlm.nih.gov/pmc/articles/PMC3226705/, (29 November 2011).

Brock, Rita Nakashima., Lettini, Gabriella. Soul Repair: Recovering from Moral Injury after War, Boston: Beacon Press, 2013.

Brownmiller, Susan. "Thornhill: Rape on the Brain". A review of Randy Thornhill and Craig Palmer, A Natural History of Rape: Biological Bases of Sexual Coercion. Boston: MIT Press, 2000, Volume 3, Number 9, Feminista. http://www.feminista.com/archives/v3n9/brownmiller.html. (Feb. 23, 2000).

Budziszewski, J. Written On The Heart: The Case for Natural Law. Downers Grove, Illinois, InterVarsity Press, 1977.

Buncombe, Andrew. "The life and death of an Iraq veteran who could take no more", http://www.theinsider.org/news/article.asp?id=1819, (25 January 2006).

Bush, George H. W. "Address on Iraq's Invasion of Kuwait (August 8, 1990)", http://millercenter.org/president/bush/speeches/speech-5529, (2016, 6 June).

Byrne, Peter. The Philosophical and Theological Foundations of Ethics. New York: ST. Martin's Press, 1999.

Campbell, R. J. The War and The Soul. New York: Dodd, Mead and Company, 1918.

Cartledge, Paul. The Spartans. New York: The Overlook Press, 2003.

_____. Thermopylae: The Battle That Changed The World. New York: The Overlook Press, 2006.

Carney, Elizabeth., Ogden, Daniel. Philip II and Alexander the Great: Father and Son, Lives and Afterlives, New York: Oxford University Press, 2010.

Center for American Progress, "In Their Own Words: Iraq's 'Imminent' Threat", https://www.americanprogress.org/issues/security/news/2004/01/29/459/in-their-own-words-iraqs-imminent-threat/, (January 29, 2004).

Chamberlain, Joshua. "Bayonet! Forward". Gettysburg, Pennsylvania: Stan Clark Military Books, 1994.

Charney, Dennis S., Deutch, Ariel Y., Krystal, John H., Southwick, Steven M., Davis, Michael. "Psychobiologic Mechanisms of

Posttraumatic Stress Disorder", Arch Gen Psychiatry. 1993;50 (4):294-305. (April, 1993).

Charter of the United Nations and Statute of the International Court of Justice, Chapter 1, Purposes and Principles, Article 1 (4), https://treaties.un.org/doc/publication/ctc/uncharter.pdf, (2016, 6 June).

Chersi, Fabian., Mirolli, Marco., Pezzulo, Giovanni., Baldassarre, Gianluca. "A spiking neuron model of the cortico-basal ganglia circuits for goal-directed and habitual action learning", Neural Networks, Volume 41, (2013).

Chopra, Deepak. Peace Is the Way. New York: Harmony Books, 2005.

Clement, Catherine. Gandhi: The Power of Pacifism. New York: Harry N. Abrams, 1996.

Coleman, Stephen. Military Ethics: An Introduction with Case Studies. New York: Oxford University Press, 2013.

Cowan, Ross. Roman Legionary. Great Britian: Ospery Publishing, 2003.

Crawford, Neta. "The Justice of Preemption and Preventive War Doctrines". In Mark Evans, Just War Theory: A Reappraisal. Great Britain: Palgrave MacMillan, 2005.

Crosby, Donald. Battlefield Chaplains, Lawrence, Kansas: University of Kansas, 1994.

Daimyo, The Everything Japanese Guide, http://www.japanese123.com/daimyo.htm, (May 2009).
Daniels, James, Howden, Emily, and Kuhlbars, Richard. Silent Wounds: The Hidden Cost of War. Irmo, South Carolina: Virtual Life Solutions, 2007.

Dayton, Tian. "Scared Stiff: The Biology of Fear",
http://www.tiandayton.com/scared-stiff-the-biology-of-fear, (3 July,
2015).

Dear, I. C. B. and Foot, R. D., Tarawa, capture of. The Oxford
Companion to World War II. Oxford University Press. 2001.
Encyclopedia.com. 24 Jul. 2009 <http://www.encyclopedia.com>.

"Declaration of Independence (Preamble),"
http://users.wfu.edu/zulick/340/Declaration.html, (31 October,
2017).

Delaney, Eileen. "The Relationship between Traumatic Stress, PTSD
and Cortisol",
http://www.med.navy.mil/sites/nmcsd/nccosc/healthProfessionalsV2
/reports/Documents/ptsd-and-cortisol-051413.pdf, (July, 2015).

Democracy Now, "U.S. Broadcast Exclusive–"Fallujah: The Hidden
Massacre" on the U.S. Use of Napalm-Like White Phosphorus
Bombs,"
http://www.democracynow.org/2005/11/8/u_s_broadcast_exclusive_
fallujah_the, (November 08, 2005).

Department of Veterans Affairs Department of Defense, " VA/DoD
Clinical Practice Guideline for the Management of Post-Traumatic
Stress," http://www.healthquality.va.gov/ptsd/ptsd_full.pdf, (2004,
January).

Dersin, Denise. Editors of Time Life Books. What Life Was Like
When Rome Ruled the World. Alexandria, Virginia: Time Life
Books, 1997.

Diggersrealm, Fallujah Investigation - Evidence Of Atrocities, IED's
and Weapons Caches [Pics And Images],
http://www.diggersrealm.com/mt/archives/000452.html, (June 6,
2009).

Donn, Jeff., Hefling. "Wounded vets from Iraq, and families, now
suffer economically,"

http://www.nctimes.com/articles/2007/10/01/military/5_20_889_29_07.txt, (29 September, 2007).

Drez, Ronald. remember d-day. Washington, D.C.: National Geographic Press, 2004.

Duhigg, Charles. "Soldiers trained to kill, not to cope," http://seattletimes.nwsource.com/html/nationworld/2001984566_combat21.html, (July 21, 2004).

Eisen, Susan V., Schultz, Mark R., Vogt, Dawne., Glickman, Mark E., Elwy, A. Rani., Drainoni, Mari-Lynn., Osei-Bonsu, Princess E., Martin, James. "Mental and Physical Health Status and Alcohol and Drug Use Following Return From Deployment to Iraq or Afghanistan", http://www.ncbi.nlm.nih.gov/pmc/articles/PMC3496463/, (March, 2012).

Ellul, Jacques. The Theological Foundation of Law. New York: Doubleday & Company, 1960.

Euston, David R., Gruber, Aaron J., McNaughton, Bruce L. "The Role of Medial Prefrontal Cortex in Memory and Decision Making", Neuron, Volume 76, Issue 6, p1057–1070, http://www.cell.com/neuron/abstract/S0896-6273(12)01108-7?_returnURL=http%3A%2F%2Flinkinghub.elsevier.com%2Fretrieve%2Fpii%2FS0896627312011087%3Fshowall%3Dtrue&cc=y=, (2012, December 20).

Evans, Mark. Just War Theory: A Reappraisal. New York: Palgrave MacMillian, 2005.

Evans, Michael., Ryan, Alan. The Human Face of Warfare: Killing, Fear and Chaos in Battle. St. Leonards, NSW: Allen & Unwin, 2000. eBook Collection (EBSCOhost), EBSCOhost (accessed August 26, 2015).

Ferguson, Niall. The Pity of War. New York: Basic Books, 1999.

Fields, Rick. The Code of the Warrior: In History, Myth and Everyday Life. New York: Harper Perennial, 1991.

Figley, Charles., Nash, William. Combat Stress Injury: Theory, Research, and Management, (New York: Routledge, 2007).

Figueroa, Teri., Walker, Mark. "The 'Pendleton 8': A look at the 7 Marines and Navy corpsman charged in Hamdania incident", The North County Times, July 23, 2006, http://www.nctimes.com/articles/2006/07/23//news/top_stories/21_0 8_547_22_06.txt (March 3, 2009).

Finley, Erin. "Fields of Combat: Understanding PTSD Among Veterans of Iraq and Afghanistan", (Ithaca: ILR Press, 2011).

Finnis, John. Natural Law and Natural Rights. Oxford: Clarendon Press, 1980.

Finucane Anne., Alexandra, Dima., Ferreira Nuno., Halvorsen, Marianne. Basic emotion profiles in healthy, chronic pain, depressed and PTSD individuals. Clinical Psychology & Psychotherapy.

Fontana, Alan., Rosenheck Robert. "Trauma, change in strength of religious faith, and mental health service use among veterans treated for PTSD", Journal of Nervous Mental Disease, Volume 192, Issue 9, (2004, September), pp. 579-584.

Fox, James Alan., Levin, Jack. Extreme Killing: Understanding Serial and Mass Murder. Sage Publishing: Thousand Oaks, CA.

Frankena, William. Ethics. Englewood Cliffs, New Jersey: Prentice Hall, 1973.

Frantzen, Allen J. Bloody Good: Chivalry, Sacrifice, and the Great War, Chicago: University of Chicago Press, 2004.

Freedberg Jr, Sydney J. "Thin line separates aggressive fighting from war crimes", http://www.govexec.com/dailyfed/1007/101207nj1.htm, (October 12, 2007).

Frenkel, Karen. "Continuing Effects of 9/11," http://www.sciammind.com/print_version.cfm?articleID=1878E90B -E7F2-99DF-3F4B426F6533D13A, (August, 2007).

Friedman, Matthew. "Post-Traumatic Stress Disorder", https://www.acnp.org/g4/GN401000111/CH109.html, (2000).

Frye, David. "Greco-Persian Wars: Battle of Thermopylae", http://www.historynet.com/greco-persian-wars-battle-of-thermopylae.htm, originally published in Military History Magazine, (January/February, 2006).

Fuchs, Josef. Natural Law: A theological Investigation. New York: M. H. Gill and Son, 1965.

Fuentes, Gidget. "6 Navy Crosses for Darkhorse," https://www.leatherneck.com/forums/showthread.php?t=47652, (June 11, 2007).

Fulkerson, Norman. "Through the Valley of Death," http://www.tfp.org/through-the-valley-of-death/, (8 May, 2012).

Fundukian, Laurie and Wilson, Jeffrey. Eds. The Gale Encyclopedia of Mental Health, Second Edition, Volume 1 A-L. New York: Thomson Gale, 2008.

Fussell, Paul. Wartime: Understanding and Behavior in the Second World War. New York: Oxford Press, 1989.

Gallagher, Jim. Viking Explorers, (New York: Chelsea House, 2000), p. 62, http://0-web.ebscohost.com.dbpcosdcsgt.co.san-diego.ca.us/ehost/detail?vid=18&hid=8&sid=77fdbe8d-43fc-41e5-88bd-b637fd5e0a5c%40sessionmgr108&bdata=JnNpdGU9ZWhvc3QtbGl2ZQ%3d%3d#db=khh&AN=9210912.

Geisler, Norman. Ethics: Alternatives and Issues. Grand Rapids, Michigan: Zondervan Publishing House, 1971.

George, Robert. In Defense of Natural Law. Oxford: Oxford University Press, 1999.

Gibbon, Edward. The History of the Decline and Fall of the Roman Empire. New York: Penguin Books, 2000.

Giles, Kevin. "Jan. 27: This Marine's death came after he served in Iraq", http://www.startribune.com/local/11605966.html, (January 29, 2007).

GoldFarb, Lyn. "Japan: Memories of a Secrets Empire, Samurai," http://www.pbs.org/empires/japan/enteredo_8.html, (2003).

Goldstein, Donald, Dillon, Katherine and Wenger, Michael. D-Day Normandy. New York: Brassey's, 1994.

Goleman, Daniel. Emotional Intelligence, Bantam Books, New York, 1995.

_____. Working with Emotional Intelligence. New York: Bantam Books, 2006.

Goodman, Amy. "Ex-U.S. Marine: I Killed Civilians in Iraq", Rush Transcript," http://il.democracynow.org/2004/5/24/ex_u_s_marine_i_killed, (May 24, 2004).

Google,http://www.google.com/archivesearch?hl=en&q=medal+of+honor+grenade&um=1&ie=UTF-8&scoring=t&ei=YvbnSdmZLIOitwfi84iNBg&sa=X&oi=timeline_result&resnum=12&ct=title.
Gottlieb, Paula. "Aristotle on Non-contradiction," http://plato.stanford.edu/entries/aristotle-noncontradiction/#1, (February 2, 2007).

Gravett, Christopher. English Medieval Knight 1300-1400. Great Britian: Osprey Publishing, 2002.

Gray, J. Glenn. The Warriors: Reflections on Men in Battle. New York: Harper Torchbook, 1970.

Griffith, Paddy. Battle Tactics of The Civil War. New Haven: Yale University Press, 1989.

_____. Forward into Battle. Novato, California: Presidio Press, 1991.

Grossman, Dave. On Combat. China: Warrior Science Publications, 2008.

_____. On Killing. New York: Back Bay Books, 1996.

Gula, Richard. Reason Informed by Faith. New York: Paulist Press, 1989.

Hadas, Moses. Imperial Rome. New York: Time-Life Books, 1965.

Haddock, Vicki. The Science of Creating Killers/ Human reluctance to take a life can be reversed through training in the method known as killology, http://www.sfgate.com/science/article/THE-SCIENCE-OF-CREATING-KILLERS-Human-2514123.php, (13 August, 2006).

Hafemeister, Thomas., Stockey, Nicole. "Last Stand? The Criminal Responsibility of War Veterans from Iraq and Afghanistan with Posttraumatic Stress Disorder," Indiana Law Journal, Volume 85: Issue 1, (2010).

Hailey, Elizabeth. "Spartan Women," http://people.uncw.edu/deagona/amazons/spartanwomen2.htm. (May 2009).

Hampshire, Stuart. Morality and Conflict. Cambridge, Massachusetts: Harvard University Press, 1983.

Hanel, Rachael. Knights: Fearsome Fighters. Minnesota: Creative Education, 2008.

Hartle, Anthony. Moral Issues in Military Decision Making. Lawrence, Kansas: University Press of Kansas, 2004.

Hartmann, Nicolai. Moral Phenomena. New Brunswick, New Jersey: Transaction Publishers, 2002.

Hastings, Max. Warriors: Portraits From the Battlefield. New York: Alfred A. Knopf, 2005.

Hauser, Marc. Moral Minds. New York: Harper Collins Publishing, 2006.

Heckel, Waldemar and Jones, Ryan. Macedonian Warrior: Alexander's elite infantryman. Great Britian: Osprey Publishing, 2006.

Hedges, Chris. "The Death Mask of War", https://www.adbusters.org/magazine/72/The_Death_Mask_of_War.html, (23 July 2007).

Henry, Patrick. "Give Me Liberty or Give Me Death", A Chronology of US Historical Documents, http://www.law.ou.edu/ushistory/henry.shtml, (March 23, 1775).

Hinde, Robert. Why Good Is Good: The Sources of Morality. New York: Routledge, 2002.

Historic Foundations of Japan's Military Aggression. "Japan under Shoguns 1185-1853," http://www.users.bigpond.com/battleforAustralia/foundationJapmilaggro/Shogunate.html, (May 2009).

History Reference Center, Early Explorations. Everyday Life: Exploration & Discovery, http://0-web.ebscohost.com.dbpcosdcsgt.co.san-diego.ca.us/ehost/detail?vid=8&hid=115&sid=62ac5a90-fd1e-4dc2-

a5df-
3934873dc946%40sessionmgr102&bdata=JnNpdGU9ZWhvc3QtbG
l2ZQ%3d%3d#db=khh&AN=25262399, (2005).

Hochgesang, Josh, Lawyer, Tracye, Stevenson, Toby. "The
Psychological Effects of the Vietnam War",
https://web.stanford.edu/class/e297c/war_peace/media/hpsych.html,
(July 26, 1999).

Hoge, Charles W., Castro, Carl A., Messer, Stephen C., McGurk,
Dennis, Cotting, Dave I., and Koffman, Robert L. "Combat Duty in
Iraq and Afghanistan, Mental Health Problems, and Barriers to
Care", http://content.nejm.org/cgi/content/full/351/1/13#T1, (July 1,
2004).

Holmes, Richard. Acts of War: The Behavior of Men in Battle. New
York: The Free Press, 1985.

Howard, Sethanne., Crandall, Mark. "Post Traumatic Stress
Disorder, What Happens in the Brain?", Washington Academy of
Sciences, (Fall 2007).

Hugo,Victor. Les Miserables, New York: Dodd, Mead and
Company Publishers, 1971.

Hussein, Saddam. "Saddam Hussein: In His Own Words",
http://www.au.af.mil/au/awc/awcgate/iraq/sadquots.htm, (2002, 18
October).

Ikegami, Eiko. The Taming of the Samurai. Cambridge,
Massachusetts: Cambridge Press, 1995.

Information About, "Hypaspist,"
http://www.informationdelight.info/encyclopedia/entry/Central_Busi
ne...%20www.seattleluxury.com/encyclopedia/entry/Central_Busine
ss_District/hypaspist, (November 3, 2008).

International Humanitarian Law - Treaties & Documents, "Protocol
on Prohibitions or Restrictions on the Use of Incendiary Weapons

(Protocol III). Geneva, 10 October 1980,"
http://www.icrc.org/ihl.nsf/FULL/515?OpenDocument, (October 21, 2009).

"invincible." Webster's Revised Unabridged Dictionary. MICRA, Inc., http://dictionary1.classic.reference.com/browse/infincible, (15 May. 2009).

Jelinek, Pauline. "Number of troops diagnosed with post-traumatic stress disorder jumped roughly 50 percent in 2007," http://www.defenselink.mil, (May 27, 2008).

Johnson, Caitlin. "Vet Kills Himself After VA Turns Him Away", http://www.cbsnews.com/stories/2007/03/13/earlyshow/main256253 7.shtml, (March 13, 2007).

Johnson, Gordon S. "Iraq Vet Accused Of Killing Wife Suffers From PTSD", http://tbilaw.com/blog/iraq-vet-accused-of-killing-wife-suffers-from-post-traumatic-stress-disorder/, (29 December, 2012).

Johnston, David. A Brief History of Justice. West Sussex, United Kingdom: Wiley-Blackwell, 2011.

Jolly, Vik. "Saluting a Marine's bravery: LCpl Christopher Adlesperger", http://www.leathern eck.com/forums/showthread.php?71820-LCpl-Christopher-Adlesperger, (14 April, 2007).

Jones, Ann. They Were Soldiers: How the Wounded Return from America's Wars: The Untold Story, Chicago: Haymarket Books, 2013.
Jones, Brent. "U.S. Marines will shift to Afghanistan," http://www.usatoday.com/news/washington/2008-12-08-marine-afghanistan_N.htm, (December 8, 2008).

Joyner, James. "Desmond Doss, Pacifist Medal of Honor Recipient, Dies at 87", http://www.outsidethebeltway.com/desmond_doss_pacifist_medal_o f_honor_recipient_dies_at_87/, (24 March, 2006).

J.T.O., "Murderers who have served in the U.S. Military: A Database", https://ajaor.wordpress.com/2012/12/05/murderers-who-have-served-in-the-u-s-military-a-database/, (05 December, 2012).

Junger, Ernst. Storm of Steel. London: Penguin Books, 2003.

Karlin, Mark. "'They Were Soldiers' Author Discusses High Cost of War for America's Veterans", http://www.truth-out.org/news/item/19992-how-easily-americans-forget-the-physically-and-psychologically-wounded-veterans-of-the-post-9-11-wars-a-national-shame#, (13 November 2013).

Keegan, John. The Face of Battle. England: Penguin, 1978.

_____. The History of Warfare. New York: Vintage Books, 1994.

Keegan, John., Holmes, Richard. Soldiers: A History of Men in Battle. New York: Konecky & Konecky, 1985.

Kelly, Orr. Never Fight Fair! Navato, California: Presidio Press, 1995.

Kent, Zachary. World War I: The War to End Wars. New Jersey: Berkeley Heights,1994.

Kershaw, Alex. The Bedford Boys. Cambridge, Massachusetts: Da Capo Press, 2003.

Kreitzer, Anatol C., Malenka, Robert C., "Striatal plasticity and basal ganglia circuit function", Neuron, Volume 26, Issue 4, (26 November, 2008).

Krulak, Victor. First To Fight. Annapolis, Maryland: Naval Institute Press, 1984.

Kudo, Timothy. "I killed people in Afghanistan, Was I right or wrong?", (2013, January 25), https://www.washingtonpost.com/opinions/i-killed-people-in-afghanistan-was-i-right-or-wrong/2013/01/25/c0b0d5a6-60ff-11e2-b05a-605528f6b712_story.html.

Kuhnhenn, Jim. "VA review finds 'significant and chronic' failures", http://bigstory.ap.org/article/obama-hear-update-veterans-affairs-problems, (June 27, 2014).

Ladd, Dean., Weingartner, Steven. Faithful Warriors, A Combat Marine Remembers the Pacific War. Annapolis, Maryland: Naval Institute Press, 2007.

Lamothe, Dan. "Honor or insult for a fallen Marine?", http://www.marinecorpstimes.com/news/2008/09/marine_peralta_09 2808/, (September 30, 2008).

Lanius, Ruth., Miller, Mark., Wolf, Erika., Brand, Bethany., Frewen, Paul., Vermetten, Eric., Spiegel, David. "National Center for PTSD, Dissociative Subtype of PTSD", http://www.ptsd.va.gov/professional/PTSD-overview/Dissociative_Subtype_of_PTSD.asp, (3 January, 2014).

Lekic, Slobodan. "Troops already outnumber Taliban 12-1," http://www.google.com/hostednews/ap/article/ALeqM5jWM24PqW pJg-935bFXbYANhGJ_lQD9BJLDVO0, (27 October, 2009).

Lewis, C. S. The Abolition of Man. San Francisco, California: Harper Collins, 2001.

_____. Mere Christianity. San Francisco, California: Harper Collins, 2001.

Liberzon, Israel., Taylor, Stephan F., Amdur, Richard., Jung, Tara D., Chamberlain, Kenneth R., Minoshima, Satoshi., Koeppe, Robert A., Fig, Lorraine M. "Brain Activation in PTSD in Response to Trauma-Related Stimuli", Biological Psychiatry, Volume 45, Issue 76, (1 April, 1999).

Liberzon, Israel., Sekhar Sripada, Chandra. "The functional neuroanatomy of PTSD: a critical review", Progress in Brain Research, Vol. 167, (2008).

Lisman, John., Sternberg, Elizer. "Habit and Nonhabit Systems for Unconscious and Conscious Behavior: Implications for Multitasking Journal of Cognitive Neuroscience", Volume 25, Issue 2, (February 2013).

LItz, Brett., Orsillo, Susan. "The Returning Veteran of the Iraq War: Background Issues and Assessment Guidelines," Excerpt from the Department of Veterans Affairs National Center for PTSD, http://www.ncptsd.va.gov/ncmain/ncdocs/manuals/iraq_clinician_gu ide_ch_3.pdf, (2 June, 2009).

Litz, Brett T., Stein, Nathan., Delaney, Eileen., Lebowitz, Leslie., Nash, William P., Silva, Caroline., Maguen, Shira. "Moral injury and moral repair in war veterans: A preliminary model and intervention strategy", Clinical Psychology Review, Volume 29, Issue 8, (2009 December), Pages 695–706, http://www.ptsd.va.gov/professional/newsletters/research-quarterly/v23n1.pdf.

Lowry, Rich. "Sgt. Rafael Peralta, American Hero", http://www.nationalreview.com/lowry/lowry200501110730.asp, (January 11, 2005).

Luttrell, Marcus. Lone Survivor: A Conversation, History vs Hollywood. (2016, March 10), Marcus Luttrell Responds to Controversy over Freeing the Goatherds, http://www.historyvshollywood.com/video/lone-survivor-controversy/.

Luttrell, Marcus. Marcus Luttrell Interview, (2007, August 9). Marcus Luttrell, author of "Lone Survivor", interviewed by Matt Lauer on The Today Show on June 12, 2007. https://www.youtube.com/watch?v=irC4K7Q4JCo

Luttrell Marcus., Robinson, Patrick. Lone Survivor. New York: Little, Brown and Company, 2007.

Macgregor, Mary. "Stories of the Vikings", http://www.heritage-history.com/?c=read&author=macgregor&book=vikings&story=discoveries, (August, 2015).

Maguen Shira, Litz, Brett. "Moral Injury in Veterans of War", National Center for PTSD, "PTSD Research Quarterly", (2012), Volume 23/No.1, ISSN, 1050 -1835, http://www.ptsd.va.gov/professional/newsletters/research-quarterly/v23n1.pdf.

Maguen, Shira., Lucenko, Barbara., Marmar, Charles., Litz, Brett., Seal, Karen., Knight, Sara., Reger, Mark., Gahm, Gregory A., "The impact of reported direct and indirect killing on mental health symptoms in Iraq war veterans." Journal Of Traumatic Stress [serial online]. February 2010;23(1):86-90 5p. Available from: CINAHL Complete, Ipswich, MA. Accessed March 4, 2016.

Marcinko, Richard. Rogue Warrior. New York: Pocket books, 1992.

Marshall, S. L. A.. Men Against Fire. Gloucester, Massachusetts: Peter Smith, 1978.

Martin, Thomas R. "An Overview of Classical Greek History from Mycenae to Alexander," http://www.perseus.tufts.edu/hopper/text?doc=Perseus%3Atext%3A1999.04.0009%3Achapter%3D6, (2016, 6 May).

Martinez, Marco. Hard Corps: From Gangster to Marine Hero. New York: Random House, 2007.

McGirk, Tim. Collateral Damage or Civilian Massacre in Haditha?, http://www.time.com/time/world/article/0,8599,1174649,00.html, (March 19, 2006).

McMahan, Jeff. "On the Moral Equality of Combatants", The Journal of Political Philosophy: Volume 14, Number 4, 2006, pp. 377–393, Web. 18 January, 2016.

Meagher, Robert. Killing from the Inside Out: Moral injury and Just War. Eugene, Oregon: Cascade Books, 2014.

Mejia, Camilo. Road from Ar Ramadi. New York: The New Press, 2007.

Melber, Ari. "For vets, rehab rather than prison", http://www.msnbc.com/the-cycle/vets-rehab-rather-prison, (July 19, 2014).

Messina-Dysert, Gina. "Rape and Spiritual Death", Feminist Theology. vol. 20 (2) 120-132. (January 2012).

Microsoft Encarta Online Encyclopedia 2009, "Chemical and Biological Warfare," http://encarta.msn.com/encyclopedia_761558349_4/Chemical_and_Biological_Warfare.html#howtocite, (1997-2009).

Military Times Hall of Valor, "Rafael Peralta, Awards and Citations, Navy Cross", http://valor.militarytimes.com/recipient.php?recipientid=3655, (July, 2015).

MilitaryTimes, Honor the Fallen, "Army Sgt. Dennis P. Weichel Jr.", http://thefallen.militarytimes.com/army-sgt-dennis-p-weichel/6568133, (29 April, 2016).

Miller, Franklin. Reflections of a Warrior. Novato, California: Presidio Press, 1991.

Mockenhaupt, Brian. "I Miss Iraq. I Miss My Gun. I Miss My War," http://www.esquire.com/features/ESQ0307ESSAY, (June 26, 2007).

Montgomery, Victor. Healing Suicidal Veterans, New Jersey: New Horizon Press, 2009.

Moore, G. E. Principia Ethica. Cambridge: University Press, 2002.

Moran, Lord. Anatomy of Courage. New York: Avery Publishing, 1987.

Moreland, J. P. and Nielsen, Kai. Does God Exist: The Debate between Theists and Atheists. Amherst, New York, 1993.

Moreland J. P., Craig, William Lane. Philosophical Foundations For A Christian Worldview. Downers Grove, Illinois: Intervarsity Press, 2003.

Mortenson, Darren. "Violence subsides for Marines in Fallujah", http://www.nctimes.com/news/local/military/article_f67f8c4c-275c-541e-837b-5265fc69e2ee.html, (April 11, 2004).

Moseley, Alexander. "Just War Theory," Internet Encyclopedia of Philosophy, http://www.iep.utm.edu/justwar/, (February 10, 2009).

_____. "Pacifism," Internet Encyclopedia of Philosophy, http://www.iep.utm.edu/pacifism/, (April 19, 2005).

Murchison, William. Reclaiming Morality in America. Nashville, Tennessee: Thomas Nelson Publishers, 1994.

Murphy, Audie. To Hell and Back. New York: Owl Book, 2002.

Murphy, Andrew. "Training warriors in ancient Sparta," http://www.helium.com/items/795298-training-warriors-in-ancient-sparta, (May 2009).
Murphy, Mark. "The Natural Law Tradition in Ethics." http://plato.stanford.edu/entries/natural-law-ethics. (9 January, 2004).

Nadelson, Theodore. Trained to Kill. Baltimore, Maryland: The Johns Hopkins University Press, 2005.

National Coalition for Homeless Veterans, "Background and Statistics," http://nchv.org/index.php/news/media/background_and_statistics, (29 December, 2017).

Neiberg, Michael. Fighting The Great War. Cambridge, Massachusetts: Harvard University Press, 2005.

Newhouse, Eric. Faces of Combat: PTSD and TBI, Washington: Issues Press, 2008.

Nitobe, Inazo. Bushido: The Warrior's Code, Santa Clara, California: Ohara Publications, 1979.

Now. "Over 50 ISIS child soldiers killed in 2015", https://now.mmedia.me/lb/en/NewsReports/565591-over-50-isis-child-soldiers-killed-in-2015, (20 July, 2015).

Nussbaum, Greg. "Nathan Hale", http://www.mrnussbaum.com/nathanhale.htm, (2006).

O'Brien, William. The Conduct of Just and Limited War. New York: Praeger Publishers, 1983.

O'Connor, D. J. Aquinas and Natural Law. New York: Macmillan, 1968.

OFFICE OF THE SECRETARY OF DEFENSE, "Review of Medal of Honor Nomination
(Sergeant Rafael Peralta (deceased), USMC), INFORMATION PAPER",
http://media.utsandiego.com/news/documents/2012/03/01/DOD_rep ort_on_Peralta_2008.pdf, (2 June, 2008).

Orend, Brian. "War," http://plato.stanford.edu/entries/war/, (July 28, 2005).

Ouellette, Judith A. "Habit and Intention in Everyday Life: The Multiple Processes by Which Past Behavior Predicts Future Behavior", Psychological Bulletin, Volume 124, Issue 1, 1998.

Page, Hugh. "Viking Society," Berkshire Encyclopedia of World History, 2005, Vol. 5, History Reference Center, http://0-web.ebscohost.com.dbpcosdcsgt.co.san-diego.ca.us/ehost/detail?vid=7&hid=8&sid=77fdbe8d-43fc-41e5-88bd-b637fd5e0a5c%40sessionmgr108&bdata=JnNpdGU9ZWhvc3QtbGl2ZQ%3d%3d#toc.

"Paralumun". "Rape Survival, Defense and Healing." Paralumun: New Age Womens Village. http://www.paralumun.com/rapesurvival.htm (5 January, 2004).

Park, Michael. The Silver Shields: Philip's and Alexander's Hypaspists, http://www.academia.edu/2397748/The_Silver_Shields_Philips_and_Alexanders_Hypaspists, (2016, 8 May).

Pfarrer, Chuck. Warrior Soul. New York: Presidio Press, 2004.

Philipps, Joshua. None of Us Were like this Before: American Soldiers and Torture. New York: Verso, 2012.

Plato, The Republic. As translated by Desmond Lee. London: Penguin Classics, 2007.

Porpora, Douglas. Landscapes of the Soul. New York: Oxford Press, 2001.

Prigerson, Holly G., Maciejewski, Paul K., Rosenheck, Robert A. "Population Attributable Fractions of Psychiatric Disorders and Behavioral Outcomes Associated With Combat Exposure Among US Men", http://www.pubmedcentral.nih.gov/articlerender.fcgi?artid=1447389, (January 2002).

Proser, Jim., Cutter, Jerry. I'm Staying with my Boys: The Heroic Life of Sgt. John Basilone, USMC, New York: St. Martin's Press, 2004.

Ramde, Dinesh. "Benjamin G. Sebena Gets Life For Killing Police Officer Wife", http://www.huffingtonpost.com/2013/08/09/benjamin-g-sebena_n_3734411.html, (October 9, 2013).

Rand Corporation, For Release, "One In Five Iraq and Afghanistan Veterans Suffer from PTSD or Major Depression", http://www.rand.org/news/press/2008/04/17/, (April 17, 2008).

Ratti, Oscar and Westbrook, Adele. Secrets of the Samurai. Rutland, Vermont: Charles E. Tuttle Company, 1973.

Rawls, John. Justice is Fairness. London, England: Belknap Press of Harvard University Press, 1971.

Reno, Jamie. "Medicating Our Troops Into Oblivion": Prescription Drugs Said To Be Endangering U.S. Soldiers", http://www.ibtimes.com/medicating-our-troops-oblivion-prescription-drugs-said-be-endangering-us-soldiers-1572217, (2014, April 19).

Rhodes, Bill. An Introduction to Military Ethics. Santa Barbara, CA: ABC-CLIO, 2009.

Rice, Hugh. God and Goodness. Oxford: Oxford University Press, 2000.

Rico, Johnny. Blood Makes the Grass Grow Green. New York: Presidio Press, 2007.

Richard Rodgers. "Audie Leon Murphy: Memorial Web-Site," http://www.audiemurphy.com/welcome.htm, (August 18, 2009).

Rigby, Andrew. "Forgiveness and Reconciliation in Jus Post Bellum," Mark Evans, Just War Theory.

Robinson, Kara Mayer. reviewed by Joseph Goldberg, MD, "Sociopath vs. Psychopath: What's the Difference?"

http://www.webmd.com/mental-health/features/sociopath-psychopath-difference, (2005-2015).

Rocheleau, Matt. "Veterans, grannies protest war", http://www.dailycollegian.com/2.10120/1.1345440-1.1345440, (February 3, 2009).

Rodgers, Richard. "Audie Leon Murphy: Memorial Web-Site," http://www.audiemurphy.com/welcome.htm, (August 18, 2009).

Roozendaal, Benno., McEwen, Bruce S., Chattarji, Sumantra. "Stress, memory and the amygdala", Nature Reviews Neuroscience 10, 423-433 (June 2009).

Rowland, Michael. "Albert Jacka: the 'Australian Achilles' whose bravery saw him awarded the country's first Victoria Cross of the war", http://www.abc.net.au/news/2015-04-23/albert-jacka-the-australian-achilles/6360196, (22 April 2015).

Russell, Bill. god is not here: A soldier's struggle with Torture, Trauma and the Moral Injuries of War, (New York: Pegasus, 2015).

S. J., "Anatomy of Fear," Graphic is found at http://hardanxiety.blogspot.com/fight_or_flight.html. The Fight-or-Flight.

Sanders, Laura. "Military combat marks the brain", Science News, Vol. 182, Issue 7, (10/6/2012).

Sapolsky, Robert. "Why Stress is Bad for Your Brain", Science, Volume 273, (August 1996).

Sargent J.F., Koski, Dustin. "The 6 Most Aggressively Badass Things Done by Pacifists", http://www.cracked.com/article_20157_the-6-most-aggressively-badass-things-done-by-pacifists.html, (23 December, 2012).

Scarre, Chris. Chronicle of the Roman Emperors. London: Thames and Hudson, 1995.

Scherer, Glen and Fletcher, Marty. World War I. New Jersey: Berkeley Heights, 2006.

Scott, Michael J., Stradling, Stephen G. Counseling for Post-Traumatic Stress Disorder, (Thousand Oaks: CA, SAGE Publications, 2006).

Seck, Hope Hodge. "Eyewitnesses respond to claims challenging Peralta's MoH account", http://archive.marinecorpstimes.com/article/20140222/NEWS/30222 0009/Eyewitnesses-respond-claims-challenging-Peralta-s-MoH-account, (22 February, 2014).

Seger, Carol A., Spiering, Brian J. "A Critical Review of Habit Learning and the Basal Ganglia", http://www.ncbi.nlm.nih.gov/pmc/articles/PMC3163829/#, (2011).

Sekunda, Nicholas. Greek Hoplite, Great Britian: Osprey, 2000.

Shay, Jonathan. Achilles in Vietnam. New York, NY: Scribner, 1994.

_____. Odysseus in America. New York: Scribner, 2002.

Shin Lisa, M., Liberzon, Israel. "The Neurocircuitry of Fear, Stress, and Anxiety Disorders", Neuropsychopharmacology (2010) 35, 169–191; (22 July 2009).

Shin, Lisa., Rauch, Scott., Pitman, Roger. "Amygdala, Medial Prefrontal Cortex, and Hippocampal Function in PTSD", Annals of the New York Academy of Sciences. 2006, Vol. 1071 Issue 1, pp. 67-79, (2006, July 15).

Shriver, Donald. An Ethic For Enemies. New York: Oxford University Press, 1995.

Shwartz, Mark. "We've evolved to be smart enough to make ourselves sick",

http://news.stanford.edu/news/2007/march7/sapolskysr-030707.html,
(7 March, 2007).

Siddle, Bruce. Sharpening The Warrior's Edge. Belleville, IL:
PPCT Research Publications, 1995.

Singer, Peter. How are We to Live? Amherst, New York:
Prometheus Books, 1995.

Sites, Kevin. "The Unforgiven",
http://aeon.co/magazine/psychology/how-do-soldiers-live-with-their-
guilt/, (November 2004).

_____. "Killing Up Close", http://www.vice.com/read/killing-up-
close-0000001-v20n1/page/1, (January 28, 2013).

Slim, Hugo. Killing Civilians: Method, Madness, and Morality in
War. New York: Columbia University Press, 2008.

Smith, David. The Most Dangerous Animal, New York: St. Martin's
Press, 2007.

Sontag Deborah., Alvarez, Lizette. "War Torn, Part III",
http://www.nytimes.com/2008/01/27/us/27vets.html?pagewanted=all
, (27 January, 2008).

Sorabji, Richard and Rodin, David. Eds. The Ethics of War.
Burlington, Vermont: Ashgate Publishing Limited, 2007.

Southwick, Watson. "The emerging scientific and clinical literature
on resilience and psychological first aid. A practical guide to PTSD
treatment: Pharmacological and psychotherapeutic approaches",
http://eds.a.ebscohost.com.library.gcu.edu:2048/eds/pdfviewer/pdfvi
ewer?sid=63f7f891-aaf3-4e8e-a589-
4aaa9460af38%40sessionmgr4001&vid=12&hid=4208, (July 18,
2015).

"Sparta: Famous quotes about Spartan life",
https://www.pbs.org/empires/thegreeks/background/8c_p1.html, 12 October, 2017.

Special Series, War Torn Part I. "A series of articles and multimedia about veterans of the wars in Iraq and Afghanistan who have committed killings, or been charged with them, after coming home", http://www.nytimes.com/interactive/2008/01/12/us/20080113_VETS _DATABASE.html, (January 12, 2008).

Spinner, Jackie. "7 Marines Killed in Blast Near Fallujah, Apparent Suicide Attack Is Deadliest for Troops Since April; 3 Iraqis Slain", http://www.washingtonpost.com/wp-dyn/articles/A64921-2004Sep6.html, (September 7, 2004).

Staff writer, "ISIS accused of crimes against humanity," Al Arabiya News (2l04, November 14), http://english.alarabiya.net/en/News/middle-east/2014/11/14/ISIS-commits-crimes-against-humanity-in-Syria.html.

Stockton, Robert. The Millennium Fulcrum Edition, 3.0, Lewis Carroll, Alice's Adventures in Wonderland, "Advice from a Caterpillar," Chapter V, http://www.cs.cmu.edu/~rgs/alice-table.html, (14 December, 2009).

Storm, Tania., Marianne Engberg and Christian Balkenius. "Amygdala Activity and Flashbacks in PTSD: A Review", https://www.lucs.lu.se/LUCS/156/LUCS156.pdf, (2013).

_____. "Dysregulation of emotional responses due to amygdala hyperactivity resulting from PFC hypoactivity, has been suggested as one of the components of the PTSD pathology (Koenigs and Grafman, 2009; Shin, 2009.

Strachan, Hew. The First World War. London, England: Penguin Books, 2003.

Szoldra, Paul. "Marine Sgt. Rafael Peralta Deserves The Medal Of Honour For What He Did In Fallujah Or He Deserves Nothing", http://www.businessinsider.com.au/rafael-peralta-2014-1, 11 January, 2014.

The Associated Press, "'I can't forgive myself': U.S. veterans suffering alone in guilt over wartime events", (2013, February 22), http://www.cbsnews.com/news/i-cant-forgive-myself-us-veterans-suffering-alone-in-guilt-over-wartime-events/.

The Holy Bible: New International Version. Grand Rapids: Zondervan, 1996, c1984, S. 1 Sa 17:11, I Sa 17:32, I Sa 17:40, and Judges 7.

The Universal Declaration of Human Rights. http://www.un.org/en/documents/udhr/, (10 September, 2009).

Thornhill, Randy, and Palmer, Craig. A Natural History of Rape: Biological Bases for Sexual Coercion. Cambridge, Massachusetts: The MIT Press, 2000.

Tollefson, James. The Strength Not to Fight—An Oral History of Conscientious Objectors of the Vietnam War. Boston: Little, Brown and Company, 1993.

Trafton, Anne. "How the brain controls our habits", http://newsoffice.mit.edu/2012/understanding-how-brains-control-our-habits-1029, (29 October, 2012.

Tripp, Jessica., McDevitt-Murphy, Meghan., Henschel, Aisling. "Firing a Weapon and Killing in Combat Are Associated With Suicidal Ideation in OEF/OIF Veterans". Psychological Trauma: Theory, Research, Practice, And Policy [serial online]. October 12, 2015; Available from: PsycARTICLES, Ipswich, MA. Accessed March 4, 2016.

Turnball, Stephen. Samurai: The Warrior Tradition. London: Arms and Armour Press, 1996.

_____. Samurai Warfare, New York: Sterling Publishing Co., 1996.

_____. Samurai Warlords: The Book of the Daimyo, London: Blandford Press, 1989.

_____. Samurai Warriors. London: Blandford, 1987.

Twenge, Jean. Generation Me. New York: Free Press, 2006.

United States Marine Corps, History Division, "Major General Smedley D. Butler, USMC", http://www.mcu.usmc.mil/historydivision/Pages/Who's%20Who/A-C/Butler_SD.aspx, (29 April, 2016).

Unto the Breach. Brian R. Chontosh Navy Cross citation. http://www.victoryinstitute.net/blogs/utb/2003/03/25/brian-r-chontosh-navy-cross-citation/, (16 December, 2017).

U.S. Department of State, 2004 Press Releases: "Terrorists using mosques and schools as weapons caches, U.S. reports", http://iraq.usembassy.gov/iraq/041111_fallujah_briefing.html, (November 11, 2004).

Van Creveld, Martin. The Culture of War. New York: Random House, 2008.

_____. The Transformation of War, New York, The Free Press, 1991.
Van der Kolk, Bessel. "The Assessment and Treatment of Complex PTSD", http://www.traumacenter.org/products/pdf_files/complex_ptsd.pdf, (2001).

Van Der Vat, Dan. D-Day: The Greatest Invasion. New York: Madison Press Book, 2003.

Varley, H. Paul. Samurai. New York: Delacorte Press, 1970.

406

Veteransinc.org, "Statistics", http://www.veteransinc.org/about-us/statistics/, (June 24, 2015).

Warren, James A. American Spartans: The U.S. Marines: A Combat History from Iwo Jima to Iraq, (New York: Pocket Books, 2005),

Weapons and Warfare ~ History and Hardware of Warfare, "Silver Shields", https://weaponsandwarfare.com/2015/12/31/silver-shields/, (2016, 6 May).

Webster, Henry Kitchell. Early European History, Forgotten Books.org, http://books.google.com/books/p/pub-4297897631756504?id=rXSqwPFMn3oC&printsec=frontcover&dq=isbn:1606209353&source=gbs_summary_r&cad=0#PPA3,M1, (2008).

Wellborn, Jack. "The Vietnam Connection: Charles Heads' Verdict", http://heinonline.org/HOL/LandingPage?handle=hein.journals/ciiafe n9&div=6&id=&page=, (1982).

West, Bing. No True Glory: A Frontline Account of the Battle for Fallujah. New York, Bantam Book, 2005.

Wheeler, Richard. A Special Valor. New Jersey: Castle Books, 1996.

Wilkinson, Philip. Gandhi: The Young Protester who Founded a Nation. Washington, D.C.: National Geographic Press, 2005.

Wilson, James. The Moral Sense. New York: The Free Press, 1993.

Wong, David. "Relativism", A Companion to Ethics, Peter Singer, ed., Malden, Massachusetts: Blackwell Publishers, 2000.

Wong, Leonard., Kolditz, Thomas A., Millen, Raymond A., Potter, Terrence M. "Why They Fight: Combat Motivation in the Iraq War," http://25thaviation.org/history/id871.htm, (July, 2003).

Wong, Michael. The Truth Set Him Free: Ehren Watada vs. the U.S. Army, http://www.inthemindfield.com/2011/03/25/the-truth-set-him-free-ehren-watada-vs-the-u-s-army/, (March 25, 2011).

Woodruff, Bob., Hill, James., Hennessey, Jaime. "Unstable Soldiers Redeployed to Iraq", http://www.veteranstoday.com/2008/10/24/unstable-soldiers-redeployed-to-iraq/, (October 24, 2008).

Workman, Jeremiah. "24 Insurgents Killed, 3 Marines Rescued, 1 Navy Cross: A Reluctant Hero Is Made", http://www.getthegouge.com/insider/waronterror/stories.asp?print=Y&ID=264, (2009 U.S. NAVAL INSTITUTE).

YouTube. (Mar 10, 2012). 2-10-12 The O'Reilly Factor: Chris Kyle 'American Sniper'. https://www.youtube.com/watch?v=tDyAT1TVQ9Q.

Zimmermann, Tim. "Getting There First," U.S. News & World Report, (08/16/99-08/23/99, Vol. 127 Issue 7, p71), http://0-web.ebscohost.com.dbpcosdcsgt.co.san-diego.ca.us/ehost/detail?vid=11&hid=115&sid=62ac5a90-fd1e-4dc2-a5df-3934873dc946%40sessionmgr102&bdata=JnNpdGU9ZWhvc3QtbG12ZQ%3d%3d#db=khh&AN=2124008.

Zoroya, Gregg. "Some upset Marine sergeant won't receive Medal of Honor", http://www.usatoday.com/news/military/2008-09-17-Medal-of-Honor_N.htm, (November 18, 2008).

Made in the USA
San Bernardino, CA
17 April 2019